THE HISTORY OF
CHRISTIAN THEOLOGY

Volume 2: The Study and Use of the Bible

Editor: Paul Avis

THE HISTORY OF CHRISTIAN THEOLOGY

Editor: Paul Avis

VOLUME 1 THE SCIENCE OF THEOLOGY

Gillian R. Evans
Alister E. McGrath
Allan D. Galloway

VOLUME 2 THE STUDY AND USE OF THE BIBLE

John Rogerson
Christopher Rowland
Barnabas Lindars SSF

THE HISTORY OF
CHRISTIAN THEOLOGY

Volume 2: The Study and Use of the Bible

Editor: Paul Avis

John Rogerson
Christopher Rowland
Barnabas Lindars SSF

Marshall Pickering, Basingstoke

Wm. B. Eerdmans Publishing Co., Grand Rapids

Marshall Morgan and Scott
Marshall Pickering
3 Beggarwood Lane, Basingstoke, Hants RG23 7LP, UK

Copyright © 1988 Paul Avis
First published in 1988 by Marshall Morgan and Scott Publications Ltd
Part of the Marshall Pickering Holdings Group
A subsidiary of the Zondervan Corporation
and
Wm. B. Eermans Publishing Co., 255 Jefferson Ave. SE, Grand Rapids,
Mich. 49503

Eerdmans ISBN 0-8028-0196-X
Marshall Morgan and Scott ISBN 0 551 01519 5

Text set in Linotron Plantin
By Input Typesetting Ltd, London
Printed in the United States of America

THE HISTORY OF CHRISTIAN THEOLOGY

The History of Christian Theology aims to provide an extended introduction to religious thought in the Christian tradition from an
historical perspective. It presents the unfolding of Christian thought
in its various departments: doctrine, ethics, philosophical theology,
the study and interpretation of the Bible, interaction with the
sciences and with other religions. The various volumes of the *History*
will eventually constitute a set of fundamental resource books of
wide usefulness in religious education and in ministry. The approach
aims to combine clarity of presentation and ease of reference with
academic integrity and theological depth.

Editor

THE STUDY AND USE OF THE BIBLE

The second volume of *The History of Christian Theology* is devoted to the history of the study and use of the Bible in the Christian church through the centuries. It describes the changing approaches to the interpretation and application of the holy scriptures, the primary source of Christian theology, from the ways in which the New Testament writers employed Old Testament texts, to the latest developments in the sociological and structuralist approaches to the Bible. Major coverage is given to the place of the Bible in the early church, at the Reformation, and in the modern critical movement. The questions of the inspiration, interpretation and authority of the Bible today are also constructively considered.

Owing to the specialisation of scholarship in modern biblical study, between the Old Testament and the New, these are covered separately by John Rogerson and Barnabas Lindars SSF respectively. A significant feature of this volume is the attention given to the inter-testamental period and its literature, including the Apocrypha, an understanding of which is essential, both to see where later Old Testament trends were leading and to give the origin and background of important themes of the New Testament. As the history of the scientific study of the inter-testamental literature is largely confined to the recent past, Christopher Rowland has taken the opportunity to include an introduction to this less familiar field and to present the significance of inter-testamental research for the study of the canonical scriptures.

In its combination of clarity, scope and detail, the present volume of *The History of Christian Theology* should prove to be an exceptionally useful account of an important subject.

Editor

CONTENTS

PART I

THE
OLD TESTAMENT

THE INTERPRETATION OF THE OLD TESTAMENT IN THE NEW

1. INTRODUCTION

For the Christians of the New Testament period, what we today call the 'Old Testament' was Scripture, inspired by God, and authoritative for understanding what God had done for mankind in the life, death and resurrection of Jesus. Paul wrote that

> whatever was written in former days was written for our instruction, that by steadfastness and by the encouragement of the scriptures we might have hope (Romans 15:4).

The writer of II Timothy (whether Paul or a Paulinist) reminded Timothy of

> how from childhood you have been acquainted with the sacred writings which are able to instruct you for salvation through faith in Christ Jesus,

and he continued with the affirmation:

> all scripture is inspired by God and profitable for teaching, for reproof, for correction, and for training in righteousness, that the man of God may be complete, equipped for every good work (II Timothy 3:15–17).

The Impact of Jewish Tradition

Because Jesus and his first disciples were Jews, the scriptures which they accepted as authoritative were the Jewish scriptures. Indeed, not only did the earliest church inherit its scriptures from the Jews, it also inherited from them various methods of interpretation, as well as actual interpretations. For example, Balaam is never mentioned in the New Testament except as an example to be avoided (II Peter 2:15–16; Jude 11), yet a modern reader of the Balaam story in Numbers 22—24 could be forgiven for thinking that Balaam was a good person. After all, he refused to curse Israel, the task for which he was hired, and instead only proclaimed what God put into his mouth to say. However, Jewish interpretation of Balaam fastened upon the tradition, most fully expressed in Numbers 31:16, that Balaam encouraged the people to turn from God, and interpreted the whole Balaam story in such a fashion as to show the wickedness of all his actions. The New Testament tradition accepted this understanding of Balaam. Again, in Hebrews 11:21, Jacob is said to have bowed in worship 'over the head of his staff'. Standard translations of Genesis 47:31 say that he bowed himself 'upon the head of his bed'. In his account of Jacob's actions, the New Testament writer was following a tradition reflected in the Septuagint which read the Hebrew consonants mth as matteh (staff) rather than mittah (bed). Other examples of Jewish exegesis will be mentioned later. However, in the use of the Jewish scriptures by the earliest church there is a new factor at work which stamps a new meaning upon the scriptures: the life, death and resurrection of Jesus.

The Fulfilment of the Scriptures
In the New Testament account of the ministry of Jesus, it is claimed that Jesus himself was responsible for teaching his disciples that his ministry was a 'fulfilment' of the scriptures. According to Mark 14:21, Jesus described his impending betrayal and death with the words

the Son of man goes as it is written of him.

Luke 24:13–27 describes a conversation between the risen Christ and two disciples who are walking from Jerusalem to Emmaus, in which Christ 'beginning with Moses and the prophets' interprets 'in all the scriptures the things concerning himself'. This exposition is preceded by the exclamation:

O foolish men, and slow of heart to believe all that the prophets have spoken. Was it not necessary that the Christ should suffer these things and enter into his glory? (Lk. 24:25–6).

In the Fourth Gospel, Jesus says to his opponents

you search the scriptures, because you think that in them you have eternal life; and it is they that bear witness to me (John 5:39).

This is not the place to go into the question of the relationship between the 'Jesus of history' and the picture of him that is present in the Gospels. It would be surprising, however, if the new and radical way in which the first Christians interpreted the Jewish scriptures was entirely their invention, and owed nothing to Jesus himself. The Gospel tradition, at many levels, indicates that Jesus both understood his mission in a way that ran counter to the assumptions and expectations of his closest followers as well as his opponents, and also saw his mission as in some sense a fulfilment of the scriptures. However, we can content ourselves at this stage with C.K. Barrett's observation that

the gospel story as a whole differs so markedly from current (i.e. first century) interpretation of the Old Testament that it is impossible to believe that it originated simply in meditations on prophecy; it originated in the career of Jesus of Nazareth. (*Cambridge History of the Bible*, vol I, p.405.)

Granted the centrality of Jesus for the earliest church's use of the Old Testament, it is not surprising that in giving an account of the life of Jesus the New Testament writers saw that at almost every point, his life had fulfilled one scripture or another. His virgin birth had been foretold in Isaiah 7:14 (Matt. 1:23). His birth in Bethlehem in Micah 5:2 (Matt. 2:6), the flight to Egypt in Hosea 11:1 (Matt. 2:15), the slaughter of the innocent children by Herod in Jeremiah 31:15 (Matt. 2:18), his upbringing in Nazareth in a prophecy not identified or identifiable (Matt. 2:23). John the Baptist's ministry preparatory to that of Jesus had been foretold in Isaiah 40:3 and Malachi 3:1 (Matt. 3:31), while Jesus's removal from Nazareth to Capernaum had been foretold in Isaiah 9:1–2 (Matt. 4:14–16). The general effect of his ministry had been foretold in Isaiah 42:1–4 (Matt. 12:17–21) and his use of parables in his teaching accorded with Isaiah 6:9–10 and Psalm 78:2 (Matt. 13:14–15,35).

2. THE PASSION OF JESUS

The story of Jesus's passion was full of allusions to the Old Testament, including the description of at least two actions on the part of Jesus himself in which he is presented as deliberately seeking to fulfil Old Testament prophecies. Thus, the triumphal entry into Jerusalem is meant to evoke Zecharaiah 9:9 (Matt. 21:5), and the cleansing of the temple to exemplify Isaiah 56:7, Jeremiah 7:11, or Psalm 69:9 (Matt. 21:13). In the crucifixion narrative, the division of the garments of Jesus among the soldiers (John 19:24), the piercing of him with a lance (John 19:36–7) and his cry 'I thirst' all have Old Testament counterparts (John 19:28). The use of the Old Testament by the earliest church thus far described had, then, two main functions. The first was to provide a sort of running commentary on the life of Jesus, so that his life could be seen to be the constellation of many Old Testament prophecies. The second main function, carrying on from the first, was to indicate that the one who had died, to human eyes, a death that betokened ignominy and failure, was in fact the long-expected Servant of God. There was thus a strong apologetic and interpretative factor in the use of the Old Testament in the account of the life and death of Jesus.

In the Fourth Gospel and the New Testament epistles, the apologetic and interpretative factors were developed in the direction of propounding the meaning and abiding results of the work of Jesus. In the Fourth Gospel, the discourse about Jesus as the bread which came down from heaven (6:26–40), the good shepherd (10:1–18) and the true vine (15:1–8), seen against their Old Testament backgrounds, describe the new life which is now available to those who are united to Christ, are under his protection and are nourished by his risen life. In the Pauline epistles and the Epistle to the Hebrews, the fundamental paradox of early Christian use of the Old Testament is wrestled with – the relationship of the Old Testament law to those who have faith in Christ.

3. THE OLD TESTAMENT LAW

There must have been among the earliest followers of Jesus Jews who could accept that Jesus was the promised Messiah, but who did not see that this entailed that they should give up their life-long observance of the Mosaic law. It would also be natural for such people to insist that even converts from among the Gentiles should take it upon themselves to live in obedience to God's law revealed in the Jewish scriptures. In those parts of the New Testament from which we learn about the struggle between the 'legalists' or 'Judaisers' and those who held the point of view represented most effectively by Paul, we see the struggle only from the side of the victorious Pauline 'party', the group that successfully contended that although the work of Christ 'fulfilled' the Old Testament law, it also put that law into a new perspective, in the light of which the Christian was to obey it in the spirit of love and faith in Christ Jesus, and not according to the letter of the minute performance of commandments.

The Analogy of Faith

In presenting the view that the work of Christ had freed the Christian from the obligation to be circumcised and to observe the minutiae of the Jewish law, Paul based his case squarely upon the exegesis of the Old Testament. In some instances, he used methods of exegesis familiar to us from the rabbinical literature. For example, in Romans 4 he used the device known as *gezera shava*, the argument by analogy from one passage to another, to show that the righteousness which God reckoned to Abraham was on the basis of faith and not on the basis of works. At issue was the interpretation of Gen. 15:6

> and he (Abraham) believed the Lord; and he reckoned it to him as righteousness.

Paul understood the verse in the light of Psalm 32:1–2

> Blessed are those whose iniquities are forgiven, and whose sins are covered;
> blessed is the man against whom the Lord will not reckon his sin.

Basing himself upon the point that in the Psalm, the forgiveness referred to is forgiveness that is based entirely upon the graciousness of God – the recipients would not be 'blessed' if the forgiveness was what God somehow owed to them – Paul interpreted the righteousness that God reckoned to Abraham as an act of divine graciousness. It was not something that God owed to Abraham because Abraham had done something that entitled him to it; it was an act of divine graciousness in response to Abraham's trust in God's promise that his offspring would be as numerous as the stars of heaven.

Allegorical Interpretation

However, more importantly for later exegesis of the Old Testament, Paul defended his position with the use of methods that can be loosely described as allegorical and typological. The most elaborate example of an 'allegory', which itself contains 'types' as well as examples of stricter methods of Jewish exegesis is to be found in Galatians 4:21–31. Without insisting upon exact definitions of the terms 'allegory' and 'type', two points can be made. First, Old Testament passages which in their context were meant to be taken as historical, were interpreted by Paul in a symbolic manner. The narratives about Abraham, Sarah and Hagar in Genesis 16 and 21, which on a surface reading tell us about events which happened to people who were certainly believed by Paul and his readers to have been real people, are interpreted by Paul to refer to Jews (and 'Judaising' Christians) and Gentile Christians. Jews (and 'Judaising' Christians), although the physical offspring of Sarah, are the spiritual offspring of Hagar, while Gentile Christians, although the physical offspring of Hagar are the spiritual offspring of Sarah, and thus children of God's promise to Abraham. This complex interpretation, whose many steps cannot be charted here, depended among other things upon what we may loosely call 'types', that is, persons or institutions in the Old Testament prefiguring or anticipating Christ and his work, or Christians and their institutions, or the opponents of Christianity. Thus in Gal. 4:25, Hagar is a 'type' of (corresponds to) Jerusalem, which in turn denotes Judaism and Jewish Christianity, which Paul believes to be in spiritual slavery.

Typology
Nowhere in the New Testament is 'typology' to be found so clearly as in the Epistle to the Hebrews, one of whose purposes is to interpret the work of Christ in priestly terms. The fact that Jesus did not have a priestly lineage is overcome by linking him with Melchizedek, and by making him the subject of the declaration

> Thou art a priest for ever after the order of Melchizedek (Psalm 110:1).

Christ is therefore superior to the priestly house of Levi; yet the ordinances of the Jerusalem temple serve as a context and as a foil for the understanding of Christ's work in priestly terms. Just as under the Old Covenant the blood of sacrificial animals effected purification from sin, so the shed blood of Christ effects the purification of the consciences of those who serve the living God (Hebrews 9:13–14). Again, there is a correspondence between the Old Covenant and that inaugurated by Christ, in that the death of Christ which annuls the Old Covenant and makes possible the New corresponds to the deaths of the animals whose shed blood ratified the Mosaic covenant (Hebrews 9:15–22). Another correspondence which also points up a difference is perceived between the high priest entering the Holy Place each year, having first offered a sacrifice for his own sins, and Christ, who did not need a sacrifice for himself, entering into the very presence of God having nonetheless offered himself as a sacrifice for sin (Hebrews 9:24–28).

So far in this chapter, we have seen the Old Testament used in the New Testament in order to set the ministry of Jesus in the context of God's eternal purposes, to vindicate Jesus as the Servant of God, and to interpret his work, especially as this affected the relationship of Christians to the observance of the Old Testament law. However, other usages of the Old Testament in the New can also be found.

4. THE OLD TESTAMENT AS A GUIDE TO CHRISTIAN LIVING

Important for discussion later in this book is the use of the Old Testament as a guide for Christian living. The Old Testament provides for Christians examples of men and women of faith, prayer, and perseverance (Hebrews 11:4–39; James 5:11, 17–18). It also provides examples to be avoided, in the cases of characters such as Cain (I John 3:12), Balaam (II Peter 2:15ff.) and Jezebel (Revelation 2:20). A crucial question is whether the Old Testament is used in order to give detailed guidance to Christians about how to conduct their everyday lives.

Christian Use of the Law
In the church's use of the Old Testament in the post-New Testament period, Old Testament laws played an important part in the regulation of Christian life. For example, the prohibited degrees of marriage implied in Leviticus 18 and 20 became the basis for regulating Christian marriage. In the post-Reformation period, in some of the reformed churches, the Old Testament laws regarding the sabbath were applied as closely as possible to the Christian Sunday. In view of what has been said above about Paul's arguments concerning the relation of the law to the work of Christ, was the later Church correct in drawing so extensively upon the Old Testament for the purpose of regulating Christian behaviour?

An examination of the New Testament indicates that there are few examples where specific Old Testament laws or pieces of teaching are detailed for observance by Christians. One notable instance concerns divorce, in which the apparent inadmissability of divorce contrary to its provision in Deuteronomy 24:1–4, is based upon Genesis 2:24 (Mark 10:1–12). Romans 13:8–10 seems to envisage that Christians will observe the Ten Commandments, although the point is also made that what the commandments prescribed in the field of relations with other people can be summed up in the teaching 'you shall love your neighbour as yourself'. Although this latter commandment is itself from the Old Testament (Leviticus 19:18) it lacks specific content, and puts the onus upon the Christian to define the scope of both 'neighbour' and 'love'. Another of the few specific references to the Old Testament for guidance about Christian conduct is in I Timothy 2:11–14, where a subordinate status of women is justified on the grounds of Genesis 2:7, 21–22 and Genesis 3:1–6.

Natural Law

In seeking to evaluate the significance of the comparative lack of reference to the Old Testament in the matter of providing guidance for Christian behaviour, we must bear in mind that most of the New Testament letters were written to Gentile Christian churches. Where Paul was the author of the letters, he seems to have held the view that while Gentile Christians enjoyed the freedom granted to them by Christ, they needed to exercise that freedom in proper obedience to law. For Gentiles, this law was not necessarily the Old Testament law, but rather the natural law, failure to observe which occasioned God's wrath (Roman 1:19–32; 2:14–16). Paul's preference, when dealing with Gentiles, for the natural law over against the Old Testament law probably did not spring from a total rejection of the latter, but rather from his conviction that it was not necessary for *Gentile* Christians to observe the *Jewish* law.

What, then, was Paul's attitude to the Old Testament law when dealing with Jewish Christians, of whom he was one himself? The Acts of the Apostles presents Paul as an observer of the law. At Chencreae he makes what is presumably a short Nazirite vow, in accordance with which he cuts his hair to mark the termination of the period of the vow (Acts 18:18). In Acts 21:23–26, Paul carries out the suggestion of the leaders of the Jerusalem church that he should pay the expenses of shaving the heads of four men who had taken a vow, thereby demonstrating that he lives 'in obedience of the law' (Acts 21:24). In his speeches to the Jews in Jerusalem, Paul describes himself as a Pharisee (Acts 23:6).

Paul and the Law

The question of how far modern critical scholarship is prepared to accept the accuracy of the presentation of Paul in Acts is irrelevant for our present purposes. Until the rise of modern critical scholarship, the picture of Paul in Acts was accepted as authentic, and it could thus be used in the question concerning the part that Old Testament law should play in Christian life and legislation. Outside of Acts, Paul described the Old Testament law as 'holy' and 'spiritual' (Romans 7:12, 14) and the commandment as 'holy and just and good' (Romans 7:12). In I Corinthians 7:18, Paul advised Jews who became Christians (his language is: 'Was any one at the time of his call already circumcised? Let him not seek to remove the marks of circumcision') to continue, as C. K. Barrett puts it 'with his own appointed way of obedience' (*The First Epistle to the Corinthians*, London 1968, p.168).

It has not been the intention of the preceding paragraphs to attempt to deal comprehensively with the problem of 'Paul and the Law'. The intention has been to indicate that, in spite of the very few examples of actual uses of the Old Testament to regulate Christian behaviour, the New Testament contains material that indicates that, at least for one branch of the New Testament church, the Old Testament law had authority and some sort of binding power. Further, whatever Paul's attitude to the observance of Old Testament laws, the Old Testament itself remained for him the supreme authority for interpreting and understanding what God had done for mankind in Jesus Christ.

5. APPEAL TO THE OLD TESTAMENT

The Eternal Sonship of Jesus

It remains for three further types of usage of the Old Testament in the New to be considered, before the chapter is concluded. The first concerns the use of the Old Testament in christological arguments designed to prove the eternal sonship of Jesus. Probably the most conspicuous example of this usage is found in the opening chapter of the Epistle to the Hebrews. Here, passages from the Psalms and 2 Samuel 7 are quoted as either addresses of God to Jesus, or an address of God to his angels to worship Jesus; also, there is a direct ascription to Jesus of what the Psalmist in the Old Testament addresses to God. Another example, this time from the Fourth Gospel, quotes from Isaiah 6:10 in such a way as to indicate that in his vision, Isaiah saw the glory of Christ (John 12:39–41).

The Authorship of Old Testament Books
The second Old Testament usage in the New concerns information
about the authorship of Old Testament books. The New Testament
seems to imply that Moses was the author of the Pentateuch
(Matthew 19:7), that David was the author of the Psalms attributed
to him (Acts 2:25, 34; 4:25), that Isaiah was the author of Isaiah
42:1–4 (Matthew 12:17–21), and that Jeremiah was the author of
Zechariah 11:12–13 (Matthew 27:9). These ascriptions played a role
in Old Testament interpretation until at least the 19th century;
and indeed, some Christians today would regard the matter of the
authorship of parts of the Old Testament as settled on the basis of
what the New Testament states.

Christ in the Old Testament
The third approach to Old Testament interpretation in the New,
and a very significant one, was that which found Christ already
present in the Old Testament. The most obvious example is found
in I Corinthians 10:4, in which a spiritual rock which followed the
Israelites during the wilderness wanderings is said to have been
Christ. No doubt the background to this passage is very complex,
as modern commentators indicate. C. K. Barrett, who uncovers
the wealth of allusions and possible influences behind the passage,
nonetheless clearly states that the well referred to 'was not a mere
representation of Christ, but a scene of his activity' (*The First Epistle
to the Corinthians*, p.222). This is certainly how the earliest Christian
expositors read the passage, and it provided a legitimation for
seeking many other instances of the presence of Christ in the Old
Testament.

Summary
In summing up this chapter, I must freely admit that several aspects
of the use of the Old Testament in the New have not been treated.
For example, no attempt has been made to consider how far New
Testament exegesis of Old Testament passages is similar to, or
possibly influenced by, the methods of exegesis found in Philo and
in the Qumran scrolls. The omissions are deliberate. The main
purpose of the chapter has been to isolate those features of Old
Testament use in the New Testament that were significant in the
subsequent history of the church. These features can be listed as
follows: a) The ministry of Jesus is a completion of God's purposes
begun in the Old Testament. b) Not only the ministry of Jesus in
general, but aspects of it in particular, are foretold in the Old
Testament. c) The work of Jesus is anticipated in Old Testament

'types', that is, in certain Old Testament persons and institutions. d) The work of Jesus makes parts of the Old Testament superfluous, or sets their usefulness in a new context. The Old Testament, however, retains its authority as God's revelation. e) The fact that the Old Testament anticipates or foreshadows the work of Jesus indicates that it is permissible to interpret it 'allegorically', that is, not literally and not historically. At the same time, events and persons in the Old Testament understood historically can be used as examples for the edification of Christians. f) The Old Testament can be used to prove the unique sonship of Jesus. g) The New Testament indicates who were the authors, under God's inspiration, of some of the parts of the Old Testament. h) Jesus Christ can be found in the Old Testament.

The items listed here by no means cover everything that would later constitute Christian use of the Old Testament. For example, the integrity of the opening chapters of Genesis as true accounts of the origin of the world and of mankind would be defended on its own merits, and attempts to reconcile Genesis 1 with the science of the 5th or the 12th or the 16th centuries would proceed similarly. However, in the history of Christian use of the Old Testament, constant reference to its usage in the New would be made, especially when the so-called biblical theology of the late 18th and early 19th centuries sought to interpret the Old Testament in a fashion not determined by doctrinal assumptions. It was also the case that in the centuries following the period of the New Testament church, exegesis of the Old Testament followed very closely the lines laid down in the New Testament itself.

FOR FURTHER READING

R. M. Grant, *A Short History of the Interpretation of the Bible*, London 1963, chapter 3.

C. K. Barrett, 'The Interpretation of the Old Testament in the New' in *The Cambridge History of the Bible* vol.I (1970) pp. 379–394.

G. W. H. Lampe, K. J. Woollcombe, *Essays on Typology*, 1957.

B. de Margerie, *Introduction a l'histoire de l'exégèse*, vol. I, Paris 1980.

A. T. Hanson, *Jesus Christ in the Old Testament*, London 1965.

THE APOSTOLIC FATHERS AND THE APOLOGISTS (c. A.D. 70–220)

The title 'Apostolic Fathers' is usually employed to denote a group of writings composed roughly between A.D. 70 and 150. It is possible, although not demonstrable to the point of reasonable certainty, that two of the Apostolic Fathers are at least as old as some parts of the New Testament. Thus I Clement has been dated in the reign of Vespasian (A.D. 69–79), and the *Didache* is believed by some to refer to New Testament tradition, but not to any books of the New Testament in any written form. Of the remaining Apostolic Fathers to be considered in this chapter, the letters of Ignatius, bishop of Antioch, date from towards the end of his episcopate (traditionally dated A.D. 69/70 – 107/8), the Epistle of Barnabas dates from c. A.D. 130–132, and the *Shepherd of Hermas* from c. A.D. 140. In most of these texts, a further development of the uses made of the Old Testament in the New is evident.

The Person and Work of Christ
The use of the Old Testament to show that the work of Christ was foreseen by the Hebrew writers is not as prominent in the Apostolic Fathers as in the New Testament. This is not surprising, since the Fathers were writing mainly in order to give instruction about the Christian life, rather than to interpret the person and work of Jesus. However, in the letter of Ignatius to the Magnesians, ch. 9, the Old Testament prophets are described as the disciples of Christ, who waited for Christ as their teacher, and whom Christ raised from the dead when he came. In I Clement 16, the humility of Christ is illustrated not from his earthly life, but from Isaiah 53 and from Psalm 22:6–8:

I am a worm and no man . . .

Clement draws from these two Old Testament passages the exhortation

> Ye see, beloved, what is the example which has been given for us; for if the Lord thus humbled himself, what shall we do who have through him come under the yoke of his grace? (I Clement 16:17)

Another example under this heading can be found in I Clement 36:2–5 where the high priesthood of Jesus is proved from Psalm 104, Psalm 2:7 and 110:1. These citations are all to be found in Hebrews 1, and thus Clement may be referring to Hebrews if he is not citing *Testimonia*.

Typology
Not far removed from the attempt to show that the Old Testament foresees the ministry of Jesus is the 'allegorisation' of the Old Testament in terms of Jesus, or the discovery of 'types' that point forward to him. In this usage, the Epistle of Barnabas excels among the 'Apostolic Fathers'. A famous passage from Barnabas 9:7–8 argued that when Abraham circumcised 318 men of his household, he was 'looking forward in spirit to Jesus'.

> The ten and the eight are thus denoted – Ten by I and Eight by H. You have (the initials of the name of) Jesus. And because the cross was to express the grace (of our redemption) by the letter T, he says also, 'Three Hundred'. He signifies, therefore, Jesus by two letters, and the cross by one.

Exegesis of the Old Testament, in some ways no less fanciful than the example just given, also proved to Barnabas's readers that the scapegoat of Leviticus 16 and the red heifer of Numbers 19 were 'types' of Christ (Barnabas, ch. 7–8). That the cross of Christ was often announced in the Old Testament was indicated by Moses raising his hands to form a cross during Israel's battle against Amalek (Exodus 17:8–13; the Old Testament says nothing about the actual position of Moses's hands) and by the familiar incident of the brazen serpent (Numbers 21:6–9; cp. John 3:14–18) (Barnabas 12:2–7). The cross was also foreseen in a text not otherwise attested:

> When a tree shall be bent down, and again rise, and when blood shall flow out of wood . . . (Barnabas 12:1)

If some of the 'Apostolic Fathers' were adept at finding 'types' of Jesus in the Old Testament they had not yet developed to any degree the belief that Jesus himself was active in the Old Testament. This idea is implicit in the passage quoted above from I Clement 22, where Christ himself, through the Holy Spirit, addresses his followers in the words of Psalm 34:11–17 beginning:

Come ye children, hearken unto me (I Clement 22:1–8).

Examples of Faith

One of the most prominent uses of the Old Testament by the 'Apostolic Fathers' is that in which the leaders of Israel are held up as examples of faith. I Clement chs. 9–12 exhorts readers to contemplate the examples of Enoch, Noah, Abraham, Lot, and Rahab the harlot. In I Clement 17 is an exhortation to imitate those who 'went about proclaiming the coming of Christ', namely Elijah, Elisha and Ezekiel among the prophets, and Abraham, Job and Moses. In ch. 18 David is set forth as an example of humility on the basis of his words in Psalms 51 and 69. In chapter 55, Judith and Esther are given as examples of women of faith and courage.

An interesting appeal is made to the Old Testament in I Clement 41:1–4 so as to emphasise the importance of order in the church. The point is made that the Jewish sacrifices are not made anywhere and by anyone, but in Jerusalem on a specific altar and by specified ministers. Thus, in the church, it is necessary to recognise the importance of God-given orders of bishops (*episkopoi*) and deacons (*diakonoi*).

The Old Testament Law in Christian Life

Another prominent concern in the 'Apostolic Fathers' is that of the place of Old Testament law in the life of Christians. Before this is illustrated, however, it is worth noting that the 'Apostolic Fathers' present some interesting negative evidence about the use of Old Testament law in this period. The *Didache*, which purports among other things to guide its readers in the way of righteousness, makes hardly any reference to the Old Testament. The same is true of that part of *The Shepherd of Hermas* which sets out twelve commandments for Christian living. Only one, that relating to divorce, has an Old Testament origin, and even so, it is most likely that the author is dependent upon Matthew's gospel rather than on the Old Testament itself.

On the positive side, we find numerous repudiations of 'Judaising', as well as attempts to give a spiritual interpretation to the Mosaic laws. The most explicit repudiation of the Jewish law is probably to be found in Ignatius's letter to the Magnesians 8:2–3:

. . . if we still live according to the Jewish law, we acknowledge that we have not received grace. For the divinest prophet lived according to Christ Jesus.

In ch. 10 Ignatius declares:

It is absurd to profess Christ Jesus, and to Judaize. For Christianity did not embrace Judaism, but Judaism Christianity, that so every tongue which believeth might be gathered together to God.

I Clement 29:2–3 uses three Old Testament passages, Deuteronomy 32:8–9, and Numbers 18:27 and II Chronicles 31:14 combined, to show that God elected the Church.

The most conspicuous spiritualising of the Mosaic law is to be found in Barnabas. The writer is clear that Old Testament sacrifices are not required, and he quotes the polemical prophetic messages against sacrifice in his support (Isaiah 1:11–14, Jeremiah 7:22). Barnabas declares

he has . . . abolished these things, that the new law of our Lord Jesus Christ, which is without the yoke of necessity, might have a human obligation (2:5–6).

He quotes Isaiah 58:6–10 against the Jewish fasts, and on the basis of Exodus 32, the incident of the Golden Calf, he declares that Israel has lost the covenant (chs. 3, 14). The examples of Jacob displacing Esau and Ephraim becoming superior to Manasseh (Genesis 48:13–19) illustrated how the Church had become superior to Judaism (Ch. 13).

On specific points, Barnabas denies that the Mosaic ordinances about clean and unclean foods apply to Christians, because, he claims, Moses meant them to be understood 'spiritually'. Thus, the prohibition on eating pork means (spiritually)

Thou shalt not join thyself to men who resemble swine (10:3)

The other unclean creatures are similarly 'spiritualised' to represent types of persons whose company a Christian should avoid. The Jews misunderstood these scriptures and received them according to fleshly desire, as if he had merely spoken of (literal) meat (10:9).

The Old Testament statements about the sabbath are no more to be taken literally by Christians than are those about unclean creatures. The Old Testament statements about the Sabbath, read in the light of Genesis 1, mean that God will accomplish all things in six thousand years:

> Therefore, my children, in six days, that is, in six thousand years, all things will be finished. 'And he rested on the seventh day'. This meaneth, when his Son, coming (again), shall destroy the time of the wicked man, and judge the ungodly, and change the sun, and the moon, and the stars, then shall he truly rest on the seventh day (15:4–5).

Further exegesis of Old Testament passages justifies the fact that Christians observe not the seventh, but the eighth day, the day of Christ's Resurrection (15:8–9).

Summary

To sum up this section on the law: Christ is both foretold in the law, and abolishes it. If its precepts are binding upon Christians, they must first be interpreted 'spiritually'.

There are not many examples of Old Testament exegesis in the 'Apostolic Fathers' which break ground not already anticipated in the New Testament. A possible example of a more creative approach is to be found in ch. 4 of I Clement. Here, the writer takes the key word 'envy', and traces examples of it through the Old Testament. Thus, Cain envied Abel, Esau envied Jacob, his brothers envied Joseph, Aaron and Miriam envied Moses, Dathan and Abiram envied Moses, and Saul envied David. All these envious people met with disaster of one sort or another, and in addition, there was persecution for the faithful servants of God.

The 'Apostolic Fathers', then, expected their Christian readers to use the Old Testament in the light of God's revelation in Jesus Christ. Christ was foretold in the Old Testament, and he spoke in the Old Testament; he was pre-figured in institutions such as circumcision, the scapegoat and the red heifer. The Old Testament, read literally, furnished examples of faith, humility and heroism, and it indicated the sufferings to be expected by God's faithful servants. At the same time, its legal sections were not to be read literally. The Old Testament provided only very general examples for Christian behaviour, while its specific demands were to be read 'spiritually', whereupon they, too, became general precepts such as avoiding the company of certain types of person.

It is to be noted, in conclusion, that some references to the Old Testament in the 'Apostolic Fathers' are to otherwise unknown forms of the passages, and that some of the references are not known from the extant Old Testament or Apocrypha and Pseudepigrapha. No distinction is made between what Protestants were later to designate as 'Old Testament' and 'Apocrypha'. The claim can be found, especially in Barnabas, that the 'spiritual' interpretation of the Old Testament came as a special gift of illumination from God (Barnabas 9:9).

2. THE APOLOGISTS

With the writing of the Apologists (I deal here with Justin Martyr c. 100–165, Irenaeus c.130–c.200 and Tertullian c.160–c.225) we meet not only a new type of Christian literature but also new uses of the Old Testament. The Apologists were defending Christianity on two fronts: against Roman pagans and Jews on the one hand, and against heretical Christian-type sects on the other. In the present section I shall not deal with the defence of the Apologists against the Roman pagans and the Gnostics, but consider only the defence against the Jews and against Marcion. Marcion was the founder of a rival Church round about A.D.144 which spread all over the Roman empire. What he did to the Old Testament will be explained later. What makes the defence against the Jews and Marcion so interesting, however, is that these antagonists represented two extremes. The Jews rejected the claims of Christians that Jesus was the promised, suffering Messiah. Marcion, believing himself to be the restorer of the pure Pauline gospel, denied that the Old Testament had any place at all in Christian life and thought. The Apologists, therefore, had to develop the Christian use of the Old Testament so as to demonstrate to Jew and to Marcionite alike that the Old Testament was a Christian book.

Justin Martyr

The most important defence against Jews is that by Justin in his *Dialogue with Trypho*, although he also used arguments drawn from the Old Testament in his *First Apology* addressed to the emperor Antoninus Pius. Not surprisingly, Justin covers ground with which we are already familiar: the use of texts such as Isaiah 7:14, 52:13

– 53:12, Psalms 22, 45:6–7, 110:1 referred to Christ; the prefiguring of the cross in Moses's outstretched hands, and in the paschal lamb. Because he is defending Christianity and not exhorting his fellow-Christians, he does not refer to Old Testament characters as examples of faith or heroism. Where he breaks new ground is in his handling of the Mosaic law, and in his demonstration of the divinity of Jesus.

On the Mosaic law, Justin argues from the lives of all the generations, from Abraham to the mother of Moses, that observance of Sabbaths and the Mosaic law is not necessary for salvation (*Dialogue with Trypho*, ch. 9). From the lives of Enoch, Abraham, Lot and Melchizedek, he argues that circumcision is not necessary for salvation (ch. 19). The reason why these institutions were given to the Hebrews and enjoined upon them, was that the Israelites were sinful. God did not require the sacrifices and observances for their own sake; they were needed to regulate a wayward people (chs. 21–22). With the coming of Christ, they are now entirely abolished, since he has established the New Covenant promised in Jeremiah 31:31–2 (ch. 11). In response to the Jew Trypho's question whether it is possible for a believer in Jesus to observe the Mosaic law, Justin allows the possibility only

> if he does not strive in every way to persuade other men..to observe the same things as himself, telling them that they will not be saved unless they do (Ch. 47).

Justin's argument about the divinity of Christ moves the use of the Old Testament into a new area of theological concern. It is one thing to demonstrate that the Old Testament foretells a suffering Messiah who will be resurrected and come again at his second advent, and that Jesus is the one foretold; it is quite another thing to show that the Messiah is the divine Word, begotten from the Father's power and will, who became incarnate in Jesus.

In his demonstration of the divinity of Jesus, Justin first argues from passages such as Genesis 18, 32:22ff., and Exodus 3:1–6 that the Old Testament speaks of a Lord who is not the Father above, yet who acts fully in accord with the will and purpose of the Father (Chs. 56ff.). In particular, Justin linked Genesis 18:10

> I will surely return to you . . .

spoken by one of the three messengers who appeared to Abraham, with Genesis 21:12

but God said to Abraham 'be not displeased because of the lad . . .'

The 'returning' spoken of in Genesis 18:10 was identified with God's speaking in Genesis 21:12, from which it was proved that one who was called God appeared to Abraham, Jacob and Moses, yet he was distinct from the Father above who created all things. Similar arguments follow, based upon the incident of Jacob's wrestling (Genesis 32:32ff.) and Moses at the burning bush (Exodus 3:1-6) (Chs. 58–60).

This demonstration from passages of the Pentateuch, reinforced by familiar texts such as Psalm 45:6-7 cited as

thy throne, O God, is for ever and ever

leads on into Proverbs 8:21ff., which is taken to be the very words, through Solomon, of

the Word of Wisdom, who is himself thus God begotten of the Father of all things, and Word, and Wisdom, and Power, and the Glory of the Begetter . . . (Ch. 61)

The familiar words spoken by the eternal Word in Proverbs 8:21ff. include

The Lord made me the beginning of his ways for his works.

Thus Justin seeks to prove from the Old Testament

that Christ being Lord, and God the Son of God, and appearing formerly in power as Man, and Angel, and in the glory of fire as at the bush, so also was manifested at the judgement executed on Sodom (Ch. 128).

This is not an attempt to 'spiritualise' the Old Testament for its own sake. Whatever we may think today of Justin's interpretations, we cannot miss the intensity of his personal faith in Jesus which led, not only to his martyrdom, but to his attempt to find in the scriptures a demonstration of the deepest truths of Christianity.

Two other features of Justin's use of the Old Testament can be noted. First, we have in chs. 98–106 of the *Dialogue with Trypho* a detailed exposition of Psalm 22, in which Justin tries to relate the details of the Psalm to the events of the life of Jesus, including the identification of the psalmist's enemies with the opponents of Jesus.

Secondly, the dispute between Jews and Christians about the true text of the Old Testament occupies two chapters. Justin, in chapter 72, charges the Jews with having removed certain 'Christological' passages from the Old Testament.

We now know that the Jews, rather than the Christians, had the more reliable versions of the Old Testament. However, Justin's use of the Old Testament in no way depended upon the disputed passages.

Marcion

In the *Dialogue with Trypho*, it was common ground between Justin and Trypho that the Old Testament was the revelation of the Father above, creator of things seen and unseen. In Marcion, the Church had to contend with a believer in Jesus Christ, who maintained that the Old Testament was the revelation of a God who had nothing at all to do with Jesus. Marcion could have agreed with Justin that the Mosaic law was applicable only to the Hebrew nation and that it had no binding force upon Christians. At this point, however, the similarities ended.

Marcion believed that Jesus was the son of a God who was totally different from the God who created the visible universe and who was revealed in the Old Testament. This God of Jesus had his own heaven, his own mode of existence and his own attributes; but these were different in kind from those of the Creator of the visible universe, and could be spoken of only approximately by means of human language (Tertullian, *Against Marcion*, Bk. I ch. 9). The God of our visible world had no knowledge of the God revealed by Jesus, a fact indicated by the claim in Isaiah 45:5 and similar passages:

I am the Lord, and there is no other, besides me there is no God.

Jesus had come into the world, in the 15th year of Tiberius, as the envoy of the unknown God (Tertullian, Bk.I ch. 15). Jesus had assumed a human form, but had not been born as man, since to have done so would have involved him in assuming what belonged to the God of the visible world (Tertullian Bk.III, ch. 10). Jesus had, however, died upon the cross in order to free mankind from obligation to the God of the visible world, an obligation occasioned by mankind's failure to observe the law. By his humility and self-offering, Jesus offered the grace of his otherwise unknown Father to mankind. Marcion's attitude to the Old Testament was not entirely hostile. Its histories were true, its characters were real, and its law was valid for the people for whom it was intended. The God of the visible world revealed in the Old Testament was a real God. The main point, however, was that this God had nothing to do with the God revealed by Jesus, and did not even know of his existence.

Marcion was partly led to this position by the belief that the God of the Old Testament, although truly a God, suffered from defects which were made plain in the Old Testament revelation of him. He had not, apparently, foreseen the disobedience of Adam and Eve, and when he met them in the garden following their disobedience, he did not know where they were, or whether or not they had in fact disobeyed him. He had called to Adam

Where are you?

and had responded to Adam's reply that he was hiding because he was naked:

who told you that you were naked? (Tertullian, Bk.II ch. 25)

In the story of Cain and Abel, God was ignorant of Abel's murder, and asked:

Where is Abel your brother?

In various places, God 'repented' of what he had done. He had acted cruelly in hardening the heart of Pharaoh, and unjustly in telling the Israelites who were about to leave Egypt to borrow (i.e. steal) jewellery of gold and silver etc. from the Egyptians. God's necessity to change his plans was further illustrated by the fact that Saul, the first chosen king was rejected, and that Solomon also fell away from God. Such a God could not be the supreme God revealed by Jesus.

Given that Marcion put a literal interpretation upon even rhetorical questions, it is not surprising that he rejected the 'allegorical' or 'typological' exegesis that was used by orthodox Christians to point the Old Testament to Jesus. Marcion held that Jesus was not foretold in the Old Testament, and the messianic prophecies referred either to a universal Messiah of this world who was yet to come, or they had been partly fulfilled in notable Hebrew kings (Tertullian Bk.III ch. 6).

In some instances, Marcion followed the Old Testament exegesis of Gnostic writers. The astonishing assertion that, in his descent to Hades, Christ redeemed Cain, the Sodomites, the Egyptians 'and all the nations who walked in all sorts of abomination', whereas Abel, Enoch, Noah, the Patriarchs and the prophets were not saved by Christ, can be paralleled from Gnostic writers (Irenaeus, *Against Marcion*, Bk.I ch. 27).

Barbara Aland has argued strongly that Marcion was not a Gnostic, and that his position sprang basically from a strong emphasis on the fallenness of man and upon the graciousness of the God of Jesus. We cannot discuss this here, nor do more than note that, in order to support his views, Marcion compiled a New Testament 'canon' consisting of St. Luke's Gospel and 10 Pauline epistles, all censored so as to remove allusions to the Old Testament that implied a connection between Jesus and the Old Testament. Marcion's importance for the present work is that he challenged orthodox Christians to preserve those fundamental elements of the Gospel – human fallenness and divine grace – while holding on to the Old Testament and to the belief that Christ's redemption was wrought by the God of the visible universe.

Irenaeus
It was not easy to refute Marcion on the ground where he had chosen to fight; for he had altered the text of the New Testament to suit his theories, and, like all reductionists, he could dismiss any argument brought against him. Irenaeus, in his defence of orthodoxy against Marcion, could do little more than repeat the now familiar arguments that the Old Testament foretold the advent and passion of the Son of God, that Christ and the eternal word spoke in the Old Testament, and that the Old Testament law was given to the Israelites to direct them away from idolatry and rebelliousness. Irenaeus also appealed to New Testament passages to show that Abraham and the righteous of the Old Testament were *not* excluded from the salvation wrought by Christ, and that the two covenants, Old and New, were the work of one and the same householder bringing out of his treasure things old and things new (Matthew 13:52). (*Against Heresies*, Bk. IV, 8:1)

Although Irenaeus follows the established teaching that the Mosaic law is not binding upon Christians, we may perhaps detect a movement towards a more positive literal evaluation of the Mosaic law. He used the Old Testament to distinguish between the true

Mosaic law and the 'traditions of the elders' which latter are rejected (*Against Heresies* IV 8:1). He affirms that the true law and the Gospel agree on the substance of the First and Great Commandment (IV 12:3), and he argues that Jesus did not teach anything contrary to the true law but contradicted only 'traditions of the elders' (IV 13:1). In trying to refute specific points of Marcion, especially those relating to God's 'immoral' commands to the Israelites to despoil the Egyptians, and God's 'immoral' behaviour in hardening Pharaoh's heart, Irenaeus replied that the Egyptians owed far more to the Israelites than the latter took from them when they left Egypt, and that God was entitled to punish those who he knew would not believe in him (IV chs. 29–30).

An interesting passage occurs in Book II of *Against Heresies* where, pointing to things in the Bible that come in fours (the Gospels, the four-faced cherubim), Irenaeus speaks of four principal covenants being given to the human race:

> one, prior to the deluge, under Adam; the second, that after the deluge, under Noah; the third, the giving of the law, under Moses; the fourth, that which renovates man, and sums up all things in itself by means of the gospel, raising and bearing men upon its wings into the heavenly kingdom.

Irenaeus does not seem to have developed this idea of various covenants; but we shall find it later in the 'covenant theology' of one of the wings of the Reformation.

Tertullian

Tertullian's defence of orthodoxy against Marcion is a much more trenchant and successful effort, even allowing for the fact that Tertullian was a master of the techniques of ridicule and sarcasm. His opening attack concentrated upon Marcion's allegation that there was a God apart from, and higher than, the God of the visible universe. In the first place, such a proposition could not be proved, because, by definition, nothing in the created universe hinted at the existence of such a God. Tertullian preferred to go along with those philosophers who saw evidence of the divine in the created universe, and he identified that divine with the God revealed in the Old and New Testaments (*Against Marcion* Bk. I chs. 12–13). Secondly, if Marcion's God had only first manifested himself in Jesus, then he was morally deficient in not having come to the rescue of mankind when such rescue was first needed (Bk.I, ch. 22).

The second thrust of Tertullian's defence sets out from the Old

Testament itself, and is concerned with Marcion's denigrations of the God portrayed there. The accusation that God ought to have foreknown the disobedience of mankind is countered by the assertion that the possibility of disobedience was an essential part of the freedom bestowed upon mankind by God, (Bk.II ch. 7). Against the charge that the devil, who instigated the fall, was a being created by God, Tertullian described the 'fall' of Satan, identifying the prince of Tyre in Ezekiel 28:11–16 with the devil (Bk. II ch. 10). Incidentally, in expounding Ezekiel 28:11–16, Tertullian distinguished between two creations: that in Genesis 1:1 – 2:3 was an 'ideal world formulated in the mind of God', that of Genesis 2:4–5 was a creation of man in the actual world, with the animals of Genesis 2:18–20 understood as *angels*.

In dealing with other charges of Marcion against the God of the Old Testament, we see Tertullian beginning to wrestle with the problem of the meaning of religious language. He criticises those who, from things human, form conjectures about things divine, and who suppose that passions ascribed to the deity are as corruptive of God's character as they are of human character. He writes

> We read of God's right hand, his eyes, his feet: yet these are not to be supposed exactly the same as a man's, just because they partake of the same designation . . . equally great must be the difference of divine mind and human, though their sensations are referred to in the same terms (Bk. II ch. 16).

Granted this point, Tertullian could dismiss Marcion's assertion that God changed his mind about Saul and Solomon, and that on other occasions he 'repented'. These reversals on God's part were not the result of lack of foresight, or just plain unpredictability:

> It is to be understood as neither more nor less than a simple reversal of a previous decision, such as can be brought about without any adverse judgement upon that other (Bk. II ch. 24).

Tertullian's refutation of the charges of God's 'Immorality' followed the lines found in Irenaeus.

In Books IV and V of his *Against Marcion*, Tertullian argues from the New Testament, criticising Marcion's excisions from the text, and showing that the Old Testament is often implicit in the New, even if it is not quoted. A section on Paul, Marcion's true interpreter of Jesus, shows Paul's indebtedness to the Old Testament, and even sees an Old Testament reference to Paul's conversion! The passage

Benjamin is a ravening wolf: until morning he will still devour, and in the evening will distribute food (Genesis 49:27)

is referred to the Benjamite Paul, whose early life (the 'morning' of Genesis 49:27) was devoted to harassing the Lord's flock, but whose later life (the 'evening') is devoted to feeding Christ's sheep as the apostle of the Gentiles (Bk. V ch. 1).

Summary

To conclude this chapter, we must recognise that the achievements of the Apologists were impressive. They asserted that the Old Testament had relevance for all mankind, because without it, it was impossible to understand the advent and mission of the Saviour of mankind. Moreover, the mystery of the nature of divine being was already to be found in its pages, so that the Incarnation of God was anticipated by the divine appearance to some of the heroes of Old Testament faith. We find in the Apologists the beginnings of a concern with the nature of religious language, and how this affects the divine attributes. The christological and 'typological' exegesis is further developed. Although modern exegesis, for reasons given later in the book, can go only part of the way with the Apologists, there is no denying the fact that in their situation, the Old Testament was the living Word, confirming and deepening their faith in Christ.

FOR FURTHER READING

R. M. Grant, *The Apostolic Fathers*, New York 1964.

J. A. Fischer, *Die Apostolischen Väter*, Munich 1956.

The Apostolic Fathers (Ante-Nicene Christian Library) *The Writings of Justin Martyr and Athenagoras* (Ante-Nicene Christian Library), Edinburgh 1892.

E. Evans, *Tertullian: Adversus Marcionem*, Oxford 1972.

E. C. Blackman, *Marcion and his Influence*, London 1948.

The Writings of Irenaeus (Ante-Nicene Christian Library), Edinburgh 1884.

Barbara Aland, 'Marcion. Versuch einer neuen Interpretation', *Zeitschrift für Theologie und Kirche* 70 (1973) pp. 420–44.

3

THE EXEGETICAL SCHOOLS
OF ALEXANDRIA AND
ANTIOCH

1. THE SCHOOL OF ALEXANDRIA: CLEMENT

An event of considerable importance for Christian biblical studies was the founding, some time in the 2nd century, of the Catechetical School in Alexandria. Alexandria was a centre of learning, as well as the home of the allegorical method of interpreting the Bible, as this method had been practised by Jews and especially by Philo. The first known director of the school was Pantaenus, who is widely held to have been in charge from a little after A.D.180 to his death in A.D.199. Pantaenus's chief assistant and successor was Clement of Alexandria, who is believed to have been born in Athens of pagan parents in c. A.D.150. He is usually regarded as the head of the Catechetical School from A.D.200–202, when he was forced to leave Egypt during the persecution under Septimus Severus. Clement died in A.D.215. His successor as head of the school, Origen, was born in A.D.185, probably in Alexandria, his father dying as a martyr in the persecution that forced the departure of Clement. At the age of 18, Origen took over the Catechetical School and brought to it a distinction higher than that attained even by his illustrious predecessor. Origen remained in Alexandria until 231, when he was excommunicated, after which he moved to Caesarea. During the Decian persecutions, he was greatly tortured, and died in Tyre in A.D.253, not having fully recovered from his physical sufferings.

In the surviving writings of Clement, there is little hint of controversy with Jews. Rather, Gentiles are addressed, and in particular, Gentiles with an interest in philosophy. Clement strives to show how Christ is the supreme source and content of knowledge in its most profound sense, and in using the Old Testament, his approach is that Christ has spoken in the Old Testament, and that what he said there was both anterior to, and the source for, all that was best in Greek philosophy.

The Logos and the Law
Clement's book *The Instructor* presents the Divine Word as the teacher and trainer of mankind from the beginning.

> . . . . our Instructor is the holy God Jesus, the Word, who is the guide of all humanity. The living God himself is our Instructor . . . (Bk.I ch. 7)

Clement argues that the Divine Word was the Instructor of Abraham, Jacob and Moses, and he emphasises the Johannine verse that the law was given *through* Moses (John 1:17), the implication being that it was not given *by* Moses. This means that Clement has the highest possible view of the Mosaic law. It is the teaching of the Divine Word himself. It is not the *cause* of sin but an indicator of sin where it is disobeyed (*Miscellanies*, Bk.II ch. 7). It is not contrary to the gospel but in harmony with it. It is therefore binding upon all mankind, and it was the source of the laws formulated by Plato (*Misc.* Bk.I ch. 25).

However, not every part of the Mosaic law is to be understood in the same way. In his work *Stromateis* (*The Miscellanies*) Clement divides the Mosaic writings into four elements:

> the historic, and that which is specially called the legislative, which two properly belong to an ethical treatise; and the third, that which relates to sacrifice, which belongs to a physical science; and the fourth, above all, the department of theology, 'vision'. . . . (Bk.I ch. 28)

The historic part presumably is the narrative traditions of the Pentateuch, which Clement certainly understands historically, although examples of 'spiritualising' interpretation of historical narratives can be found (Bk.I ch. 21).

Mosaic Legislation
To the legislative part of the Mosaic writing, Clement appears to assign any Pentateuchal law whose literal observance presents no problem. Thus, Clement commends the Deuteronomic laws about not completely reaping a field in order that the poor may benefit, as well as the laws about letting the land lie fallow. The law about not yoking together an ox and an ass recognised the lack of agree-

ment between the animals, while the prohibition against setting a
kid in its mother's milk is directed against those

> that kick the bellies of certain animals before parturition, in order
> to feast on flesh mixed with milk (and) make the womb created
> for the birth of the foetus its grave . . . (Bk.II ch. 18)

In some cases, it is necessary to apply the 'spirit' of a law to a small
degree. The prohibition against a man wearing a woman's clothes
(Deuteronomy 22:5) is designed to ensure that males behave in
a manly fashion. The privileges of Deuteronomy 20:5–7 giving
exemption from warfare to certain classes of people not only ensure
that the army will consist of totally dedicated soldiers; good reasons
can be given for allowing the exemptions in their own right. On the
question of punishing adulteresses, Clement appears to hold that it
is right that they should be stoned to death.

> . . . The law is not at variance with the gospel, but agrees with
> it. How should it be otherwise, one Lord being the author of
> both? (Bk.II, ch. 23)

Concerning sexual relationships, the regulations of Leviticus 18:20,
22 are cited so as to prevent perversions (*Instructor* Bk.II ch. 10).
    Clement, then, more than any other father we have so far
considered is prepared to quote the Mosaic law as a basis for Christian and general obedience. He also alludes extensively to Proverbs
and Ecclesiasticus. He is obliged to spiritualise parts of the law,
however. In dealing with the clean and unclean beasts he says

> The Instructor, by Moses, deprived them (the Jews) of the use
> of innumerable things, adding reasons – the spiritual ones hidden;
> the carnal ones apparent, to which indeed they have trusted . . .
> (*Instructor* Bk.II ch. 1)

The 'hidden meaning' of the division between clean and unclean
creatures was the distinction between the Church, and Jews and
heretics (*Miscellanies*, Bk.VII ch. 18). The different creatures also
represent different types of person.

Allegorical Interpretation
If Clement has a 'reputation', it is for what today seems very far-
fetched exegesis. Examples of this can certainly be found. For

example, Clement understands by Abraham's preference for Hagar over Sarah that Abraham is

choosing only what was profitable in secular philosophy;

and when he said to Sarah 'Behold thy maid is in thy hands' (Genesis 16:6) he 'manifestly' meant:

I embrace secular culture as youthful, and a handmaid, but thy knowledge I honour and reverence as true wife (*Miscellanies*, Bk.I ch. 21).

An unusual interpretation of Psalm 150 can be found in *The Instructor*, in which Clement identifies the various musical instruments mentioned with parts of the human body and personality, which unite to praise God. The psaltery is the tongue, the lyre is the mouth struck by the Spirit, the timbrel and dance means

the Church meditating on the resurrection of the dead in the resounding skin (Bk.II ch. 4).

With Clement, then, we have reached more explicitly than hitherto the point of the complete harmony of the Old and New Testament. I am not suggesting that Clement is the first to present such a harmony, but merely that he appears to do it more explicitly than his predecessors. The antithesis between the law and the gospel is overcome. One and the same Instructor gave both not merely to Jews and Christians, but to all mankind.

2. THE SCHOOL OF ALEXANDRIA: ORIGEN

Of the writings of Origen, many have perished because of the charges of heresy that were brought against his works, after his death. In particular, his Old Testament homilies and commentaries have survived only in fragments. However, in two of his surviving works, *On Principles* and *Against Celsus*, enough material is present to enable his approach to the Old Testament to be reconstructed. After dealing with Origen as an interpreter of the Old Testament, I shall mention his work as a textual critic.

Origen as Interpreter

Like Clement, Origen is popularly regarded as a leading exponent of 'spiritual' or 'allegorical' interpretation. This is true in the sense to be explained shortly. On his own admission, however,

> the passages that are true in their historical meaning are much more numerous than those which are interspersed with a purely spiritual signification (*On Principles* Bk.IV ch. 1).

Origen certainly did not hesitate to regard much of the history recorded in the Old Testament as authentic, and he also accepted that an Old Testament law such as

> honour thy father and thy mother

was to be observed in its literal and obvious sense (*Principles* Bk.IV ch. 1). But it is certainly the case that Origen was primarily concerned with the spiritual sense or senses of Scripture.

We may classify the reasons for Origen's concern with hidden senses of Scripture under several headings.

First, Origen acknowledged that, read at its face value, the Old Testament at times contradicted common sense and reason. Thus he saw difficulty in Genesis 1 that the sun was not created until the 4th day, yet days 1–3 had morning and evening (*Principles* Bk.IV ch. 1). Origen's solution was that it was obvious that the statements of Genesis 1 could not be taken literally. Again, in Mosaic law, Origen discovered absurdity and impossibilities. An example of the former was the command to regard as a clean beast the goat-stag which appeared in the Greek version of Deuteronomy 14:5, a creature that simply did not exist. An example of the impossible was the command to remain sitting for the whole of the sabbath day, which was how Origen understood Exodus 16:29. These were just some of the examples of 'stumbling blocks' and 'offences', introduced by God into the legal and historical material of the Old Testament so as to prevent it from being read entirely at the surface level.

Second, Origen wished to avoid the charge that the God of the Old Testament was immoral, or that his character could not be reconciled with what is enjoined in the New Testament. 'Immoral' passages were no more to be taken at face value than Greek myths in the hands of their allegorisers. Thus, the encouragement given in Psalm 137:8–9 to dash the heads of Babylonian children against the rocks is interpreted as follows:

The infants of Babylon, which means confusion, are the confused thoughts caused by evil which have just been implanted and are growing up in the soul. The man who takes hold of them, so that he breaks their heads by the firmness and solidity of the Word, is dashing the infants of Babylon against the rock (*Against Celsus* Bk.VII ch. 22).

Origen, indeed, is very unsympathetic to any suggestion that the Old Testament contradicts the New, and even at the literal level he can find in Lamentations 3:29

let him give his cheek to the smiter, and be filled with insults

an Old Testament parallel to the injunction in the Sermon on the Mount about turning the other cheek (*Against Celsus* Bk.VII ch. 25).

Thirdly, Origen is concerned about the status of religious language, and thus rejects a literal interpretation of any passage in which God is presented anthropomorphically, or is seen to have 'passions'. Thus, Genesis 2–3 with its anthropomorphic language about God planting a garden (Genesis 2:8), taking one of Adam's ribs while he slept (Genesis 2:21) etc. cannot be taken literally (*Against Celsus* Bk.IV chs. 37–8).

Fourthly, Origen was convinced that the Old and New Testaments, taken together, demanded a spiritual interpretation. In addition to the obvious Pauline passages which supported this view, such as Galatians 4:21–31 and I Corinthians 10:1–11, Origen appealed to such passages as the prayer in Psalm 119:18

Open my eyes, that I may behold wondrous things out of thy law

to indicate that there must be hidden things in the law that could be understood only with divine help (*Against Celsus* Bk.IV ch. 50). Again, when Paul spoke of an

Israel after the flesh (I Corinthians 10:18 – the words in the Greek 'after the flesh' are left untranslated, e.g. by R.S.V.)

he implied that there existed also an 'Israel after the Spirit' and that thus there was a spiritual interpretation of the Old Testament (*Principles* Bk.IV ch. 1). Indeed, it was possible to go further and posit not only an 'Israel after the Spirit' but an Egypt, a Babylon and a Tyre, etc. 'after the Spirit'. And this latter type of exegesis was fully justified by passages such as Ezekiel 28:11–19 where it was impossible that an actual king of Tyre was being addressed (*Principles* Bk.IV ch. 1).

Origen believed that although Christ, the Divine Word, was foretold in the Old Testament, and spoke in it, it was not until the Incarnation that the veil which hid its spiritual meaning was removed. Moreover, there were pragmatic reasons why the Mosaic law needed a spiritual interpretation, with the coming of Christ:

> it did not fit in with the calling of the Gentiles that they should conduct their society according to the literal interpretation of the law of Moses, since they were subject to the Romans. Nor was it possible for the structure of life of the ancient Jews to remain without any modification if, for instance, they were to obey the form of life enjoined by the gospel (*Against Celsus* Bk.VII ch. 26).

Origen's view of Scripture can be summed up as follows. Every part of Scripture has a spiritual meaning. Many, but not all, parts have also a 'literal' meaning. When read spiritually, the Bible has a harmony from beginning to end: and its intellectual and moral difficulties disappear.

Origen as Textual Critic
We have already seen that in controversy with Jews, the early fathers insisted that the Jews had removed from the Hebrew Bible passages which pointed clearly to the coming and passion of Jesus. The early fathers read the Old Testament not in Hebrew, but in the Greek translation that derived from the work of Jewish scholars in Alexandria, and which was known as the Septuagint. Origen appears to have learnt sufficient Hebrew to enable him to appreciate the considerable differences that existed at some points between the Hebrew Bible and the Septuagint. In his letter to Africanus he wrote:

> through the whole of Job there are many passages in the Hebrew which are wanting in our copies, generally four or five verses, but sometimes, however, even fourteen, and nineteen, and sixteen . . . In Jeremiah I noticed many instances, and indeed in that book I found much transposition and variation in the readings of the prophecies . . .

In an attempt to establish an edition of the Septuagint that

conformed as closely as possible to the Hebrew, but without under-
mining the authority that the Septuagint had come to have for the
Church, Origen compiled while at Caesarea, his *Hexapla*.

The Hexapla

This massive work, estimated to be 6,500 pages long, set out in six
parallel columns the Hebrew (in Hebrew script), a transliteration of
the Hebrew into Greek, and the translations of Aquila and
Symmachus, the Septuagint, and the translation of Theodotion. In
some sections the number of columns was reduced to five, in others
it was enlarged to seven or eight, and in the case of the enlargement
Origen utilised translations that he had discovered in his travels,
including one discovered near Jericho, and possibly concealed in a
wine jar. A work called the *Tetrapla*, containing the four columns
of the four principal Greek versions was compiled either before or
after the *Hexapla*.

In the fifth column of the Hexapla, containing the Septuagint,
Origen seems to have transposed the text where this was necessary
to make it conform to the Hebrew order. Where the Septuagint
contained material not in the Hebrew, or lacked what was in the
Hebrew, the fifth column was marked with text-critical signs derived
from Alexandrian practice.

Origen's Influence

S. R. Driver in his Notes on Samuel, described Origen's labours as
'a step in the wrong direction' (p.xliii). His attempt to align the
Septuagint more closely to the Hebrew affected the subsequent
purity of the text of the Septuagint, thereby obscuring its value as
a witness to a Hebrew text-type *different* from that of the traditional
or Masoretic Hebrew text. However, Origen's work, both in the
field of interpretation and textual criticism, mark him out as one of
the greatest minds ever given over to biblical studies; his utter
commitment to the Christian revelation given in the Bible also led
him to suffer persecution. In spite of the official disapproval from
which his works suffered after his death, his influence was to be
considerable for many centuries.

3. THE SCHOOL OF ANTIOCH

To describe the exegetical school of Antioch, it will be necessary to
go both backwards and forwards in time: backwards to a representative of the so-called first Antiochene school who pre-dated the

Apologists Irenaeus and Tertullian, and forwards to the so-called later Antiochene school whose most notable representatives were active in the second half of the 4th century. This dislocation of the historical sequence can be justified on the grounds that the contrast between the Alexandrians and the Antiochenes enables some of the most fundamental issues in the use of the Old Testament in the early church to be seen at their clearest.

Discussions of the school of Antioch usually stress the strong influence of the Jewish literalist tradition of Antioch upon the Christian interpreters of that place. In what follows, no attempt will be made to identify or evaluate the Jewish influence. This is not to deny or denigrate the Jewish influence, but rather to allow the results of some of the greatest Antiochenes to be presented in their own right. Where they differed chiefly from the Alexandrians was in their conviction that the primary level of interpretation was the *historical* level. Whereas for the Alexandrians, and in particular Origen, narratives in the Old Testament that contained anthropomorphisms or which offended reason or morality were not to be interpreted historically, the Antiochenes adopted an historical interpretation wherever possible. How they dealt with anthropomorphisms etc. will be discussed later. With regard to prophecies and psalms that were generally understood to be Messianic, the Antiochenes allowed for a 'fuller' sense alongside the historical sense. Thus, they understood passages to refer to Christ, the church and the spreading of the gospel; but they did this only in certain clearly defined circumstances, as will be illustrated below.

Theophilus of Antioch
The chief known representative of the 'first' Antiochene school, Theophilus of Antioch, became bishop of Antioch round about A.D.169. His main extant work, *To Autolychus*, is probably older than the works of Irenaeus and Tertullian discussed in chapter 2. In his vindication of Christianity, Theophilus lays great stress on the Old Testament as a book of history, which contains the authentic history of God's dealings with the Jewish nation. Theophilus goes to great lengths to establish a biblical chronology from the creation to his own day (III, 24–5). The Old Testament also reveals to mankind that the God to whom it bears witness is the creator of the universe. This is possible because the human writers were inspired and instructed by God, and thus able to write about things that happened before or after their own times.

However, the Old Testament is given a Christian interpretation by Theophilus. He uses Psalm 45:1 understood to mean my heart has vomited forth a goodly word

to show that God has generated the Logos, and that through the Logos God made all things (John 1:3). This same Logos also spoke through Moses and the prophets. Thus Theophilus can retain Genesis 3 as authentic history, without conceding that God had been confined to one particular place. This is his solution to the problem of anthropomorphisms.

Genesis 1 is defended as an authentic account of how the world was created, the account being inspired by the Logos of God. However, the difficulty that light is created before the sun is tacitly acknowledged. The light created on the first day comes from the Logos.

In Book III of *To Autolychus*, Theophilus uses the Old Testament to indicate what behaviour God requires. He quotes from the 10 commandments, and from Exodus 23:6–8. R. M. Grant argues that Theophilus presents a 'radical' view of the Decalogue by omitting the commandments about taking God's name in vain and about observing the Sabbath, substituting in their place 'commandments' from Exodus 23 (R. M. Grant, *To Autolychus* p.xviii), but this may build too much on an argument from silence. Theophilus is at pains to show the harmony between the laws of the Old Testament and the New. Thus, the injunction in the Sermon on the Mount to love one's enemies is balanced by a text from Isaiah 66:5

Say to those who hate you . . .
'you are our brothers . . .' (II, 14)

Of Theophilus's attitude to the ceremonial law there is no indication.

Diodore of Tarsus

More than two hundred years separate Theophilus's appointment as bishop of Antioch in A.D.169 from that of Diodore as bishop of Tarsus and Cilicia in A.D.378. Diodore is the first great representative of the later Antiochene school whose works exist in any number, although he certainly had his predecessors, especially Lucian of Antioch (d. A.D.310) who was responsible for the important Lucianic rescension of the Septuagint. The best preserved of Diodore's works is his commentary on the Psalms, from which we get a good idea of how Antiochene exegesis was both 'historical' and Christological. David is held to be the author of the Psalms, but, by the gift of prophecy, some of the Psalms refer historically to the times of later kings and prophets, the exile, and even the Maccabean period. Diodore's treatment of Psalms 2 and 22 show the two extremes of Antiochene exegesis. Psalm 2 is about the Lord (Jesus), and tells how the Jews handed him over to Herod and Pilate, how he will save those who believe, and how he will crush those who do not believe. The 'today' of 'Today I have begotten thee' refers to what will happen in the future. The invitation

Ask of me, and I will make the nations your heritage

is given to the incarnate Christ. Diodore rejects the Arian interpretation that God is addressing the Logos before the creation, with the argument that the Logos cannot be invited to ask for things that do not yet exist. The verse refers to the honour accorded by the Gentiles to the incarnate Christ (*Commentarii in Psalmos* pp.11–15).

Against this thoroughly Christological interpretation of Psalm 2, Diodore firmly rejects the idea that Psalm 22 has anything to do with Christ, in spite of the use by Jesus of the opening words of the Psalm on the cross (*Comm.* p.142). Diodore's reason for a completely 'historical' interpretation is that the sufferings described in the Psalm do not correspond to those of Christ. In his interpretation of Psalm 24, Diodore sees the setting of the Psalm as the return of the exiles from the Babylonian exile. However, he notes that some refer 24:10b to Christ's ascension, and does not rule out this possibility (*Comm.* p.242). Good examples of Diodore's more exact criteria for referring Psalms to Christ are found in Psalm 40:6, where the demand for obedience not sacrifice 'conforms greatly to the things of Christ', and Psalm 45:6–8 where only Christ can be addressed as God and can reign for ever.

Theodore of Mopsuestia

A much more restrained use of Christological interpretation of the Old Testament is found in the work of probably the most remarkable Antiochene – Theodore of Mopsuestia (c. A.D. 350–428). Theodore appears to have worked with an unorthodox canon of the Old Testament, excluding from it as 'inspired' Scripture the Wisdom literature, and some of the 'historical' books such as Chronicles and Ezra – Nehemiah, on the grounds that these works contain merely human wisdom or merely human historical information.

The work of Theodore's most fully preserved is his commentary on the minor prophets, and in this work, the main hermeneutical principle appears to be that a prophecy is to be understood Messianically only if it is thus used in the New Testament (see *Patrologia Graeca* vol.66). Mere allusion is not sufficient; thus, Theodore makes no reference to the New Testament uses of, for example, Hosea 1:10 and 2:23 in Romans 9:25–6 or of Hosea 11:1 in Matthew 2:15. However, writing on Joel 2:28–32, the promise that God will pour his spirit upon all mankind, Theodore explains that the Old Testament contains veiled information that is only fully realised in the coming of Jesus (vol. 66, cols. 229, 232).

A firm rejection of the application of a passage to Christ is found in the treatment of Micah 4:1–3 (Cols. 364–5). How can the words

for out of Sion shall go the law, and the word of the Lord from Jerusalem

refer to Christ, who taught (John 4:21) that God did not require worship from a particular place, but required his followers to worship in spirit and in truth? The words of the prophecy, then, clearly referred to the re-establishment of the Jewish law and worship in Jerusalem after the return from exile.

John Chrysostom

The other great representative of the Antiochene School was John Chrysostom (354 – 407), who combined the historical interpretation of his predecessors with doctrinal and didactic gifts. This makes his writings both voluminous, and explorative of theological doctrines to a degree not found among the earlier Antiochenes. His expositions of the Psalms contain, as well as sensible and straightforward teaching at a practical spiritual level, long critiques of the various heresies that were serious in his day. A short, and illuminating, exposition is that on Psalm 117, which is seen as looking forward to the acceptance of the Gospel by the nations, who are thereby called upon to worship God. The phrase

his truth endures for ever

is understood to mean that what is contained in the Old Testament is a type or figure of what is to come in the New Testament (*Patrologia Graeca* vol.55 cols 327–8).

Summary

To sum up the Antiochenes and their significance, it can be said that they served as a constant reminder to later interpreters that there was a primary 'historical' sense to much of the Old Testament.

They were against the *arbitrary* discovery of anticipations of the New Testament in the Old. They were ready to illustrate points in the Old Testament about faith or wickedness from New Testament quotations; they were ready to see Old Testament passages as applying to Christ. Yet this latter possibility had become apparent only after the coming of Christ himself. He provided the light in terms of which it was now possible to understand what otherwise did not make sense at the historical level – passages such as those that spoke of a universal or an eternal reign of a King. Perhaps the contrast between the exegesis of Alexandria and Antioch can be summarised by saying that whereas the Alexandrians devised a hermeneutic which enabled them to apply to Christ Old Testament passages that did not seem at all likely to have such an application, the Antiochenes first identified a number of Old Testament passages which were much more self-evidently 'fulfilled' by Christ, and then devised a hermeneutic to explain the correspondences. In this regard, they were much closer to modern Old Testament exegesis than their Alexandrian counterparts.

FOR FURTHER READING

J. Quaesten, *Patrology*, vol 2, Utrecht/Antwerp 1953.

Clement of Alexandria, *The Instructor* (Ante-Nicene Christian Library) Edinburgh 1884.

Clement of Alexandria, *The Miscellanies* (Ante-Nicene Christian Library) Edinburgh 1882.

Origen, *On Principles* (Ante-Nicene Christian Library) Edinburgh 1895.

B. de Margerie, *Introduction a l'histoire de l'exégèse* vol.I.

Origen, *Homilies on Genesis* (Sources Chrétiennes, vol.7) Paris 1976.

H. Chadwick, Origen's *Contra Celsum*, Cambridge 1953.

Origen *Letter to Africanus* (Ante-Nicene Christian Library) Edinburgh 1895.

N. R. M. de Lange, *Origen and the Jews*, Cambridge 1976.

H. B. Swete, *An Introduction to the Old Testament in Greek*, Cambridge 1902.

S. R. Driver, *Notes on the Hebrew Text and the Topography of the Books of Samuel*, Oxford 1913.

G. Downey, *A History of Antioch in Syria*, Princeton 1961.

R. M. Grant, *Theophilus of Antioch: 'Ad Autolycum'*, Oxford 1970.

J. M. Olivier, *Diodori Tarsensis, Commentarii in Psalmos*, Corpus Christianorum, series Graeca 6, Turhout 1980 for Psalms 1–51.

L. Pirot, *L'oeuvre exégetique de Théodore de Mopsueste*, Rome 1913.

4

JEROME AND AUGUSTINE

1. JEROME

Career

'The most important single work produced by the Church Fathers
on any of the prophetic writings of the Old Testament, commenting
upon the original Hebrew text, and showing a complete mastery of
all the literature of the Church on the subjects touched upon to the
time of composition, is without question St. Jerome's Commentary
on the book of Daniel.' Whether or not W. M. Smith's extravagant
claim is justified will not be considered here (See G. L. Archer,
Jerome's Commentary on Daniel p.5); it is however, a notable introduction to one of the most remarkable and influential early Christian
commentators on the Old Testament. Its subject, Jerome, was born
in A.D.347 of Christian parents, in Stridon, whose site was probably
in what is today north-western Jugoslavia. He received his secondary
and higher education in Rome, where he was baptised at some point
before A.D.366. In A.D.372 he left Europe for the Near East,
travelling through Athens and Asia Minor until he reached Antioch,
where he lived in a Greek-speaking household. From 374/5, for two
or three years, he lived the life of a desert monk, which time was
spent in improving his knowledge of languages, especially Greek.
It was during this period also that he began to learn Hebrew. From
376/7 to 378/80 he was back in Antioch, from where he moved to
Constantinople before returning to Rome in 382. In Rome he
became secretary to Pope Damasus, and began gathering about him
the wealthy Roman women who would accompany him to
Bethlehem in 385–6 and who would largely finance the monastic
foundations which he was to establish there. From 386 to his death
in 420, Jerome's house was in Bethlehem, although he journeyed
from there, for example, to Caesarea to refer to the original of
Origen's *Hexapla*. From roughly 391 to 405, Jerome translated the

Old Testament from Hebrew into Latin, thus providing the basis of what was to become the standard Bible of the Western Church until the Reformation. Jerome's work will be considered under two headings: first, his Hebrew scholarship and second, his work as a commentator.

Mastery of Hebrew
Jerome's achievement in mastering Hebrew, in an age when there were no grammars, lexicons or concordances, was outstanding. His special works and commentaries provided the western church with the only knowledge of the Hebrew of the Old Testament that it possessed, until the revival of Hebrew learning in the 12th century. In his translation from the Hebrew into Latin, Jerome provided a version which often reproduced the literalisms of the Hebrew, and occasionally, he allowed himself to import Christian sentiments into the translation. Further, the translation seems to have varied according to how Jerome happened to feel at any one time. Whether it is fair to judge the translation by modern standards is a difficult question. In terms of Jerome's own time, it was a monumental achievement; by modern standards, the rendering is mostly fair, if not without unevenness.

Jerome used his knowledge of Hebrew extensively in his Old Testament commentaries; he also wrote several works dealing specifically with the Hebrew text of the Old Testament, of which the most notable example was the *Hebrew Questions on Genesis* of around A.D.391. Jerome's desire to treat the whole Old Testament in the manner of *Hebrew Questions on Genesis* was to be disappointed.

A good deal of the content of the *Hebrew Questions on Genesis* concerns the mistakes that were to be found in the Septuagint and in the Latin translations that were dependent upon it, as well as wrong opinions about the Hebrew text. Some apologists maintained that the Hebrew of Genesis 1 began with the words

In the Son, God created the heaven and the earth (*Hebraicae Quaestiones in libro Geneseos* p.3).

At Genesis 28:19, the Septuagint and Latin versions gave the former name of Bethel as 'Ulammaus' – conflating the Hebrew words ulam (meaning 'but, indeed') and luz (the actual name) (*Heb. Quaest.* p.34). At Genesis 31:7 and 31:41, the Hebrew *monim* ('times, occasions') was translated as 'sheep' by the Septuagint (*Heb. Quaest.* pp.39–40). The Hebrew word *abrek* in Genesis 41:43 was taken to mean a 'herald' in the Septuagint and the Latin versions, although

Aquila rendered it 'bowing the knee'. In Genesis 49, the Septuagint varied considerably from the Hebrew. Thus the verses about Issachar, which begin in the Hebrew

Issachar is a strong ass crouching between the sheepfolds

read in the Septuagint and Latin versions

Issachar desired what was good resting between the allotted land (*Hebr. Quaest.* p.54).

All these mistakes and many others, Jerome corrected by means of fresh translations from the Hebrew, and by comments on the Hebrew text. On occasion, he professed not to know how or why the Septuagint had translated the Hebrew in the way it had; why, for example, the Hebrew *mittah* (bed) was rendered by 'staff' at Genesis 47:31 and 'bed' at 48:1 (*Hebr. Quaest.* p.51).

Jerome was also able to correct more serious matters. The chronology of the life of Methuselah in the Septuagint and the Latin version had Methuselah living for 14 years *after* the Flood without having entered the ark (*Hebr. Quaest.* pp.8–9). The problem vanished if the Hebrew and Samaritan chronology was followed. Other information provided by Jerome included alternative renderings of the Hebrew of Joseph's many-coloured coat in Genesis 37:3, so that it could be a coat of long sleeves, or one reaching to his ankles (*Hebr. Quaest.* p. 45); and there was also a discussion of Genesis 6:3, which Jerome took to mean that God's spirit would not judge mankind for ever – an indication of God's mercy (*Hebr. Quaest.* p.9).

The *Hebrew Questions on Genesis* also contains many etymologies on names, which are then given a 'spiritual' or even sometimes christological meaning. Other passages are also interpreted to refer to Christ or to the Holy Spirit, for example, Genesis 1:2, where the Hebrew *merahepet* (was brooding) is likened to a bird hatching its chicks, which life-creating activity is appropriate to the Holy Spirit who gives life to all (*Hebr. Quaest.* p.3).

Influence of Didymus on Jerome

As a commentator, Jerome was strongly influenced by the 'origenist' Didymus the Blind (c.313–398), whom Jerome visited in Alexandria in 385/6 immediately before settling in Bethlehem. The discovery of manuscripts of Didymus's works in Egypt in 1941 has afforded the opportunity to see one of the influences at work on Jerome. In the light of Didymus's exegesis, it is not difficult to see why Jerome, for all his concern with the Hebrew text and its correct literal translation, regarded the 'spiritual' sense as the real crown of interpretation.

In his commentary on Genesis, Didymus recognises the value of the literal sense for 'the crowd', but he is magisterial in his execution of a 'spiritual' sense. Thus, while the literal sense of Genesis 6:2, which speaks of the union of the angels of God with the daughters of men, has value in teaching that nothing must be undertaken without God, the spiritual sense is that God united to men reflection, piety and wisdom so that they may bring forth the virtues in their lives (*Sur la Genèse* pp.22–3). In his commentary on Zechariah, Didymus took as different an approach as possible from the literal Theodore of Mopsuestia. The latter's disavowal that Zechariah 9:9–10 has any reference to Jesus has an astonishing counterpart in Didymus. For him, the daughter of Zion denotes the attentive soul, because the name Zion means 'observing (invisible and eternal things)' as well as 'keeping the commandment'. The coming one, whom Zechariah announces is, of course, Jesus (*Sur Zacharie* pp.687).

Jerome's Exegesis

Returning to Jerome, we find in his commentaries attention to Hebrew scholarship combined with Christological and 'spiritual' interpretation. For example, writing on the Psalms, Jerome refers many individual Psalms to Christ, as well as to David (*Comment. in Psalmos* pp.177–245). In Psalm 3, the 'holy hill' from which God answers the psalmist can refer both to the Son of God and to the church. In Psalm 4, the references can only be to Christ, since the psalmist possesses a righteousness not appropriate even to David. In Psalm 5:2 the phrase 'my King and my God' refers to Christ, who is king and God of the church. Again, the whole of Psalm 17 pertains to Christ in the person of David; and so on.

Commentary on Daniel

In view of the laudatory references to Jerome's commentary on Daniel with which the chapter began, a summary of its contents will not be out of place. Of all Old Testament books, Daniel is probably the one that most readily lends itself to 'historical' interpretation, precisely because its own 'allegorical' style calls for some unravelling in historical terms. Jerome's commentary remains strictly within the confines required by the text. Although he accepts the book as the work of Daniel, the 6th century exile to Babylon, he believes that through inspiration, the book refers to some events that happened after the time of Daniel, but before the time of Jerome himself. In Daniel 2, the four empires signified by the gold, silver, bronze, and iron mixed with clay are respectively the Babylonians, the Medes and Persians, the empire of Alexander the Great and his successors, and finally, the Roman empire. The mixture of iron and clay signifies the fact that Rome depended upon barbarians to support it. The stone made without hands which smashes the structure made up of the four metals is Jesus, born of a virgin, who has crushed all empires (*Comment. on Daniel.* p.32).

Again, in Daniel 7, Jerome identifies as the Roman Empire the fourth beast which trampled upon the three preceding beasts. Interestingly, Jerome devoted some space to refuting the views of the pagan philosopher Porphyry (c.232–c.305), who identified the 'little horn' that grew on the head of the fourth beast (Daniel 7:8) with Antiochus Epiphanes, the persecutor of the Jews in the first half of the 2nd century B.C. This identification is accepted by most contemporary critical scholars. In Jerome's opinion, the 'little horn' represented a future human ruler who would be used by Satan. The figure of 'one like a son of man' (Daniel 7:13) was Christ.

In interpreting chs. 8 and 11, Jerome made indentifications that are accepted by modern scholars. Thus, the ram defeated by the he-goat in vv.4–7 referred to the defeat by Alexander the Great of the Persian empire, and the division of the large horn of the he-goat when it died was the division of Alexander's kingdom at his death. In interpreting ch.8, Jerome allowed that the 'little horn' of 8:9ff was Antiochus Epiphanes. In discussing Daniel 11, Jerome allowed that the text of vv.3ff. referred to the events of the struggle for the land of Israel between Antiochus the Great and the Ptolemies at the beginning of the 2nd century B.C. In commenting on ch.9, Jerome devoted much space to differing theories about the meaning of the 70 weeks and the 62 weeks.

Elsewhere, Jerome expounded the text in a dignified Christian fashion. He was obviously much in sympathy with the ascetically inclined Daniel and his companions, and praised Daniel's apparent refusal of gifts (Daniel 5:17). He saw in the book a noble expression of God's government of the world. The favour shown to Daniel in ch.1 was not the goodness of perverted men, but the working of divine mercy. The restoration of Nebuchadnezzar after his madness was a sign of God's sovereign control, which control was also recognised by the response of the three men thrown into the fiery furnace (Daniel 3:18). In interpreting this passage, Jerome did not identify the fourth person in the furnace as Christ, on the grounds that it was unlikely that an ungodly king would be vouchsafed a vision of the Son of God. Jerome understood Daniel 3:25 to refer to an angel, who pre-figured Christ.

The nearest one comes to overt spiritualising is in the comments on Daniel 5:4, where the gods of gold, silver, bronze, iron, wood and stone refer to heretics and abusers of God. Those of gold rely on human reason, those of silver rely on eloquence and rhetoric, those of bronze and iron on fables and divergent ancient traditions, and those of wood and stone rely on absurdities. On the other hand, Jerome firmly resisted the 'spiritualising' of Origen, who saw in Nebuchadnezzar's repentance a 'type' of the conversion of the devil.

Clash with Augustine

To conclude the section on Jerome, I refer to a dispute between Jerome and his younger contemporary Augustine, which is documented by J. N. D. Kelly (*Jerome, his life, Writings and Controversies* pp.269–272). The dispute concerned the interpretation of Peter's actions, alluded to in Galatians 2:11–12, when Peter refused to eat with Gentile Christians in Antioch and was rebuked by Paul. Porphyry, who, in exploiting the clash between Peter and Paul, had once again identified a major issue that would engage modern scholars, had been 'answered' by a whole succession of Christian writers who asserted that Peter had only pretended to observe the Jewish law and that Paul had only pretended to rebuke him. Jerome followed this interpretation, but Augustine rejected it on the grounds that such behaviour would amount to deliberate dishonesty. It was common ground, however, between Jerome and Augustine, that Christians were not bound by Jewish (Old Testament) regulations about food laws. If Augustine accepted Peter's behaviour at its face value, he also believed that the Jewish Apostles were allowed the privilege of observing the Jewish law provided that they did not trust in this observance for salvation.

Summary

In Jerome, Christian Old Testament scholarship found a great linguist, interpreter, translator and mediator of earlier scholarship. In a sense, he combined what was best in both the Alexandrian and Antiochene schools. He made it clear to his successors that the Old Testament was an oriental book written in an oriental language and set in the oriental past. At the same time he fervently expressed his belief that the coming of Jesus showed that the Old Testament was a book of illumination and hope for all mankind.

2. AUGUSTINE

Jerome's younger contemporary, Augustine, did not possess great linguistic equipment. He knew no Hebrew, and his knowledge of Greek was not extensive. Unlike Jerome, he did not enjoy the life of a scholar. At the time of his ordination he regarded himself as unprepared for his ministry from the point of view of his knowledge of the Bible. His work on biblical interpretation was carried out in the midst of the demanding life of a bishop of the church in North Africa. Yet arguably, he brought Old Testament interpretation to a level even higher than that of Jerome, if one considers his achievement in bringing together detailed exegesis and an original overall view of the Bible.

Augustine was born in Thagaste in Roman North Africa in A.D.354. He studied in Carthage and his home city of Thagaste, and he travelled to Rome in 373 where, ten years later he founded a school of rhetoric. Whilst in Milan, he came under the influence of Ambrose, and he was baptised in 387. In 391 he was ordained priest, and about five years later he became bishop of Hippo in North Africa, in which office he remained until his death in 430.

'The City of God'

Augustine wrote three commentaries on Genesis (one incomplete), a collection of sermons on the Psalms, and several more general works on the Old Testament. However, he dealt with the Old Testament in many other works, for example, in his treatise on biblical interpretation *De doctrina Christiana*, in the *De spiritu et littera*, and above all in the masterpiece of his mature years *De civitate dei* (*The City of God*). In what follows, I shall concentrate on *The City of God*, since this brings together all Augustine's skills as theologian and interpreter. The work is also one of the greatest expositions of the Old Testament taken as a whole ever to be produced by a Christian theologian. The exposition that follows is indebted to R. A. Markus's study *Saeculum: History and Society in the Theology of St. Augustine*, from which the next remarks are derived.

The City of God was begun in A.D.413, soon after the sack of Rome in 410 by the Goths. Ostensibly, it was a reply to pagan criticisms of the time, that the downfall of Rome was the result of that city's abandonment of its gods and its acceptance of Christianity. However, even before the fall of Rome, Augustine had abandoned the belief that the Christian Roman Empire was the fulfilment of biblical prophecy, a belief popularised by Eusebius of

Casesarea, and widely held at the end of the 4th century (Markus pp.47ff.).

By the time that he came to write *The City of God*, Augustine had 'secularised' in his thought both the Roman Empire and its history. He had come to regard the Bible as prophetic history, that is, a composition whose purpose was not only to record past events, but to indicate in the way in which the record was presented how the hidden purposes of God had been operative in the history of Israel and the advent of Jesus. The sacred record thus gave no clues to the meaning of contemporary secular history; rather, it set before mankind the story of two realms, or cities, and it bade mankind either to seek to enter the divine city, or to remain in its counterpart.

The Two Cities
The title 'The City of God' was taken by Augustine from the Psalms, and the work of the same name is designed, from book eleven onwards, to show that the whole Bible is the story of two cities: the heavenly, and the earthly or diabolic. At the outset, we notice that Augustine's scheme cuts across the division between Old and New Testaments. The Old Testament is not a preparation for the establishment of the heavenly kingdom by Christ, although the coming of Christ has brought significant changes. Again, the Old Testament is not about this-worldly blessings while the New Testament is about heavenly blessings. In fact, both the Old and New Testaments describe both cities from their inception to their end, and the city of God is as much present, in a sense, in the Israel of the Old Covenant as it is present, in a sense, in the New. Thus Augustine presented an approach to the Bible which, while allowing for the radical significance of the coming of Jesus, still maintained the essential unity of the testaments (*The City of God* Bk. 10, ch.25).

According to Augustine, the city of God is for the majority part composed of angels, and is situated in heaven. It began, or was founded, when God created the angels on the first day of creation, for what is meant by

Let there be light (Genesis 1:3)

is nothing other than the creation of the angels (Bk.11 ch. 9). The city of the devil (as it must be called from the heavenly perspective) established itself when some of the angels chose to follow their own interests, as opposed to using them wholly in the life and service of God. They 'fell' by their own choice, and their existence is implied in the division between light and darkness in Genesis 1:4 (Bk.11 ch.20).

The creation of the first man and woman in Genesis 1–2 was the creation of a pair who would not have experienced death if they had not disobeyed God's commandment. They would have procreated offspring, but not by physical contact, had they remained fully obedient. In choosing to disobey, they brought not only upon themselves but upon their descendants a two-fold death: the dissolution of body and soul at the end of earthly life, and the eternal punishment after the final judgement (Bk.14 ch.26). Their disobedience created the conditions for the existence of the city of God and its opposing earthly city in the world of mankind. Because all mankind was now subject to death at the end of a natural lifespan, those humans, destined to be members of the city of God were also subject to death. They were thus pilgrims and strangers in this world.

The founders among mankind of the cities of God and of the earthly city were Abel and Cain. Cain, the murderer of Abel, is said to have founded a city (Genesis 4:17), and Augustine compares the murderous origin of the earthly city with the story of the fratricide of the founders of the city of Rome, Remus and Romulus (Bk.15 chs 1,6). It is important at this stage, however, to point out that Augustine does not make the simple identifications

Israel/the Church   equals   City of God
the nations/the state   equals   earthly city.

He allows that within both Israel and the Church, good and bad, members of both cities, are mingled (Bk.11 ch 1). He allows that in Old Testament times, non-Israelites such as Job were members of the city of God (Bk.18 ch 47). On the other hand, he does not regard human political organisations as wholly bad. If a country, by going to war, achieves a just end, it cannot be blamed or condemned. A political organisation has its own appropriate goods, which are not to be despised. However, at the end of the day, these goods are not those of the city of God, and will not lead mankind to that city (Bk. 15 ch 4; Bk. 19 chs 5ff.). We thus see that Augustine maintains a subtle and complex balance between the earthly and the heavenly, the two interacting spheres in which the believer is obliged to live and work, the nature of whose intersection and their conflicts is clarified in the inspired scriptures.

Having described the establishment of the two cities from their heavenly and earthly points of view, Augustine traces their history up to and through the Flood, and on into Israelite history. It is in dealing with the latter that Augustine shows most clearly what he means when he says that biblical history is primarily prophetic rather than simply an inspired factually correct record of the succession of past events. It is also here that Augustine contextualises his view of the relation between historical and 'spiritual' interpretation, and between prophecy that has an 'earthly' and a 'heavenly' fulfilment (Bk.17 chs 3ff.).

Biblical Interpretation
The historical events recorded in the Old Testament are, for Augustine, sacrosanct and above criticism. This is as true for the story of the Garden of Eden as for the rest (Bk.13 ch 21). It does not follow from this, however, that Old Testament history is exhaustive in its accounts of events, nor that it always related events in the exact sequence of their occurrence (Bk.15 ch 8). Again, it is not the case that all events are 'significant'. Some are completely without significance, and are there only as necessary adjuncts to truly significant happenings (Bk.16 ch 2). This having been said, Augustine makes it clear that the primary function of Old Testament history is to testify to the existence of the city of God by anticipating the coming of Christ, who makes possible for all mankind the reversal of the curse of the disobedience of Adam.

In establishing this point, Augustine refers to many familiar passages in Psalms and prophetic books which were standard prophecies of the coming of Christ (Bk.17, Bk.18 chs 18ff.). But he also saw the interplay of the forces of the two kingdoms in the events of Israel's history. Thus, the condemnation of the priesthood of the house of Eli (I Samuel 2:27–36) points to the abrogation of the Aaronic priesthood with the coming of Christ. The rending of the kingdom from Saul (I Samuel 15:23) foreshadows the loss of the kingdom to the Jews when they reject Christ as their king. Augustine also notes that after the division of the kingdom at the death of Solomon, we are not left with two kingdoms, one good and the other bad. In Judah as well as in Israel there is a need for prophetic rebuke, and although the northern kings are adjudged to be more impious than those of the southern kingdom, it is in the northern kingdom that were to be found the 7,000 who had not bent the knee to Baal. This parallels the position the church finds itself in after the coming of Christ. Although in a sense it is the city of God on earth, it still contains both good and bad, who will finally be divided at the judgement. In the closing books of *The City of God*, Augustine describes the thousand-year rule of Christ and the final judgement, matters pertaining mostly to the New Testament.

So far, this exposition has been concerned with Augustine's grand design, and with the total view of the meaning of existence and history in terms of which the Bible is interpreted. But *The City of God* involves much detailed exegesis, of which some examples will now be given.

Examples of Exegesis
It has already been noted that while Augustine holds biblical history to be sacrosanct in its accuracy, he allows that it often omits information, or does not have it in strict chronological sequence. These concessions are part of his defence of the authenticity of the history. This same defence also leads him into other areas in which he deals with problems that were to exercise all thoughtful readers of the Old Testament until the rise of the critical method.

A good example is Augustine's treatment of the Flood and of the ark built by Noah (Bk.15 chs 27ff.). He notes in his own day those who doubt that there could have been a Flood of such great proportions, or that there would have been room in the ark for all living creatures. On the latter point, he argues that it was not necessary for *all* living creatures to enter the ark. Those that lived normally in water would not need to enter, nor was it necessary for there to be male and female of sexless creatures such as bees. Again, in the case of remote islands, it was likely that the earth produced the animals to be found on them after the Flood as hinted in Genesis 1:24

Let the earth bring forth the living creature (Bk.16, ch 7).

Augustine's defence of the Flood narrative therefore involved a certain freedom with the text which would have been frowned on by some orthodox 19th century writers. In dealing with Genesis 1, Augustine was well aware of the problem of light being created before the sun, and of there being days and nights before the creation of the sun and moon. As we have seen, he understood the light to be the angels; the exact nature of the days remained a mystery.

Another problem concerned the existence of giants before the flood, and the tremendously long lives lived by such as Methuselah. On common sense grounds, Augustine argued that the days and years referred to in Genesis 5, where Methuselah and others are mentioned, could be no different from the days and years of the Flood narrative in Genesis 6, and that it was clear that ordinary days and years were meant in the Flood narrative. Thus there was no reason to suppose that Methuselah's 969 years were anything other than normal years. Augustine conceded, however, that an explanation was needed for the fact that some patriarchs in Genesis 5 did not beget children until there were aged 150 or more. One of several possible explanations was that in those times, people reached physical maturity much more slowly than in later times. The existence of giants could be substantiated by the vast size of tombs of ancient heroes, and by people of extraordinary stature even in Augustine's own time (Bk.15 ch 23).

If Augustine was prepared to defend the historical authenticity of the Old Testament, he also defended the moral integrity of the heroes of faith in the Old Testament. Thus, Abraham, in fathering a son through his wife's servant, was not to be blamed, because he did this action without lust (Bk.16 ch 25). His marriage to Keturah was also not the result of fleshly lusts, but a foreshadowing of the 'carnal people' who thought that they belonged to the New Covenant. Jacob did not act fraudulently when he deprived Esau of his blessing; his action enabled Christ to be proclaimed to the nations when Isaac blessed him. Again, in anointing the stone after his heavenly vision, Jacob practised no idolatry but foreshadowed Christ (Bk.16 ch 37–8).

It is clear from these examples that Augustine, like most of his generation, indulged in the 'spiritualising' of the Old Testament, and there are many such examples in *The City of God*, of which a not untypical example is the interpretation of the door of Noah's Ark in terms of the wound made in the side of Christ (Bk.15, ch 26). We also find strenuous attempts to prove that God does not move, come to know, repent, and so on, these expressions all being figures of speech (Bk.16 ch 5).

Conclusion

For all this, the impressive thing about *The City of God* is that it is an attempt to take the Old Testament seriously as history, and to consider how secular and sacred history are to be regarded in relation to each other. In some respects, it is an anticipation of the notion of *Heilsgeschichte* (Salvation History) of the 19th century, but without the philosophical assumptions of the latter. Indeed, Augustine's view that biblical history's main function is to give a clue to the hidden divine imperatives that are at work in secular history, is remarkably modern.

On other matters of the Old Testament Augustine believed in the superiority of the Septuagint over the Hebrew, for all that he drew extensively upon Jerome's etymologies of Hebrew names, and commended Jerome's Hebrew learning (Bk.18 ch 43). He regarded a training in rhetoric as a valuable preparation for handling biblical language. On the laws of the Old Testament, he held that some, like those dealing with sacrifice, circumcision and the sabbath foreshadow the Christian dispensation, while laws such as the Ten Commandments had a validity in themselves as divine law.

With the age of Jerome and Augustine, we may say that the Christian use of the Old Testament reached a point after which there was room only for fine tuning for the next six hundred years or so. The next chapter will deal with some aspects of that fine tuning.

FOR FURTHER READING

J. N. D. Kelly, *Jerome, His Life, Writings and Controversies*, London 1975.

H. F. D. Sparks, 'Jerome as Biblical Scholar' in *Cambridge History of the Bible* vol.1 pp.510–540.

G. L. Archer (trans.), *Jerome's Commentary on Daniel*, Grand Rapids, Michigan 1958.

Jerome, *Hebraicae Quaestiones in libro Geneseos*, in *Corpus Christianorum, Series Latina* (C.C.L.) vol.72; *Commentarioli in Psalmos*, C.C.L. vol. 72.

Didyme L'Aveugle, *Sur Zacharie* (Sources Chrétiennes vol. 83, Paris 1962); *Sur la Genèse* (Sources Chrétiennes vol. 244, Paris 1978).

Gerald Bonner, *Saint Augustine of Hippo. Life and Controversies*, London 1963.

Gerald Bonner, 'Augustine as Biblical Scholar' *Cambridge History of the Bible* vol. 1, pp.541–563.

R. A. Markus, *Saeculum: History and Society in the Theology of St. Augustine*, Cambridge 1970.

Augustine, *The City of God* (there are many translations, including those of Marcus Dods in the *Nicene and Post-Nicene Fathers* vol. II, E. B. Pusey in the *Everyman* library, H. Bettenson in the *Penguin* classics, and the edition in the *Loeb* Classical Library).

5

THE FIFTH TO THE NINTH CENTURIES

1. THE APOSTOLICAL CONSTITUTIONS AND CYRIL OF ALEXANDRIA

One particular feature of the interpretation of the Old Testament that this first section of the book will attempt to trace is how, after being virtually rejected or spiritualised by the early Church, the Mosaic law came to play an important role as a lawbook for Christians. The attempt to trace this development will not be particularly successful in the period up to about A.D.1200, since little is known about the origin and growth of canon law before A.D.1200. An interesting text, one that may not have been influential but whose existence is worth notice, is the *Apostolical Constitutions*, thought to have been compiled in Syria some time in the 4th century, possibly from earlier sources. If this dating is correct, then a consideration of the *Constitutions* in the present chapter violates the chapter heading. However, a consideration here will enable us to preserve a general clear outline of the use of the Old Testament in the Church.

Mosaic Laws

The most explicit treatment of the Mosaic law in the *Constitutions* occurs in Sections 4–6, Chapters 19–30 of Book VI; but there are many unusual references to the law, as well as unusual applications of other parts of the Old Testament elsewhere in the work. The section 'Of the law' (Ante-Nicene Library, vol. 17, pp.162–170) affirms that Christ did not come to abolish but to fulfil the law, and explains this process in terms that we have already met elsewhere. A distinction is made between the decalogue and the laws given before the worship of the Golden Calf (Exodus 32), and those given after this act of apostasy. It is pointed out that laws in Exodus 21ff. often take the form of what modern scholarship has defined as 'casuistic law', that is, laws beginning with the word 'if', and outlining a possible case that may arise. The *Constitutions* make the point that many of these pre-Golden Calf laws do not, therefore, restrict liberty, but allow possibilities (p.164). Exodus 20:24 does not say 'make an altar of earth', it says 'if you make an altar, make it of earth'. The point is also made that no sacrifices are commanded before the Golden Calf incident but only after it.

It follows from the distinction between the period before and after the Golden Calf apostasy that the sacrificial regulations and the levitical instructions are a particular legislation for the Israelites in virtue of their apostasy. These regulations do not represent natural law, as is indicated both by the fact that Christ abolished them, and that the prophets and psalmists declare them to be, strictly speaking, unnecessary. Christ fulfils the law by abolishing the sacrificial and levitical legislation that was applicable only to apostate Israel, and by giving a new depth of meaning to the Ten Commandments in the Sermon on the Mount. Christians who wish to observe Jewish rules of purity are severely criticised. If they believe that child-bearing or menstrual blood defiles a person, then they are denying the Holy Spirit, because his indwelling is not affected by external factors (p.171).

However, it is clear from the remainder of the *Apostolical Constitutions* that the distinction before and after the Golden Calf incident is an over-simplification. Elsewhere, a distinction is made between the 'original law' and the 'additional precepts', and one of the tasks of a bishop is that he should learn to distinguish carefully between them (p.29). How he is to do this is not stated, but presumably the task is more complex than dividing law into the pre– and post-Golden Calf eras. Early in the work, two examples are given of 'additional precepts' that are binding upon Christians: men must not comb their hair in order to make it curl or shine, nor may they shave (p.19).

Christian Applications
The *Constitutions* urge upon Christians that they should read and meditate upon the Mosaic law, and Deuteronomy 6:7 is paraphrased

Thou shalt meditate in his law day and night . . .

Christians who do this will have 'the glorious law of the Lord God'. Then follows the interesting statement:

'when thou readest the law, think not thyself bound to observe the additional precepts; though not all of them, yet some of them' (p.20).

If the *Constitutions* themselves do not make it clear which are and are not 'additional precepts' or which of the latter are binding upon Christians, we can at least outline how the Mosaic law is to affect Christians. I shall consider in turn church order, administration of justice and worship.

The Christian ministry is seen to parallel that in the Old Testament. In one passage (p.58), bishops are likened to the high priests, presbyters to the priests, and deacons to the levites. The offering of tithes and first-fruits to clergy is supported with reference to the tithes etc. that were due to the levites (p.56). In one curious passage, the bishop is even described as an earthly god to his congregation, on the grounds that God is referring to bishops when he says:

I have said, ye are gods (Psalm 82:6)

and

Ye shall not speak evil of the gods (Exodus 22:28) (p.58).

Many Old Testament passages are used to show that there are privileges that pertain only to clergy. Saul and Uzziah are examples of kings punished for trying to usurp the priestly office (p.59).

The bishop as a judge in the administration of church justice is grounded upon Deuteronomy 19:17

both parties to the dispute shall appear before the LORD, before the priests and the judges who are in office in those days (p.75).

The Old Testament laws about witnesses are to be enforced (three are preferred) while sentences are to be varied, as was the case in the Old Testament.

On the question of worship, one interesting feature is the importance accorded to the sabbath. The sabbath does not, of course, overshadow the day of Resurrection; but it certainly is more important than the other days of the week, and the command is given:

every Sabbath-day excepting one (that is, Holy Saturday), and every Lord's day, hold your solemn assemblies and rejoice (p.143).

To sum up, the *Apostolical Constitutions* indicate a very real move in at least one part of the church towards re-admitting the Mosaic law as a law book for the life of the church. Theory (the division into pre- and post-Golden Calf laws, or the distinction between 'original' and 'additional' precepts) is outrun by practice – something that we shall find again.

Cyril of Alexandria

With the view in the *Apostolical Constitutions* of the Mosaic law in the history of God's dealings with Israel, it is interesting to compare the position maintained by Cyril of Alexandria (Archbishop of Alexandria) A.D. 412–444. Recent research on Cyril as an Old Testament scholar has shown him to be strongly influenced by Jerome, but also to break new ground in his interpretation of the historical sense of the text (A. Kerrigan, *St. Cyril of Alexandria. Interpreter of the Old Testament*, Rome 1952). In particular, Cyril seems to have had a great interest in the geography of Palestine and surrounding nations, and to have alluded frequently to the legends of the Jews, as well as to pagan writers.

Cyril's view of the history of Israel is based upon Leviticus 19:23–5, a law which forbids Israelites to eat the fruit which a fruit tree produces in its first three years, directs them to regard the fruit of the fourth year as dedicated to God, and allows them to enjoy the fruit of the fifth year (Kerrigan pp.170f.). On the assumption that the first three years represent the periods of Moses, Joshua and the Judges, Cyril concludes that in this period of Old Testament history the law was

impure, loaded with the coarseness of history and having the dark shadow around it as worthless refuse.

The fourth year represents the period of the prophets, some of whom set aside the legal enactments, and proclaimed the advent of Christ. Examples of this are Hosea 6:6ff.

For I desire steadfast love and not sacrifice, the knowledge of God, rather than burnt offerings

which is taken to mean that charity and the knowledge of Christ are more pleasing to God than animal sacrifice; and Joel 1:13, 19 which are held to proclaim the cessation of the Mosaic sacrifices (Kerrigan pp.171ff.).

During this fourth period, the prophets were 'purifying' the law and making it holy so that it could become 'eatable' during the fifth period, that of Christ's advent. Cyril's view of the law, is, strictly speaking, less favourable to its use as a Christian lawbook than is the case with the *Apostolical Constitutions;* but it shares with the latter a 'dispensational' view of the law.

2. GREGORY THE GREAT AND BEDE

Effects of the Upheavals of the 5th to 9th Centuries
Together with Augustine and Jerome, Gregory the Great and Bede were the most influential interpreters in the early middle ages. They worked in a very different world compared with that of Augustine and Jerome, although Augustine had seen the beginnings of the fall of the Christian hegemony that had once stretched from Britain to Asia Minor, Syria-Palestine and Egypt. The western part of the Roman Empire had fallen to the 'germanic' peoples in the first half of the 5th century, and by A.D. 475 was divided into ten or more kingdoms. Britain had been invaded by the Angles and Saxons. By the time of the death of Theoderic the Great, king of the East Goths in 526, Central Europe, including Italy, had come to be dominated by two main kingdoms, the Franks in the north and the East Goths in the south. The political power of Christianity was strengthened in the 6th century, when the Franks, who were orthodox Christians since the time of Clovis (king from 482–511) expanded at the expense of the Arian East Goths, and the Eastern Roman Emperor Justinian re-conquered Italy and part of North Africa. Further shocks were to follow, however, especially in the 7th century, when the rise and triumph of Islam wiped out much of the Eastern Roman Empire. In the 8th and 9th centuries in Western and Central Europe a growing together of kingdoms and church culminated in the coronation of Charles I (Charlemagne) by Pope Leo III in 800. Even so, the Carolingian Empire suffered various crises of succession to the throne and, after 887, was sorely pressed by Magyar invasions from the East. Britain was invaded from Denmark during the 9th century.

The affect of all this unrest upon Old Testament scholarship is not easy to determine. There were obviously great losses. For example, Origen's *Hexapla* perished with the Moslem conquest of Palestine, and the great centres of Antioch and Alexandria ceased to exercise the Christian influence that they had done in their heyday. One presumes that the political upheavals were not conducive to scholarship, and it is certainly the case that from the 6th century onwards, it was in the monasteries that Old Testament learning was kept alive. This state of affairs continued into the 12th century, when cathedral schools began to play a significant role. The next major development would be the establishment of universities.

Gregory the Great

Gregory the Great, Pope from A.D. 590–604, was a monk who, in spite of having endowed a number of monasteries including that to which he belonged, had worked his way through the monastic ranks to the position of Abbot. From 579–586 he was a papal representative in Constantinople, where he gave the monks the lectures that were to become the *Moralia* on the book of Job (references are to *Morales sur Job* in Sources Chrétiennes 32, Paris 1975). Other Old Testament works would include homilies on Ezekiel, the books of Kings and the Song of Songs. As a sample of his work, I shall outline Gregory's lectures on the opening of the Book of Job.

There are three expositions of Job 1:1–5, a literal exposition, an allegorical and a moral exposition. The classification 'literal' does not convey exactly what the modern reader might understand from the term. The purpose of the 'literal' exposition is certainly as didactic as the other expositions, and in it, Gregory interprets scripture from scripture, as though the Bible were a seamless robe. We can, over-simplifying, distinguish the three expositions by saying that in the literal exposition, Gregory uses Job as an historical example of a man of great faith, from whose piety the modern believer can learn much. The allegorical exposition is essentially Christological and an exploration of the meanings of biblical symbols, while the moral exposition likens Job to the soul of the individual believer, identifying Job's possessions with the possessions of the soul.

In the first exposition, Gregory begins by noticing that Job is identified as living in a non-Israelite country, the land of Uz (pp.175 ff.). This is an immediate pointer to his virtue. It is easier to be virtuous in a place where others are virtuous; it is much harder where one is surrounded by the wickedness that Gregory supposed typified the land of Uz. It is next pointed out that Job's implicit virtue is confirmed explicitly by the text that states that in addition to being blameless and upright, Job turned away from evil. Thus Job's large possessions were no hindrance to his virtue, while his children, by inviting each other to feasts, exhibited a degree of harmony that was to their father's credit. The fact that Job offered sacrifices on behalf of his children in case they had offended against God unwittingly, gave Gregory the chance to reflect upon the high probability that where people feasted together, they would become the victims of sensuality. The text from Exodus 32:6:

the people sat down to eat and drink, and rose up to play

indicated the danger of the kind of gaity that had no motive, which was engendered by feasting.
Two factors completed the portrait of the exemplary patriarch. The first was his perseverance. Job continually offered the sacrifices on behalf of his children (Job 1:5c). The second was the contrast between the description of Job as the

greatest of all the people of the east (Job 1:3)

and the humble resignation with which he could say at the end of the chapter:

The LORD gave and the LORD has taken away; blessed be the name of the LORD (Job 1:21).

One piece of Christological interpretation is present in the literal exposition of Job 1:1–5. On the basis of Job 1:5, Gregory inferred that Job offered sacrifices on the eighth day, after the seven sons had each given a feast that lasted a day. This eighth day was an indication of the Resurrection day, which was also the eighth day (p.187).

The allegorical interpretation of Job 1:1–5 begins with a Christological reference (pp.189 ff.). The name 'Job' means 'the one who suffers' and Uz means 'the counsellor'. Thus Job's name points to Christ, who suffers, and who lives in the land of Uz when he reigns in the hearts of believers, to guide and counsel them. The number of Job's children (seven sons and three daughters) gives rise to various speculations. Seven is a number of perfection, as shown by the fact that God rested on the seventh day, and that the seventh day was the sabbath. Further, seven represented the apostles, since seven is comprised of 3 plus 4 which amount to 12 when multiplied. 3 and 4 also signify that the Trinity is preached to the four corners of the earth. The three daughters can be linked to the three saints of Ezekiel 14:14, Noah, Daniel and Job. These three men represent respectively the priests (Noah guided the ark as priests guide the church), the celibate (Daniel abstained from the luxuries of Babylon) and the faithful married.

On the animals possessed by Job, Gregory was able to trace different threads of meanings of symbols. Camels, for example, can indicate pagans deformed by vice who come to faith. A camel can also indicate Jesus as in the dominical saying to the Jews:

you strain at a gnat
and swallow a camel (Matthew 23:24).

Camels, unclean animals, can also designate Samaritans. The sacrifices offered by Job on behalf of his children typify the sacrifice
offered by Jesus to his Father on behalf of the faithful.
The moral sense (pp.215 ff.) can be briefly characterised by saying
that the seven sons represent the seven gifts of the Spirit (Isaiah
11:2), and the three daughters represent faith, hope and charity.
The invitations of Job's sons to their sisters to attend their feasts
indicated that Christian gifts had to be exercised in harmony, and
in accordance with faith, hope and charity. Job's rising up early to
offer sacrifice on behalf of his children symbolises the individual
making daily prayers on his own behalf for the strengthening of his
Christian virtues.
   On Job 2 (pp.255 ff.), one of Gregory's concerns is to explain
how it was possible that Satan could appear before God. If only the
pure in heart see God, then how could Satan do so? The answer is
that Satan could not look upon God, even though God could look
upon Satan. Gregory's literal exposition of this chapter contains
some interesting studies of biblical language. God's question to
Satan 'where have you come from?' cannot be taken literally,
because to do so would deny God's omniscience. The phrase is
compared to God's question to Adam 'where are you?'. This latter
question shows not that God was ignorant of Adam's whereabouts,
but that he was passing judgement on Adam. Similarly, the question
to Satan about where he had come from expresses not ignorance,
but judgement.
   The spiritual and moral interpretations of Job 2 follow the lines
already established in ch. 1. Job, as the one whose name means 'the
sufferer', represents Christ, and Job being given into the power of
Satan typifies Christ being given into Satan's power at the crucifixion. In the moral exposition, God's permission to Satan to afflict
Job is interpreted to mean permission given to Satan to tempt the
human soul. Various moral lessons are drawn from the misfortunes
that overcame Job.

Comment
If this sample of Gregory's exposition is representative, two
comments are possible. The first is that it is unlikely that anyone
today could interpret the Old Testament in a similar fashion. Yet,
secondly, it cannot fail to arouse our admiration. Whatever else the
writer of Job may have intended, he certainly saw Job as an example

of a very pious man. Gregory, in his literal expositions, certainly did not betray the author's intention in drawing out to the full the virtues of Job. In the context of the Christian spirituality of his day, Gregory's exposition can be judged as profound and effective. If today we find it foreign, this may be as much our fault as the fault of 6th century Christian piety.

Bede

The other great western commentator to be considered here, Bede, was born in Northumbria, and spent his working life in the monastic foundation of Jarrow-Wearmouth, dying in Jarrow in A.D.735 at the age of about 63. His Old Testament works included expositions of the Hexaemeron (the six days of creation), the Pentateuch, Samuel and Kings, Proverbs, and the Song of Songs, as well as books on the Tabernacle and the priestly ornaments. It is, I hope, not unfair to describe Bede as a mediator of the learning of the great commentators who had gone before him, rather than as an original commentator in his own right. The Old Testament points unmistakably to Christ as stated by Paul in I Corinthians 10:11:

> these things . . . were written down for our instruction, upon whom the end of the ages has come (*Corpus Christianorum*, Series Latina, CX, 1962, p.9).

Thus Bede has no hesitation in providing allegorial interpretations, for example, of Samuel and Kings.

In the exposition of Samuel, Bede makes constant use of explanations of names, and sees almost everything in terms of Christ and the Church. The two wives of Elkanah, Hannah and Peninnah are the Church and the Synagogue respectively. The capture of the ark by the Philistines represents the gospel being taken from the Jews and given to the Gentiles. On the other hand, while in Philistine captivity, the ark, in the house of Dagon (who is a fish, and therefore Leviathan, and thus a figure of Satan), accomplishes a triumph over the powers of the evil one.

In the period briefly surveyed, the allegorical and mystical interpretation of the Old Testament reached a high point. For the remainder of the Middle Ages, although these approaches were still very much in evidence, there was a renewal of interest in the west in the historical and scientific interpretation of the Old Testament, as the next chapter will show.

FOR FURTHER READING

G. le Bras, *Histoire du Droit et des Institutions de l'Eglise en Occident*, Vol.I, Prolegomenes, Paris 1955.

H. Daniel-Rops, *The Church in the Dark Ages*, London 1959.

6

THE NINTH TO THE FIFTEENTH CENTURIES

This period can be divided into three phases for our purposes: 9th – 11th centuries, 12th – 13th centuries, 14th – 15th centuries, with the middle period being by far the most important.

1. THE NINTH TO THE ELEVENTH CENTURIES

The 9th – 11th centuries can be seen as preparation for the so-called 12th century renaissance. In this period, the reforms in education initiated by Charlemagne (d. A.D.814) resulted not merely in an improved educational system. They led to a surge in the provision of materials for study, as new copies of classic Christian and pagan texts were made and corrected, and a new form of handwriting was developed. The great representatives of this period were Alcuin (c. 735–804) Rabanus Maurus (d.856) and Rabanus's pupil Walufrid Strabon (d.846). Alcuin, a Northumbrian, head of the episcopal school at York, and later the director of Charlemagne's Palatine School at Aix-la-Chapelle, is best known for his revision of the text of the Vulgate. As a commentator on the Old Testament he wrote works on Genesis, Ecclesiastes, the penitential Psalms and the Song of Songs. He is above all a compiler and transmitter of the views of others, especially Augustine, Jerome and Bede.

Rabanus Maurus is also seen as a compiler in his commentaries on the historical books of the Old Testament, Proverbs, Wisdom, Ecclesiasticus, Jeremiah and Ezekiel. As Beryl Smalley has written, to study scholars such as Rabanus 'is to study their sources' (*The Study of the Bible in the Middle Ages*, Oxford 1983(3) p.38). However, Rabanus made an attempt to set out rules for interpreting the Bible, based upon Augustine's *De doctrina Christiana*, in his *De clericorum institutione* – a work which itself draws deeply upon the Old Testament. Walufrid Strabon was once believed to be the father of the *Glossa Ordinaria*, which will be discussed later. While this view is no longer entertained, it is based upon the practice already current in the 9th century of adding glosses from Christian authorities to the biblical text either in the margin or between the lines. This same period saw a revival in the study of Hebrew among Christians. Beryl Smalley notes (*Study* p.43) that there were many attempts by scholars at least to learn the Hebrew alphabet, and that a Bible corrected by Theodulf, bishop of Orleans, had been compared with the Hebrew text. The 11th century seems to have been something of a blank period in Old Testament scholarship. According to Beryl Smalley, no important commentary was written for a century and a quarter after the death of Remigius of Auxerre (c. A.D.908), and even compilations were few for the same period (*Study*, p.44). A reason for this may have been the closure of the monastic schools as monks concentrated on liturgy and worship, and their libraries were used only by a few scholarly Abbots.

2. THE TWELFTH AND THIRTEENTH CENTURIES

The renaissance of the 12th century was prepared for by the growth in importance of the Cathedral schools. Both teachers and students alike seem to have moved around somewhat from school to school, and as a result of the teaching there began to be developed the 'glosses' by which the students recorded alongside the biblical text the teachings of their masters. An attempt to standardise the glosses was first made at the Cathedral school in Laon, under Anselm of Laon, and once the Laon system was introduced into Paris it became a standard form of commentary on the Old Testament in the form of the *Glossa Ordinaria*. The glossing of the Pentateuch, the major prophets, Lamentations and possibly the historical books is now attributed to the Laon master Gilbert the Universal. The glosses are drawn mainly from Jerome, Augustine, Bede, and Gregory, with some references to Walufrid Strabon.

Along with the method of the *gloss*, there developed in the 12th century the method of *quaestio*. This was a use of dialectic derived from the study of the liberal arts to interrogate the biblical text, so as to seek for truth in the process of overcoming the questions that the text raised. A master of this method was Peter Abelard.

Abelard

Abelard's major writing on the Old Testament, the commentary on the Hexaemeron, had no influence in the history of Old Testament scholarship, since it was addressed to the nuns of the convent of the Paraclete. However, Abelard remains a fascinating and important figure in the 12th century, and his work as an exegete is not without interest. As a student, he had attended the school at Laon at the time when the *glosses* were being standardised. However, he had moved to Chartres, where the teaching was more concerned with the liberal arts, and where he became familiar with pagan classics such as Plato's *Timaeus*.

In his exposition of the narrative of creation, Abelard used the *Timaeus* to provide the general framework of his approach, and he understood the biblical text to say that before God created the world as an act he first ordered and constituted it as an archetype through his reason (references are to Eileen F. Kearney, *Master Peter Abelard, Expositor of Sacred Scripture*, Diss. Graduate School, Marquette Univ., 1980). Abelard also considered the narrative in the light of the science of his day without, however, providing satisfactory answers. The question about how there could be waters overhead i.e. how could a lighter element, air, support a heavier element, water, was solved by the observation that it is the will of God. Abelard also distinguished between two accounts of creation without, of course, contemplating two authors or sources. He also distinguished between the intention of the author (Moses) and the intention of God (Kearney, p.103).

Abelard's main thrust in interpretation was towards the literal sense. Yet, as with Gregory on the book of Job, the literal or historical sense could contain much that was figurative or allegorical (Kearney, p.48). However, Abelard does provide moral and mystical expositions, and in the latter there is an interesting discussion of the law which will lead to the main subject of the present chapter, the understanding of the Old Testament law in the 12th – 13th centuries. Abelard associates the six days of creation with six phases in salvation history (Kearney, pp.137ff.).

Day 1, the confusion of the elements signifies the world before the law.

Day 2, the separation of the waters alludes to those who escape the Flood.

Day 3, the land emerging from the waters and producing life resembles the giving of the law which lifts people from earthly to spiritual values.

Day 4, the creation of the light signifies the prophets who come after the law and look for the coming of Christ.

Day 5, the production of living beings by the water anticipates the renewal of those who undergo Christian baptism. Day 6, man being placed in paradise looks forward to man restored to paradise after the Lord's passion.

An Unknown Contemporary

Roughly contemporary with Abelard was a glossator of the book of Leviticus, whose work has been discovered by Beryl Smalley (*Studies in Medieval Thought and Learning from Abelard to Wyclif*, London 1981, pp.27–48). Smalley estimates that the glossator taught in a cathedral school in northern France before the middle of the 12th century. She describes him as 'a pioneer of biblical scholarship in a modest way'. His work is characterised by the attempt to make sense of the levitical law as a viable code even though it has been superceded in the coming of Christ. This differed from the many previous approaches to the levitical law which pointed out supposed contradictions and absurdities in order to move straight to the spiritual sense which the law was believed to have for Christians. This unknown glossator went so far as to claim that penance and the Old Testament sacrifices remitted actual sin because they prefigured Christ's sacrifice on the cross.

The discussion of the literal meaning of the law, together with a renewed interest in 'literal' exegesis in general, seems to have typified the 12th and 13th centuries. This interest was caused, among other things, by contacts between Jewish and Christian scholars and by the emergence of a literal form of interpretation among Jews, exemplified in the work of Rashi.

The Victorines

The revival of Christian interest in the literal sense of the Old Testament is nowhere better illustrated than at the school of the Abbey of St. Victor at Paris, which was founded in 1110. The first of the great Victorines was Hugh, who taught at St. Victor from about 1125 until he died in 1142. Hugh set out from the standard classics of his day, but he went beyond what they said, and he sought also to study the Old Testament in Hebrew. This involved conversations and consultations with Jewish scholars. Hugh's achievement has been described as the proper reinstatement of the literal or historical sense of the Old Testament. This, he believed, should be studied with the help of Hebrew and with the aid of all that could be known about the history of the biblical world, its geography and the manners and customs then in force. He believed the text thus studied provided a sacred history and that the sacred history provided the framework in terms of which theology and doctrine should be studied.

Hugh's emphasis on the historical sense did not exclude the other, deeper, senses; neither did his understanding of the literal sense exclude from it deeper dimensions. An interesting point is that he paid some attention to a problem that was to exercise orthodox protestant minds in the 19th century – the problem of whether messianic prophecies referred to the historical circumstances in which they were given, or whether they merely looked forward to the coming of Christ. Hugh, in the spirit of Theodore of Mopsuestia, preferred to refer prophecies to their historical circumstances except in cases such as Joel 2:28, where the prophecy was used in the New Testament as a prophecy of the coming of the Holy Spirit. According to Beryl Smalley, Hugh, a century before Thomas Aquinas, had grasped the idea that in the first instance, the intention of the writer is the clue to understanding prophecy and metaphor (*Study*, p.101).

The other great Victorine is Andrew, who studied under Hugh, and who taught at St. Victor until 1147 and from about 1155–1163. Andrew took the exposition of the literal sense and openness to Jewish sources of information a step beyond what had been achieved by Hugh. Although he employed the standard classical commentators, he was not afraid to disagree with them, or to state that they had been wrong. On occasions, he preferred Jewish exegesis to that of the classical Christian commentators. We also find in his writings the suggestion that the biblical writers were not subject to an overpowering revelation at the point at which they wrote, but that they may have indulged in research, or at any rate have received their traditions from others. In the case of the narrative of creation, while Andrew did not rule out the possibility that God had directly revealed the past to Moses, he preferred the view that

> Adam and his descendants would commit the creation carefully to memory . . . even in writing . . . So might it come to the knowledge of Moses who sought it by careful research (Smalley, p.132).

In his literal expositions, Andrew sometimes left open the question of whom a text might refer to, allowing, for example, that Isaiah 51:5

> my just one is near at hand

might mean Cyrus, or Christ, or the Messiah awaited by the Jews. Andrew's exposition of Isaiah 53 referred the passage entirely to the Babylonian captivity of the Jews, the 'man of sorrows' being a collective term for the Jews in captivity.

Dr. Smalley has traced the influence of Andrew upon the Old Testament exegesis of the century following his death by noting the number and distribution of the manuscripts of his work (*Study*, pp.173ff.). She states that whereas to their contemporaries Hugh of St. Victor seems like a second Augustine, Andrew seemed like a second Jerome. Andrew also had a notable pupil, Herbert of Bosham, who excelled in Hebrew studies beyond the achievements of Andrew. Herbert was capable of consulting the *Mahberet*, a lexicon of the 10th century compiled by Menahem ibn Saruk, he may have used the *Targumim*, and he may have been able to read Aramaic also. Whether or not his influence was great, he is evidence for the importance which Hebrew assumed for some 12th century Christian exegetes.

The Old Testament Law
In spite of the growing interest in the literal sense of the Old Testament, the tradition of Origen and Gregory received powerful advocacy in the form of a commentary in 20 books on Leviticus by Ralph of St. Germer of Flaix (Smalley, *Studies in Medieval Thought*, pp.49–96). It was written 'towards the middle of the 12th century', and was intended as a contribution by a Benedictine monk towards helping his fellow Benedictines answer objections to Christianity put forward by Jews. The view taken of the Old Testament law by Ralph was that it was prophetic because Moses was a prophet. However, it had value to the Jews in promoting obedience on their part, for all that the law contained contradictions and impossibilities. Ralph's books enjoyed considerable popularity right on into and through the 13th century.

The cause of literal interpretation on the other hand, was greatly strengthened when *The Guide of the Perplexed*, a masterpiece of biblical exegesis by the Jewish philosopher Maimonides (1135–1204) was translated into Latin only some 30 years after its original composition in Arabic in about 1190. For the purposes of the present chapter, it need only be noted that among other matters, the *Guide* attempted to give a rational explanation for the precepts of the law, understanding the purpose of the law as being to unite the ancient Israelites, to keep them from paganism, and to instil into them a deep fear and reverence for God. Texts such as Jeremiah 7:22 which, on the face of it, indicates that God did not instruct the Israelites in the wilderness to offer sacrifice to him, were taken by Maimonides to mean that in the first instance, God required that the Israelites should worship only him, and that the sacrificial law was a means to that end.

In its Latin version, the *Guide* was studied by Christian scholars, especially by William of Auverne who, in his *De legibus* of about 1230, set about defending the literal sense of the law (Smalley, *Medieval Thought*, pp.138–156). This law, given by God himself, was eminently fitted to serve the needs of the Israelite people of the time. They were a simple people, and the law enabled them to behave in a manner approximating to the law of nature. The law also taught them about God's mercy as well as his justice, and was effective in cleansing the worshippers from sin and in deepening their fellowship with God.

William strongly attacked those who argued that the Old Testament law was contradictory or absurd. To suppose this was to attribute mockery and deception to Moses. On the contrary, the whole meaning of the law was contained in its literal sense. With the coming of Christ it was no longer valid, but this did not mean that it contained hidden meanings that were not meant to benefit those to whom the law had been first given. William did not reject the possibility that the law could have an inner or spiritual meaning for Christians; but he seems to have been better at showing that the law must have deeper meanings (cp. Psalm 119:18) than at explaining what those meanings were.

William had stated an extreme point of view. In his turn, he was 'corrected' by John of La Rochelle who, somewhere between 1228 and 1249, wrote the *Tractatus* which forms part of the *Summa* ascribed to Alexander Hales (Smalley, *Medieval Thought*, pp.157–161). In the *Tractatus* the threefold division of the law into moral, judicial and ceremonial is made to correspond to the law of nature (moral), the punishment of evil (judicial) and the law of grace (ceremonial). William's defence of the rational nature of the law is accepted in so far as it can be fitted into a conservative framework. The spiritual senses of the law are, however, upheld.

Aquinas
It was left to Thomas Aquinas to mediate between the literal and the spiritual senses, and this he did by giving full weight to each, and by carefully setting their proper limits.

At the outset, he considered the objection that the Old Law (as the Old Testament Law is referred to) was not good, because of the passage in Ezekiel 20:25

I gave them statutes that were not good,
and ordinances by which they could not live.
(*Summa Theologiae*, ed. Bourke and Littledale, vol.29, pp.2 ff.)

Aquinas's reply implies that the two lines are complementary, and that what is meant by 'not good' is that the Israelites 'could not live' by the Old Law in the sense that it did not confer the grace by which sins are cleansed. On the other hand, the Old Law was good in that it forbade sins contrary to reason, and was framed so as to achieve a particular end, to bring men to eternal happiness. It did not follow from this that the Old Law was perfect; in absolute terms it was not. But in terms of those to whom it was given, namely, the Israelites, it was entirely appropriate.

Like many commentators before him, Aquinas distinguished between the moral, the ceremonial and the judicial content of the Old Law. The moral law contained the obligations of the natural law, and was binding upon all men precisely because it was natural law. However, as revealed by God, the moral law went beyond the natural law by adding precepts that human reason could not attain. The ceremonial and judicial laws were to be seen as particular applications of natural law. In the case of ceremonial laws, their aim was to direct men to the worship and service of God. The judicial laws were applications directed to the life of Israel at a specific time. Because they were applications, the ceremonial and judicial laws were not universally binding. The moral law, also, was not immutable at the level of the letter. The precepts of the Ten Commandments, the supreme expression of the moral law, were immutable in essence, but needed to be interpreted. Thus, it had been permissible to break the sabbath law when acting for human welfare.

Nowhere is Aquinas's defence of the rationality of the law interpreted according to the letter better expressed than in his defence of the various sacrifices. This section, significantly, contains several references to Maimonides. The main question at issue is

can a suitable reason be given for the ceremonies connected with the sacrifices? (*Summa* vol.29, p.136.)

Aquinas considers fourteen objections, including the points that the kinds of animals to be offered to God did not include the best possible, that God did not need the sacrifices (cp. Psalm 50:13), that inward contrition was preferable to sacrifice, and that the various distinctions of which animals should serve for which sacrifices together with the differing ways in which they should be killed (i.e. burned in whole or part) were strictly unnecessary.

Aquinas's defence is not only a justification of the rationality of the literal sense; it is also a justification of the figurative sense whereby all the ceremonies point to Christ. Thus, God did not order the sacrifices because he needed them; he did so in order to prevent idolatry, to direct the minds of the worshippers to God, and to prefigure the redemption of mankind by Christ. The animals required in sacrifice were deliberately not those used by other peoples for the purpose of idolatry. Also, they were the cleanest for the purposes of providing food for human consumption. In addition, they more appropriately prefigured Christ than did the unclean animals. Here, Aquinas quoted the Gloss on Leviticus 1

> Christ is offered in the calf to signify the power of the cross; in the lamb, to signify innocence; in the ram, his dominion; in the goat, the likeness of sinful flesh. The turtledove and pigeon signified the union of his two natures (*Summa*, vol.29, pp.144–5).

In justifying the various animals and their types of killing, Aquinas showed how different types of offence required different sacrifices, by means of which the different status of the offence or the gravity of the offence were underlined. The remainder of the ceremonial law in all its intricacies is similarly treated.

An interesting question that is considered is the status of sacrifices that existed *before* the giving of the Old Law. Aquinas admitted that sacrifices and holocausts were offered by the men of old, and that even before the law, 'exceptional men endowed with the prophetic spirit' were led to institute worship which, while not belonging to the Old Law, also prefigured the mystery of Christ.

That part of the *Summa Theologiae* dealing with the Old Law is an achievement which shows that 13th century Old Testament exegesis at its best was scholarly, critical and sensitive. In the hands of Aquinas, the literal sense is treated seriously and rationally, and in great detail. A proper understanding of the literal sense is necessary if the spiritual senses are to be properly handled. Aquinas's insistence on defending spiritual senses is a mark of his conservatism. Yet it expressed also a deep theological concern. An important issue in the 13th century was whether Old Testament laws and sacraments of themselves justified the worshippers. The answer of Aquinas was that up to a point, they did. For example, the rite for readmitting the leper achieved that end. Where the old ceremonies fell short was in not being able to cleanse from sin in the inner sense. Yet, when the old ceremonies were performed, the

> minds of the faithful . . . could be united by faith with Christ incarnate and suffering, and in this way be justified by Christ (*Summa*, vol.29, pp.236–7).

The old ceremonies did not of themselves cleanse from sin, but enabled the faithful to appropriate that which was to be made available through Christ. Thus, Aquinas's insistence that the law had a deeper sense, in that it prefigured Christ, was not merely a sign of his conservatism. It was part of his understanding of salvation under the Old Law. That the Old Law prefigured Christ was not apparent to the people of Old Testament times; but their profession of faith in God which the Old Law made possible linked them to the work of Christ which was implicit in the ceremonies of the Old Law.

Beryl Smalley has written of Aquinas that, although he was not primarily a biblical specialist, he made possible a new approach to biblical scholarship. While he safeguarded the spiritual senses of scripture, seeing them as senses intended by God, he allowed the literal sense to come fully into its own. The literal sense was what was intended by the human author, and it included metaphor, imagery and parable. It was to be studied with all scholarly means available. No longer could the literal sense be regarded as unimportant or second best (D. E. Nineham (ed.) *The Church's Use of the Bible Past and Present*, London 1963, p.60).

3. THE FOURTEENTH AND FIFTEENTH CENTURIES

Dr. Smalley mentions, among those who developed the literal exposition in the wake of Aquinas, the latter's pupil Ptolemy of Lucca, who wrote a literal account of the work of creation aimed at harmonising with Genesis the natural science of the day, and Reminius of Florence, who lectured on the literal sense of the Song of Songs. He regarded the literal sense as the expression of Solomon's love for his bride who was Pharaoh's daughter, a dark beauty.

Nicholas of Lyre
Among other notable scholars of the 14th century were Pierre Auriel, who compiled a manual on the literal sense of the whole Bible, and Nicholas of Lyre, whose *Postilla* became a classic, and

was published in many editions along with the *Glossa ordinaria*. Dr. Smalley explains that whereas the glosses were interlinear or in the margins, the *Postilla* were comments written in blocks alternating with the biblical text (*Study of the Bible*, p.270).

Nicholas (1270–1340) drew extensively upon Hebrew scholarship, particularly that of Rashi, and while not ruling out Christological interpretation of psalms, interpreted the majority of them in relation to Old Testament history. His commentary on the Song of Songs embraced both Jewish and Christian approaches. Whereas traditional Jewish interpretation saw the book as expressing the relationship between God and Israel, while for Christians it expressed the relationships between Christ and the church, Nicholas divided this exposition into two, unequal parts. Chs. 1–6 preferred the Jewish approach and Chs. 7–8 the Christian.

Joachim of Fiore

In making this division, Nicholas may have been influenced by a form of Joachimism. Even if he was not, the chapter must mention Joachim of Fiore (c. 1135–1204) even at the risk of breaking the historical sequence. Joachim was a Cistercian monk who was allowed to found his own order in 1196. He was an earnest student of the spiritual meanings of the Old and New Testament, and fashioned a type of dispensationalism that expected the early arrival of a new age. In his work, which was to inspire successive generations of apocalyptists, we find the most extreme triumph of the spiritual over the historical interpretation of the text. To characterise Joachim's thought briefly is impossible. As one of his foremost interpreters has put it, his mind had a kaleidoscopic quality, for ever forming new patterns. He is sometimes presented as having advocated a dispensational scheme of three ages, those respectively of the Father, the Son and the Holy Spirit. However, there seems to have been a complex dialectic in his thinking between 'twos' and 'threes' arising from the tension between the two parts or covenants of the Bible and the three persons of the Trinity. With regard to the two parts of the Bible, Joachim found many correspondences between them, at the levels of their institutions and their chief actors. Thus, Abraham, Isaac and Jacob are in concord with Zachariah, John the Baptist and Christ. On the other hand, the patterns of three within the Old and New Testaments (of which the concord between Abraham, Isaac and Jacob and Zachariah, John the Baptist and Christ is an example) point to the persons of the Trinity and the three 'ages'. Yet the third age will not be an abrogation of the dispensations of the two covenants, but a development of them into a new quality of life.

Returning for a moment to Nicholas of Lyre, if his interpretation of the Song of Songs, is influenced by Joachimism, it is in the weakened sense of the dispensationalism that derived from Joachim's works, a dispensationalism that had radical implications where the belief in the imminent arrival of a third age was understood to involve radical reforms of Church institutions.

Wycliffe

To conclude the chapter, brief reference is made to Wycliffe, who certainly called for radical reform of the Church, and who is often thought of as a precursor of the Reformation. So far as his use of the Old Testament is concerned, his standpoint was rather different from that of Luther and the 16th century reformers. Wycliffe commented on the whole of the Old Testament, and in so doing he was heavily dependent on those who had preceded him. Beryl Smalley describes his recipe for comments as follows:

> use Auriol's *Compendium* as a mould, pour in Lyre, flavour with Augustine, and sprinkle with Grosseteste (*Study of the Bible*, p.256).

Further, he had no hesitation in employing the three or fourfold method of interpretation. Where he seemed to anticipate the later reformers, this resulted from his conversion from philosophical nominalism to realism, following Plato and Augustine in particular. Having been trained in philosophy, and having adopted a realist standpoint, he expected the Bible to confirm the results of his philosophical reasoning. This being so, there were no contradictions in the Bible, and apparent contradictions were functions of the ignorance of the interpreter rather than shortcomings of the text. The value of the study of Greek and Hebrew was that it gave access to metaphysical truth, in that the names of things in Scripture corresponded to metaphysical realities.

It was from Wycliffe's view of the concord between a philosophical (realist) account of the world and the Bible that there developed his sense of the all-sufficiency of Scripture, which sense he then turned against the Church of his day on the grounds that it did not accord with scriptural teaching. It would appear, then, that Wycliffe's similarities with later reformers were more superficial than real. True, in both of them we find a kind of *sola scriptura*, and a critique of the Church in the light of scripture. But the underlying assumptions of Wycliffe seem to have been as different from those of Luther as the latter's appear to have been from the Protestant Orthodoxy that succeeded him. Exactly what was new in the exegesis of the Old Testament in the first flush of the Reformation will be discussed next.

FOR FURTHER READING

H. Daniel-Rops, *The Church in the Dark Ages*, pp.421 ff.

C. Spicq, *Esquise d'une histoire de l'exégèse latine au Moyen age*, (Bibliotheque Thomiste XXVI), Paris 1944.

B. Smalley, *The Study of the Bible in the Middle Ages*, Oxford 1983 (3rd ed.).

B. Smalley, *Studies in Medieval Thought and Learning from Abelard to Wyclif*, London 1981.

R. Loewe, 'Herbert of Bosham's Commentary on Jerome's Hebrew Psalter. A preliminary Investigation into its Sources', *Biblica*, xxxiv (1953) pp.44–77, 159–192, 275–298.

B. Smalley, 'The Bible in the Middle Ages' in D. E. Nineham (ed.), *The Church's Use of the Bible Past and Present*, London 1963, p.60.

M. Reeves, *Joachim of Fiore and the Prophetic Future*, London 1976.

K. R. Firth, *The Apocalyptic Tradition in Reformation Britain 1530–1645*, Oxford 1979.

B. Smalley, 'Wycliffe's *Postilla* on the Old Testament and his *Principium*' in *Oxford Studies Presented to Daniel Callus* (Oxford Historical Society N.S.Vol.XVI) Oxford 1964 pp.253–296.

7

FROM THE REFORMATION TO THE ENLIGHTENMENT

At the beginning of the 16th century, on the eve of the Reformation, the interpretation of the Old Testament was largely governed by the theory of the four-fold sense of Scripture. The literal sense, especially in the hands of interpreters who were sympathetic to Jewish methods of interpretation, was an historical sense, giving information about the history and religion of Israel. A specifically Christian interpretation was derived from the spiritual senses of Scripture, by means of which the text was made to refer to Christ, and deductions were made about doctrine, morals and application to Christian life.

1. LUTHER

The Reformation, especially as exemplified in the writings of Luther, brought profound changes to the interpretation of the Old Testament. In some respects, these changes did not last for more than a generation or two in the form that Luther had introduced them. The writings of Luther, however, took on new significance two hundred years after his death, and played an important part in the rise of the historical critical method in the 18th century.

Influences on Luther
Luther's breakthrough to a new understanding of the Old Testament depended, of course, on the work of those who preceded him. He was heir to the humanist revival of learning at the end of the 15th and the beginning of the 16th century, a movement associated particularly with the name of Erasmus (1466/69 – 1536). Also, the beginnings of Hebrew scholarship among Christians, a milestone in which was the publication of a Hebrew grammar by J. Reuchlin in 1506, had a part to play. As a professor of Biblical Studies at the

University of Wittenberg, Luther was part of a larger movement of reform and new discovery in the fields of education and scholarship. Luther also owed much to other biblical interpreters, and in particular to Faber Stapulensis (c.1455–1536). It is generally agreed that Luther worked out his distinctive approach to the Old Testament sometime between 1513 and 1519. Experts disagree about whether the distinctive approach was already latent in the lectures on Psalms given in 1513–15, or whether these early lectures represent the last work of the 'medieval Luther' before the reformer began to work towards an entirely new approach from 1516. Whatever view one takes, all are agreed about the importance, for Luther's development, of the commentary on the Psalms by Faber Stapulensis, which Luther used for his 1513–15 lectures. Faber redefined the meaning of the literal sense of the text by dividing it into two, into a literal historical sense and a literal prophetic sense. The literal prophetic sense was that which interpreted the text of the Psalms with reference to Christ. It was not an allegorical or spiritual reading of the text, but a literal reading designed to make clear the prophetic intention of the author. It differed from the literal historical sense in the way that the spirit differed from the letter. The letter, typified by Jewish historical interpretation of the Psalms, kills. The spirit, a literal prophetic reading of the Psalms with reference to Christ, gives life.

Before Luther began to work out his own special approach to the Old Testament, there existed, in the commentary of Faber, a method of interpretation that in effect abolished the need for the four-fold sense of Scripture. If there was a literal sense that referred to Christ, there was no need for spiritual senses in order to find him in the text. Luther found in Faber's commentary a method of interpretation in which reference to Christ was the fundamental aim.

The Old and New Testaments
Luther's special contribution has been described either as the development of the distinction between letter and spirit into the distinction between Law and Gospel, or as the discovery that the idea of promise is fundamental to interpreting the Old Testament. Either way, the effect of Luther's distinctive approach was to rescue the Old Testament from the dilemma that if it was interpreted historically, it became an account of the history and religion of Israel and if it was interpreted prophetically or spiritually, it became completely subservient to the New Testament. Luther rediscovered the Old Testament as a history of faith, which, at the level of its historical

interpretation, had much to say to Christians living in his own times. This can also be put in a different way by saying that whereas earlier interpretation could find in the Old Testament many examples of how Christians should live, Luther found many examples of God at work among his people.

Luther's special understanding of the relation between Law and Gospel enabled him to reformulate the distinction between the Old Testament and the New. It was not the case that the Old Testament was the Law and the New Testament was the Gospel. Law and Gospel were to be found in both Testaments. In the Old Testament, God acted on behalf of his people, and some responded in faith. The notion of promise as a fundamental key to Old Testament interpretation depended upon an analogy between the people of Israel and the church. The former looked forward to the first coming of Christ, the latter to the final coming of Christ. Both communities lived in faith and hope, looking forward to a coming of Christ, the church, of course, having the advantage of knowing Christ's first coming. However, the similarity between the two communities was sufficiently strong for it to be possible to apply the historical sense of the Old Testament to contemporary Christian life. Men and women of faith in the Old Testament could be seen as having much in common with Christians living in the turbulent world of Luther's days.

In view of what had just been said, it is no surprise to learn that Luther found himself very much at home in the Old Testament world as he found it in the text, and that he identified himself easily with Old Testament characters. One of his favourites was Samson. Luther felt an affinity with the man who had stood alone against overwhelming odds. He approved what Samson had done in killing many Philistines in his official position as Judge (it would have been a crime to have killed them as a private individual). He believed that God must have been rich in mercy and forgiveness to Samson, in view of the man's many shortcomings. In short, Luther could see in Samson an anticipation of the Gospel, in that Samson was empowered by God's spirit to act on behalf of God's people, and was forgiven for disobeying the command not to cut his hair, by being given the strength to kill many of his and God's enemies in his final act of defiance.

Luther's wish to interpret the text historically so as to relate it to contemporary Christian life led him, at times, into surprising, and forced exegesis. His interpretation of the Song of Songs is a striking example. Where Jewish interpretation had regarded it as expressing the relationship between God and Israel, and Christians had found in it an expression of Christ's love for the church, Luther argued that the Song was sung by Solomon in praise to God for establishing and preserving the kingdom over which Solomon ruled. ' . . . every kingdom, principality, or state which has the Word and true worship of God . . . is deservedly called "the people of God" and has every right to place this song, and Solomon's state, before itself as an example . . . to proclaim and marvel at His divine mercy and power, by which He protects His own against the snares of the devil and the tyranny of the world' (*Luther's Works*, vol.15, St. Louis 1972, pp.191–2). If Hebrew were a language which differentiated between masculine and feminine when attributing something to a possessor in the first person singular, Luther's interpretation would have been grammatically impossible. In the event, he was able to envisage Solomon as the speaker, even when the context demands that it is a young woman.

A wrong impression will have been given by what has been written so far, if it is assumed that Luther's interpretation of the Old Testament concentrated upon the historical sense in order to apply it to Christian life. The picture is far more complex. Readers of Luther's lectures and commentaries on the Old Testament will find many examples of a prophetic literal sense in which the text is referred to Christ. Again, not every part of the Old Testament was regarded by Luther as suitable for his historical Christian interpretation. He was unenthusiastic about Esther, and gave no lectures on Joshua, Samuel, Kings and Chronicles, except for his treatment of David's last words in 2 Samuel 23:1–7. In this latter piece, he argued strongly for evidence in the Old Testament for the existence of the Divine Trinity, as well as for the fact that 'the God who led the children of Israel from Egypt and through the Red Sea . . . is the very same God and none other than Jesus of Nazareth, the Son of the Virgin Mary, whom we Christians call our Lord and God' (*Luther's Works*, vol.15, p.313).

It is impossible here to do justice to the complexities of Luther's Old Testament interpretation, but, to conclude this section, brief mention will be made of his treatment of three important topics.

Creation and fall (Luther's Works, *vols.1–2*)

Luther's handling of Genesis 1 and 2 is marked by sensitivity to the scientific and philosophical questions raised by the text, by an awareness of the history of interpretation of the chapters, and by a pragmatism that rigorously excludes what he holds to be idle speculation. The two chapters are taken to complement each other, with 2: 7–24 being an enlarged account of what God had done on the 6th day.

Moses had written the account for unlearned people, and for this reason Luther vehemently denies that there are hidden meanings behind the plain sense of the words. Moses called a spade a spade. Nevertheless, the text cannot be read without guidance. On the old questions of the nature of the days of creation and of the light that was created before the sun, Luther asserted that they were days and light in the sense in which we know them. The light, however, was crude and coarse, and only reached its perfection when there was added to it the light of the sun. On the astronomical question of the size of the sun and moon in relation to other stars, Luther claimed that the text referred to their superior brightness, not to alleged superior mass. Even so, Luther accepted the evidence drawn from eclipses that the moon derived its light from the sun, and was not, strictly speaking, a 'light' in itself.

The threefold division of the world into heaven, earth and waters seemed to contradict philosophical speculation about the four basic elements of earth, air, fire and water, as well as current views about the nature and number of the heavens. Luther did not dismiss such speculations. He regarded them as 'useful for teaching because they are the result of plausible reasoning and contain the foundation for the arts' (vol. 1, p.27). Provided that theology reserved to itself the right to proclaim the sovereignty of God as creator and sustainer of the world, reasonable speculation about its nature had positive value.

Traditional interpretation of Genesis 1–2 had not only dealt with philosophical and scientific questions, but with theological questions such as the origin of angels and the devil and their fall, and the nature of the image of God in man. The first of these two matters would still be dealt with in some detail in the mid–19th century by a scholar of the calibre of Franz Delitzsch! Luther was radically dismissive in his treatment. That there were such things as angels, including fallen ones and the devil, was clear from the Bible, including the New Testament; what we could not know, however, was when they originated and how they fell. God had not seen any necessity to make these things known. Some had attempted, on the basis of Isaiah 14:12 'how you are fallen from heaven, O Day Star, son of Dawn' to formulate a doctrine of the fall of the devil, but Luther, while sympathetic to this approach, would not require others to accept it.

On the image of God in man, Luther was even more radical, and a discussion of this issue brings us to the most striking feature of his treament of creation and fall, his insistence that we today can know nothing of the creation as God originally made it, including the nature of man. Luther's view of the fall in Genesis 3 and of the flood in Genesis 6–9 was that these happenings had destroyed the world as originally created by God until such time as they would be restored and transcended by the completion of God's redemptive work in Christ. All that we could know for certain was that we lived in a corrupted world characterised by human sin, violence and injustice, and that the created order was also filled with the violence of wild animals and with many harmful, useless or downright vile creatures, such as vermin. But it had not been like this at the beginning. God had declared his created order to be 'good', something that was no longer true.

In man's state of corruption, it was idle, in Luther's view, to speculate about man's nature prior to the fall. Yet speculation about the 'image of God' was an important aspect of theology, of which Luther had to take account. Where he allowed himself to speculate about the matter, it is significant that he did this not in abstract but in practical terms. He tried to envisage what it was like for Adam to be in perfect relationship with God: 'he was without the fear of death or of any other danger, and was content with God's favour' (vol.1, p.63).

Adam and Eve, in their pre-fall life in Paradise (it lasted, according to Luther, for only one day, since they were created on the 6th day and fell on the 7th), were surrounded by no danger. The wild beasts were not wild, and Adam could command them as we today command a trained dog. Procreation, if it had taken place before the fall, would have been without shame or guilt or pain. Adam would have lived in complete blessedness before being taken into God's sabbath rest.

The fall changed all this, and produced the situation familiar to us today. The tree whose fruit was forbidden was to Adam and Eve a sort of church, in that it was a means of allowing them to express their obedience to God's command. It was also their undoing, as the serpent, then a beautiful little animal that went upright, was used by Satan to tempt Eve to eat the forbidden fruit and to get her husband to eat it also. The fruit itself was harmless. We do not find in Luther the theories of the late 18th century about the fruit being sufficiently poisonous to shock but not to kill the couple. Luther works out the offence and its consequences in terms of disobedience to the divine Word. In the altered state of mankind there is an alteration to the world. God's 'resting' after the creation refers only to resting after completing his ideal creation. The new situation brought about by man's disobedience requires new actions on God's part. The earth is cursed and now bears not only thorns and thistles, but many other apparently useless creatures. The wild animals become truly wild. The flood will distort things even further, so that it will be impossible for later generations to locate paradise or the river that flowed out of it. But hope is indicated in Genesis 3:15 in the promise of the work of Christ, even hope for Adam and Eve. They are not restored to the life they lost, but they are given hope of restoration to that life.

Luther's treatment of creation and fall is dominated by his clarity of vision about the purpose of the Bible, which is to proclaim God's grace in Christ to a fallen world. His realistic assessment of the created order led him to one of the most radical statements ever about the effect of the fall on creation. Luther would not deny that the 'heavens declare the glory of God' and that they are wonderfully made. He did, however, deny their perfection as we now know them in our fallen state, and if they taught us anything about God it was not that he existed as designer, but that he was abundantly gracious, through his provision for the needs of mankind, to creatures that strictly deserved only judgement and punishment.

The Old Testament Law.
We have already seen that in the centuries immediately preceding the Reformation, the literal sense of the Old Testament law had been treated with greater respect than in earlier centuries, without this leading to the abandonment of its spiritual interpretations as pointing to Christ. Luther was faced with the situation that some of the extremist wings of the Reformation wanted to enforce aspects of the Old Testament law upon Christians. His treatment of the subject is vigorous and radical (*Luthers Werke*, vol.16, Weimar 1904, pp.363–393).

The Old Testament law has no binding force upon Christians as *law*. The law was given to the Jews, not to the heathen, and is binding only upon Jews. This point is reinforced by Luther with respect to the beginning of the Ten Commandments: 'I am the Lord your God who brought you out of the land of Egypt' (Exodus 20:1). God brought only the Jews out of Egypt, not anyone else, and thus his words are not law for any except the Jews. The point is further supported by the fact that in the New Testament, the early church did not observe the sabbath. Luther followed the accepted view that the Ten Commandments were 'natural law', written on the hearts of the heathen. If they were important to Christians, it was not because Moses had framed them at God's command, but because they were written on the human heart.

Of the many commandments in the Old Testament that were not ceremonial, and that were not known to the heathen, Luther took the view that they could be useful examples to follow, provided this was done voluntarily, and thatt one stopped following the examples when one wished. As examples, Luther cites giving a tenth of one's wealth to God, or providing a son for a childless widow by levirate marriage. These are good examples, but they are not laws to be enforced upon Christians.

At the same time that he rejected the enforcement of Old Testament law upon Christians, Luther had a high regard for Moses, and could even find in the Old Testament instances of a new law that pointed to the Gospel. Moses was honoured as an example of a pious man, but more especially as one who had anticipated the coming of Christ in a series of prophecies, beginning with Genesis 3:15.

Biblical criticism.
Luther was not a biblical critic in the sense that the term came to be understood from the 18th century onwards; but his attitude to the Old Testament was far more radical than that of many Protestants in the centuries that followed him. On matters of authorship, he was prepared to call the Pentateuch 'Mosaic' as opposed to being wholly written by Moses. The account of Moses's death was written by Joshua or Eleazar, and Moses may have used sources of the early chapters of Genesis. The prophetic books, especially Isaiah, Jeremiah and Hosea did not display a coherent order, and were possibly not complete, or not put into order by the prophets themselves.

Within the Old Testament canon, Luther certainly prized some books above others, and his lack of enthusiasm for Esther and certain historical books has already been pointed out. His view of the word of God in the Old Testament was that it could not be equally and uniformly found there. If asked whether the Old Testament was the Word of God or whether it contained the Word of God he may well have chosen the latter. For Luther stressed that it was necessary to see who spoke a word, to whom, and in what circumstances. The command to Abraham to offer his son Isaac was a word only to Abraham, and there were many similar instances. Luther's use of the Old Testament was governed by a number of dialectical principles: what leads to Christ, the tension between law and Gospel, the relation between promise and fulfilment.

Any brief treatment of Luther's use of the Old Testament is bound to be inadequate. What is written here is done in the hope that it will encourage readers to go to Luther himself, and to gain from his many insights, in spite of the great difference between his thought and ours.

2. CALVIN

Luther and Calvin Compared

To turn from Luther's expositions of the Old Testament to those of Calvin is to move into a different world. It is true that they seem to have much in common. In their expositions of Genesis, for example, they agree among other things that Moses is writing for unlearned people and is not setting out a scientific treatise; that the fall had obliterated the divine image in man and that the existence of such things as thorns, thistles and vermin are God's punishment for the fall; that the giants referred to in Genesis 6:4 were not of gigantic stature but were mighty in other ways. But in spite of these and other similarities there are important differences between the two reformers.

At the formal level, Calvin is a much more systematic commentator. He had set out his basic theological position in his *Institutes of the Christian Religion*, and, taking this for granted, his aim as a commentator was to elucidate the biblical text in front of him, usually verse by verse. Luther is much less systematic, and often rushes off into general theological discussions that are excited by the text, but which take him away from the strict exegesis of the text itself.

Calvin is more scholarly than Luther in that he appears to have a firmer grasp of Hebrew, or at any rate, to use his Hebrew in ways more convincing to the modern reader than Luther's use of Hebrew. He also seems to be theologically sharper than Luther. In discussing the plural mode of address in Genesis 1:26–7 'let us make man in our image . . .' Luther was content to take these as the words of the divine Trinity. Calvin, however, rejects this interpretation, lest it be used as a support for Sabellianism, the doctrine that the 'persons' of the Trinity are merely three modes of divine operation, and not three 'persons' with distinctive characteristics (Calvin, *Genesis*, Edinburgh 1975, p.71).

Again, Calvin is far more concerned than Luther to establish details about the text with the help of secular knowledge. Luther, we have seen, was sceptical about the possibility of locating the

Garden of Eden. Calvin was not only more confident, but he drew extensively upon works of classical authors dealing with the geography of Mesopotamia, on the basis of which he provided a map to explain the details of Genesis 2 8–14, and asserted that the Garden of Eden was in the Tigris/Euphrates region (*Genesis*, p.120).

At the level of the handling of the literature, and of seeing it in the light of philosophy and natural science, Calvin again scores over Luther. He makes frequent reference to literary figures of speech, especially metaphor and synecdoche, and is particularly concerned to underline that God does not repent or see or move in the sense in which these words are used in normal speech (*Genesis*, p.113). This is not, of course, an innovation on Calvin's part; but it shows his conscious acceptance of a philosophical tradition going back through Augustine. In reconciling the Genesis cosmology with the science of his day he is also much more forthright than Luther. The cosmology, written by Moses for unlearned people, dealt only with things naked to the eyes. It was also accommodated to an uneducated understanding. Hence it is not a source for astronomy or physics (*Genesis*, pp.86–7). Calvin's view here contrasts remarkably with that of British defenders of the Mosaic cosmology in the 19th century, for whom it was heresy to argue that the primary purpose of the cosmology was theological not scientific.

Deeper Differences

If we look for deeper differences between Luther and Calvin, we find ourselves considering an important and complex matter that is vital for the position of the Old Testament in the Christian church. Luther, as we have seen, had a far from straightforward view on the relation between the Old Testament and the New. His dialectic of law and gospel led him to find both of these present in the Old Testament as well as in the New, and the primary purpose of the law was to bring people to the realisation that only through the gracious word of the gospel could they have pardon and hope before God. Once God's grace had been experienced, the law continued to function as a constant reminder of the constant need for grace. In their Old Testament formulation, however, laws were not binding upon Christians, even though Christians might choose, for a time, to follow them. The Ten Commandments, as we have seen, were not even considered to be binding upon Christians according to Luther. If they had any value it was because they were part of the law written on the heart of mankind, and not because they were given by Moses.

Luther's essentially prophetic and soteriological understanding of the Old Testament was not well fitted to be applied to the world of everyday living, and seemed to some to make too many concessions to antinomianism. Within the Lutheranism of the generations following Luther, it became necessary to identify a third use of the law, one which could be used to regulate daily living. The steps towards this will be described later. On the Reformed side of the Reformation as represented by Calvin, there was a much earlier move towards a simpler and more practically applicable view of the Old Testament, a view which in its more extreme form even required the enforcement of the Old Testament sabbath as the Christian Sunday.

Calvin saw the difference between the Old and New Testaments as one of administration. In both, the one just and gracious God deals with his people, but in the case of the Old Testament, the administration is incomplete, although people of faith in Old Testament times received an anticipation of salvation through Christ. Calvin was firmer than Luther about the purpose of the law, especially the Ten Commandments. It was certainly in accordance with the natural law, and its precepts were to be taken seriously by Christians. However, in Calvin, there is a note of caution that is missing from later Calvinism. With regard to the sabbath, Calvin asserts that it is necessary, as a matter of discipline, for Christians to set aside one day; but he does not insist that this day should be Sunday. A congregation should be free to set apart whatever day it chooses. We can see Calvin here being as equally concerned as Luther not to collapse the gospel into legalism.

Calvin's Achievements
Before turning to the considerations that placed the Old Testament on a footing very different from that envisaged by Luther, it can be said of Calvin as an Old Testament commentator that his primary concern was for the literal historical sense of the text, informed by his overall Christian perspective. His commentaries, written with scholarship, sensitivity and clarity, were the most distinguished contributions in this genre by any reformation leader and deservedly had a great readership in the following generations. Where necessary, his interpretation was Christological, as is witnessed by his commentaries and sermons on Isaiah 52:13 – 53:12.

3. BULLINGER

Covenant Theology
On the Reformed side of the Reformation there were several developments which brought about the elevation of the Old Testament to an important position in Christian life and politics. One such development was the rise of covenant theology of the type advocated by Heinrich Bullinger (1504–1575) the Zürich reformer. Bullinger rejected the idea that God had, by an eternal decree, predestined some to salvation and the rest to damnation. How this doctrine of 'double predestination' affected the use of the Old Testament will be seen later. Bullinger preferred to construct his theology upon a reading of the Old Testament as the history of the covenant, in which God pledged himself to mankind on condition that mankind, in turn, pledged itself to God.

The covenant was made with Adam after the fall and inaugurated a period which lasted until the time of Moses. In his grace and mercy, God promised redemption to the faithful through Christ (Genesis 3:15), and those who believed during this period were in no way inferior to Christians after Christ's coming. The covenant was renewed with Noah and Abraham, and Abraham was given a new sign of the covenant, namely, circumcision.

The period from Moses to John the Baptist was an interregnum between the first period and that inaugurated with the coming of Christ. The Ten Commandments embodied both God's will for all mankind at all times, and were also a summary of the covenant made from the time of Adam. The ceremonial and judicial laws, which were given after the Ten Commandments, added nothing to the latter, but were rather an application to the special circumstances of the Israelites of the basic requirements of the second table of the Ten Commandments. They were an aid to observing the covenant, and in their ceremonial form they helped to preserve the Israelites from idolatry. The ceremonies were also types of Christ.

Although the period of the Law, from Moses to the coming of Christ, was a time of much turning away from God, it was important because it established many things that were applicable to Bullinger's own times. During this period, God willed to establish an organised church, with priests who had the oversight of ecclesiastical matters and the prophets who also addressed themselves to everyday life. There was also the office of magistrate, older than the time of Moses, but established especially after the Exodus to prevent anarchy, to restrain wrongdoing, and to ensure the observance of the covenant. As well as appealing to Romans 13, Bullinger appealed to Exodus 18:21 as an example:

Choose able men from all the people, such as fear God, men who are trustworthy and who hate a bribe; and place such men over the people as rulers of thousands, of hundreds, of fifties and of tens.

The history of Israel down to the time of Ezra indicated the role of Judges and of good kings in exercising the magistrate's office.

With the coming of Christ, there was restoration of the covenant faith of the period before the time of Moses. The New Covenant, foreseen by Jeremiah (31:31), was the renewal of the one original covenant, but now without the ceremonial and judicial law (i.e. the 'Old Covenant'). Christ and his apostles lived in the different circumstances that they were under the rule of hostile nations. The conversion of Constantine enabled a return to take place to the conditions intended by God, in which a Christian magistrate could fulfil his office. Following the abuses of the pre-Reformation church, the Reformation enabled the covenant situation to be restored completely. Bullinger's view has been thus summed up:

Reformation, as a restitution of the covenant between a people and God, encompassed all matters in the commonwealth both ecclesiastical and civil, and must be effected according to the law of God. It should include schools, laws, courts, economic matters, and any other matters that 'pertain to the welfare of the Church and the commonwealth' . . . The magistrate ought to obey the law of God and carry through a complete reformation, both ecclesiastical and civil. Bullinger's favourite examples of such reform came from the kings of Judah such as Josiah, Jehoshaphat, and Hezekiah (J. W. Baker, *Heinrich Bullinger and the Covenant*, Athens, Ohio 1980, p.102).

4. BUCER AND HIS INFLUENCE

Another important representative of a type of covenant theology was the Strasbourg reformer Martin Bucer (1491–1551). Experts have found it difficult to place him within the many movements that made up the Reformation. He was certainly influenced by Luther, but made use of the Old Testament in a manner very different from that of the Wittenberg professor. He is best approached as an essentially practical and pastoral man, who drew upon those aspects of reformation teaching that best served his practical ends.

His most important book for our purpose, *De regno Christi* (On the kingdom of Christ) was written in England shortly before Bucer's death and was dedicated to Edward VI of England (*Library of Christian Classics*, vol. 19, Philadelphia and London 1959). It expressed Bucer's opinion of how the Reformation should be carried out by the king, and it covered very many aspects of both ecclesiastical and civil life including, under the latter heading, education, poor relief, luxury, honest gains, marketing and public inns. It is no part of the present work to ask how far the Reformation in England was affected by *De regno Christi;* what will be examined is its use of the Old Testament.

Use of the Old Testament
Bucer's basic view of the validity of Old Testament civil and ceremonial laws is summed up as follows:

> We being free in Christ are not bound by the civil law of Moses any more than by the ceremonial laws given to ancient Israel, insofar as they pertain to external circumstances and elements of the world (p.319).

He goes on to argue, however, that

> since there can be no laws more honorable, righteous, and wholesome than those which God, himself, who is eternal wisdom and goodness, enacted, if only they are applied under God's judgement to our own affairs and activities, I do not see why Christians, in matters which pertain to their own doings should not follow the laws of God more than those of any men (p.319).

This is a rather neat solution of what to do with those parts of the Old Testament that were classified as part of the civil law. Bucer acknowledges their relativity to their times and circumstances, but asserting that for all that, they derive from God, he recommends their adoption rather than 'the laws of men' in modern circumstances where they are appropriate. This opens the way for an extensive use of the Old Testament in setting out how the kingdom of Christ is to be established in a country such as England, according to God's laws.

The Godly Prince

The responsibility for establishing the kingdom rests firmly upon the king, as is indicated by the examples of devout kings in the Old Testament.

> Worthy of your majesty's consideration and conscientious imitation are the examples of men like David, Solomon, Asa, Hezekiah, Josiah and Nehemiah, whom the Scriptures praise resoundingly for their piety and the sound administration of their kingdoms (p.266).

The king will perform this task by a combination of methods including decrees, education, evangelism and the proper ordering and support of the church. Magistrates will play an important role, and, like Bullinger, much is made by Bucer of Exodus 18:21, and the example of Jehoshaphat (2 Chronicles 17:7–12).

At the level of administration of justice, reference is made to Old Testament penalties in ways that are surprising to modern readers. The death penalty is approved of not only for capital offences, but for blasphemy, violation of the sabbath, adultery, rape and certain types of false testimony. In each case the Old Testament is referred to, and Bucer concludes that

> no one knows better or provides more diligently what is for man's salvation than God. In these sanctions of God, we see that he judges that the death penalty should eliminate from his people whoever had openly defected from him or held him in contempt or persuades others to do the same . . . (p.379).

Here, then, is an attempt to institute a society based upon an Old Testament framework of civil law and a New Testament concept of the church.

The use of the Old Testament in *De regno Christi* is not confined to its legal parts. In the opening section of the work, Bucer expounds prophecies of the establishment of the kingdom of Christ, in a way that seems forced to modern readers, e.g.:

> 'House of Jacob, come and let us walk in the light of the Lord' . . . it is shown that no one is to be reckoned of the house of Jacob, that is, of the true Church of Christ, who does not enthusiastically frequent sacred assemblies and invite those whom he can to the same . . . (pp.193–4).

Trends in Covenant Theology
As the 16th century progressed, there developed a type of covenant theology which envisaged two covenants – a covenant of works which God made with Adam at creation and a covenant of grace made with Adam after the fall. The former was required by God of all mankind, but sin made it impossible to fulfil. The covenant of grace contained all matters and means of mankind's redemption, had been renewed to Abraham and Moses among others, and had received its culmination in Jesus. The effect of this theory of the double covenant was that the Old Testament came into its own as indicating the way in which God wished human society and daily life to be ordered. To the objection that the law, according to 2 Corinthians 3:6–7, was a ministry of death and a killing letter, it was rejoined that in 2 Corinthians Paul was speaking of the law without Christ, 'whereas otherwise of the law (being considered in the covenant that is in Christ) it is truly said by the prophet in the Psalms: "the law of the Lord is perfect, converting the soul . . . " ' (Psalm 19:7–8) (J. Knewstub on Exodus 20).

Another tendency within the Reformed wing of the Reformation that affected the use of the Old Testament was a development that has been traced within English Calvinism which arose from the separation between faith and assurance. Within the context of belief in double predestination (the view that some were decreed for salvation and the rest for damnation before the creation of the world), there arose the question of whether people could know if they belonged to the elect. One answer was that they could know, if their obedience to God was such as to indicate that they were empowered by his Spirit to keep his law. An important text in the discussion was 2 Peter 1:10.

be the more zealous to confirm your call and election, for if you do this you will never fall.

The confirmation of election involved obedience to God's law, much of which was to be gained from the Old Testament.

Thomas Watson
To conclude this section of the Reformed part of the Reformation, reference is made to Thomas Watson's exposition of the Ten Commandments. Watson belonged to the latter part of the 17th century, but his exposition sums up succinctly the many tendencies on the Reformed side in the 16th and 17th centuries. Much of what

he says can be paralleled by writers back to Calvin. (T. Watson, *The Ten Commandments*, Edinburgh, 1965.) On the law and the gospel Watson writes

> The moral law requires obedience, but gives no strength. . . . but the gospel gives strength; it bestows faith on the elect; it sweetens the law; it makes us serve God with delight.

On how the moral law is both abolished and in force he explains that it is abolished to believers in respect of justification and of its curse. But though a Christian is not under the condemning power of the law yet he is under its commanding power.

On the Ten Commandments themselves, Watson sets out certain rules on the basis of *synecdoche*, meaning in this case that more is intended than is written. Thus, where a duty is commanded, its violation is forbidden, and when a sin is forbidden, the contrary duty is commanded. The occasion or circumstances that may lead up to a forbidden sin are also forbidden; in the case of the prohibition of adultery, wanton glances are thus also forbidden. If greater sins, such as idolatry are forbidden, so are lesser sins of the same class, such as superstition. It is also possible to be an accessory to someone else's breaching of the commandments, for example, by commanding a person to do what is unlawful, or by failing to prevent wrongdoing when it was in a person's power to prevent it. Where a Christian falls short in obedience, God

> will accept of sincere obedience; he will abate something of the degree, if there be truth in the inward parts. He will see the faith, and pass by the failing. The gospel remits the severity of the moral laws.

5. MELANCHTHON AND DEVELOPMENTS IN LUTHERAN THEOLOGY

Having tried to deal briefly with the Reformed side of the Reformation, I return to the Lutheran side. Luther's view that even the Ten Commandments were not binding upon Christians, although Christians might adopt them if they wished because they were an expression of universal moral law, is a very different viewpoint from what we have just been considering. However, Lutheranism had to come to terms with the need to provide ethical guidance, and it did this by gradually admitting a third use of the law, for the guidance of Christians.

Philip Melanchthon
An important step on the road to this position, which was finally embodied in the Formula of Concord of 1580, was Melanchthon's *Loci Communes*, first published in 1521, and destined to become the basic work of early Lutheran systematic thought (Library of Christian Classics, vol.19). Although Melanchthon's work helped to move Lutheranism towards greater formalism, and, ultimately, rigid orthodoxy, the 1521 edition of the *Loci communes* accords very closely with Luther's teaching on law and gospel, and thus on the use of the Old Testament.

Melanchthon defines the Old Testament as a promise of material things linked with demands of the law. Thus, possession of the land of Canaan, and prosperity in the land of Canaan are conditional upon Israel observing the obligation of the covenant. By contrast, Melanchthon writes, 'the New Testament is nothing else than the promise of all good things without regard to the law and with no respect to our own righteousness . . . And here you see what the fullness of grace is; it is a veritable prodigality of divine mercy . . . it bestows salvation gratuitously without regard for our righteousness or our works . . . Who could believe this report?' (pp.120–1).

Dividing the Old Testament law into its three traditional parts, the moral, civil and ceremonial, Melanchthon argues strongly that the moral commandments, the Ten Commandments, have been abrogated by the New Testament. To say that Israel merely offended against the ceremonial law is to misread the Old Testament, and consequently, when Jeremiah (31:31 ff.) says that the Old Covenant will be replaced by the New, he is referring not just to ceremonies but to the whole law. The Christian is set free from law altogether and, led by the Spirit, is devoted to love and fear God and to serve his neighbour. If the spiritual man fulfils the Ten Commandments, it is because he cannot do otherwise. If the moral law of the Old Testament is abrogated, it is the more so that the ceremonial and civil laws are abrogated (p.127).

Nevertheless, there is a passage in the *Loci communes* that is similar to what is found, for example, in Bucer's *De regno Christi:*

. . . . judicial or ceremonial laws have not been so abrogated that one sins if he acts according to any one of them. But because Christianity is a kind of freedom, it is in our power to use this or that or leave it alone, just as it is in our power to eat and drink. As for the rest, I should like Christians to use that kind of judicial code which Moses laid down and many of the ceremonial laws as well. For since in this life we have to have judicial laws, and, it seems to me, ceremonial ones, it would be better to use those given by Moses than either the Gentile laws or papal ceremonies (p.126).

However, the difference between this position and that of Reformed protestantism must not be overlooked. The latter would have argued that the moral law as expressed in the Ten Commandments was binding upon Christians, not optional, and that the civil laws were a much more serious expression of God's will for mankind than implied by Melanchthon. The latter's view that Christian freedom conferred the freedom to adopt ceremonies would not have appealed to those who argued that what was not specifically commanded in the Bible by way of ecclesiastical organisation and observance, was not allowed. Again, Melanchthon's stress on the unconditional nature of God's grace as offered in the gospel did not accord either with the covenantal theology that stressed human obedience as a condition within the covenant, or the predestinarianism that, on the basis of 2 Peter 1:10, sought in obedience to the law a confirmation of election.

Later Lutheranism
Within later Lutheranism there was a development towards something that resembled at some points the Reformed view of the law and use of the Old Testament. In the fundamental work of J. Gerhard (1582–1637), the Ten Commandments were identified with the moral law, the purpose of their promulgation being to restore to mankind the knowledge of God's law which had been partly perverted by sin. Moral law was also to be found elsewhere in the Old Testament, and was to be distinguished, by reason, from what in the Old Testament was temporary (i.e. for Israel only) ceremonial and judicial law. Although the Ten Commandments became the basis of civil legislation in some areas of Lutheran influence, the civil laws of the Old Testament were not so treated. In some cases, Roman law was recommended. Christians were held to be duty bound to obey magistrates unless conscience forbade obedience, while those in authority were to be bound to obedience to God. Thus, although external circumstances forced Lutheranism to provide concrete guidelines for morality and society, this was achieved as closely as possible in the spirit of Luther, even if there

was a blurring of his law/gospel dialectic. A different use of the Old Testament resulted compared with the Reformed tradition.

It has not been the aim of this section so far to give an account of the course of the Reformation in England and on the Continent; instead, the attempt has been made to fix the main lines of the use of the Old Testament. As a result, many names that could have been mentioned are passed over in silence. For example, it would have been possible to chronicle William Tindale's shift from an initial Lutheran position to a position in which the Old Testament law was seen as part of Christian obedience. No attempt either has been made to describe the rise of the complex and elusive phenomenon known as Puritanism, and there is no specific material on 'Puritan use of the Old Testament'. Yet it is hoped that the broad outlines presented here do justice to the main possibilities of Old Testament use that were available in the complex years of the 16th and 17th centuries.

Sabbatarianism

This section can end with a brief allusion to sabbatarianism. As against the views of early reformers such as Calvin, that any day of the week could be observed as the Lord's day, there developed at the end of the 16th century a sabbatarianism that has been admirably defined as follows:

> the Sabbath derives from the creation and so antedates both Man's fall and the Mosaic law. . . . that the hallowing of the Lord's day in place of the Sabbath was of apostolic or even divine appointment . . . so that the Sabbath is still in force in this altered form, commemorating the second creation in Christ's resurrection, and robbed only of some of its ceremonial detail (P. Collinson, in *The Godly People*, London 1983, p.429).

With this sort of use of the Old Testament we reach almost the opposite extreme from Luther's conception of the freedom which the Gospel has brought with it.

6. THE BEGINNINGS OF BIBLICAL CRITICISM

Introduction

The remainder of this chapter, and indeed the remainder of this part of the book, will be concerned with the beginnings and development of what is known as the historical critical method. In some ways this will give a distorted picture of how the Old Testament was being used in the church. The historical critical method is the preserve of scholars. It was developed by learned men and was propagated through universities. The churches initially resisted it and only gradually and reluctantly came to terms with it; and, arguably, the greater majority of people who constitute the church know little or nothing about it even today.

However, it is unavoidable that the historical critical method should become the main concern for the remainder of this part of the book. At its worst, the method can be destructive and frivolous. At its best it begins from questions that arise genuinely from the text, and it seeks to understand the text in the light of everything that can be learned from scholarship in a number of disciplines. Further, questions posed by the historical critical method touch on the central question of the authority of the Old Testament in the church.

Before the attempt is made to trace the beginnings of the historical critical method, however, it is necessary to remind readers that even in the so-called pre-critical era of Old Testament study, many critical questions were considered and dealt with. The difference between pre-critical and critical scholarship was that the latter set different doctrinal limits from the former in terms of which to deal with critical matters. The most fundamental difference was in relation to the unity of the Old and New Testaments. Although what I am about to say is probably an over-simplification, it can be said that pre-critical scholarship accepted the primacy of the New Testament in deciding critical matters in the Old Testament. That Moses had written all or much of the Pentateuch was established on the basis of New Testament passages such as Mark 7:10:

For Moses said, 'Honour your father and your mother'

and Mark 10:3–4

(Jesus) answered them, 'What did Moses command you?' They said, 'Moses allowed a man to write a certificate of divorce . . .'

Of course, there are many critical questions raised by the Old Testament text that are not touched on in the New Testament; but the latter provided a frame for reference which generally determined critical matters. Although, as we shall see shortly, orthodox pre-critical scholars did not defend the entire Pentateuch as the writings of Moses, they would have regarded any substantial attack on

Mosaic authorship as an attack on the New Testament and the authority of Jesus. For critical scholars the bond between the Old and New Testaments had been loosened to the point that Old Testament critical matters were to be decided without reference to the New Testament.

Matthew Poole

A good example of a pre-critical scholar handling critical questions is the Puritan Matthew Poole. His *Annotations on the Holy Bible* were published in 1683–5, and were based, from Isaiah 59 onwards, on his *Synopsis Criticorum* (1669–76), since Poole only lived to complete the work as far as Isaiah 58. The *Synopsis criticorum* was a compendium of scholarly views on the books of the Bible from all ages and countries, and Poole's knowledge of this critical work is evident in his *Annotations*.

Poole accepted that Moses wrote almost the entire Pentateuch, except for Deuteronomy 34, which was written

> by Eleazar, or Joshua, or Ezra, or some other man of God, directed herein by the Holy Ghost: this being no more impeachment to the Divine authority of this chapter, that the penman is unknown, which also is the lot of some other books of Scripture, than it is to the authority of the acts of the king or parliament, that they are written or printed by some unknown person (*A Commentary on the Holy Bible*, Edinburgh 1962, vol.1 p.407).

He also conceded that Numbers 12:3, 'the man Moses was very weak',

> might be added, as some other clauses were, by some succeeding prophet (p.286).

On the authorship of the Psalms, Poole thought that Psalm 126 was 'composed by Ezra, or some other man of God, at the return of Israel from Babylon' (vol. 2 p.195), while of Psalm 137 he wrote

> the penman of this Psalm is uncertain; the occasion of it was unquestionably the consideration of the Babylonian captivity; and it seems to have been composed either during the time of that captivity, or presently after their deliverance out of it (vol.2, p.201).

The book of Chronicles, although substantially by Ezra, contained a few additional passages that were added by later prophets (vol.1 p.774).

In commenting on Isaiah 40–66, Poole sees those chapters as prophecies about the Babylonian exile. The one raised up by God in Isaiah 42:2 is possibly Cyrus, and although the servant mentioned at Isaiah 42:1 is probably Christ, Poole mentions the alternative possibility that the servant is Cyrus, or Israel, or the Jews (vol.2, p.418). Poole's interpretation of Daniel 8:9ff. regards the verses as a prophecy of the events of the second century B.C. when Antiochus Epiphanes ousted Onias from the priesthood and sold it to Jason and then Menelaus (vol.2, p.834). It is only a short step from saying that Isaiah 40–66 envisages the Babylonian captivity to saying that these chapters were composed in the 6th century; it is only a short step from saying that Daniel 8:9ff. refers to events of the 2nd century B.C. to saying that the book was written in the 2nd century. Such steps were soon to be taken, and similar steps were already being taken when Poole's *Annotations* were published.

The Situation in Holland, England and Germany

In dealing with the beginnings of historical critical scholarship I shall look separately at Holland, England and Lutheran Germany. Although the situation in each of these countries was very different, contacts between them were also important for stimulating the progress of critical studies. Holland in the 17th century has been described as 'a swarming ant-heap of different sects' all of which

> were engaged in an endless succession of pitched battles, Armi-
> nians and Gomarians, Cocceians, Voetians, Trinitarians, anti-
> Trinitarians . . . , each and every doctrinal view and shade of
> opinion about Grace, about the Scriptures, about the Right of
> Conscience, about Toleration, and even about the Civil Power,
> were ranged one against another in angry dispute (P. Hazard,
> *The European Mind 1680–1715*, Harmondsworth 1973, p.118).

In Holland, this free-for-all produced not only the freedom in which critical opinions could be expressed, but also a desire on the part of some to rise above the sectarian in-fighting by suggesting a type of belief in which reason could adjudicate between conflicting views.

In England the situation was very different. The main parties accepted the right of the secular authority to control matters civil and religious, but were in conflict about the type of secular authority. In England, critical studies of the Old Testament arose partly as a protest against the Old Testament model for reforming kings, such as we noticed in Bucer's *De regno Christi*.

Lutheran Germany lacked the political unity of England, and found religious unity in adherence to the doctrine believed to have been delivered by Luther. However, the rise of pietism at the end of the 17th century produced a type of subjective religion that laid far greater stress on individual experience than on faithfulness to Lutheran doctrine. This led to a shift in the understanding of Luther from the re-discoverer of authentic Christian doctrine to the champion of the freedom of the individual believer. In the mid–18th century, Luther would be claimed as the champion of the right of the individual scholar to handle the Old Testament according to the historical critical method.

Although Holland, England and Lutheran Germany proceeded along differing paths, they were all equally affected by the vast changes that were taking place in the general understanding of the world and of man's place in it. The 16th and 17th centuries were a time of scientific discovery, of the exploration of unknown parts of the world, and of the rise of a new type of philosophy which sought for certainty not in external authorities but in the necessary truths of reason as approved by the human mind. The enlightenment, complex phenomenon though it was, has been described as the transition from defining man in relation to a divinely-ordered universe, to defining the world in terms of human reason and experience.

Grotius

Indications of a new direction in Old Testament studies can be seen in the *Annotata ad Vetus Testamentum* of Hugo Grotius, published in Paris in 1644. Grotius (1583–1645) studied at the University of Leiden, and absorbed its humanist spirit, and was also attracted to the supporters of Arminius. Arminius himself was a professor at Leiden at the beginning of the 17th century, and his work was characterised by tolerance, and by the use of the philosophy of Peter Ramus in this theology. Grotius was a victim of the triumph in Holland in 1618 of the orthodox calvinistic parties, and escaped in 1621 to Paris from a life sentence in prison. Later in his life he became a diplomat in the service of Sweden.

His work on the Old Testament exhibited the severing of the traditional bond between the two testaments that was a hallmark of the critical method. Grotius, although comparatively traditional in his view of authorship of Old Testament books nonetheless advocated a literal historical interpretation that understood the text solely in terms of the circumstances of the writers. Whereas Poole would allow that the servant in Isaiah 42:1–4 might be a figure such as Cyrus but that the servant of Isaiah 52:13–53:12 could only be Christ, Grotius affirmed that in the latter passage the servant was Jeremiah. The Old Testament law was set aside by the lawyer Grotius, not on the Lutheran ground that Christians were free from it, but on the pragmatic grounds that it was archaic and incomplete. The relation between Old and New Testaments was reformulated as follows. The Old Testament was to be interpreted historically. As such, it formed the background to the New Testament, and in some places had intrinsic spiritual value. Otherwise it does not have any great practical religious importance for Christians.

Spinoza
A little over 25 years after Grotius's *Annotata*, Spinoza's *Tractatus Theologico-Politicus* was published (1676). Spinoza (1632–1677) was born in Amsterdam of Jewish parents, was excommunicated by the Jewish community in Amsterdam in 1656, and lived in later life first near Leiden and then near the Hague. The *Tractatus* was to become an influential work in the area of biblical criticism, expecially in the following century.

Setting out from observations made by the medieval Jewish commentator Ibn Ezra, Spinoza argued that the traditional belief that Moses wrote the Pentateuch was 'ungrounded and even irrational' (*Chief Works of Benedict Spinoza*, trans. R. H. M. Elwes, London 1909, p.126). It could be argued at many points that the Pentateuch was later than Moses, and that what Moses had written was a law book that was used by the real author of the Pentateuch – Ezra. Ezra was also the probable writer of Joshua, Judges, I & II Samuel and I & II Kings. In reaching this conclusion, Spinoza drew attention to the presence in these books of allusions to Deuteronomy, and argued that Deuteronomy itself was the law book set forth and explained by Ezra as detailed in Nehemiah 8:8 (pp.127–130).

Although Ezra had written the 12 books Genesis to II Kings (including Ruth), Ezra's work was, according to Spinoza, unfinished, and put into its final form by later revisers, who also used additional sources. The result was that the twelve books contained many repetitions, contradictions and discrepancies, which Spinoza described in some detail. In so doing, he drew attention to features of the text that would be explained by later critical scholarship in terms of different sources or separate redactions. Among his views on the date of authorship of other Old Testament books, Spinoza

held that Chronicles had probably been written after Judas Macca-
beus restored the temple in 164 B.C. (pp.133–151).

Spinoza, no doubt anticipating the furore that his opinions would
excite, excused himself graciously by saying that he was pointing
out errors in the Old Testament in order to prevent

> the clear and uncorrupted passages being accommodated to and
> corrupted by the faulty ones . . . No book ever was completely
> free from faults, yet I would ask, who suspects all books to be
> everywhere faulty? Surely no one, especially when the phras-
> eology is clear and the intention of the author plain (pp.154–5).

Spinoza, then, comes before us as a tolerant, rational person, whose
aim in criticising the text is not to be destructive, but to clear away
errors that have arisen in the processes of compilation, so that the
plain and clear passages will not be obscured by being harmonised
with corrupt passages on the grounds of a prior view of the self-
consistency of scripture. In so doing, Spinoza was enunciating
another important principle of historical critical scholarship, that
theories of consistency and authority must arise from the text, and
must not be imposed upon the investigation of the text.

Richard Simon
Another important principle of historical-critical scholarship was
advocated from an unexpected quarter – it breaks into the strict
geographical sequence of this chapter – namely, Catholic France.
Richard Simon (1638–1712) a member of the Oratory in Paris
published in 1678 his *Histoire critique du Vieux Testament*. This was
largely devoted to demonstrating the need for a new translation of
the Old Testament, one based not upon the traditional Hebrew text,
but on a critical text established with the help of the ancient
versions. But Simon's book was also an attack on Protestantism.
The Second Helvetic Confession of 1566 required belief in the divine
inspiration of the traditional Hebrew text including its vowel points.
Simon argued that the Hebrew text was corrupt in some places, and
that the vowel points had been taken over from Arabic by Arabic-
speaking Jewish grammarians of the middle ages. Protestants, in
effect, based their faith upon a text whose original form was in
some parts lost or corrupted. Simon also attacked the view that the
authority of biblical books rested upon their authenticity, that is,
the belief that they had been written by inspired individuals such
as Moses, Joshua, Samuel and David. Simon suggested that there

had been scribal schools in ancient Israel, and that the biblical books had passed through many hands before reaching their final form.

Jean le Clerc

Simon's *Histoire critique* was immediately banned by his own church, and much of his subsequent life was spent in conflict with his ecclesiastical superiors. It was 'answered', however, by Jean le Clerc, who was born in Geneva in 1657, but who made his home in Amsterdam, where he was a professor of Hebrew, and a follower of Arminius. Le Clerc is best known for his *Ars critica* of 1697, a handbook on the study of ancient languages and texts, which includes a section on Classical Hebrew, in which it is argued that the vowel points were added in the Christian era by Jewish scholars who did not know how Hebrew was originally pronounced. Le Clerc advocates the study of Hebrew in the light of other Semitic languages, and advocates a cautious use of emendation based upon the ancient versions and comparative philology. In 1685 Le Clerc published some 'observations' on Simon's *Histoire critique*. He rejected Simon's view that the Pentateuch was written by public scribes, preferring instead a view that it was based upon various documents, some of which were pre-Mosaic. Spinoza's view that Ezra wrote the Pentateuch was rejected on the grounds that the Samaritans possessed the Pentateuch, and that they separated from Judah in the 8th century. The Pentateuch must pre-date the separation. Clericus also wrote commentaries on the Pentateuch and the historical books in which he adopted a strictly philological, historical and rationalist approach. Miraculous happenings were given natural explanations, and 'messianic' passages were interpreted according to the events of the Israel's history.

By the end of the 17th century in Holland, then, there had begun to emerge, especially in Arminian circles, an approach to the Old Testament that put its study in historical terms above its study as inexorably linked to and determined by the New Testament. In England a similar movement developed out of the 17th century clashes between those who advocated a state church and those who wanted freedom from religious coercion, and between Puritans and Anglicans. There were also important philosophical developments, to which John Locke made a lasting contribution, and which had the effect of exalting reason as the criterion for acceptance of all truths and beliefs.

Hobbes

As early as Thomas Hobbes's *Leviathan* of 1651 we find a desire to reject traditional views on the authorship of Old Testament books, in favour of an approach based upon the internal evidence of the books themselves. This entailed that the Pentateuch was written after the time of Moses, although Deuteronomy 11–27 was ascribed to Moses himself. Similarly, Joshua, Judges and Ruth had been written long after the events recorded in them, as witnessed by phrases such as 'in those days' or 'until the day'. Hobbes's discussion of prophets concluded that prophets were not simply predictors of the future, but had also the role of speaking in the present on behalf of God to man and vice versa.

Deism

The acceptance of the primacy of reason in matters of truth and faith led to Deism, a complex phenomenon, but one that sought a universal religion that taught one God, the importance of good works, and the hope of immortality for the righteous. With such a controlling religious philosophy, the role of the Old Testament was reduced to that of reinforcing religious and moral truths in those of its parts that reason could approve. But, of course, there were many parts of the Old Testament that began to seem repulsive to 'enlightened' thinkers. The Old Testament was both rationalised, as in Toland's *Hodegus* or its morality sharply criticised, as in Thomas Morgan's *Physico-Theology* of 1741.

Basil Willey has neatly summed up the situation in the following words:

> Towards the close of the seventeenth century the prestige of Scripture, though outwardly unchallenged, had actually diminished appreciably. It was not so much that men rejected it as 'false'; it was rather that as 'natural religion' came more and more to seem all-sufficient, 'revelation' began to appear, if not superfluous, at least secondary, and perhaps even slightly inconvenient. An age which discovered God effortlessly in the starry heavens above, and in the moral law within, could not but be embarrassed by having to acknowledge dependence upon the annals and legends of an unenlightened Semitic tribe (*The Seventeenth Century Background*, Harmondsworth 1962, p.73).

7. LUTHERAN PIETISM

If Lutheran Germany seemed to lag behind Holland and England in matters critical, this was partly because of the development of Pietism, usually held to date in Germany from the publication of P. J. Spener's *Pia desideria* in 1675. However, the Pietists made very considerable contributions to Old Testament scholarship in the late 17th and early 18th centuries, which laid the foundations for the lead that Protestant Germany was to establish from the late 18th century onwards.

Pietism was a reaction against the Lutheran orthodoxy of the 17th century, and it stressed personal experience, especially experience of conversion and holiness. It accorded the Bible a fundamental place in the Christian life, and in practice this meant that the Old Testament was interpreted in a traditional manner as touching questions of authorship. At the same time, it has been argued that the individualism of Pietism was a reflection of the spirit of the Enlightenment, and 19th century orthodox Lutheran writers blamed Pietism's lack of stress on adherence to doctrine for the rise of biblical criticism. Their point was that Pietism, by implying an approach to the Bible that related its interpretation to individual Christian experience rather than to the doctrinal insights of the Reformation, was opening the door to a kind of critical individualism that would eventually undermine the traditional understanding of the Bible's authority.

One of the important achievements of Pietism was its involvement, through Spener and A. H. Francke (1663–1727) of the founding of the University of Halle in the 1690s, with which were to be associated foundations such as the *Collegium orientale* (1702). This latter foundation of Francke's was designed to equip gifted students with the knowledge of Semitic and Slavonic languages, and is evidence of the stress placed by Pietism upon the study of biblical languages and versions.

Halle became a centre for Pietist scholarship and learning; but Pietist scholarship did not necessarily follow the paths intended by Spener and Francke. The philosopher Christian Wolff developed, within the limits of Pietist orthodoxy, a philosophy of knowledge of God and the world which was thought to be sufficiently dangerous as to result in Wolff's expulsion from Halle in 1723. One of the features of Wolff's system that made him suspect was his acceptance of the Leibniz distinction between necessary and contingent truths. Necessary truths were truths of reason, whereas contingent truths included what was known from history. Consequently, Wolff assigned a lower place to history than to deductive reason, and although he dealt explicitly with how the Bible should be interpreted, his system was bound to question the authority of texts such as the Old Testament whose testimony was expressed in large measure through historical narrative.

S. J. Baumgarten

A scholar who stands as the bridge between a pietistic faith informed by Wolff's philosophy, and the rationalising critical scholarship of the later 18th century in Germany is S. J. Baumgarten (1706–1757). Baumgarten's scholarly output and activity were enormous and amazingly varied. On the one hand he published many biblical commentaries whose purpose was to expound the text for the spiritual building-up of the readers. On the other hand, through a sort of library bulletin, he introduced to the German public the latest literature, including the works of the English deists which were hostile to the Old Testament.

In his commentaries, Baumgarten's views of the authorship of Old Testament books were more traditional than those of the Puritan Poole. We have seen, for example, that the latter would date Psalm 137 to the Babylonian exile. Baumgarten, on the other hand, argued strongly for the view that all Psalms whose author is not named were by David, and that David could have written about the exile by means of prophetic insight. Again, Baumgarten takes Psalm 109 to be the words of Christ condemning those Jewish leaders who rejected him and clamoured for his execution. In Poole, it is acknowledged that David is a type of Christ, but the typological interpretation is evident only here and there in Poole's commentary. Baumgarten, then, offers an approach to the Old Testament in which Christ is seen to be speaking or to be implied in many passages.

At the same time, Baumgarten conceded much to what would later become commonplace in critical scholarship. The biblical authors, although inspired by God to the extent that he influenced the language which the writers employed out of their individuality, were not preserved from errors in matters of fact and history. Baumgarten maintained that, in practice, there were no historical errors in the Bible, but this was a conclusion that had to be justified by scholarly research, not by appeal to belief in inspiration. Baumgarten even maintained that, at the level of philological and historical interpretation, an unconverted scholar could be correct and a converted scholar could err. But Baumgarten distinguished between two levels of understanding, a 'natural' understanding which included philology and history, and a 'supernatural' understanding which approached the Bible as a communication from God. Only a converted person could interpret the latter.

J. S. Semler

It is not difficult to see that the only thing that separated Baumgarten from the later historical-critical position is his assumption of a supernatural understanding of the Bible. Take that away and you are left with biblical authors who, in theory, could have made errors of fact and history, and whose veracity is to be checked by scholarly investigation. Baumgarten's student, who has also been called the father of modern biblical criticism, took the step of abandoning belief in the 'supernatural understanding' of the Bible. J. S. Semler (1725–1791) substituted for the supernatural understanding a view of the word of God which he believed to go back to Luther himself. Semler, indeed, was something of a Luther scholar, basing himself on original manuscripts as opposed to unreliable printed editions of Luther's works. He believed that the purpose of the Bible was to speak the word of assurance to the believer that the believer was accepted through God's grace. This was quite a separate matter from the right of a Christian to handle the biblical text freely and critically. With Semler, Luther became the patron saint of free enquiry into matters of biblical origins and authorship.

In practice, Semler valued only those parts of the Old Testament that mirrored the spirit of the New Testament. He was not bound by the traditional limits of the Old Testament canon. Even traditional dogmatic formularies were not exempt from historical and critical investigation. By 1770, the right of free and critical handling of the Old Testament was established in Protestant Germany. The Old Testament was freed from its subservience to the New, and to Christian dogma. But was a free and critical spirit, guided by reason, sufficient for its correct interpretation? This was to become and remain the crucial issue for the Old Testament in the Christian church.

FOR FURTHER READING

G. Ebeling, 'Die Anfänge von Luthers Hermeneutik' ZThK 48 (1951) pp.172–230.

J. S. Preus, *From Shadow to Promise. Old Testament Interpretation from Augustine to the Young Luther*, Cambridge, Mass. 1969.

H. Bornkamm, *Luther und das Alte Testament*, Tübingen 1948.

R. Hermann, *Die Gestalt Simsons bei Luther*, Berlin 1952.

Arnold Williams, *The Common Expositor. An account of the Commentaries on Genesis 1527–1633*, Chapel Hill 1948.

T. H. L. Parker, *Calvin's Old Testament Commentaries*, Edinburgh 1986.

J. W. Baker, *Heinrich Bullinger and the Covenant. The Other Reformed Tradition*, Athens, Ohio, 1980.

J. S. Coolidge, *The Pauline Renaissance in England*, Oxford, 1970.

R. T. Kendall, *Calvin and English Calvinism to 1649*, Oxford 1979.

W. A. Clebsch, *England's Earliest Protestants 1520–1535*, New Haven and London 1964.

H. Graf Reventlow, *Bibelautorität und Geist der Moderne*, Göttingen 1980, E. T. *The Authority of the Bible and the Rise of the Modern World*, London, 1984.

E. W. Zeeden, *The Legacy of Luther*, London 1954.

K. Scholder, *Ursprünge und Probelme der Bibelkritik im 17. Jahrhundert*, (FGLP 10, 33) 1966.

Carl Bangs, *Arminius. A Study in the Dutch Reformation*, Grand Rapids, Michigan 1985.

J. W. Rogerson, *Old Testament Criticism in the Nineteenth Century*, London 1984.

E. Hirsch, *Geschichte der neuern evangelischen Theologie* vol.2. Münster 1984 (reprint).

D. G. Kramer (ed.), *A. H. Franckes Pädagogische Schriften, nebst der Darstellung seines Lebens und seiner Stiftungen*, Langensalza 1885(2).

The introduction by H. W. Arndt to C. Wolff, *Vernünftige Gedanken von den Kräften des menschlichen Vestandes* in *Gesammelte Werke*, Hildesheim, 1965 (repr.) Apt.1 Vol.1.

M. Schloemann, *Siegmund Jacob Baumgarten. System und Geschichte in der Theologie des Überganges zum Neuprotestantismus* FKDG 26, Göttingen 1974.

G. Hornig, *Die Anfänge der historisch-kritischen Theologie. Johann Salomo Semlers Schriftverständnis und seine Stellung zu Luther.* FSTR 8 Göttingen 1961.

Y. Belaval and D. Bourel (eds.), *La siècle des Lumières et la Bible* Paris 1986 (Bible de Tous les Temps,7).

8

FROM 1750 TO 1890

1. 1750 TO 1799: MICHAELIS TO HERDER

Introduction
The end of the previous chapter may have given the false impression
that the establishment of the historical critical method was the
achievement of one man – Semler. Semler, indeed, made a significant contribution; but he was only representative of a deep change
that took place in Protestant Germany around the middle of the
18th century.

The change came about partly as a response to the dissemination
of English deist attacks on the Old Testament as well as the re-
publication of books such as Spinoza's *Tractatus* and Simon's *Histoire
critique*. In the case of the English deist writings, these were made
available in some cases in German translation; otherwise, they were
known, together with anti-deist writings, by means of library bull-
etins such as that begun by S. J. Baumgarten.

Protestant German scholarship responded to the deist writings by
switching attention to history. The study of the history of Christian
doctrine was begun in a serious fashion, as was the history of biblical
religion. The interest in history answered the deist attacks in the
following manner. The deists poured scorn on aspects of Christian
doctrine that seemed contrary to reason, and on parts of the Old
Testament that seemed immoral or incredible. Historical study
enabled Christian doctrine to be understood in the light of its origins
at particular times and situations, and Old Testament belief and
morality to be evaluated in their particular historical and cultural
setting. Such an approach aimed genuinely to preserve the integrity
of what was being attacked by the deists; but this was achieved at
the expense of abandoning authority as it had been traditionally
understood. In the case of the Old Testament, the stress on its
historical particularity meant that it ceased to have any real contri-

bution to make to Christianity, other than being part of the background to the New Testament. Paradoxically, this did not mean that the Old Testament was ignored in theological faculties. As we shall see, Old Testament study went on apace; but it was the Old Testament studied as an ancient eastern book. Exegesis became the elucidation of the literal and historical sense of the text. Of the few scholars that space allows to be mentioned, I shall deal with J. D. Michaelis, J. C. Döderlein, J. G. Eichhorn, J. P. Gabler and J. G. Herder.

J. D. Michaelis

Michaelis (1717–1791), like Semler, came from the Halle pietist background, and was a student of S. J. Baumgarten. For much of his life he was a professor of Oriental Languages at Göttingen. His most famous work, his *Commentaries on the Law of Moses* (1770–75) was a painstaking elucidation of the Pentateuchal legislation in the light of the social world of ancient Israel. Its major thesis was that the laws of Moses were appropriate to the ancient Israelites in their particular situation, and are not to be applied to other peoples and times. It sums up well the scholarly mood of the time – the Old Testament had lost its place in Christian theology, but nonetheless remained the object of deep and detailed study in its own right. Michaelis published many papers on the social background of the Old Testament, published a new translation of the Old Testament with notes of a rationalising tendency, and was influential in the mounting in 1761 of the scholarly expedition to the East sponsored by King Frederick V of Denmark. The purpose of the expedition was to accumulate knowledge about the geography, customs, flora and fauna of the East, some of which would hopefully shed light on obscure Old Testament passages.

J. C. Döderlein

J. C. Döderlein (1746–1792) has been described as greater in the esteem of those in his time than even Semler. He was not a Baumgarten student, but studied in Altdorf, where he became a Professor in 1772, moving to Jena in 1782. His most significant work, for the history of biblical criticism, was his Isaiah commentary of 1775. This work, perhaps for the first time in Old Testament study, seriously considered the possibility that Isaiah 40–55 was written during the Babylonian exile. Döderlein also noticed the considerable difference in style of chapters 40 onwards compared with what went before. In his exposition of passages such as Isaiah 42:1–4 and 60, Döderlein referred the text to events in the 6th century. The servant of 42:1–4 was Cyrus, and ch. 60 referred to the return from the exile.

J. G. Eichhorn

J. G. Eichhorn (1752–1827) studied in Göttingen under Michaelis, and after teaching in Jena (1775–88) moved to Göttingen where he remained until his death. In 1779 he published anonymously a series of articles on the opening chapters of Genesis which marked the inception of the so-called mythical school. Eichhorn argued that Genesis 1–3 were authentic records about the experiences of the first man and woman to be created. In order to be understood correctly, the supernatural embellishments had to be stripped from them. Mankind in its infancy had no knowledge of scientific causes, and ascribed to supernatural powers what modern readers would understand in a normal secular way. Thus approached, Gen 2–3 was a story about earliest mankind. The original couple had lived in a fertile garden, had been slightly poisoned by eating a particular fruit, and had fled in terror from the garden on hearing the thunder of a storm, which thunder they interpreted as the expression of divine judgement.

In 1780–85, Eichhorn published an *Introduction to the Old Testament* in which he argued that the early chapters of Genesis were composed from two sources. Eichhorn had been preceded in this suggestion by J. Astruc in 1753, but it was his advocacy of the documentary hypothesis that set the agenda for subsequent investigations. Eichhorn defended the substantial Mosaic authorship of the Pentateuch in the first edition of his *Introduction*.

J. P. Gabler

J. P. Gabler (1753–1826) studied in Jena and Göttingen, and was Professor in Altdorf (1785–1804) and Jena (1804–26). He shared many of Eichhorn's views, and in 1790 produced an edition of Eichhorn's essays on Genesis 1–3 with extensive additional comments of his own. In his inaugural lecture delivered in Altdorf in 1785 he is generally thought to have inaugurated 'biblical theology'. What he did was to advocate a study of the Bible that was free from dogmatic presuppositions. At one level it would describe the history and development of theological ideas in the Bible; at the higher level it would evaluate these ideas and select those that should command acceptance. Dogmatic theology would then be the translation of these accepted ideas into forms for practical use.

J. G. Herder

A related, but highly individual approach to the Old Testament was adopted by J. G. Herder (1744–1803). Herder did not hold an academic appointment, but was a *Superintendent* of the Lutheran Church, first in Bückeburg (1771–1776) and finally in Weimar (1776–1803). However, Herder was to have a greater influence on subsequent Old Testament study than any of those mentioned so far in this chapter.

Herder agreed with his contemporaries that the Old Testament must be studied from the standpoint of its historical particularity. He went beyond them in being prepared to see in the earliest traditions of the human race (as he supposed parts of the Old Testament to be) not simply interesting specimens of archaic and naive conceptualisings of the world, but intuitions of reality that were of value in their own right. Gabler and Eichhorn understood 'myth' in the sense of a naive and prescientific conceptualising of 'normal' events that described these events in terms of the supernatural. For Herder, myth was a poetic expression of an experience of nature, which was not to be rationalised or explained away.

One of Herder's most important works for Old Testament study was 'On the Spirit of Hebrew Poetry' in which the attempt was made to elucidate the particular genius that Herder believed Hebrew poetry to have. Another important writing was 'The Oldest Record of Mankind' in which Genesis 1 was interpreted as God's communication to earliest mankind about the creation of the world. Behind Genesis 1 was earliest mankind's experience of sunrise which gradually dispelled the mists and disclosed a natural world of beauty and order. Herder believed, and endeavoured to prove by comparative studies, that the Genesis account of creation was the source for all the other creation stories in the ancient world. For Gabler and Eichhorn, the Old Testament text had virtually become a means to an end, the end being the history of the theological development of the Hebrews. Herder, perhaps because he was a man of literature, valued the text in and for itself. It is true that, in practice, he saw the text primarily as a record of human experience, but he offered to subsequent generations of scholars a way of interpreting the Old Testament that allowed its literature, and its poetic genius to stand in their own right, resistant to attempts to dismiss them as the product of an ancient, unenlightened people.

Conclusion

By the end of the 18th century, a profound change had taken place in the religious life of Protestant Germany. The various reactions to deism from 1750 onwards, with their attention to history, resulted in new hymn books, new devotional books, and a reduction in the number of church festivals. Sermons had become pre-eminently occasions for instruction in morals. Theologically, Old Testament scholars were divided into three groups: rationalists who denied miracles and stressed the primacy of morals, supranaturalists who affirmed the miraculous in theory but often mildly explained it away in practice, and neologists. Gabler and Eichhorn are usually described as neologists, and they adopted a mediating position. They fought for freedom on two fronts: freedom from being tied to church dogmas, and freedom from the all-sufficiency of human reason. An historical approach to biblical texts and to church dogmas enabled them to steer their middle course.

By the end of the 18th century in Germany the critical study of matters of authorship and of sources of Old Testament books had been accepted in many universities, and a growing number of scholars was beginning to advocate positions that were to become widely, if not universally accepted in modern scholarship. These included the division of parts of the Pentateuch into three sources, the deutero-Isaiah theory, and the identification of distinctive 'Servant Songs' in Isaiah 40–53. By way of contrast, Britain, whose deist literature had played a part in the changes that had taken place in German theology, was affected by pietist movements such as the Methodist revival, and showed no inclination to engage in critical scholarship. Indeed, the institutional framework did not exist in England (as distinct from Scotland) to encourage the growth of a body of scholarship actively engaged in critical matters.

2. 1800 TO 1865: DE WETTE

de Wette

In the first decade of the 19th century there appeared a work that marked a turning-point in Old Testament study, and which posed a question which has ever since remained fundamental for any Christian use of the Old Testament. The work was *Contributions to Old Testament Introduction* (1806–7). The writer was a young scholar named Wilhelm Martin Leberecht de Wette (1780–1849). De Wette was born near Weimar, and attended, among other schools, one in Weimar that came under Herder's authority. Herder made a lasting impression upon de Wette, as did the plays and writings of Schiller. When de Wette became a student of Philosophy and Theology at Jena in 1799 he soon became dissatisfied with his rationalist and neologist teachers, and discovered in the philosophy of J. F. Fries the answer to his need to combine a critically rational approach to faith with a deep respect for the biblical documents.

Fries was a disciple of Kant, and much could be written about Kant's own use of the Old Testament and of the influence of his critical philosophy on the theology of rationalists and supranaturalists. The distinctive contribution of Fries was that he linked religion with aesthetics. Experiences of beauty in art and literature and of what was awesome in nature were experiences of eternal values. Furthermore, the creators of art and literature gave expression, in their work, to intuitions of eternal values. Religion was similarly a way in which eternal values were grasped and made available in institutional forms.

Fries's philosophy enabled de Wette to give expression to his own convictions that religious texts were more than expressions of merely human experience; they were intimations of something eternal. They could thus be studied in their own right, and could also be a means of coming to an understanding of the eternal values which they sought to express. One facet of Fries's system was particularly important. He believed that naive and spontaneous graspings of eternal values were more authentic than elaborate and self-conscious forms. As applied to religion this meant that developed dogmas had lost sight of something that was more authentically grasped in simple stories. It was therefore not the case that religions necessarily progressed; they might degenerate in their mediation of eternal values.

De Wette's *Contributions* had two main aims. The first was to attack the work of scholars such as Gabler and Eichhorn whose mythical interpretation regarded the early chapters of Genesis as a means of recovering scraps of history about earlier mankind. De Wette, and there are echoes of Herder here, wanted to treat the texts as literature in their own right, literature that gave expression to the way in which the Hebrew spirit had grasped eternal values. His method of attack was to deny that it was either possible or desirable to recover history from the narratives of the Pentateuch. Historically speaking, they reflected an age much later than that which they claimed to portray; but this did not matter, since their proper interpretation was concerned with them as literature expressing eternal values.

The second aim of the *Contributions* was to present a picture of the history of Israelite religion that differed radically from that implied by the Old Testament itself. According to the Old Testament, Israel's laws, priesthood and ritual were given through Moses prior to entry into the promised land. According to de Wette, the religion that Moses bequeathed to his people was very simple. The importance of priests and the necessity for elaborate ritual had developed only gradually in Israel. Further, de Wette drew a sharp distinction between what he called Hebrew religion and Judaism. The latter, for which de Wette had little enthusiasm, had developed after the exile, and was a distortion of Hebrew religion at its best. Here, we can detect Fries's view that spontaneous religion is superior to elaborate and self-conscious religion.

In presenting his alternative view of the history of Israel's religion, de Wette raised many questions that are still key issues in Old Testament interpretation. First, he attacked the reliability of the books of Chronicles, books which suggest that the Mosaic institutions were indeed in place and functioning from the time of David and Solomon. Against the prevailing view, de Wette argued forcefully that the writers of Chronicles had merely read back the conditions of their own day (4th century B.C.) into earlier times. The evidence of Samuel and Kings was to be preferred, which showed that, during the early monarchy, there were many sanctuaries at which sacrifices were offered, and there was no centralised priesthood with exclusive priestly rights. The centralisation instituted by Josiah in 621 B.C. was a decisive step in the progress of Hebrew religion to the form that it assumed after the exile.

De Wette wrote not from a standpoint of destructive and negative criticism, but with a zealous faith which was a combination of aesthetic mysticism and post-Kantian philosophy. He believed that the Lutheran Reformation had been a movement for freedom, and that the new critical discoveries of his time embodied the true spirit of the Reformation. Already in his *Contributions* of 1806–7 there was to be found much of the position to be advocated by Wellhausen in 1878. That his position, after initial support from contemporary scholars, was eclipsed for over 40 years from the 1830s was for reasons that must now be outlined. By way of summary it can be said that de Wette's work was tarnished by association with that of the radical hegelians Vatke and Strauss, was opposed by a resurgence of Lutheran orthodoxy, and was regarded as inferior to the so-called positive criticism of scholars such as Ewald.

Reactions to de Wette

Strauss's *Life of Jesus* and Vatke's *Biblical Theology* were published in 1835. The former concerns us only in that the negative attitude to the historical value of Old Testament Pentateuchal traditions adopted by de Wette seems to be applied by Strauss to the Gospels. Vatke's work differed significantly from that of de Wette. In particular, he adopted a hegelian view of religion as essentially involving progress, as a result of which he did not detect a degeneration of Israelite religion after the exile. Rather, the Persian period (540–333) marked the highpoint. However, de Wette was blamed for having started a process that led inevitably to Vatke and even Strauss. In passing, it must be said that Vatke's *Biblical Theology* is a penetrating work of scholarship that draws attention to many problems latent in the Old Testament regardless of hegelian theories of religion.

By 1835, a strong tide of Lutheran orthodoxy was running in many parts of Germany, spearheaded by the Berlin Old Testament professor E. W. Hengstenberg (1802–1869). This orthodox movement reasserted the importance of interpreting the Bible in accordance with Lutheran formularies, especially the Augsburg Confession, whose three-hundredth anniversary fell in 1830. Hengstenberg and his followers opposed the views of Israelite religion advocated by de Wette and Vatke because they varied from the Old Testament's own account. Also, they stressed the unity of the Bible in the sense that they believed that the Old Testament prophets foretold the atoning work of the suffering Messiah. Theirs was a return to the position of the orthodoxy of a hundred years earlier, albeit backed by the knowledge that research had accumulated in the meantime. Among the followers of Hengstenberg were C. F. Keil and (with slight reservations) Franz Delitzsch, whose commentary on the Old Testament is still available in English translation.

The so-called positive criticism was championed by H. Ewald (1803–1875) and popularised by C. C. J. Bunsen (1791–1860). It had close contacts with classical scholarship, and regarded books such as Genesis as valuable information about the history of tribes which had been personified in the characters and families of Abraham and Jacob. Ewald's *History of Israel* (1843–1848) was the first modern critical work of its genre. It traced the history back to the tribes before the Exodus, and was generally much more constructive about the work of Moses and the establishment of the priesthood and rituals than was the case with de Wette.

3. 1865 TO 1890: GERMANY

From 1865 onwards, however, there was a movement back towards the de Wettian position. In 1866, K. H. Graf's *The Historical Books*

of the Old Testament re-stated the de Wettian view that the books
of Chronicles gave an unreliable account of the history of Israelite
religion; and he added something that de Wette would have denied,
namely, that the priestly cultic traditions of Exodus, Leviticus and
Numbers were composed *after* the exile. In 1875, B. Duhm argued
in his *The Theology of the Prophets* that the 8th century prophets
had made fundamental contributions to Israelite religion, and that
they preceded rather than followed the religion of Israel in its
priestly and cultic form. Another important factor was that there
was a renewal of interest in the Documentary Hypothesis, to be
found already at the end of the 18th century in the work of Eichhorn
and others.

J. Wellhausen

In his *History of Israel* (1878) Julius Wellhausen drew together many
of the strands of contemporary research, and combined them into
a brilliant synthesis which, whether it was to be accepted or rejected,
became a work that could not be ignored. Wellhausen is popularly
known as the chief advocate of the four-document hypothesis of the
composition of the Pentateuch, the sources being designated by the
letters J (Jahwist), E (Elohist), D (Deuteronomist) and P (Priestly
writing). This popular view, though correct, is so incomplete as to
amount to a parody.

In his history, and its second edition in 1883 known as the
Prolegomena, Wellhausen divided the history of Israel into three
main periods: the early monarchy, the 7th century, and the period
of the return from exile. Each period had a different religious
character. The first was a period of spontaneity, with many sanctuaries and no priesthood with exclusive rights. The second period
saw a decisive movement towards centralisation, in the reformation
of Josiah. During and after the exile the Jerusalem priesthood gained
exclusive power, and Israel became a theocracy ruled by priests
and committed to elaborate sacrificial rituals. To each period there
corresponded a pentateuchal document or documents. The first
period was reflected in J and E, which were composed in the 9th–8th
centuries B.C., and reflected the conditions of those times in their
portrait of the Patriarchs building altars and offering sacrifices
without the presence of priests. The second period was closely
connected with Deuteronomy, which was substantially the law book
discovered in the temple in 622 and the basis for Josiah's reforms.
Its demands for a single sanctuary were something new in Israelite
religion. If the law of the sanctuary was ancient, then it had been
ignored by Samuel and Elijah and had been unfamiliar to Amos, all

of which was unlikely. The period of return from exile was to be associated with the priestly legislation of Exodus – Numbers, of which there was no trace in the earlier books such as Samuel and Kings.

Wellhausen had reasserted the basic de Wette position of 1806–7, but with greater clarity, and with the help of the Documentary Hypothesis, which had not been a concern of de Wette. However, the overall position remained the same in respect to the history of Israel's religion. Little could be known about the time of the Patriarchs, and much of what was attributed to Moses had developed much later. The exile marked a turning point, and was a transition from the spontaneity of Israelite religion at its best, especially as seen in the prophets, to the legalism of post-exilic Judaism. Wellhausen's position did not find universal acceptance in Germany. Scholars such as August Dillman and Rudolph Kittel argued that most of the levitical laws about the cult were earlier than the exile, and had been written down during the early monarchy. Kittel in particular was far more positive than Wellhausen about what could be known of the Patriarchs and Moses. However, Wellhausen had won possession of the centre of the stage. Those who disagreed with him were obliged to fight the battle at the points where Wellhausen had laid down the challenge, and as time went on, even conservative scholars such as Franz Delitzsch came to admit that Wellhausen was right in many details.

The General Position in Germany 1750–1890

It is now necessary to look back over the period just surveyed and consider what was going on in the use of the Old Testament in the German Protestant churches. The relationship between the university Theology faculties and the church was, of course, very close, and future clergy did their training in the faculties. Because Germany was divided into a number of states, each with its independent Lutheran or united Lutheran and Reformed Church, the theological climate could vary from place to place and from university to university. Old Testament studies in Tübingen, Erlangen, Leipzig, Rostock and Berlin (during Hengstenberg's ascendency) tended to be more conservative than elsewhere. Some faculties, such as Halle, housed scholars of both conservative (Tholuck) and critical persuasion (Gesenius, Hupfeld). On the whole, there was no unified view of how to use the Old Testament. The Hengstenberg party fought for the authority of the traditional doctrinal statements. Ewald believed that God disclosed himself in history, and that positive critical study of the Old Testament would make clear what

God had taught Israel, and through Israel, mankind. The followers of de Wette were interested in the spirit of the biblical literature rather than an historical process that could be reconstructed from it. Others were content to treat the Old Testament as an interesting ancient document. This was true of Wellhausen. Although he was basically a devout man, he disliked organised religion, and in 1882 he resigned from his chair at Greifswald because he did not feel that he could conscientiously continue to teach future clergy. He was to spend the remainder of his teaching career in oriental faculties. This general lack of agreement about the use of the Old Testament was a reflection of the general theological scene in Protestant Germany. In scholars such as Schleiermacher, Hofmann, Rothe and Ritschl Germany produced people who were willing to speculate creatively about Christian theology around the core of the doctrine and experience of justification by faith. German theologians were also willing to be sensitive to contemporary philosophy. Thus the general scene was one in which there were schools of thought centred around key figures or based in particular faculties, the schools being in dialogue and sometimes sharp opposition with each other. Old Testament study flourished within this milieu, and shared its characteristics.

4. 1865 TO 1890: BRITAIN

In Britain the story of the use of the Old Testament was quite different. Britain entered the 19th century with nothing comparable to the 20 Protestant German university faculties with their growing body of critical scholarship, and showed little desire to further the critical enterprise at all. From the 1830s there was a determined attempt to keep German criticism out of Britain at all costs, and the barriers that were created did not begin to crumble until the 1880s, although they were quite badly shaken in the 1860s.

T. H. Horne
A good illustration of the state of Old Testament study in Britain in the early decades of the 19th century is furnished by T. H. Horne's *Introduction to the Critical Study and Knowledge of the Holy Scriptures* which enjoyed several editions in the 1820s and 1830s. It is a massive work of four volumes and over 2,500 pages, and is encyclopaedic in its coverage of the nature of the biblical languages, texts and versions, customs and social organisation, the geography of the Bible lands, and the different types of biblical literature and

how to handle them appropriately. There are also extensive annotated bibliographies of commentaries and general works of biblical introduction, including reference to works by German scholars, including Semler who is sharply criticised. Combined with this massive erudition there are certain very slight liberal tendencies, or at any rate concessions to difficulties that might be felt by sensitive readers. Thus Horne allowed that the order of the chapters of Joshua had suffered 'accidental derangement', as was also the case in I Samuel, where it was obvious that ch.17 should come in between 16:1–13 and 16:14–23. He also allowed that elsewhere, e.g. Genesis 11:31 and 12:1 the Bible did not relate events in the order in which they had occurred. Horne also dealt fully with discrepancies that critical scholarship explained in terms of the combination of originally separate sources, such as the command in Genesis 6:19–21 to take two pairs of all creatures into the ark and the command of 7:2 where seven pairs of clean animals are to be on board (*Introduction* 1825 edition vol.1 pp.545–6, 578ff., vol.II p.36).

However, Horne's *Introduction* expresses a strict orthodoxy in which God, as author of the Bible, has expressed himself in a way free from contradiction. Although there are three main dispensations of faith, those of the Patriarchs, Moses and the Gospel, these are in harmony for all that the first two are completed by the third. Horne vigorously rejects arguments brought against the morality of the Old Testament. On God's command to Abraham to sacrifice his son Isaac, Horne defends the right of 'the Supreme Lord and Giver of Life' to take it away when he pleases. Abraham's act would have been murder if there had been no divine command; given the command, it was an act of obedience (vol. I p.563). On the command of Joshua to kill the Canaanites sparing no one, Horne argued that God not only had a right to punish wicked nations, but that it was clear that 'in the course of his Providence' he actually did punish nations by means of war, famine and disease. The example of Joshua was thus only a particular instance of a general principle. The Canaanites were wicked and deserved to be destroyed (vol.I pp.566–7). On the conduct of David, Horne distinguished between the King's private conduct and his public official conduct. As touching the latter, David was always a man after God's heart (vol.I p.571). The whole Bible, then, was a communication from God, and was to be interpreted as the expression of the character of one who was consistent, and whose sovereign authority placed him above moral cavils that might be brought by opponents or doubters of divine revelation.

Presumably, if historical critical scholarship had gained no footing

in Britain, the Old Testament would have continued to be interpreted along the lines of Horne's *Introduction*. Many scholars were,
indeed, to spend a lifetime defending the basic principles enshrined
in Horne, scholars such as E. B. Pusey who was able to exert
considerable influence from the chair of Hebrew at Oxford, which
he occupied from 1828 to 1882.

H. H. Milman

In 1828–9 a *History of the Jews* was published by H. H. Milman,
later Dean of St. Paul's, which, it was later claimed on good authority, was the first decisive inroad of German rationalist theology
into England. In fact, this claim does not bear close examination.
Milman's *History* was a very traditional re-telling of the Old Testament story, illuminated by references to classical writers and the
accounts of travellers to the East. It was perfectly ready to accept the
miraculous, and dismissed, for example, the idea that the redness of
the Nile when Moses allegedly turned it to blood was a natural
phenomenon. Milman preferred to accept the plagues as miracles,
even if he pointed to natural explanations for the feeding of the
Israelites in the wilderness by means of manna.

For all that it contained nothing new or outrageous, Milman's
History met with a storm of protest that necessitated the withdrawal
of the work from John Murray's 'Family Library' series. It is difficult today to discover what all the fuss was about. Perhaps the
outcry reflected opposition between traditionalists and those with
broader sympathies; perhaps some were offended that it was possible
to write about the Old Testament as though it was like secular
history. Whatever the truth, the outcry shows how different the
situation was in Britain in 1830 compared with Germany.

Thomas Arnold

I turn next to mention the sermons and expositions of the Old
Testament published by Thomas Arnold from the late 1830s. The
contrast with Horne is interesting, and we see present a theme that
was to become the main key to understanding the Old Testament
in Britain for the rest of the 19th century and for the first half of
the 20th century. Horne, we have seen, in defending alleged
immoral parts of the Old Testament such as the wars of Joshua,
asserted God's right to order the destruction of wicked people.
Arnold, on the other hand, asserted that God's commands in the
Old Testament were adapted to the understanding of the people to
whom they were addressed in the times in which they lived. In
other words, seeming immoral commands were not to be justified

by appeal to divine privileges, but on the grounds of the immature moral understanding of the Israelites in earlier times. From this it followed that the Old Testament was not to be read, together with the New, as a communication of the divine will and character. Rather, it was a witness to an historical process in which God had guided and educated his people from a rudimentary understanding of his will to something more enlightened. At the same time, Arnold saw positive value even in stories such as the conquest of Canaan. An important theme shared by the Old Testament and the contemporary world was the battle between good and evil. This battle was evident in the book of Joshua, and although Joshua's behaviour as recorded there could not be replicated by Christians, Joshua's commitment to the side of good was a challenge to Christians to be resolute in the struggle between good and evil as they found it in their own times.

The idea that history was a process guided by God, and that the Old Testament was a witness to this process was an idea that was strongly represented in Germany in the 1830s, and it may indeed have constituted the most significant influence of German thought on British liberal theology. When, in 1860, the barriers of orthodoxy received a nasty jolt, the ideas of God guiding the historical process and of the Old Testament being the record of God's education of Israel were very prominent.

Essays and Reviews

The 1860 'jolt' was caused by the publication of seven essays, six of whose authors held office or who were prominent in the Church of England. *Essays and Reviews* was thus not seen simply as an expression of opinion on the part of seven private individuals, but as a concerted attempt to launch a new standpoint within the Church of England. Two of the essayists were arraigned before the Court of Arches and the Judicial Committee of the Privy Council and two counter volumes maintaining orthodox positions were published entitled *Aids to Faith* (1861) and *Replies to Essays and Reviews* (1862). Compared with the radicalism of de Wette's *Contributions* of 1806–7, *Essays and Reviews* was very moderate indeed, and insofar as it dealt with the Old Testament, it was most closely in touch with the work of Ewald as popularised by Bunsen, to whose *Bibelwerk* an entire essay was devoted.

The essay on Bunsen argued that the latter's researches had historically dated Abraham and Moses, had vindicated the historical reality of the Exodus, and had shed much light generally on the Old Testament by placing it within a general historical context of which contemporary knowledge was rapidly growing. What, we might ask, was objectionable about any of this? The answer was that Bunsen denied the Mosaic authorship of the entire Pentateuch, questioned the unity of authorship of books such as Isaiah, Zechariah and Daniel, and interpreted prophecies historically, so that Isaiah 7:14 referred not to Christ but to a child to be born in the reign of Ahaz. It must also be said that Bunsen was a *bête noir* to the High Church party, who objected to the joint Anglican-Lutheran bishopric in Jerusalem, the setting up of which owed much to Bunsen, and to Bunsen's views on the history of the early church.

On the Old Testament front, the objectors to *Essays and Reviews* rejected the developmentalist approach to biblical interpretation, which saw the Old Testament as the story of divine education. Not only was this approach to be found in the essay by R. Williams on Bunsen, but in the essay by F. Temple which opened the volume, and was entitled 'The Education of the World.' The orthodox objectors stood for interpreting the Bible as a unity, according to the doctrinal 'rule of faith', and as possessing a harmony such that Old Testament prophecies referred to Christ.

J. W. Colenso

The next jolt to orthodoxy came in 1862 with the publication of part I of J. W. Colenso's *The Pentateuch and the Book of Joshua critically examined*. Colenso was a missionary bishop working in Natal, South Africa. That a bishop, whose traditional role was to preserve the doctrine of the church, should publish such radical speculations about the Old Testament was bad enough, quite apart from the implications of the radical speculations themselves. In practice, Colenso's observations reproduced some of the deist attacks on the Old Testament of the previous century, and are not unlike the attacks made by the German H. S. Reimarus and published anonymously and posthumously in the 1770s. One of Colenso's arguments was that it was impossible that 600,000 adult males could have taken part in the Exodus as claimed at Exodus 12:37-8. This would have given a grand total of over two million Israelites altogether crossing the Red Sea and journeying through the wilderness, which was absurd for many reasons, which Colenso spelled out devastatingly. The conclusion from this was that the narrative account of the Exodus and wilderness wanderings was historically unrealiable in many details.

Part I of *The Pentateuch and Joshua* was followed by six more parts, of which the last appeared in 1879, bringing the size of the whole work to some 3,500 pages. During the years that intervened,

Colenso developed from being an anachronistic deist to a critical scholar of considerable attainment. He increasingly entered into dialogue with German and Dutch scholarship, and began to move towards a position which, while not being in any way identical with Wellhausen's, shared much with it. Thus Colenso argued for the unreliability of the picture of Israelite religion given in the books of Chronicles, and he also believed that those parts of Exodus – Numbers that contained levitical legislation about sacrifices and purity were written after the exile. He advocated a modified form of the Documentary Hypothesis, and claimed that the book of the law found in the temple in Josiah's reign in 622 B.C. consisted of Deuteronomy 5–26,28.

In another book I have dealt with Colenso in some detail, and it is not possible here to chronicle the opposition that he faced in both Britain and South Africa for his radical views. I believe, however, that Colenso has been treated less fairly than he deserves in subsequent treatments of the history of the 19th century church. He was a devout man, a far-sighted missionary, and a courageous advocate of the rights of the Zulu people. As an Old Testament scholar he applied himself to serious critical study in a way unrivalled by any Anglican scholar before his time. It has been suggested that his contribution to critical Old Testament study in Britain was to break up the hard soil of the objections of the orthodox. It was certainly true that, only a few years after his death, even those who had been trained in the orthodox positions came to realise that these could no longer be defended, and that a new way of handling the Old Testament in the Church was necessary.

Two alternative lines of approach were championed in the 1870s in Britain within orthodox circles. One was essentially a restatement of a fundamental tenet of the liberal Anglicans of earlier decades, namely, that the Old Testament was the record of the divine education of the Hebrew people. The other owed much to direct contacts with Germany, and argued that historical criticism was a necessary tool for a true Reformation understanding of the Old Testament. Interestingly, both approaches were to lead to an acceptance in Britain of a modified form of the Wellhausen position.

J. B. Mozley

We can see the progress of the divine education view in J. B. Mozley's *Ruling Ideas in Early Ages*, published in 1877 but based upon lectures delivered in Oxford in 1874–5. The burden of Mozley's position is that the Old Testament must not be seen in terms of its parts but in terms of the whole. If one looks at the end-product, the Old Testament will be seen to be a cumulative process in which each stage leads to something higher. This is illustrated by Genesis 22, God's command to sacrifice Isaac. According to Mozley, only someone could sincerely believe that God could give the command to destroy a human life who lived in a primitive age in which there was no developed sense of individual rights. Such was the situation at the time of Abraham, and indeed, the rights of individuals were not clearly stated until the time of Ezekiel. What is remarkable about Mozley's lectures is that they show how quickly the position had changed in orthodox circles since the replies to *Essays and Reviews* only just over a decade earlier. Mozley was one of the early supporters of the High Church movement in England, and he became Regius Professor of Divinity at Oxford in 1871. We find him adopting a completely different position from the opponents of *Essays and Reviews*, for whom the Bible had a unity based upon God's unchanging character, not a unity based upon his gradual leading of the Hebrews from lower to higher stages of moral and religious understanding.

W. R. Smith

The other main approach to a new understanding of the Old Testament was advocated, not without personal loss and tragedy, by a member of the Free Church of Scotland, William Robertson Smith. Smith became Professor of Old Testament at the Free Church College in Aberdeen in 1870 at the age of 24. He had studied in Bonn, Göttingen and Heidelberg, and had come to value the work of two German systematic theologians in particular, Richard Rothe and Albrecht Ritschl. Smith was a fervent evangelical and seems to have caught from Germany two convictions that were to determine his work. The first was that the Old Testament at its best was an account of God dealing graciously and personally with his people. The second was that historical critical scholarship, by showing that the formal priestly and sacrificial religion of the Old Testament was a late development, was a method granted by God to the church to enable the true, gracious religion of the Old Testament to be recovered. In his later apology, *The Old Testament in the Jewish Church* (1881) he was to accuse his opponents of betraying the Reformation by rejecting the historical critical method.

In May 1876 there began a series of investigations into Smith's views that led eventually to his trials and his dismissal in 1881 from his Aberdeen post. He moved to Cambridge in 1885 and remained there until his death in 1894. The proceedings against Smith were occasioned by his articles 'Angel' and 'Bible' in the 9th edition of the *Encyclopaedia Britannica*, and while he was on trial he delivered in 1880 and 1881 a series of lectures later published as *The Old Testament in the Jewish Church*. This is a highly original and novel approach to the Old Testament, which, starting with the Authorised Version of the Bible of 1611, works back to the actual method of composition of the original biblical autographs. The argument is far too detailed and elaborate to be summarised here, and only one or two points can be made. The first is that Smith accepted the Wellhausen view of the composition of the Pentateuch and of the history of Israelite religion. Secondly, he attacked the idea that the authority of the Old Testament was equally distributed through its pages. There was far more of Christ in the prophets and psalms than in the Pentateuch, he declared, a fact that could be checked by the use made of the Old Testament in the New. Further, Christians were not to be bound by traditional Jewish ideas of the extent of the Old Testament canon. The Reformation stood for the freedom of Christians to discriminate in their handling of the Old Testament between books that were the foundation of the new covenant and those that were not.

S. R. Driver

Smith's book did not create a 'school' in Britain; it was probably too Lutheran to do that. It had the effect, however, of bringing to general attention the results of historical criticism in a powerfully argued form, and in the context of a passionately-held evangelical belief. The next major influence on the establishment of the historical critical method in Britian was that of S. R. Driver, who succeeded Pusey as Regius Professor of Hebrew in Oxford in 1882. Driver worked on two fronts. He advocated the progressive education view, and he painstakingly examined the historical and literary arguments for the Wellhausen position until he was sufficiently convinced of them to lay them before the public in what is still arguably their finest presentation in English, in his *Introduction to the Literature of the Old Testament* (1891).

Driver was also interested in reconciling science with religion, a topic that has so far not been mentioned in this chapter. That there has been no such mention may surprise those readers whose view of the 19th century is that it was a great battle between science and religion, between evolution and creation. My own reading suggests that the major battles were fought in the 1820s, when the findings of geologists suggested that the world was thousands (sic) of years old, and not created in 4,004 B.C. as one authoritative estimate of biblical chronology had it. The orthodox reply to these charges was that the fossil evidence collected by geologists had been distributed where it was by means of the flood recorded in Genesis 6–9. The geologists' evidence did not, therefore, discredit the biblical chronology, but confirmed the truth of a universal Flood (Horne, *Introduction*, vol.I pp.169ff). Darwin's *Origin of Species* (1859) seems to have made little impression on Old Testament circles. Neither Colenso nor *Essays and Reviews* discuss it. Some liberal Anglicans held that Darwin had provided support for a new version of the argument from design for God's existence.

By the time that Driver became Regius Professor, what we might call social Darwinism had become prevalent, and he addressed himself to the problem of reconciling Genesis with popular science in a sermon delivered in 1883 entitled 'Evolution compatible with faith'. While not trying to identify the 'days' of creation with the successive geological eras that were now scientifically established, be described the days as evidence for a series of stages 'each the embodiment of a Divine purpose'.

Conclusion

The developmentalist approach to the Old Testament, whose roots went back to the 1830s in Britain, completely triumphed in the 1880s as the historical-critical method began to find acceptance in establishment circles that had hitherto opposed it. So completely did it triumph that it had the effect of modifying the British acceptance of Wellhausen in one important respect. It will be remembered that Wellhausen, like de Wette, made a distinction between Hebrew religion and post-exilic Judaism, which latter marked a decline in Israel's faith. British developmentalists, though, could not accept this. If the revelation of God in the Old Testament was progressive, it had not gone fundamentally backwards. The development of the levitical system was thus seen as a necessary way of preserving the Old Testament faith against the onset of Greek culture following Alexander the Great's conquest of Judah in 332. Also, it could be pointed out that only during the exile had Israel attained a pure monotheism and a true understanding of the rights of the individual.

By way of broad generalisation, it can be said that by 1890 in Britain there were two main attitudes to the Old Testament. The first, almost certainly held by the vast majority of churchgoers, was a simple version of the sort of orthodoxy expressed in Horne's *Introduction* in the 1820s. The second, maintained by the majority of those in university and theological colleges, involved an acceptance of the Wellhausen position within the context of belief in the Old Testament as the record of God's progressive revelation of himself to his people. That this latter view often amounted in practice to branding the Old Testament as largely obsolete explains why, in the 20th century, as this view was propounded in schools and colleges, the Old Testament was increasingly thought to have little relevance to theology and church.

FOR FURTHER READING

A. O. Dyson, 'Theological Legacies of the Enlightenment: England and Germany' in S. W. Sykes (ed.) *England and Germany. Studies in Theological Diplomacy*, Frankfurt am Main/Bern 1982, pp.55ff.

J. W. Rogerson, *Anthropology and the Old Testament*, Oxford 1978, reprint Sheffield 1984, pp.3ff.

J. W. Rogerson, *Myth in Old Testament Interpretation*, Berlin 1974.

J. W. Rogerson, *Old Testament Criticism in the 19th Century. England and Germany*, London 1984.

Klaus Leder, *Universität Altdorf. Zur Theologie der Aufklärung in Franken*, Nürnberg 1965, pp.161–244.

J. H. Hayes and F. C. Prussner, *Old Testament Theology. Its History and Development*, London 1985, pp.62–6.

R. A. Riesen, *Criticism and Faith in Late Victorian Scotland*, Lanham 1985.

9

FROM 1890 TO THE 1930s

1. ANCIENT NEAR EASTERN STUDIES

The Rise of Assyriology
The previous chapter concentrated deliberately upon the growth of
the historical critical interpretation of Old Testament texts, the
changing view of the history of Israelite religion which culminated
in Wellhausen's *History of Israel* (1878) and reactions to this critical
work in both Germany and Britain. Nothing was said about a branch
of study that was in its infancy and adolescence for much of the
19th century, and which rapidly grew to adulthood before the end
of the century, transforming Old Testament study in the process. I
have in mind the discipline known generally as Assyriology.

The work of Ewald and Bunsen in the mid–19th century on the
History of Israel made use of the rapidly developing discipline of
Egyptology, and of newly-discovered inscriptions such as those in
Punic and Phoenician, which shed light on some of ancient Israel's
near neighbours. Ewald also studied the methods of history-writing
used by Arab historians. However, the decipherment and publication of Babylonian and Assyrian texts was, from the 1870s, to
have a transforming influence upon Old Testament study.

The first steps towards the decipherment of the cuneiform writing
employed in ancient Persian, Babylonian and Assyrian were taken
as early as 1802 by a German schoolmaster G. F. Grotefend
(1775–1853). Other important contributions were made from the
1850s by a French diplomat P. E. Botta, an Irish clergyman, Edward
Hincks and an English military adviser to the Shah of Persia, H.
C. Rawlinson. The importance of Assyriology came to the notice of
the general public when, in 1872, a young scholar named George
Smith working at the British Museum announced at a public lecture
the discovery of a Babylonian version of the Flood story. The
remainder of the century was to witness the accumulation of

materials from ancient Babylonia and Assyria, the emergence of a more detailed understanding of ancient Near Eastern history based upon original texts, and attempts to prove that practically everything in the Old Testament was derived from Babylon!

Arabian Studies

Before we turn to the contribution of Assyriology, however, we must notice that theories that were to have lasting influence in Old Testament study were advanced in the 1880s and 1890s on the basis of Arabic sources. After his dismissal from Aberdeen, and his removal to Cambridge in 1885, W. R. Smith concentrated upon Arabic studies. His pioneering work *Kinship and Marriage in Early Arabia* appeared in 1885 and argued that among the ancient Semites, including the ancestors of the Hebrews, the earliest form of social organisation had been matriarchal not patriarchal, and that religion had been a form of totemism, in which the social units identified themselves closely with an animal or other natural object which was the totem god. Smith believed that the Old Testament contained relics of the matriarchy in texts such as Genesis 2:24: 'therefore shall a man leave his father and his mother and shall cleave unto his wife', and of totemic religion in the names of the mothers of the Hebrew tribes, Rachel and Leah, which meant respectively 'ewe' and 'bovine antelope'. Smith's *Lectures on the Religion of the Semites* (1889) developed further the totemic theory of ancient Semitic religion in a way that supported the de Wette/Wellhausen view of early religion as something essentially spontaneous. Smith argued that sacrifice in early Semitic religion was the means of establishing *communion* between a group and its totem god, when the flesh of the animal representing the god was consumed by the worshippers. Smith believed that communion sacrifices were the earliest type of sacrifice in ancient Israel, and that the notion of propitiation had developed later.

Smith's use of Arabian sources to illumine the Old Testament represented a trend in the anthropology of his day. This anthropology, deeply affected by evolutionary thinking, believed that all peoples had evolved through identical stages of culture, but at vastly different speeds, so that modern 'primitives' might still only be in the cultural infancy that modern western people had long since left behind. Given such an assumption, which was to last well into the 20th century in Old Testament study, Smith could use Arabic sources from the 6th century A.D. to reconstruct the religion and social organisation of the ancestors of the Old Testament Israelites. Smith, and Wellhausen, who also devoted some of his later years to Arabian studies, were accused of ignoring the newly-discovered Babylonian and Assyrian materials. Their reply was that these materials might be ancient, but that they were not primitive Semitic, since Babylonian and Assyrian culture rested upon an earlier non-Semitic Sumerian culture.

The scholars who utilised the new Assyriological material did so in various ways. In Britain, Assyriology was appealed to by those who wanted to reject the Wellhausen view of the history of Israelite religion. One of the arguments used was that since the Old Testament was discovered to be quite recent in comparison with Egyptian and Assyriological sources, there was no reason to be so sceptical about the claim made in the Old Testament about the work of Moses, for example. Other uses of Assyriological material made it either a foil for the Old Testament, or tried to dispose of the Old Testament altogether as containing nothing that could not be found in Babylonian texts.

H. Gunkel

A seminal work which made use of the Babylonian material, and which was to inspire other treatments, was H. Gunkel's *Creation and Chaos at the Beginning and End of Time* (1895). Its argument is not always easy to follow, but can perhaps by summarised by saying that although Genesis 1 is a late composition, occasioned by the development from the 6th century of a distinctive Israelite belief in creation, fragments and remnants of the ancient Sumerian and Babylonian creation stories were familiar to ordinary Israelites from soon after the occupation of Canaan. Gunkel examined the Old Testament references to Rahab, Leviathan, the dragon, the deeps and the binding of the sea, in order to maintain that these passages showed that Israelites were thoroughly familiar with stories about the struggle of the gods with the forces of chaos, as represented by storms and floods. When an Israelite belief in creation developed, a version of the Babylonian story was taken and was re-expressed in terms of orthodox Yahwism. The orthodox version henceforth ousted all rivals, but could not eliminate the many traces in the Old Testament of knowledge of the Babylonian story, in which creation resulted from the victory of the god of order over the god of watery chaos.

Gunkel believed that Babylonian influence had been mediated to the Israelites via the culture of the Canaanites. He regarded as Babylonian in origin the sabbath, the cherubim in the temple, weights and measures, the sundial. However, he did not deny uniqueness to the religion of the Old Testament. A comparison of Genesis 1 with the Babylonian creation story showed obvious fundamental differences. Gunkel, then, wanted to use the Babylonian material in order to elucidate some of the shared assumptions behind Old Testament texts, wanted to place ancient Israel within a more precisely defined cultural context than had been possible hitherto, and wanted also to point out where orthodox Old Testament religion was distinctive.

Bible and Babel

A very much more radical view was taken by the Assyriologist Friedrich Delitzsch in two lectures, delivered in 1902 and 1903 before the German Oriental Society and in the presence of the German emperor. He maintained that when the Israelites entered Canaan they found a land 'completely pervaded by Babylonian culture'. Delitzsch went on to detail all the parts of the Old Testament that he believed could be paralleled from Babylonian sources, the implication being that the Old Testament was derivative. These parallels did not stop at creation, the fall, the flood, the sabbath, the ten commandments, and the Israelite laws. Delitzsch attacked the heart of the Old Testament itself. Yahweh was not a name unique to the Old Testament, and monotheism had been known among Semitic nomads as long ago as 2,500 B.C. before the settlers in Babylon had succumbed to its polytheism. The prophetic attacks upon Babylonian polytheism and idolatry were misdirected. Babylonians did not really confuse the idols with the gods they represented, and the Israelite record on idolatry was not sufficiently good to enable the prophetic criticism of Babylon to be convincing. Delitzsch rejected the Old Testament as inspired or as containing special divine revelation. For him, the Reformation was a stage on the road to truth, and truth now required that the Old Testament be left behind, now that its utter dependence upon Babylonian culture had been demonstrated. However, few were prepared to go as far as Delitzsch. Indeed, as we shall see later, the 20th century saw an approach to the Old Testament that made a sharp contrast between Israel and her neighbours, to the distinct advantage of Israel.

Folklore Studies and Form Criticism

At the beginning of the 20th century, interest began to be taken in comparative folklore, and in the social situations within which Israelite traditions had arisen and been handed down. Again, it was Gunkel who was responsible for some of the pioneering work, beginning with his Genesis commentary (1st edition 1901, 3rd edition

1910), through his small, but important *Folk-Tale in the Old Testament* (1917), to his work on the Psalms. Gunkel accepted, with slight modifications, the four-document theory of the composition of the Pentateuch, but he wanted to go back behind the documents to the individual units of which the sources were composed, and he was interested in the social setting from which such units came. By the time he had thoroughly revised his Genesis commentary for its 3rd edition (1910) he had identified many folk-tale motifs and parallels in the patriarchal stories of Genesis, and had begun to suggest social settings for them.

2. PATHS TO OLD TESTAMENT UNDERSTANDING

As the 20th century progressed there emerged four main ways of approaching the Old Testament: the archaeological, the historical, the anthropological, and the cultic. In some cases they drew upon each other, but they were sufficiently distinct for them to be taken separately here. In some cases, they were dominated by particular countries.

Archaeology
The archaeological approach derived from the new discipline of Palestinian archaeology. An interest in identifying biblical sites went back, in the 19th century, to an American scholar Edward Robinson, who travelled in Palestine in the 1830s. From the 1860s, the land was scientifically mapped by British army engineers, and excavations were attempted on a small scale in Jerusalem. In the early 20th century archaeological expeditions were mounted to major sites such as Megiddo, Gezer, Beth-shean and Jericho, and methods were refined for dating levels of these sites by means of the pottery which they contained. Before the first World War, British, German and American expeditions were mounted, with the Americans coming to the fore after the war, especially under the leadership of W. F. Albright. Albright was to have a massive influence on Old Testament scholarship in America from the 1920s. His students came to occupy many of the most important positions in America, and it was possible to speak of an 'Albright school'. On the whole, the archaeological approach to the Old Testament was anti-Wellhausen, and hoped that archaeology would vindicate the Old Testament's account of the history and religion of Israel. Many claims were made about archaeology proving the Old Testament to be true in opposition to the theories of historical critical scholarship.

For example, an early excavator at Jericho believed that he had found the walls that fell down when Joshua fought against the city. After the second World War, a book entitled *The Bible as History*, which gave a highly exaggerated account of how archaeology proved the Bible to be true, would become a best seller. We must leave the archaeological approach for the moment, but we shall return to it later when we consider the theological position of the 'Albright school'.

The Historical Approach
The historical approach is easy to identify, and is associated particularly with Germany. Probably its most representative centre was Leipzig, where first, Rudolph Kittel, and later, Albrecht Alt, were dominant. We noticed in the previous chapter that Kittel did not accept all of the results of Wellhausen's position, and in successive editions of his History of Israel he utilised the newly-emerging Babylonian and archaeological material to present a critical, but basically traditional account of Israelite history.

This conservative trend, if conservative is the correct word, was continued by Alt, whose work was based upon a meticulous study of the Old Testament traditions together with a profound knowledge of Palestinian topography and archaeology and the ancient Near Eastern background. In an essay published in 1929 'The God of the Fathers', Alt suggested that phrases such as 'the God of Abraham', 'the Fear (or Kinsman) of Isaac', 'the Mighty One of Jacob' indicated that Abraham, Isaac and Jacob had been the founders of religious cults, and that traditions about them had been retained by their descendants who worshipped 'the God of Abraham' etc. A year later, in 1930, Martin Noth suggested that, in the period of the Judges, the Israelite tribes had been an amphictyony, that is, a tribal league with a cult centre, cultic laws and officials, and mutual obligations.

Gradually, the historical approach was beginning to push back what it thought could be known for certain about ancient Israel to the time of the Israelite settlement in Canaan. If this seemed to be meagre, it was certainly positive in comparison with the view that nothing could be known for certain before the time of David or Solomon. Also, Alt's 'God of the Fathers' view rehabilitated the Patriarchs as important religious personages. The views of Alt and Noth on Israel's settlement in Canaan were radical, however. They believed that there had been little or no conquest, and that the settlement had been mostly a matter of peaceful infiltration. Many of the stories of conquest in the book of Joshua were aetiological, i.e. stories made up to explain why certain cities were ruined, the explanations being (wrongly) in terms of an Israelite conquest. These views, as we shall see, were later to be strongly resisted by the archaeological approach. We shall return to the historical approach later, and consider its use of so-called redaction criticism.

Anthropology
The anthropological approach is the hardest of the four to pin down. I shall describe two differing forms that it took, as well as noting its contribution to the cultic approach. It benefitted, in the first place, from the persistence of evolutionary thought into the 20th century, as well as the view that all peoples had developed through roughly identical cultural stages. A general theory of the history of religion emerged, which saw it as a gradual progress from animism, (the belief that spirits dwelt at sacred springs, stones and trees) through polytheism to monotheism. The Old Testament was made to conform to this pattern, and evidence was sought for relics of animism, the presence of polytheism being clearly admitted by the Old Testament. Incidents such as that in which Jacob set up a stone at Bethel (Genesis 28:28) were seen to be evidence for animism. Examples of this kind of approach can be found in Germany as well as Britain, but it received a classical formulation in the book by W. O. E. Oesterley and T. H. Robinson entitled *Hebrew Religion. Its Origin and Development* (1930). In Britain, this approach was in tune with the idea of progressive revelation, which was to be important as late as the 1950s.

A quite different appeal to anthropology was made by H. W. Robinson in a series of books and articles beginning with his commentary on Deuteronomy and Joshua in 1907. Robinson was interested in Hebrew psychology, and in the way in which Israelites understood the relation between the individual and society. His approach to the Old Testament was influenced by Sir Henry Maine's classic work *Ancient Law* dating from the 19th century, and by the 20th century researches of the French anthropologist Lévy-Bruhl into the thought-processes of 'primitive' peoples.

Robinson argued that Hebrew psychology worked very differently from modern western psychology. In particular Israelites did not possess a notion of the limits of a person's individuality. An individual could feel completely identified with his social group, with another person in that group, or with an individual long since dead, in ways to which modern thought had no parallel. If this was accepted, one could understand why Achan's whole family was destroyed because of an offence committed only by its head (Joshua

7:24–26), why some of the Psalms switch inexplicably from 'I' to 'we' (Psalm 44:4–8), and how prophets could claim that they had stood in the 'council of Yahweh'.

Robinson, consciously or not, stood in a line of tradition going back to Herder, which emphasised the importance of the distinctive 'spirit' of the Hebrew people. Although Israel's psychology could only be rediscovered with the help of the study of 'primitive' peoples, the implication was that western psychology was not necessarily superior to 'primitive' psychology, and that the latter might be capable of insights of which modern cultures should take notice. After the second World War, this sort of approach was extended into the so-called Biblical Theology movement, a movement which laid stress on the view that Hebrew psychology and experience of reality were different from western experience, and which wanted to interpret and use Hebrew insights positively.

The Cultic Approach
The cultic approach was indebted to the anthropological approach in that it believed, in the light of anthropological studies of 'primitive' peoples, that Israelite experience of the cult was very different from the modern experience of worship. For Israelites, as for 'primitive' peoples, religious celebrations were occasions on which the whole community relived the stories that gave expression to their understanding of the world. These celebrations united the people in a common outlook, and enabled them to express their hopes and fears for their continued prosperity. However, the cultic approach was indebted not only to anthropology; it drew upon Assyriology, and especially upon what was known about the cult in Babylon, especially the observance of the New Year festival, in which the king played an important role, representing the god. The cultic approach was also indebted to the pioneering work of Gunkel, and to his classification of the Psalms, especially those identified as Royal Psalms, and Psalms celebrating the universal kingship of Yahweh (nos. 47, 93, 95–99).

When these contributions from anthropology, Assyriology and type-criticism were put together, they yielded a quite new picture of Israelite religion. The Wellhausen view tended to ignore Jerusalem as a cult centre until Josiah's reformation in 622 B.C. Prior to that time, there had been a multiplicity of sanctuaries and no central priesthood with exclusive powers. The prophets were the creative figures in the development of ethical monotheism, and the cult, with its emphasis on propitiation, was a development from the exile. Given such a view, the Psalms were thought mostly to be post-exilic, possibly even as late as the 2nd century B.C. in many cases.

The cultic view proposed that, from the early monarchy, the Jerusalem cult, centred in the king as the representative of Jahweh, had been the mainspring of Israelite religion. At the annual New Year festival, the universal kingship of Yahweh had been celebrated and re-enacted, and this celebration, influenced by Babylonian models but thoroughly assimilated to Yahwism, had been the source of the ideas proclaimed by the prophets. It had also been the source of the eschatological hope of the Old Testament, that God would establish his universal rule for all to see, and would rule through a king of the Davidic line. Thus, the cultic approach not only challenged the prevailing view of the history of Israelite religion; it rehabilitated the cult (albeit with a different emphasis from that of the Wellhausen view) and it suggested a completely new way of understanding prophecy. Since the pioneering work of Duhm on the prophets of 1875, scholarship of the prophetic books had concentrated upon distinguishing the authentic words of prophets from the additions or expansions of editors and compilers, the purpose being to expose more clearly the words and works of those believed to be the main inspiration in the development of Israelite religion. The cultic approach put the prophetic contribution into a different perspective.

Myth and Ritual

The cultic approach as described here was pioneered by the Norwegian scholar S. Mowinckel, and given classical expression in his Psalm Studies published from 1921 to 1924. It was developed in several directions by scholars in Britain, Scandinavia and Germany. In Britain, a volume published in 1935 and edited by S. H. Hooke entitled *Myth and Ritual*, inaugurated what has been called the 'myth and ritual school', although it is doubtful whether the contributors ever constituted a 'school'. In Hooke's opinion, when the Israelites entered Canaan they encountered a culture permeated with Babylonian infuence, to the extent that even Canaanite agricultural festivals which the Israelites adopted were derived ultimately from Babylonian practices. Hooke also believed that what he called 'myths' (i.e. religious traditions) were derived from rituals, and in some cases were the liturgical texts used at cultic celebrations. He thus sought a cultic origin or explanation for many Old Testament traditions. For example, the story of creation in Genesis 1 was recited at the New Year festival, while the source of the tradition about the blowing of the trumpets at the battle of

Jericho was the blowing of trumpets at the New Year festival. In the work of Scandinavian scholars such as A. Bentzen and I. Engnell, the cultic approach was developed in a direction that sought to give unity to the Old and New Testaments. The cultic festival in Jerusalem involved the ritual humiliation of the king, and his symbolic death and resurrection as a representative of the god. This ideology was implicit in passages such as Isaiah 52:13–53:12, where the servant of God suffers humiliation and, on one interpretation of the text, death and vindication beyond death. The humiliation, death and resurrection of Jesus pick up a theme which, according to this cultic view, is deeply embedded in the Old Testament. Although German scholars were not enthusiastic about extreme uses of the cultic theory, the approach was taken up by A. Weiser, except that he sought the origin of Psalms and traditions not in the Jerusalem cult but in the celebration of the Feast of Tabernacles, the autumnal harvest festival. (See *For Further Reading* at end of next chapter.)

10

FROM 1935 TO THE PRESENT

The discussion so far has brought us roughly to the mid–1930s. The picture that emerges is one of growing diversity in Old Testament study as the discipline tried to respond to an accumulation of new evidence and new ideas. During the period 1890–1930 a conviction that grew strongly in all areas was that it was no longer possible to write an Old Testament theology. It was possible to write a history of Israelite religion, and many distinguished works on that subject were produced. What it was not possible to do, many agreed, was to write about the theological content of the Old Testament in such a way as to maintain that its insights should command the attention of the modern world or make a fundamental contribution to Christian theology.

1. OLD TESTAMENT THEOLOGY

From the mid–1930s to roughly 1960 this position changed dramatically, and the matter will become the organising principle of this chapter. There were several reasons for the movement towards a desire to use the Old Testament in a positive theological way. The rise of so-called Dialectical Theology, associated particularly with the work of Karl Barth (1886–1968), threw down a challenge to the prevailing liberal theology, with its interest in the relation between the Bible and the religions out of which Judaism and Christianity were thought to have developed. Barth emphasised the sovereignty of God and the uniqueness of his word expressed in Jesus Christ. Although Barth's direct impact upon Old Testament studies was not great, his work reflected a theological change of mood which was to affect Old Testament scholarship. Another important factor at this time was the opposition to the Old Testament by those in Germany who supported Hitler. The so-called 'German Christians' wanted a Christianity freed from its Jewish antecedents. The Old Testament was at best a chronicle of Jewish ungratefulness to God, and should be abandoned altogether by the Church. Thus, Nazi opposition to the Old Testament polarised the issue with great clarity, and allowed no half-way house. If there was any case for retaining the Old Testament for church and theology, it would have to be a better one than that which saw it merely as a source for the history of Israelite religion.

W. Eichrodt

A major step forward was taken with the publication, between 1933 and 1939, of Walther Eichrodt's *Old Testament Theology*, in which a comparatively simple idea enabled the Old Testament to be transferred from the domain of the history of religion to that of theology. This idea was in effect a repudiation of a positivist view of history, and the substitution of a view of history that gave full allowance to the fact that there is a subjective element in the experiencing and narrating of historical events. In the case of ancient Israel, this subjective element was Israel's covenant relationship with Yahweh. This regulated Israel's experience of history and provided a unique standpoint for its interpretation of history. Accordingly, Eichrodt's *Theology* began at what he believed to be the decisive meeting-point between God and Israel, the covenant relationship, and only when he had fully explored the nature of the covenant, its laws and its affirmations about God, did he turn to discuss the more general topics of God and the world, and God and mankind. The covenant was not only a factor that enabled the distinctive theological outlook of the Old Testament to be described; it united the Old and New Testaments because both were concerned with 'the irruption of the Kingship of God into this world and its establishment here . . . the central passage of the NT leads us back to the testimony of God in the old Covenant' (Vol. I p.26).

Eichrodt's *Theology* stressed two points: that Israel's faith was unique, and that its interpretation of history was determined by its special relationship with Yahweh. These two points were to be emphasised by what became two dominating positions in the postwar period. They can be described as the Biblical Theology Movement which was most strongly represented in America, and the Confessional Theology Movement, which belonged almost entirely to Germany. The first was a development out of what has been called earlier the archaeological approach; the second developed from what was called above the historical approach, although it also absorbed elements of the cultic approach. We shall begin with the Confessional approach.

G. von Rad and M. Noth

Its main pioneer and representative was Gerhard von Rad (1901–1971) who, after studies in Erlangen and Tübingen, taught from 1930 for several years in Leipzig, where he worked with Alt, and shared the latter's interest in the historical approach. When he moved to Jena in 1934 he came into opposition with Nazi sympathisers who wanted to dispense with the Old Testament. In 1938 he published a seminal essay in which he sought a confessional and cultic basis for the traditions of the Pentateuch and Joshua. Starting from the so-called creed of Deuteronomy 26:5–11, which a worshipper at a harvest festival had to recite as he offered his first fruits to God, von Rad noted that the saving acts of God which the creed contained had no reference to the Sinai giving of the law. Von Rad concluded that there were two fundamental complexes of tradition behind the Pentateuch and Joshua, each of which had been associated with an ancient festival. The giving of the law was celebrated at the autumn Festival of Tabernacles, while the exodus, wilderness wanderings and conquest traditions were commemmorated at the spring Festival of Weeks. We notice that what was important about these traditions for von Rad was not how they might be used by modern scholars to reconstruct historical events, but how they functioned as part of Israel's confession of faith.

In between von Rad's 1938 essay and his *Old Testament Theology* which appeared in 1957–1960, contributions were made by Martin Noth that were not only important in themselves, but which were to be taken up by von Rad in his *Theology*. In 1944, in his *Studies of the History of Tradition*, Noth argued that the books Joshua to 2 Kings (minus Ruth, which is not placed after Judges in the Hebrew Bible) were a Deuteronomic History, that is, a work with a single unifying outlook and purpose, for all that the history's author had utilised other works, such as the so-called story of the succession to David's throne (2 Samuel 5–6, 9–20, 1 Kings 1–2). The purpose of the Deuteronomic History was, according to Noth, to explain why first Israel and then Judah and Jerusalem, had fallen to their enemies. The explanation was in terms of the disregard in Israel and Judah of God's laws, and of the prophetic warnings of impending disaster. In 1948 Noth published a second major study dealing this time with the origin of the pentateuchal traditions. Here, Noth argued that it was the Israelite amphictyony which was the institution which had enabled the disparate traditions of its members to be collected together and to be fashioned into the coherent story of the patriarchs, the exodus, the wanderings and the conquest. Noth's view of what could be known about the events from the time of Abraham to the conquest was on the whole negative. We have already seen that he largely rejected an Israelite conquest of Canaan. In his 1948 study his scepticism led him to the point of denying that Moses had played the role ascribed to him in the Pentateuch, and Noth explained how he believed that, as the traditions were handed down and worked together, the figure of Moses became so prominent.

Von Rad's *Theology* brought together three elements that have been outlined above. On the whole, he accepted Noth's researches into the history of tradition, and although probably not as sceptical as Noth, he was hesitant about how far actual events could be reconstructed from the Old Testament traditions of incidents before the monarchy. Secondly, he agreed with the implications of Noth's work on the Deuteronomic History, that earlier traditions could be taken by later writers, and could be reinterpreted in the light of new situations. Third, he remained true to his interest in traditions as expressive of Israel's faith in Yahweh.

As a result of combining these elements, von Rad's *Theology* was not an account of *the* theological outlook of the Old Testament and its implications for Christian belief. It was an account of Israel's witness to faith in Yahweh. This witness was not static, but had a dynamic relationship with the narratives of Yahweh's actions, as these were passed on from generation to generation, and reinterpreted in the light of new situations. His confessional approach enabled von Rad to integrate into his *Theology* both the results of research into the history of tradition, and a certain degree of historical scepticism. Von Rad was not indifferent to history, and he did not claim that Israel's traditions were devoid of historical foundation. What mattered most for his theological understanding was not so much what modern scholarship could reconstruct by way of historical events, but how traditions of these events gave expression to Israelite faith in Yahweh. That faith was the historical datum and the traditions were the means of its expression.

We must leave the description of von Rad at this point, not because it is complete (in fact it is incomplete, saying nothing about von Rad's treatment of prophecy and wisdom), but in order to outline the Biblical Theology position, especially as represented in the work of the Albright school. We shall see that this position contrasts strongly with that of von Rad.

2. THE BIBLICAL THEOLOGY MOVEMENT

W. F. Albright

Whereas von Rad's *Theology* was based upon research into the history of Old Testament traditions, and was reticent about the historical value of some of them, the Albright school was based upon archaeological research, and was confident that the Old Testament was basically historically reliable. This confidence is found in Albright's *From the Stone Age to Christianity* first published in 1940, and reissued in 1957 with a new introduction in which Albright reasserted 'the substantial historicity of patriarchal tradition' and considered 'the Mosaic tradition as even more reliable than I did then' (in 1940). Albright believed that archaeology confirmed the Old Testament tradition that the Patriarchs originated from Haran in north-western Mesopotamia, and that social and legal documents found at Nuzi in eastern Mesopotamia and dating from the 15th century shed important light on the legal and social practices of the patriarchs. The traditions contained in Genesis 1–11 had been 'brought from north-western Mesopotamia to the west by the Hebrews before the middle of the second millennium'.

Albright was not only very positive about the Mosaic tradition; he was convinced that 'the founder of Yahwism' taught 'the existence of only one God, the creator of everything, the source of justice, who is equally powerful in Egypt, in the desert, and in Palestine (*sic*), who has no sexuality and no mythology, who is human in form but cannot be seen by human eye and cannot be represented in any form' (*From the Stone Age to Christianity*, Anchor Books, New York 1957 – p. 272).

G. E. Wright

On the basis of such a confident evaluation of the basic historicity of Old Testament tradition, G. E. Wright, one of Albright's students, was able to publish in 1952 his book *God who Acts. Biblical Theology as Recital*. It begins with a powerful call for the rediscovery of Old Testament theology, and expresses dissatisfaction with the histories of Israelite religion of the early part of the century. Old Testament theology must not be the imposition of systematic categories upon the Old Testament (Eichrodt's theology is said to be mildly guilty of this), it must allow the Old Testament to speak in its own way. The solution is that 'Biblical theology is. . . . a theology of recital, in which Biblical man confesses his faith by reciting the formative events of his history as the redemptive handwork of God' (*God Who Acts*, p. 38).

At first sight, this seems not to be too far removed from von Rad's position, and indeed, Wright quoted extensively from von Rad's 1938 essay. There is, however, a fundamental difference between von Rad and Wright. The former is concerned with Israel's confession of its faith in Yahweh; Wright is concerned with the *objectivity* of the historical acts which form the basis of Israel's confession. It is these real acts of God within the historical process that show who and what God is through what he has done. Wright does not deny the importance of subjectivity, nor the value of re-interpretation; but 'it is . . . the objectivity of God's historical acts which are the focus of attention, not the subjectivity of inner, emotional, diffuse and mystical experience' (p. 55).

It is significant that Wright used the term 'Biblical man'. This indicated his belief that what we might call the pressure of God's actions in history upon the covenant people Israel created a unique understanding in Israel of the nature of reality. In an earlier publication, *The Old Testament Against its Environment* (1950) Wright had contrasted the Old Testament view of reality with that of the ancient Near East, in order to demonstrate that the central elements of Biblical faith were *sui generis*, and could not have developed by any natural or evolutionary process or have been borrowed from Israel's neighbours. In particular, the outlook of Israel's neighbours was determined not by history, but by attachment to the cycle of nature. Only Israel was able to transcend nature, and to understand history as a process guided by God towards a goal.

That there existed what Wright called 'Biblical man' whose distinctive views of reality were determined by God's actions in history on behalf of Israel was to become a basic part of the Biblical Theology movement. It seemed to offer the prospect of guidance in ethical issues: there could be a biblical view of work, a biblical view of the state, and so on. For New Testament studies, as the third part of this book will indicate, the implication of the existence of 'Biblical man' was that Hebrew categories were to be preferred to Greek categories, because the latter were derived from general experience whereas the former were determined by God's revelatory acts in Israel's history.

By 1960 the two dominating trends in Old Testament study regarding the theological use of the Old Testament were the confessional approach of von Rad, and the 'acts of God in history' approach of the Biblical Theology scholars. The period 1960–1985 saw the demise of the Biblical Theology school and the advent of two new main approaches which can be loosely described as structuralist and sociological. The remainder of the chapter will outline these developments.

J. Barr: Challenge to Biblical Theology

A book which initiated a new direction in Old Testament study was J. Barr's *Semantics of Biblical Language* published in 1961. Essentially it was an attack on that aspect of the Biblical Theology movement that argued, on the basis of the etymologies of Hebrew words, for a distinctive Hebraic and biblical understanding of reality. 'Biblical man', it had been supposed, could be understood via the structure of the Hebrew language, and especially its method of deriving nouns from verbal 'roots'. Barr showed convincingly that such procedures could not be scientifically justified in the light of research generally in the area of linguistics. He did not deny that there might be unique religious ideas in the Old Testament; he rejected the view that these could be discovered by suggesting that Hebrew etymology gives easy access to 'the Hebrew mind'.

Perhaps the most important thing about Barr's book was that by criticising biblical scholarship in the light of general linguistics, it showed that Old Testament scholarship could not work in a privileged vacuum, unaware of advances in disciplines such as linguistics, anthropology and philosophy. Barr followed up his 1961 book with *Old and New in Interpretation* (1966) in which, among other things, he argued against the unexamined use of the category of 'history' by the Biblical Theology movement. Not only were there many parts of the Old Testament that could not easily be brought under the umbrella of history, the category was by no means as straightforward as might be supposed.

Barr's books were an encouragement, especially to younger scholars, to be much more circumspect in their use of methods in Old Testament study, and to look for guidance to other disciplines such as linguistics and anthropology. The demise of the Biblical Theology movement, initiated by Barr's work, was hastened from several quarters. B. Albrektson's *History and the Gods* (1967) questioned the assumption that Israel's neighbours in the ancient Near East had no conception of history, while other scholars challenged Albright's assumption that Patriarchal customs could only be understood in the light of 15th century Mesopotamian law. It began to be argued that the stories of the patriarchs fitted rather into the first millennium – a return to the position maintained by Wellhausen and, before him, de Wette.

3. RECENT DEVELOPMENTS

Literary Studies and Structuralism
As the Biblical Theology movement waned, there was growing interest in what might be called literature criticism, as distinct from literary criticism which, in Old Testament studies, had come to mean the *history* of literary traditions. Literature criticism was interested in the finished form of the text, and in interpreting the text in terms of its own literary dynamics. An early pioneer was James Muilenburg who, as early as 1953, published a paper on Hebrew rhetoric, which he had delivered at the Copenhagen international congress. However, much of the impetus for literature criticism was to come from French scholarship, where the social anthropologist C. Lévi-Strauss and the literary critics R. Barthes and A. Greimas had been applying to their respective disciplines the implications of structuralism, that is, the interpretation of language and behaviour as a code, on the basis of inner structural markers and oppositions. In 1969 Paul Beauchamp's book *Creation and separation* treated Genesis 1:1–2:4a as a work with a complex literary structure of oppositions and complementarities whose elucidation could contribute to an understanding of the text. In 1971 a group of French-speaking biblical scholars and literary structuralists published the results of a two-day conference held in Geneva in which structural analyses of biblical passages were compared with more traditional Old Testament approaches. Once begun, literature criticism grew rapidly. At the 1977 Göttingen International Old Testament Congress there were hardly any contributions of this type. In 1980 in Vienna they were well represented, while in 1983 in Salamanca the presidential address by L. Alonso-Schökel was devoted to the 'two' methods of Old Testament study, the literature method and the historical approach.

Literature criticism has, in practice, run well ahead of theory; while some practitioners openly declare that the way they read a biblical text has nothing to do with the author's original intention, assuming that that can be known in any case, other practitioners feel that, by using the new literary methods, they can overturn some of the results of traditional source criticism and research into the history of traditions. Emphasis on the 'final form of the text' has, however, been a creative move. The study of prophetic traditions, for example, is much less a search for the authentic words of a prophet, all else being discarded as editorial. Prophetic books are seen as a whole, possibly deriving from prophetic schools, and having a complex history of transmission. Another movement concerned with the final form of the text is the canon criticism inaugurated at the 1977 Göttingen Congress by B. S. Childs. As far as I understand what its aims are, it is an attempt to argue that the process by which the community of faith in Israel handed down its sacred traditions was a process in which the traditions were deliberately regarded as canonical, that is, of regulative authority. In their final form they express the canonical intentionality of the community that put them into that form, and it is on the basis of that intentionality that they should be interpreted.

Catholic Old Testament Scholarship

The only serious attempt that has been made to put literary criticism on to a firm methodological basis has been in the work of W. Richter and his students, based in the Catholic Theological faculty in Munich. The mention of the Catholic Faculty is an opportunity to comment briefly on the development of Old Testament scholarship among Catholics. The pioneer of modern Catholic scholarship was M.-J. Lagrange who, in 1890, established the École Biblique in Jerusalem and in 1892 founded its journal the *Revue biblique*. Lagrange argued that the Old Testament was an oriental book, and could only properly be understood as such, in the light of oriental languages, customs and methods of literary composition. However, in the early 20th century, the Pontifical Commission issued a series of 'responses' on critical biblical matters. For example, on 26 June 1906 the substantial Mosaic authorship of the Pentateuch was upheld, and on 28 June 1908 the authorship of Isaiah 40–66 by a 6th century prophet was ruled out. This made Lagrange's position very difficult, and it was not until the mid–1930s that historical critical scholarship was given any real encouragement. The encyclical *Divino afflante spiritu* of 1944 was a major advance, and after the Second Vatican Council, Catholic scholarship was largely freed from doctrinal constraints, and became a major factor in international scholarship.

W. Richter

W. Richter proposed a programme for the scientific study of Old Testament literature in his 1971 book *Exegesis as the Science of Literature*. It took issue with much that was taken for granted in Old Testament study. It accused form criticism of being as much the comparison of content as the comparison of form, and it criticised the circularity of using a text to establish an historical setting, which historical setting was then used to interpret the text. Richter proposed a literary method which, beginning from the analysis of the language, moved from smaller to larger units of text until the final form was reached. In the years since 1971 Richter and his students have produced a stream of monographs dealing with Hebrew grammar, semantics, verbal systems, poetics, and selected texts. Their researches are based upon the latest work in linguistics and philosophical semantics, are formidably technical in presentation, and remain untranslated into English. In essence, they offer a new version of form and redactional studies of Old Testament texts based upon exacting methods and procedures, and they deserve far more attention than they have received.

Literature criticism of the Old Testament shows no sign of flagging. For students working at doctoral level there is increasing interest in areas of literary theory such as audience reception criticism, and the investigation of 'tradition' in the light of the philosophical hermeneutics of H. G. Gadamer. The theological implications of literature criticism have yet to be drawn out. Literature criticism could well make a contribution to theology by showing how the Israelite presentation of stories was part of the way in which reality was constructed and experienced in Old Testament times.

Sociology of the Old Testament
The sociological study of the Old Testament is not new but has witnessed an explosion in the past twenty years. It has several roots – the student unrest of the late 1960s, the growth of the peace movement and the women's movement, and the struggles for freedom and justice in Africa and South America of persecuted majorities. Also, there has been a development in archaeology generally towards interest in population sizes, maximal use of labour resources etc., in ancient times. The work that has probably had the greatest impact in this field is N. K. Gottwald's *The Tribes of Yahweh. A Sociology of the Religion of Liberated Israel 1250–1050 B.C.E.* (1979). In many ways it builds upon Noth's theory of the Israelite amphictyony and the role supposedly played by the amphictyony in shaping the traditions about the Patriarchs, exodus and conquest. Noth's theories have been heavily criticised, and a recent trend can be detected to date the composition of some of these traditions even later than Wellhausen proposed. Gottwald's book is massive, and contains many suggestions about the early social organisation of Israel. Its basic thesis is that Israel came into being as a revolt of disadvantaged social groups against their oppression by Canaanite city states. Early Israel was thus a liberated,

egalitarian society, and the God proclaimed by this people was one who liberated from oppression.

Gottwald's book no doubt expresses a spirit of identification with oppressed peoples today, and openly makes use of marxist theories about literature as a 'product' of a given social class (in this case, a class of liberated people). Not all sociological treatments are as radical as this. Some merely claim that they are doing in a scientific fashion what Gunkel began when he enquired about the social settings of different types of literature. Other scholars are using social studies in a comparative way, for example to shed light on how prophets and their hearers related to each other. Again, there have been re-examinations of questions such as the rise of the kingship in ancient Israel in the search for the social dynamics of this important development.

4. CONCLUSION

At the time of writing, Old Testament studies are characterised by considerable diversity. If there is unity, it is to be found in a growing awareness that many of the results of Old Testament scholarship are not as certain as they once seemed. There is progress in research, but it is not necessarily progress towards a perceived goal. Rather, Old Testament study is seen to be engaged in a dialogue with the biblical text, the dialogue being determined by questions that are raised on the one hand by the central problems facing mankind in the contemporary world, and on the other hand by concerns of vital importance to many academic disciplines within the humanities.

This may seem to be a disappointing, even a despairing conclusion to any reader who, having followed this brief account of the history of the Old Testament in the church, is looking for comforting words that somehow vindicate the Old Testament as integral to Christian theology. If there are such readers, two points can be made to them. First, if this account of the history of interpretation has shown anything, it is that from New Testament times, in each generation, the Old Testament has been in dialogue with needs that have been dictated to its interpreters by the concerns of the world in which they have lived. The present situation is no different. What may be different is that there is today a greater willingness to accept that the dialogue with the Old Testament is determined by contemporary factors, and, to that extent, can only be provisional. This leads to the second point which is that the Old Testament has an amazing continuing capacity to be a partner in a dialogue with modern interpreters. For the liberation theologians of South America it is the exodus event that gives hope for liberation. For literature critics there is ample prose and poetry in the Old Testament for interpretation. For theologians the Old Testament is still a remarkable witness to faith at a place and time in the ancient world when there was much to count against such faith. That faith, seen in the perspective of the New Testament, still challenges people to commitment or rejection.

If there is a problem, it is not created by Old Testament scholarship, but by the church. In England, at any rate, most Old Testament scholars have to work outside the church, and many churches fail to give an adequate place to the Old Testament in worship and preaching. This, compared with the New Testament church, for which the Old Testament was alone Scripture, must provide food for thought. The Old Testament is a part of the Christian Bible, and cannot be given up in any circumstances. If this rather obvious statement is to have any real meaning, the problem will have to be solved as to how the church can meaningfully join in the dialogue between the Old Testament text, biblical scholarship and the contemporary world.

FOR FURTHER READING

J. W. Rogerson, *Anthropology and the Old Testament*, Oxford 1978, reprint Sheffield 1984.

J. W. Rogerson, *Myth in Old Testament Interpretation*, Berlin 1974.

J. W. Rogerson (ed.), *Beginning Old Testament Study*, London 1983.

R. E. Clements, *A Century of Old Testament Study*, revised edition, Guildford 1983.

J. Barton, *Reading the Old Testament. Method in Biblical Study*, London 1984.

N. K. Gottwald (ed.), *The Bible and Liberation. Political and Social Hermeneutics*, Maryknoll, New York, 1983.

PART II

THE
INTER-
TESTAMENTAL
LITERATURE

1

INTRODUCTION TO THE INTER-TESTAMENTAL LITERATURE

1. What do we mean by the inter-testamental literature?

One of the particular problems confronting the student of the Bible is the temptation to regard collections of documents as being in some way related because of their inclusion in a collection of sacred texts. Artificial connections have all too frequently been made between biblical books because of their juxtaposition in the canon of Scripture, which can blur difference of emphasis, practice and belief. The rise of critical scholarship has enabled us to note the different religious emphases arising from differing regional, social and theological traditions. This is equally true of a consideration of the so-called inter-testamental literature. The inclusion of books in the Apocrypha (the collection of books found in Jerome's Vulgate but absent from the Hebrew Bible) or in a collection of extra-canonical texts like *The Apocryphal Old Testament* edited by H. F. D. Sparks should not lead us to suppose that there is necessarily any affinity between writings collected together in this particular way.

Identifying the Literature

We need to be aware of another danger also. When we speak of the Inter-testamental Literature, we might either refer to literature written round about the beginning of the Christian era or to those texts which can be dated with some certainty between the Old and the New Testaments. Problems emerge at once. Firstly we cannot be sure of the date of the latest parts of what we now call the Old Testament. Secondly we cannot be certain of the dating of many of the extra-canonical texts. Thirdly we do not know with any certainty how many may have formed part of a body of sacred scripture accepted as authoritative by some or all Jews at this period.

153

Fourthly, there is that enormous volume of Jewish literature which never was considered part of the written corpus of authoritative scripture but had from a very early stage an authority as oral tradition, in the rabbinic tradition. Fifthly, in speaking of an ongoing interpretation of the Jewish tradition we have to note that this was a problem well under way in what we now consider the canonical texts. What is more, it has to be recognised that the important step taken of translating the Old Testament into Greek was very much part of this tradition. There is a real sense in which the Septuagint also forms part of the inter-testamental literature, though its particular problems cannot be treated here.

In this study the net will be cast as widely as possible, so that some consideration can be given to Jewish literature extant from the death of Alexander the Great to the earliest examples of rabbinic literature starting with the Mishnah. There is bound to be some uncertainty over dating, particularly if mention is to be made of the continuing tradition of rabbinic interpretation in Talmuds and Midrashim.

The Variety of the Literature
This literature includes a great variety of types, ranging from the detailed legal discussions in the Talmuds to pious legend and visionary material. Take the works most familiar to us in the Apocrypha, for example. There we have examples of history writing of varying degrees of authenticity (1 Maccabees), historical romance (Tobit), epistle (Letter of Jeremiah), liturgical material (Song of the Three Young Men), additions to biblical books (additions to Daniel and Esther), wisdom literature, such as we find in the Old Testament, (Ecclesiasticus and the Wisdom of Solomon) and, if we follow Jerome's Vulgate, apocalyptic literature in the form of 2 Esdras or, as it is sometimes called, 4 Ezra. It is apparent that no hard and fast division can be made between these texts and the canonical material. Parts of the apocrypha, namely 1 Esdras, overlap with the canonical Ezra and Nehemiah. The overlap between these various works has led to a variety of suggestions to explain the similarities which exist. Illustrating the complexity of the discussion of the relationship between canonical and non-canonical, the books in the apocrypha come from widely different dates, varying from the second century BC (Ecclesiasticus and 1 Maccabees) to the end of the first century AD (4 Ezra), and, we may suspect (though certainty on this matter is out of the question) from very different social and geographical settings. In doctrine also there are differences. Wisdom and 2 Macabees speak about the afterlife (though the former concen-

trates on the immortality of the soul rather than on the resurrection of the body), whereas Ecclesiasticus maintains a traditional position in the matter over against certain contemporary doctrinal developments.

These differences in the books of the Apocrypha extend also to the rest of the non-canonical literature, and some appreciation of the different types of material is therefore appropriate.

2. TYPES OF INTER-TESTAMENTAL LITERATURE

Legal Traditions

In the light of the centrality of the Law of Moses (Torah) for Judaism it comes as no surprise to find that a dominant feature of the rabbinic traditions is concern with the interpretation and application of these laws. This legal material is found in a variety of forms. Some of the legal pronouncements of the rabbis (*halakah*) are found without any obvious connection with Scripture (as in the earliest collection of law: Mishnah). Others are found in contexts where biblical material is discussed. While some legal material certainly did arise as the result of custom, the regulations are all concerned with customs firmly rooted in Scripture. It has sometimes been asserted that the preoccupation with legal matters in the rabbinic literature and the apparent absence of such concerns in the non-rabbinic texts indicates a fundamentally different attitude towards the Law, and exhibits the differing concerns of rival groups within ancient Judaism. Such a polarisation cannot be accepted, however. Recent study has indicated that the dominant concern with law (*halakah*) in the rabbinic corpus by no means excluded the interests which surface in the non-rabbinic literature.

In the light of the central importance of the legal traditions embodied in the rabbinic literature for later Judaism, it is important to be clear about the precise nature of this material and its relationship to the biblical tradition. It is well known that a fundamental feature of the pharisaic tradition is a concern with oral tradition. This oral tradition represented the ongoing understanding of the ancient laws in the new circumstances of the Hellenistic-Roman age. It may not always be easy to detect exactly what the relationship is between the rabbinic laws and the Bible, but a glance at the subject matter, (tithes, sacrifices, female purity, festivals etc.) indicates that the starting point for all this material is Scripture itself.

The Mishnah

The earliest written collection now extant is the Mishnah, which is a collection of laws (*halakoth*) concerning a variety of aspects of Jewish life ranging from the prescription of blessings to the nature of impurity. In its present form it dates from the end of the second century AD, though it contains much earlier materials. To understand the function of the material is to understand rabbinic Judaism. God had revealed his will to Moses on Sinai, a way of living appropriate for a people which had been redeemed by him and which sought to enter a covenant with him. In the Bible some of this material is given in considerable detail, particularly as it applies to the regulation of the cult (e.g. Exodus 25ff.), but in other important areas Scripture itself is vague. The legal material now contained in the Mishnah and other rabbinic legal connections is evidence of the need felt by Jewish interpreters to make sense of the Scripture, particularly as it affected the obligations laid upon Israel to be a covenant people. The provisions in the Mishnah exhibit the concern to deal not just with general principles but the specific situations in which people found themselves. Some of this may have a rather theoretical air, the product of the academy rather than real life, but other parts clearly are responses to the situations in which Jews sought to live the way of God and needed precise advice to do so.

The Mishnah marks the first and most important stage in the ongoing application of Scripture and tradition to ever new situations. In addition to the Mishnah we have a parallel and additional Mishnah collection, the Tosefta, which is similarly organised but contains much additional material not found in the Mishnah. The mainstream of this interpretation is to be found in the Talmuds, which can be found in two recensions, the longer, the Babylonian Talmud and the shorter, the Palestinian Talmud. Both of these take the Mishnah (or parts of it) as the basis for further discussion and explanation. Not all the material in the Talmuds is concerned with legal matters. Indeed, both contain a vast array of other material ranging from stories about rabbis to scriptural interpretation. The Talmuds represent a stage in the ongoing interpretation and application of the biblical material.

The rabbinic corpus offers us the most wide-ranging evidence of legal traditions in ancient Jewish literature. Nevertheless, it should be noted that other examples of such traditions can be found elsewhere. Among the Dead Sea Scrolls, for example, the Manual of Discipline and the Damascus Document contain regulations for the organisation of the community's life with specific reference to Jewish practices like the Sabbath, and there are hints of legal discussions in the pseudepigrapha.

Historiography
Already in the Bible the reflection on Israel's past has become of central importance. It was during the Exile especially that this process was embarked on, as is evidenced by the explicit theological reflection on the history of the kingdoms of Judaea and Israel (Deuteronomic History: the books of Samuel and Kings). Interest in history did not start with the experience of judgement and Exile, however. While it is likely that the Torah came into existence in the form we now have it during the sixth century, there can be little doubt that the traditions it contains go back into the very mists of Israel's origins. They were preserved to vindicate the election of God's people and the developing understanding of the relationship between God and his people down the centuries. We may expect that the concern with genealogies so evident in post-exilic books (Chronicles and Ezra) was equally strong earlier as the priests sought to justify their basis for serving in the cult in Jerusalem.

That tradition of historiography continued after the Exile. The most obvious example (as it is now contained in the Old Testament) is the Books of Chronicles. Here we have an attempt to tell a story similar to that contained in the Deuteronomic History (1 Samuel–2 Kings) but from the perspective of a different age. There have been those who have regarded the books of Chronicles and the related books of Ezra and Nehemiah as evidence of the vindication of the cultic establishment in Jerusalem over against prophetic circles who rebelled against this settlement and looked for a new arrangement of society in fulfilment of the divine promises. Whether or not we can accept this view of a polarisation in post-Exilic society, there can be little doubt that the future hope has moved into the background: it is an article of faith rather than a vital dimension to religious outlook and practice.

What is more, it is apparent from the books of Ezra and Nehemiah that the religious settlements in Judaea owed much to the intervention of foreign Jews supported by the power of the Persian empire. Thus it may well be that the establishment of the cult in Jerusalem and the 'reforms' of Ezra and Nehemiah could well be seen as part of an imperial policy which was imposed from above, and whose purpose was closely linked with the diminution of the influence of the eschatologically orientated groups in Jewish society, for whom the status quo was not an adequate fulfilment of the divine purposes. If this be the case, it is not too difficult to see why the Books of Chronicles should serve as a means of telling the story of Israel in such a way that they served the interests of the cultic settlement in Jerusalem, supported as it was by the Persian dominion.

There was a significant tradition of historiography by Jews and others writing about Judaism, much of which is no longer extant. Among the earliest and most important extra-canonical examples of Jewish historiography is the Maccabean literature. All four books give evidence of the varying concerns of their authors, from the need to vindicate the Hasmonaean dynasty in 1 Maccabees to the questioning of that version of events in 2 Maccabees and the exploration of the vicarious value of innocent suffering in 3 & 4 Maccabees. A document like the letter of Aristeas, which purports to give an account of the origin of the Greek translation of the Old Testament (the Septuagint (LXX)) should perhaps be mentioned here.

Josephus

The best known and most important example of historiography for apologetic purposes is the writing of Flavius Josephus. Josephus was for a time a Jewish general fighting against the Romans in the First Revolt (AD 66–70). During the course of this he switched sides and became closely allied with the Flavian dynasty, hailing the Roman emperor Vespasian as the one promised by God (*Jewish War* vi. 312). Clearly that betrayal was to haunt Josephus, however much his writing might appear to indicate that he was utterly convinced that God was on the side of the Romans. His major works, the *Jewish War* (BJ) and the *Antiquities*, reveal his sensitivity towards charges of betrayal of his people. The *Jewish War* is itself an attempt to explain the origins of the war, with special attention being given by Josephus to the grievous effects that resulted from the activities of the guerrilla movement. As far as he was concerned, it was the Zealots in Jerusalem during the siege and the bandits who committed atrocities throughout the country who were primarily culpable. To be fair, however, he does not neglect to point out the growing maladministration, corruption and insensitivity of the Roman procurators who were in charge of the province of Judaea during the first century AD.

Because of his apologetic aim, Josephus' work has to be used with care (evident also in his *Vita* and *Contra Apionem*). It would be dangerous to suppose that we have in his writings an unbiased account of Zealot beliefs and practices. It is not always apparent, though occasionally we catch glimpses of the profound religious motivation of the Zealot movement. While these warnings should be noted, there can be no denying the unique place that Josephus' writings have in the literature of ancient Judaism. From the point of view of the historian, they represent an indispensable body of material for the understanding of the life of Jews in the first century AD. The works themselves have different perspectives. As the titles indicate they deal with different issues. The *Jewish War* is an account of the origins and course of the war as seen by Josephus, whereas the *Antiquities* is a retelling of the history of Israel from the creation down to the end of the first century. Neither can be regarded as complete accounts. It is apparent that for some of his material, Josephus depends on other sources as well as the Bible itself, and the *Antiquities* also offers evidence of the scriptural reinterpretation which was current at the time in the form which Josephus gives to particular narratives and religious ideas.

Historiography is not apparent in the rabbinic corpus and the difficulties in writing a coherent history of early rabbinic Judaism are great. But in concentrating on Jewish historiography we should not lose sight of the scattered references to Jews and Judaism in the writings of Greek and Latin authors, which can allow us to glimpse something of the way Judaism was perceived by intelligent contemporaries.

Apocalypses

By far the most significant writings of all the inter-testamental literature are the apocalypses. These works, which purport to offer revelations of divine secrets, are similar in form and content to the New Testament apocalypse, from which (Revelation 1:1 *apokalypsis Iesou Christou*) they derive their generic description.

The origins of this literary genre are much disputed but it is clear that in their concerns with the mysteries of God and his purposes they have a close affinity with the prophetic literature of the Old Testament. In addition, in some of their concerns, particularly the future hope, the apocalypses draw heavily on prophetic passages. Nevertheless there have been those who have argued for a link with the Wisdom tradition of Israel, and certainly in the questioning spirit which is evident in so much of the apocalypses, such a connection is not difficult to find.

There is only one apocalypse included in the canon of the Old Testament, the book of Daniel. That should not be taken as an indication that the compilers of the canon did not have much interest in the apocalyptic tradition, as it is clear that there was a lively apocalyptic oral tradition in Judaism. Of this the written apocalypses are probably evidence. This tradition has a long history. The discovery of fragments of the Enoch apocalypse at Qumran have pushed the date of this particular text back well before the second century BC, back, in other words, into that obscure period when the prophetic voice began to die out in Israel. The literary evidence of the apocalyptic outlook suggests that it continued to play a vital part within Israelite religion throughout the period of the Second Temple, and even in rabbinic circles persisted as an esoteric tradition which manifested itself in written form in the extravagant angelology of the *hekaloth* tracts, and later on in the Kabbalah.

While the apocalypses are by and large the largest repository of the future hope among the Jewish texts now extant, it would be a mistake to suppose that we have exhausted their significance once we have recognised the eschatological thrust of this literature. Other concerns intrude: for example, the vision of heaven, angelology, theodicy and astronomy. The fact that several apocalypses have turned up in the gnostic library from Nag Hammadi indicates that the relationship between apocalyptic and gnosticism, which in the past has not been obvious, needs to be reassessed, particularly in the light of the common concern of both the apocalpyses and the gnostic texts with knowledge of the divine purposes.

Testaments

In Genesis 49 and Deuteronomy 33, Jacob and Moses respectively had offered advice which included some prophecy. This genre was taken up in the inter-testamental literature, pre-eminently in the work which we now know as the Testaments of the Twelve Patriarchs. In this collection of injunctions by the patriarchs to their sons we have a mixture of eschatological prophecy and moral exhortation. There are several other works of a similar type when a famous figure from Israel's past offers advice on the brink of death to sons or people. In some cases (e.g. Test. Abraham and Slav. Apocalypse of Enoch) the testament merges with the apocalypse. Influence of this literary genre can be found in the New Testament, e.g. in Mark 13, in John 14–17, in 2 Peter, where the apostle is said to offer advice to his readers before his death (2 Peter 1.14), and also in the case of Paul (Acts 20: 18ff.).

Midrash

Midrash is a Hebrew word for interpretation and is widely used to describe the interpretative activity of Jewish exegetes. It took a variety of forms, some of which will be examined briefly here.

The most obvious form of midrash is the interpretation of scripture, verse by verse. We see this taking place in rabbinic commentaries on biblical books. It was already well established in the earliest times; we have an example of such exposition of Exodus, Leviticus and Deuteronomy in the rabbinic commentaries Mekilta, Sifra and Sifre. This exposition continued and has been collected in a variety of rabbinic commentaries. The most important of these are the Midrash Rabbah, which are commentaries on the Torah and the five Megilloth (Esther, Song of Songs, Ecclesiastes, Ruth and Lamentations). Such interpretation follows the usual rabbinic pattern, often being as much an anthology as a strict interpretation. The material contained in the various collections comes from widely different dates.

Expansion of the biblical narrative in various ways was another favourite literary method. We have already noted an example of this in considering Josephus' *Antiquities of the Jews*, which is a retelling of the biblical narrative with certain additions and modification. One of the earliest examples of this type of midrash is to be found in the book of Jubilees. This is a retelling of the biblical narrative from the creation to the Exodus, though as it is placed in the context of a divine revelation, it resembles the way in which the Temple regulations are placed in the context of revelation in the Temple scroll; thus it has distinct apocalyptic traits. A similar retelling can be found in the fragmentary Genesis Apocryphon, which is an Aramaic expansion of parts of the book of Genesis, in which various items of material extraneous to the biblical account are included and which has links with both Jubilees and 1 Enoch.

Similar to the book of Jubilees, though not set in the context of angelic revelation, is the *Biblical Antiquities* of Pseudo-Philo, which may date from the end of the first century AD. This is a retelling of the biblical narrative from creation to the death of Saul. In it, several figures, mentioned only in passing in the biblical account, come in for detailed legendary treatment (e.g. Cenez, mentioned at Judges 1.13), whereas certain incidents in the biblical narrative which one might expect to see expanded are left without such an expansion.

Targum

One particular form of midrash which should be mentioned is the *targumim*. Strictly speaking, these are not commentaries on the text, though in fact like other versions of the biblical story they contain much additional material. The targumim are Aramaic translations and paraphrases of the Hebrew Bible, the most important of them being the targumim on the Torah (though there are extant targumim on most parts of the Hebrew Bible). The targumim on the Pentateuch exist in different versions which date from very different periods. Clearly in their present form some of these targumim e.g. Targum Pseudo-Jonathan, date from the Islamic period. What few would doubt is that, however late, the targumim contain much early interpretative material, and some have felt that they can be used to interpret the way in which the Bible was read and interpreted in the first century AD. The relationship between the various targumic versions offered of the Hebrew, and the frequent addition of interpretative material, are matters of great interest to the student of ancient Jewish exegesis.

Philo

Under the heading of midrash, but in content very different from the works already mentioned, are the biblical commentaries of the Jewish philosopher Philo of Alexandria. Much of his extant work consists of commentaries on the Torah, written from the perspective of one who has been profoundly influenced by the popular philosophy of Alexandria, with its blend of Stoicism and Platonism. A reading of these commentaries would hardly give the impression that this is in fact what they are. Nevertheless, amidst the complicated exposition, which seems to owe more to Philo's Alexandrian philosophical climate than the actual words of Scripture, there can be little doubt that what we have is an attempt to read and interpret the ancestral traditions of Judaism within the specific intellectual climate of first century Alexandria.

Jewish Propaganda

Strictly speaking this should not be regarded as a separate category of literature, as it covers several works which have already been mentioned under other headings. The importance of this type of literature however, and the difficulty of categorising one example of it, the Sibylline Oracles, gives us an apportunity to mention it specifically. The Sibylline Oracles have distinct resemblances to the apocalypses. They purport to be eschatological prophecies on a variety of persons, people and places. To this extent, their conern to reveal mysteries does put them in a similar category to the apoca-lypses. The difference between them and the apocalypses however, is that whereas the latter purport to be revelations from God to an ancient biblical worthy, the Sibylline Oracles are revelations of a pagan prophetess which have been used to vindicate Judaism and its future in the sight of the pagans, and so to recommend the religion to non-Jews.

Similar apologetic aims can be (or have been) detected in the

Wisdom of Solomon, and more certainly in the writings of Philo and Josephus. Other works which may be included in this category are Joseph and Asenet which has as its major theme conversion, and 4 Maccabees, in which the theme of martyrdom and the edifying story of the Maccabean martyrs is used.

FOR FURTHER READING

J. W. Bowker, *The Targums and Rabbinic Literature*, Cambridge 1969.

J. H. Charlesworth, *The Old Testament Pseudepigrapha*, London 1983ff. (2 vol.).

G. Nickelsburg, *The Jewish Literature between the Bible and the Mishnah*, London 1981.

T. Rajak, *Josephus*, London 1983.

H. F. D. Sparks, *The Apocryphal Old Testament*, Oxford 1984.

E. Schuerer (new edn ed. F. Millar and G. Vermes), *The Jewish People in the Age of Jesus Christ*, Edinburgh 1973–87 (vol. 3).

M. Stone (ed.), *Jewish Writings of the Second Temple Period*, Assen 1984.

G. Vermes, *The Dead Sea Scrolls in English*, Harmondsworth 1975.

2

HISTORY OF THE STUDY OF THE INTER-TESTAMENTAL LITERATURE

1. CHRISTIAN USE OF JEWISH INTERPRETATION

Unlike the biblical books, the inter-testamental literature has not been the subject of scholarly activity for much more than two hundred years. While the books of the apocrypha were of course well known because of their inclusion in the canon as the result of Jerome's inclusion of them in the Vulgate, other works which had formed part of the canon of the Abyssinian church, like 1 Enoch, remained unknown until they were brought back from Ethiopia at the end of the eighteenth century. Down the centuries, a vital tradition of interpretation was maintained by Jews, testified by the Talmuds and Midrash and the interpretative abilities of scholars like Rashi, Rambam, and David Kimchi, examples of whose interpretative ability can be seen in comments on talmudic passages and the scriptures themselves.

Christian Knowledge of Jewish Literature

It would be a mistake to suppose that Christian interest in Jewish literature dates only from that time or, for that matter, that the influence of ideas contained in that literature had to await the discovery of inter-testamental writings in various translations. From the very earliest times, Christians have had knowledge of Jewish literature. The influence of Philo of Alexandria on the emerging Christian philosophy of Alexandria cannot be underestimated. The preservation of his works owes much to his appeal to Christian writers. Earlier, already in the New Testament, the Epistle of Jude quotes from 1 Enoch (Jude 14), and the Epistle of Barnabas makes reference to a prophecy by Enoch (Ep. Barnabas 4:16). There was an old tradition that Enoch was to be identified with one of the two witnesses spoken of in Revelation 11. Origen, for example, was well acquainted with Jewish rabbis and even quotes a Jewish pseudepigraphon, the Prayer of Joseph; indeed, it is him that we have to thank for our knowledge of this important Jewish work. Tertullian shows that he knew the Ethiopic apocalypse of Enoch (*de cult. fem.* 1.3) and later Jerome himself was knowledgeable about Jewish faith and practice. The preservation of many inter-testamental texts is the result of the interest of Christians. Trace of the works (though not of the ideas) has all but disappeared from the corpus of rabbinic literature. Lactantius and St. Augustine (*de civit. dei* 18. 23) were influenced by the Sibylline Oracles in their theology. Of course, the debt to the ideology of the extra-rabbinic Jewish tradition is not confined to Christianity. There are remarkable, and all too little explored, affinities with the form and content of the Quran and the religion of the prophet Muhammed. The angelic revelation to Moses as it is found in the book of Jubilees, as well as the remarkable ecstatic journeys attributed to Muhammed, all recall the apocalyptic tradition. Down the centuries, Christian writers reflect their knowledge of Jewish literature, particularly of course, the literature of the rabbis. A mine of information in this regard is Raymondo Martnin's *Pugio Fidei*, which contains a vast number of quotations from rabbinic sources of various types and dates. But it was at the Reformation that we have the most evidence of the detailed knowledge and use of Jewish material by Christian scholars. The works of various Reformation scholars in England evince knowledge of Jewish material, including the talmuds, midrash and targumim. Meanwhile, on the continent, students of the Jewish tradition like Pico and Reuchlin (both of whom were particularly interested in the Kabbalah) supported by Jewish authorities, not only studied the Jewish texts but provided Latin translations of important Jewish texts, thus disseminating knowledge of Jewish literature further.

The Influence of Jewish Literature

In England in the seventeenth and eighteenth centuries, there was a vital interest in the Jewish literature, and the emergence of a group of Hebraists, pre-eminent among whom was John Lightfoot. His *Horae Talmudicae* remains a landmark in the study of the New Testament in the light of Jewish sources. Brian Walton published the *Biblia Sacra Polyglotta* in 1657, which shows evidence of wide knowledge of Jewish material. Others at this time were using the Talmuds. For example, John Selden and Hugo Grotius were acquainted with some rabbinic material and the former utilised it in his exposition of natural rights theory.

We are dealing here with material which was published and widely utilised among the Jews. What about the inter-testamental material itself? One thing is certain: even if the finding of the inter-testamental material can only be dated from the end of the eighteenth century, there is little doubt that some of the ideas which we find, particularly in the apocalypses, were having their influence on the thought of the seventeenth centuries and earlier. There has been much interest in the apocalyptic tradition in Reformation Britain. Obviously the biblical apocalypses played the dominant role in the formulation of these ideas, but the influence of other traditions, some of them oral, others written, cannot be excluded. After all, the seventeenth century saw the emergence of the most significant messianic movement in Judaism since the emergence of Christianity, led by Sabbatai Sevi. The eschatological and apocalyptic ideas which inspired that group were probably not confined to the Jews alone and were shared by Christian circles. In the eschatological ferment which characterised some groups at this time, the Sibylline tradition played some role. The influence of such texts had a long pedigree and evidence of their importance for Joachim of Fiore can be demonstrated. Certainly in the seventeenth century, the Sibylline tradition linked with the book of Revelation and the contribution of the Joachimite ideas provided a catalyst for the eschatological enthusiasm and hermeneutic which was widely held. In the late eighteenth century the writings of William Blake reflect a blend of esotericism and mysticism, which may indicate indebtedness to a lively religious tradition, in which, among others, Jewish traditions may have had their part to play.

2. MODERN DISCOVERIES

Eschatology

Thus we can see that study of Jewish material in relation to the Christian scriptures has a long history before the discovery of the Ethiopic Bible which includes the Apocalypse of Enoch (1 Enoch), the book of Jubilees and 4 Ezra. Nevertheless the publication of this material gave a renewed impetus to the study of Jewish material, because some of these texts seemed to have a much closer affinity with the New Testament. Here, it appeared, was found the true background of the early Christian movement. What made the view convincing was the fact that both the gospels and the Apocalypse of Enoch spoke about the mysterious figure, the Son of Man, who would come in judgement. While the discovery and publication of inter-testamental literature progressed throughout the nineteenth century, it was those texts which showed an eschatological interest which continued to exercise a pervasive influence, culminating in the presentation of Jesus' message of the kingdom of God in terms which owe much to an appreciation of the eschatological dimensions found in some of the literature.

It is hardly surprising that the discovery of this material should have led scholars to suppose that here was the true soil from which the early Christian movement grew. Absent were the interminable debates about the law which seemed to characterise the rabbinic material. In its place was the eschatological enthusiasm which seemed to be characteristic of the New Testament.

Notable Scholars
In pursuing this theme we find that an account of Judaism which concentrates mainly on the non-rabbinic Jewish texts was written by *Wilhelm Bousset*, though the monumental commentary on the New Testament (*Kommentar zum NT aus Talmud und Midrasch*) in the light of Jewish material by *Paul Billerbeck* still made much use of the rabbinic sources from a wide variety of periods, as also did *F. Weber*. Such a repudiation of the rabbinic material inevitably led to a reaction, and the influential and authoritative study of *George Foot Moore* redresses the balance, though at the expense of somewhat marginalising the significance of the apocalypes in favour of the view that the rabbinic tradition was in fact the normative Judaism of Jesus' day as well of as of the subsequent centuries.

In the appreciation and publication of the inter-testamental material, the history and literary survey of *E. Schürer* has been a foundation of subsequent research, and English scholars have had a significant part to play. Pre-eminent among them was *R. H. Charles* whose edition of the Apocrypha and Pseudepigrapha of the Old Testament crowned a career of patient study of the inter-testamental literature. His editions of 1 Enoch, 2 (Slavonic) Enoch, 2 (Syriac) Baruch, Jubilees, the Ascension of Isaiah, and the Testaments of the Twelve Patriarchs were landmarks in the study of the inter-testamental literature and opened up this material to many others. His consideration of many of these texts was accompanied by often complex theories of their origins which involved a history of redaction, addition and interpolation. To some, these theories may seem rather dated. Yet it is testimony to the ingenuity of the man, and his appreciation of the character of the material and the milieu in which it originated, that still today scholars feel compelled to interact with the positions he adopts. His knowledge of the literature was summarised in his book on the after-life in Judaism and in a short introduction to the inter-testamental period. In addition to his works on the Jewish material, he wrote two commentaries on the canonical books most closely related to the apocalypses, the books of Daniel and Revelation. In both, his encyclopaedic knowledge of the Jewish sources was put to the service of interpretation, and both are still a mine of information for the study of the biblical apocalypses. It is interesting to reflect that at the time of Charles' labours over the Pseudepigrapha, German biblical scholarship was being dominated by the History of Religions School whose preoccupation was not Jewish religion, but the impact of contemporary pagan religion on primitive Christianity.

Other figures who contributed greatly to the emerging interest in the pseudepigraphs were *M. R. James* whose interest in the apocryphal writings of Judaism and Christianity led him to publish editions of the Testament of Abraham, the Biblical Antiquities of Pseudo Philo, and a collection of NT Apocrypha, and *G. H. Box* whose collaboration with *J.I. Landsman* has enabled students of the inter-testamental literature to read an important apocalypse, the Apocalypse of Abraham, in English. His studies of Jewish religion at the beginning of the early Christian era still repay study. Another who investigated the inter-testamental literature in a series of publications was *W. O. E. Oesterley*, who also wrote an introduction to the apocrypha which is now somewhat dated but is still widely used.

Gershom Scholem: Jewish Mysticism

In a very different area, but one which from the point of view of biblical scholarship is of growing importance, *Gershom Scholem* opened up the world of the Kabbalah for non-Jews. Although this material had been collected in part by *A. Jellinek*, he rehabilitated texts which had been written off by Jewish scholars in the past and revealed a Jewish world all too unfamiliar to those who viewed Judaism solely in the light of the legal discussions of the Mishnah and the Talmuds. In addition to explaining the complications of the Kabbalah and its symbolism, he made people aware of the earlier stage of this religious tradition in the so-called Hekaloth texts which speak of the journey of the mystic to the heavenly world, and the legions of angels which will confront him during that journey. His major study of Jewish mysticism has enabled the non-specialist to see how important this mystical tradition has been within Judaism from the Second Temple period to the present day. The bulk of these texts still remain unavailable to the non-specialist though the German scholar Peter Schäfer has embarked on an ambitious project to make available critical editions of the material. One text which was published, however, by a research student of G. H. Box, is the *Sefer Hekalot* or 3 Enoch. *Hugo Odeberg* offered a critical edition with abundant notes and indications of links with related Jewish material.

E. R. Goodenough: Jewish Symbolism

In opening up aspects of Judaism not widely known, mention should also be made of the multi-volume project of *E. R. Goodenough, Jewish Symbols in the Greco-Roman Period*. While strictly speaking this was not a study of inter-testamental literature, it provided an important companion to that study in the form of a collection of material on Jewish iconography and ideology. Goodenough was himself convinced that there was another Judaism alongside rabbinic Judaism which did not correspond to the strict religious disciplines of the rabbis. In collecting the material he does on Jewish art and iconography, it was his concern to offer evidence of this alternative Judaism. Whether there should be a sharp line drawn between this religious outlook and the religion of the rabbis has been questioned. What cannot be in doubt, however, is that the rabbinic image of itself as manifest in its literary remains cannot be the whole story of Judaism at the beginning of the Christian era. What is more, Goodenough has reminded us that there is more to Judaism than either the rabbinic literature or the pseudepigrapha. The religion of the Diaspora is still too little investigated. It is true that interest in Philo has been considerable from the very beginnings of the Christian church, and the contribution of this remarkable Jewish philosopher cannot be underestimated. But we are now recognising that Alexandria did not have a monopoly on Jewish life and thought outside Palestine, and the explication of the Judaism of other centres is of equal importance.

3. RECENT DEVELOPMENTS

The Jewish Matrix of Christianity

In the last twenty years, the study of Jewish literature has grown at an enormous pace. There has been a resurgence of interest in the pseudepigrapha and in the relevance of Jewish material for the study of the New Testament. It was barely thirty five years ago that W. D. Davies protested against the isolation of the apostle Paul from his ancestral religion in the face of expositions of Paul's doctrine which attributed greater influence to Greek, gnostic and other non-Jewish sources. The wheel has now turned full circle, and the major influence on all strands of the New Testament is considered to be Judaism. But it is a Judaism of the Second Temple period viewed rather differently from in the past. No longer are we presented with a view which stresses a central Jewish orthodoxy with divergent views relegated to an irrelevant periphery. That is considered to be an anachronistic assessment of second Temple Judaism. Rather, it is the *absence* of orthodoxy (and for that matter orthopraxy) and the prevalence of variety which characterises writing on the Jewish matrix of Christianity.

The Resources
The renewed interest in the Jewish background of the New Testament has led to a variety of new introductions, editions and translations of a variety of Jewish texts. The emerging international co-operation since the Second World War, and the ever growing contribution of American scholarship and resources, have yielded a firmly based and expanding scholarly enterprise which seems destined to establish study of ancient Judaism on the firmest of foundations. What characterises this resurgence of interest in Jewish studies is that, even allowing for the related concern of many of the scholars involved to explore the relevance of the Jewish material for Christian origins, there is a recognition that the various Jewish sources deserve study in their own right and should not be treated merely as a quarry from which to plunder ideas which could help New Testament exegesis. The renaissance of pseudepigrapha/Jewish studies can be characterised as respect for the texts themselves and the individuals and societies which produced them.

The story of the critical study of Jewish literature, however, does not begin in this century. Already throughout the nineteenth century for various cultural reasons there emerged what was known as the *Wissenschaft des Judentums*, whose investigations of the rabbinic tradition and Jewish culture generally paved the way for more recent investigations. Similarly, the emergence of the state of Israel has led to a fast growing intellectual enterprise in the history of Judaism, in which the study of the inter-testamental literature has not been neglected. But the most dramatic increase in study of Judaism has taken place in the USA.

The Work of Jacob Neusner

We have noted some of the investigations which have been launched into non-rabbinic materials, but particular reference should be made to the new approaches to the rabbinic material taken by the American Jew, Jacob Neusner and his disciples. In Israel there have been summaries of rabbinic thought on traditional lines by Ephraim Urbach following in the footsteps of W. Bacher, but the approach which Neusner has taken has been very different. His first major publication, *A Life of Rabban Yoharan ben Zakkai*, was on very traditional lines, similar to that taken by Finkelstein in his life of Akiba, in seeking to use the traditions available to write a life of Yohanan. In another study of Yohanan, however, Neusner showed the kind of approach which was to characterise his later study. Making known his indebtedness to the form-critical or traditio-historical method, which had become firmly established in the study of similar material in the New Testament gospels, Neusner has sought to establish the history of particular traditions in the light of the concerns of the rabbinic academies and the concerns of Judaism in a particular age. He has set himself to write a history of the mishnaic laws as well as the history of the traditions dealing with leading figures in tannaitic Judaism. His output on early rabbinic traditions is phenomenal. Nor has he neglected to make his learning and expertise available to a wider range of readers.

Whether the method which Neusner and his pupils have pursued is going to remain the most convincing explanation of the rabbinic traditions remains to be seen. If New Testament scholarship is anything to go by, it is quite likely that there will be a reaction in favour of a more positive evaluation of the authenticity of some, though obviously not all, the traditions. What Neusner has compelled students of the rabbinic texts to appreciate is the history of the tradition of these texts and the function which they play within the life of the rabbinic academies, and the literary contexts in which those traditions now appear. Neusner's detailed investigations of the early rabbinic laws is symptomatic of the wider availability of detailed and authoritative investigations of Jewish material. In the past, a lack of knowledge of Jewish sources among Christian scholars was understandable because of the prohibitive difficulties of mastering talmudic Hebrew and ideology. The enormous industry which has taken place on Judaism in the last twenty years has put ancient Judaism within the grasp of Christian students in a way which seemed impossible a generation ago. It is a mark of the achievement of Neusner and his contemporaries that research on

Christian origins would today be unthinkable without proper assessment of the Jewish setting of Christianity.

But another, in this case unexpected, event has had its part to
play in the revolution which has taken place in recent years in
connection with Jewish studies.

The Dead Sea Scrolls

The most important archaelogical discovery in recent years, which
has undoubtedly revolutionised attitudes towards ancient Judaism,
is the Dead Sea Scrolls. Just after the Second World War, fragments
of scrolls written in Hebrew and Aramaic were discovered in the
vicinity of Qumran, where there were the ruins of a settlement. This
was excavated and large numbers of manuscripts were discovered in
the caves nearby. Some of these scrolls still are awaiting publication
but the considerable number that have been published have revealed
to us the existence of a Jewish sect, which in all probability inhabited
the buildings now in ruins at Qumran. Archaeological research has
provided reasons for linking the scrolls discovered in the caves and
the nearby building.

From the writings of Josephus, Philo and Pliny, scholars had
been aware of the Essenes for some time. The similarities between
the description of the customs in Josephus' *Jewish War* and the
regulations of the community outlined in the Community Rule or
Manual of Discipline (IQS) has persuaded the majority of scholars
that the community which lived at Qumran and wrote the scrolls
were in fact Essenes or a group very similar to the Essenes. The
evidence suggests that this community perished at the hands of
Roman legionaries in c. AD 68, and it is not too fanciful to suppose
that they put into practice their fantasy of a holy war against the
sons of darkness, prescribed in the War Scroll (IQM).

While there have been exaggerated claims made about the importance of the Scrolls, particularly as far as the link with Christianity
is concerned, it is apparent now that some of the similarities with
early Christianity have been overemphasised. Certainly the study of
the gospel of John has been considerably altered as a result of the
discovery of the Scrolls. The characterisation of John as a Hellenistic
gospel of the pre-war period has been replaced by the view that
what we have is a text which is firmly rooted in Judaism, albeit of
a sectarian kind. But it is in the study of Judaism that the scrolls
have made their greatest impact. The existence of a group like this
within the fabric of first century Judaism has cast a very new light
on the character of the Jewish religion and manifested the breadth
of religious possibilities at this time. Even if we may be forced to

accept the view that the Scrolls exhibit the religious ideology of only a small fraction of the population of Israel, we have been forced to ask searching questions about the character, and indeed the existence, of mainstream or orthodox Judaism in the Second Temple Period. Before the discovery of the scrolls it would have been unthinkable to have supposed that such an idiosyncratic form of Judaism could have existed (although the existence of fringe groups has been accepted for a long time). This has undoubtedly had important ramifications for our understanding of the place of the nascent Christian movement within the whole spectrum of Jewish belief and practice. But more than this, we have been forced to recognise not only that what later emerged as orthodox Judaism (the pharisaic-rabbinic tradition) was during the period of the Second Temple one minority ideology among many, but also that the sources now extant preserve only a fraction of the evidence of the vitality and variety of Jewish life and thought during this period.

FOR FURTHER READING

J. H. Charlesworth, 'A History of Pseudepigrapha Research', in ed. W. Haase, *Aufstieg und Niedergang der roemischen Welt* II.19.1, Berlin 1979 pp. 54ff.

K. Firth, *The Apocalyptic Tradition in Reformation Britain*, Oxford 1979.

E. R. Goodenough, *Jewish Symbols in the Greco-Roman Period*, 12 vols. New Haven 1953–65.

E. Kraft and G. Nickelsburg, *Early Judaism and its Modern Interpreters*, (forthcoming).

G. Lloyd Jones, *The Discovery of Hebrew in Tudor England: A Third Language*, Manchester 1983.

R. Loewe, 'Christian Hebraists 1100 – 1890', *Encyclopedia Judaica* vol 8 col 11.

H. Maccoby, *Judaism on Trial. Jewish-Christian Disputations in the Middle Ages*, London 1982.

J. Neusner, *The Modern Study of the Mishnah*, Leiden 1973.

E. I. J. Rosenthal, *Studia Semitica*, Cambridge 1971, vol 1 pp. 327ff. (on *Wissenschaft des Judentums*).

P. Schäfer, *Synopse zur Hekhalot-Literatur*, Berlin 1981.

E. E. Urbach, *The Sages. Their Concepts and Beliefs*, Jerusalem 1975.

G. Vermes, *The Dead Sea Scrolls. Qumran in Perspective*, London 1977.

3

THE INTER-TESTAMENTAL LITERATURE IN ITS SETTING

1. THE HISTORICAL SETTING

An account of the Inter-testamental literature of Judaism would be distorted and certainly incomplete without some knowledge of the historical situation and social situation out of which the literature emerged.

Post-Exilic Judaism
Our story begins in 587 BC when the city of Jerusalem was taken by the army of Nebuchadnezzar, king of Babylon. The leading citizens were taken into exile in Babylon. The impact of this event should not be underestimated. An elaborate myth had grown up around Jerusalem, Zion, the place where God caused his presence to dwell. The book of Isaiah (cf. Psalm 46) gives us evidence of a belief in the invincibility of Zion and the special affection the city had in the sight of God. The destruction shattered these illusions and vindicated the words of the prophets who over successive generations had been predicting judgement on the city and its inhabitants, notwithstanding the divine promises. The event caused a profound reappraisal of Israel's traditions, which took place particularly among the Jews taken off into exile in Babylon. From here come the prophecies of Second Isaiah and Ezekiel with their promises of restoration and renewal (e.g. Isaiah 40ff.).

In 583 BC, Cyrus issued an edict which enabled the exiles to return to the land of Israel. The history of this period is difficult to reconstruct but from the hints which we have in the prophecies of Haggai and Zachariah it would appear that the glorious return promised by Second Isaiah did not materialise. The Temple stood in ruins (Haggai 1) and the economic situation was none too promising. Eventually the Temple was rebuilt and the life of the community once again focused on the cultic activities of the central shrine, though whether this met with the approval of all groups is a moot point.

In 458, Ezra, commissioned by Artaxerxes I, came to Jerusalem and laid down strict laws with regard to marriage of Jews with foreigners, and made the religion of the Torah central to the community in Jerusalem. Nehemiah, another envoy from Persia, came probably a little earlier. Among his measures, he rebuilt the walls of the city of Jerusalem and also engaged in promulgating religious measures e.g. payment of the priestly dues, enforcing sabbath observance and dealing with the marriages of Jews to foreigners.

Results of the Exile
Two factors of importance should be noted as a result of the experience of Exile. First and foremost, the Jews exiled to Babylon had to come to terms with separation from the promised land. The dispersion of the Jews was an important factor in the Jewish history, and its beginnings can certainly be seen in the exile-experience: how, said the Psalmist, can we sing the Lord's song in a strange land? (Psalm 137). Secondly, while it is apparent from the oracles against the nations in the pre-exilic prophets that Israel and Judah had always to reckon, because of their key geographical position, with the surrounding nations, that issue became a pressing one after the exile. The missions of both Ezra and Nehemiah indicate that the patronage of the dominant world power had its effect on religious matters in Jerusalem. The Jewish nation had to come to terms with the might of the empires of the world in a way which they had not had to do quite this way before. It became an issue of some importance to ascertain how the Jewish hopes and the Jewish confession in Yahweh, the one and only God, could square with the subordination of his chosen people.

We know all too little about this period, though it may be conjectured that writings like the books of Chronicles, the prophecy of Malachi and the later oracles of Isaiah are to be placed during the late fifth and early fourth centuries BC. They give hints of growing strife within the community and the growing importance of the cult and its hierarchy as the focus of religious life. It is probably at this time that the split between Jews and Samaritans emerges.

The Hellenistic Period
The next date of importance was the conquest of Palestine by Alexander the Great. After his death in 323 BC, control of Palestine oscillated between the Ptolemies in Egypt and the Seleucids in

Syria, both dynasties founded by generals of Alexander. The most important effect of the conquest of Alexander was the emergence of Hellenistic culture as a factor with which the people of God had to come to terms. Hellenistic cities were founded in Palestine, and in the second quarter of the second century BC there began a determined process of hellenisation in Judaea which was to have ramifications for the lives of Jews in Palestine.

In 175 BC, Antiochus IV (Epiphanes) succeeded to the Seleucid throne. By this time Jerusalem was in the hands of the Seleucids. He embarked on a process of encouraging the Greek way of life, and this was encouraged in Jerusalem by the priest Jason who ousted his brother Onias as High Priest. Greek customs and practices were instituted in the city, which led to strife between rival factions. Eventually, Antiochus, who had been compaigning in Egypt, attacked Jerusalem and after more unrest took action to proscribe Judaism. Jewish practices were forbidden and a pagan cult was established in the Temple in Jerusalem (167). Opposition to this attack at the heart of the Jewish religion was led by the Hasmonean family, the Maccabeans, and by 164 the city had been retaken, the Temple purified and the cult of Yahweh re-established there. We find reflections of this episode in Israel's history in the books of Maccabees and in the book of Daniel.

These victories led to a period of independence for Judaea as the Hasmonean family, particularly, Judas, (followed by Jonathan and Simon), successfully outwitted the Syrians, and from 141, Simon established an independent Jerusalem. He became High Priest and so the Hasmonean dynasty was founded. Simon was succeeded by John Hyrcanus, who extended Jewish rule in the area. According to Josephus it was during Hyrcanus' reign that the sects of the Pharisees and Sadducees first came to prominence. After John and his successor Aristobulus, the long reign of Alexander Jannaeus began which involved further conquests. He was succeeded by his widow, Alexandra. At her death strife between her two sons, Hyrcanus II and Aristobulus II paved the way for the intervention of the Roman general Pompey into Jewish affairs, culminating with his entry into the Temple in 63 BC.

The Roman Period

The period of Jewish independence ended when Judaea became liable to Roman tribute. Hyrcanus ruled until eventually as a result of the turbulence of the civil war between Julius Caesar and Pompey, Herod, whose father Antipater had ruled with Hyrcanus, captured Jerusalem in 37. He married the granddaughter of Hyrcanus II, but his reign was marked by brutal suppression of all opposition. Despite his close relationship with Mark Antony, Herod was confirmed as king by Octavian (Augustus) after the latter's victory at the battle of Actium. He engaged in much building work, particularly the Temple in Jerusalem, completed only a few years before its destruction in AD 70. His Idumean origins did not commend him to the Jewish people both because much of his building work placed a large financial burden on the Jewish people, and because of his ambivalence towards Jewish tradition. The last years of his reign were full of intrigue and suspicion. His death in 4 BC marked the beginning of a turbulent period. His three successors were Archelaus, Philip and Antipas. By AD 6, Archelaus had been deposed as ruler of Judaea and Samaria and the area was placed under the direct rule of Rome, an event which prompted the need for a census. This provoked a rebellion led by Judas the Galilean who objected to the holy land of Israel being assessed for the purpose of taxation. Of the other sons of Herod, Antipas ruled over Galilee until 39 AD and Philip over the other areas (north and east of Galilee).

Of the Roman procurators of Judaea the most famous was Pontius Pilate, whose period of jurisdiction coincided with the reign of the emperor Tiberius. He was deposed in 36 AD after an attack on some Samaritans. During the period of emperor Gaius' reign a major threat to Judaism from Rome came from the desire of the emperor to have a statue of himself set up in the Temple in Jerusalem, about which we hear much in Philo's Embassy to Gaius. Fortunately for the Jews, Gaius Caligula was murdered before the will of the emperor could be implemented.

After the accession of the emperor Claudius, Agrippa I became king of Judaea, having already succeeded to the territories of Philip. He was granted this position because of his friendship with Claudius being intimately involved in imperial politics. So between 41–44 the land of Israel was ruled by a grandson of Herod the Great. When he died Rome took over the control of his territories, though his son Agrippa II (whose sister Berenice had an affair with the emperor Titus) was involved in Judaean political affairs; he was indeed granted the right to nominate the High Priest.

The Jewish Revolt
During the procuratorship of Cumanus (48–52) things began to get worse. Pilgrims were murdered in the Temple at Passover time and there began to be attacks by Jewish guerrillas prominent among whom were the *sicarii*, who were responsible for a succession of

murders. Action against them was taken by Cumanus' successor, Felix. During the procuratorship of Albinus (62–64) corruption increased, and Albinus was responsible for plundering public funds. It was during the time of his successor, Florus, (64–66) that the spark which ignited the flames of revolt was finally lit. The ultimate folly was his robbery of the Temple treasury which led to revolt, epitomised by the cessation of the daily sacrifice on behalf of the emperor. The story of the revolt is told in some detail by Josephus in his *Jewish War*. The horror of the siege of Jerusalem and the fantastic religious hopes entertained give a revealing insight into the minds of some of those who led the revolt.

The war of the Romans against the Jews dragged on for four years, mainly because in AD 68 Nero died, and there was initiated a troubled year in which no less than 4 generals (Galba Otho, Vitellius and Vespasian) claimed the principate. After the succession of Vespasian his son Titus went to Judaea to complete the war against the Jews already started by his father. After a siege lasting four months during which there was untold suffering and internecine strife, the city eventually fell to Titus' legionaries in AD 70, the Temple was burnt to the ground and Titus returned home in triumph. Some of the scenes from that triumphal procession in Rome are recorded on the arch of Titus. The fortress of Masada to which some of the zealots had fled was not finally captured until 73.

Judaism after AD 70

The catastrophe of AD 70 left Judaism in ruins and it was left to Rabban Yohanan ben Zakkai and his companions to rebuild the religion from the ruins left by the events of the previous years. Whereas in the aftermath of the destruction of the First Temple by Nebuchadnezzar the rebuilding of the Temple remained a focus of the restoration of Judaism, the same cannot be said for the situation after AD 70. It is true that the hope for the rebuilding of the Temple featured in one of the prayers of the synagogue, but with the end of the sacrificial system, the end of the Sanhedrin and the decimation of the fabric of Judaism as it was known up to that date, something different emerged. This owed much to what had gone before but concentrated on the views of one particular party within Judaism, the Pharisaic party, and the interpretations of one faction within that party, the Hillelite faction. The focus of religion became the Torah and its interpretation and the place of meeting, the synagogue, as they had been for centuries among those Jews outside the land of Palestine and increasingly so within it.

Perhaps the most amazing thing about Jewish history and religion at the end of the first century and in the first half of the second century, is that the catastrophe of the First Revolt did not prevent the Jews from embarking upon other rebellions against their Roman overlords. In North Africa in the reign of Trajan there was a revolt of Jews (115–117), and Palestine again broke in revolt in 132 AD, probably as the result of Hadrian's decision to turn the ruined city of Jerusalem into a pagan city. Possibly in addition Hadrian issued a decree banning circumcision. The leader of the Second Revolt was Simeon ben Koseba (or as he is better known Bar Kochba, son of a star, because of the link with Numbers 24: 17). If the Roman historian Dio Cassius is to be believed, hundreds of thousands of men were killed in raids and many perished as the result of disease and famine.

Whereas after the First Revolt Judaism was not proscribed and, with the exception of the confiscation of the half shekel Temple Tax, few penalties were placed on the Jews, Hadrian forbade the Jews access to Jerusalem and rebuilt the city as a Roman colony. Circumcision was banned (though it was lifted in 138). From the middle of the second century the religion of the Jews was firmly in the hands of the two sects which had survived the two debacles of 66 and 132: Rabbinic Judaism and Christianity.

FOR FURTHER READING

J. H. Hayes and J. M. Miller, *Israelite and Judean History*, London 1977.
E. Schuerer op. cit., vol. 1.

2. THE SOCIAL SETTING

Identifying the Social Context
One of the most difficult and yet most important tasks of the interpreter of ancient Jewish literature is to place the various literary remains of ancient Judaism into some kind of social, as well as religious setting. The major difficulty is the fact that we are rarely in a position to know for certain what place and time a particular document comes from. As a result, we have to depend on internal evidence from the document itself to build up some kind of picture, a method which has become very characteristic of research on New Testament texts. The argument is inevitably circular, as we use the picture built from a particular document as a basis for the

interpretation of the social and religious world of the community and the writer, and then apply our findings to the interpretation of the text. Except in those cases (such as the writings of Philo and Josephus where we know the identity of the authors and a little about the settings in which the writings were written) we have to accept the inevitable subjectivism which is bound to attend judgements on this matter.

Comparative Study

There are some checks on this method, however. One of these is the comparative study of social settings and ideologies. By this we understand the use of information concerning the way in which literature and ideas functioned in other social situations, perhaps separated by a considerable amount in time and space, but linked by the use of a common set of ideas and problems and *mutatis mutandis* not dissimilar religious and social setting. This kind of approach has gained a wide hearing in recent years in the study of religious ideas, particularly on the Old and New Testaments. It has to be said at once that this method is never going to give that objective precision which some scholars would dearly love to have. All that can be said of it is that it offers another set of controls on the examination of the internal evidence of the documents.

How does this method work? As an example, one may cite the way in which the study of social anthropology has been used to illuminate the understanding of biblical eschatology. Beliefs about a new age when the iniquities of the present are removed are to be found in a variety of cultures, and this complex of beliefs and practices is called by social anthropologists 'millenarianism'. It is possible to ascertain why these views emerge and how groups cope with the non-fulfilment of their hopes. In addition we are in a position to say a little about the kind of groups within a particular society which became attached to these kinds of ideas and what factors in society at large led them to espouse them. Nevertheless, one needs to be aware that study of the use of ideas and social setting in one culture cannot always be assumed to be a model applicable in the case of every other set of similar ideas. But provided that we bear in mind the limitations of this comparative method, suggestions may be made with regard to the social setting and function of particular sets of ideas on the assumption that further research and information will also be a check on excessive optimism in the use of the theory which is enunciated.

Reconstruction

Of course, the most important way in which the literature can more easily be understood is by a more detailed knowledge of the social world of the literature, even if we frequently have to admit that *precise* connections between ancient Jewish literature and specific social formations are difficult. Few scholars would deny the importance of this, yet it is a mark of the preoccupation with the history of ideas that nothing like enough attention has been given to the material at our disposal which would enable us to build up some kind of picture of the situation of Jews in the ancient world. There are enough hints in the writings of Josephus and in the voluminous rabbinic literature to enable us to construct a social and economic picture of Judaism in various areas, even if we have to recognise that our use of these sources puts us in touch with only a very narrow band of Jewish life but also includes the projections, whether conscious or otherwise, of the ideals and prejudices of the writers concerned.

Legal Traditions

As one might expect, the central feature of the bulk of the Jewish literature is the exposition of the laws of the Torah. The character of this exposition is itself not without interest. Unfortunately the bulk of the evidence available to us comes from the rabbinic sources, which largely represent one approach to the Torah. They exhibit the particular problems which were discussed by the rabbis. In the rabbinic approach to Law we find a concern for detailed observance and comprehensive treatment, so that virtually all areas of life were brought within the framework of legal observance. What emerges from a study of the rabbinic halakah is a recognition that most ordinary Jews could not maintain complete separation from Gentiles. Thus the rulings which are offered by the rabbis reflect the need for precise guidance in situations where accidental transgression is an ever present risk. This is the religious observance of co-existence rather than separation and of limited compromise rather than black and white rules of right and wrong.

A comparison with the legal traditions which we have from a non-pharisaic-rabbinic group will enable us to ascertain another function of the laws within the rabbinic tradition. We know that the Dead Sea Scrolls reflect the beliefs and practices of a Jewish sect which cut itself off from the rest of Israel by its life in the desert. What has remained of its legal traditions indicates that it took a clear and firm line on matters of community discipline. In the matter of sabbath observance, the Dead Sea Scrolls reveal nothing of the detailed prescriptions of the rabbinic traditions. There are no signs that the writers of these legal traditions wanted to enable the pious to guard against accidental transgression and to provide means whereby they could find relief from some of the more compromising biblical regulations. It may well be that one reason for the lack of evidence of this could be the fact that at the time the scrolls were written, there was no development in the legal interpretation of the scriptures which corresponds to the minute provisions we find in the rabbinic literature. It seems more likely, however, that the principal reason for this is the fact that the scrolls are the halakah of a group which was separated from society at large. Detailed provision of the kind which we find in the rabbinic literature was inappropriate for a community which was separated from society.

At the heart of the pharisaic vision was the holiness of the people of God. They were concerned to extend the holiness of the priest when he was engaged in duty in the Temple, to the home and society at large. The democratisation of priestly holiness characterised the pharisaic-rabbinic vision. Unlike the Qumran community which was not disturbed by any threat of contamination either from non-observant Jews or Gentiles, the rabbis did not agree to a separation from society at large and a retreat into the purity of the wilderness. Thus the preservation of holiness, while the pious continued to live within society, demanded a detailed consideration of the various situations which would confront them and decisions about what was necessary to remain holy.

Diaspora Literature

In the second half of the Wisdom of Solomon we find a repudiation of the wisdom of the Egyptians and the idolatry practised by them. In the early chapters we find a description of the life of the righteous man, his persecution and vindication. It has rightly been suggested that what we have here is a counterblast against those who would have closer communion with the society around them. The pressures on Jews to compromise must have been enormous, as they sought to have some kind of integration within society and enjoy some of the privileges which a fully-fledged citizen would have enjoyed. The book of Wisdom represents a warning against those who would enjoy these opportunities of integration too much.

In the Sibylline Oracles we find the use of a pagan oracle to vindicate Judaism and its beliefs before the pagan world. Similarly in the writings of Philo of Alexandria now extant, we find a combination of philosophical ideas applied to the Jewish scriptures. There are hints throughout that there is an attempt to commend the religion to pagans: synagogues are places of reflection and study (e.g. Spec. Leg. ii. 60) and practices like the sabbath and circumcision are vindicated on pragmatic grounds (e.g. Spec. Leg. i. 2).

Such an approach from Philo should not surprise us. After all, we know that he was highly placed in Alexandrian society. His nephew was later prefect of Egypt, though he had by then apostasised from his ancestral faith. Among the aristocracy, the need to maintain a strict separation from society at large was not so pressing. The fact that Philo can utilise so much of Hellenistic philosophy is an indication that he had no worries about the appropriateness of this task. There is no suggestion in Philo's writings that the approach of the pagan philosophers should not be used in the interpretation of the Holy Scriptures. Inevitably, the use of such methods blurs the differences between the practice of Judaism and the surrounding culture, and indicates that this culture is not to be avoided at all costs by Jews. On the ideological level it is a demonstration of the greater degree of integration which some were prepared to contemplate.

Sectarian Literature

When Jews began to recommend their religion to their neighbours we may assume that it indicates a degree of integration already existing with the surrounding society, though this is not to suggest that attitudes of pagans to Jews were always positive. Those who wanted to maintain their complete separation from the pagan world did not normally need to indulge in apologetic writing. Such an activity was essentially the desire of those who felt that they had something to justify. Such a view needs some qualification, however. Among the Dead Sea Scrolls we find biblical commentaries, particularly those on the books of Habakkuk and Nahum, which relate the events and personages mentioned in the biblical text with events and persons of importance in the past life of the community. It can hardly be said that this was for outside consumption, but was written to establish the importance of the existence of this group within Judaism and its place in the desert as opposed to being part of the fabric of Jewish society. It helped the community to understand the nature of the opposition to the traditions of the community, the importance of their leadership and the basis for their novel approach to the Jewish traditions.

The inward-looking group like the Qumran community did not exist to attract adherents (though, of course, many *were* attracted to share their way of life). It is evident from various passages in these documents that there is a clear dualism, a division between light and darkness, good and evil. Needless to say, the Qumran community was on the side of light and its opponents darkness. Such a polarisation, when it is accompanied by a conviction that the division between the children of light and the children of darkness is difficult to cross, inevitably makes concern with those outside an irrelevance. The children of light would naturally be attracted to the light (IQS 3), there was no need to persuade darkness to be light, for such would be an impossibility.

Propaganda Literature
By contrast there was probably a widespread movement in first century Judaism, particularly in the Diaspora, to attract new converts to Judaism. We know from passages like Acts 13:26 that there were many sympathetic non-Jews attached to the synagogues. For these Jews (or the majority of them) the division between the children of light and the children of darkness was nothing like as clear-cut. There was a large penumbra of belief and practice, which, while not in the strictest sense Jewish, was cetainly not to be despised or excluded. Clearly, despite all the anti-Jewish propaganda that existed, Jews were anxious to recommend their religion, with its attractive qualities like monotheism, repudiation of idolatry and high ethical tone, in order to attract new adherents and widen that group of sympathisers loosely attached to the synagogues. How this position was integrated into the fabric of Jewish belief is not entirely clear, though the doctrine of the angels of the nations allowed a part for the pagan divinities within the ideological structure of Judaism without necessarily radically infringing Jewish monotheism.

3. THE HISTORICAL AND SOCIAL SETTING OF APOCALYPTIC

Scholarly Consensus
If scholarly opinion on the subject of apocalyptic is anything to go by over the last twenty years or so, the place of this literature in Jewish society would appear to be obvious. There have been a number of studies which have outlined a view of this literature which regards it as a body of protest literature of a marginalised minority. A good example of this type of approach is to be found in the work of Otto Plöger. He argued that post-exilic Judaism was characterised by a polarisation between the priestly hierarchy which located the fulfilment of the prophetic promises in the worship and life of the Temple, and another group, whose views are represented

in the writings of the apocalypses, which looked forward for a future fulfilment of the divine purposes as revealed to the prophets. It did not consider the religious settlement in Jerusalem was an adequate fulfilment of those promises. According to Plöger the view of the hierarchy is to be found in its most classic form in the writings of the books of Chronicles and the related Ezra and Nehemiah. Here, it is argued, the future hope has all but disappeared and a cultic focus is to be found.

The View of Paul Hanson

Arguing along similar lines but dealing with different texts and utilising a different method, Paul Hanson has attempted to show that the dawn of apocalyptic is to be found in the post-exilic situation in a struggle between the supporters of the restoration of the cult in Jerusalem and the upholders of the Isaianic vision of a new era in God's plan. By a patient examination of the oracles in the second half of the book of Isaiah, Hanson argues that we find here evidence of a struggle between the visionaries and the hierarchy and the gradual disillusionment of the former that their hopes can ever be fulfilled on the historical plane. Hanson argues that, as compared with the oracles of Second Isaiah (40–55), the oracles which follow manifest a retreat from concern with the fulfilment of the divine promises in history, and the transposition of the future hope onto a transcendent plane; this he considers to be the foundation of apocalyptic eschatology. Into this interpretation Hanson attempts to weave the other post-exilic writings and seeks to offer an overall interpretation of the power struggle which was going on within post-exilic society.

At the heart of Hanson's analysis is his wish to ascertain how the ideology of the minority (whose views were ultimately rejected) gradually altered, in the light of the changed circumstances in which the group found itself. Thus when we find the group thinking of the fulfilment of the divine promises coming on the transcendent plane, this is to be understood as further evidence of the marginalisation of the group and its growing alienation from society, as also is its growing hostility towards those with whom it disagrees.

Reservations

Whether it is possible to posit such a sharp difference of opinion within post-exilic Judaism is open to question. In addition, the view of apocalyptic espoused by Hanson has been criticised of late. What is more, we have to accept the severe limitations placed upon us when we seek to interpret the oracles in the final part of the book of Isaiah, and explain why it is that these oracles of the oppressed minority were accepted in due course by the majority group as the logical development of the Isaianic tradition.

It is a dangerous oversimplification to suppose that such a neat division of ideologies existed between eschatologically orientated groups and the cultic establishment. It probably does not do justice to the complexities of belief and practice at this time, as we shall argue in a moment. The Dead Sea Scrolls manifest hostility towards the Temple as it was constituted at the time, and the community which wrote them appears to have looked forward to a day when the cult was organised on the right lines.

With the Dead Sea Sect we are dealing with an obvious example of a marginalised group with a sophisticated self-conscious identity. They combined in their ideology a vitriolic abuse for the status quo, an eschatological belief of great intensity, and an unswerving conviction that the cult was central to the hopes of Judaism. The problem for them was not the apparatus of cultic activity but the way in which it was run. They could not tolerate a form of organisation which allowed the abuses of the true priesthood and tradition to be continued. For them there was no alternative but to separate themselves completely, justify this separation and wait for such time that they could, once again, restore the fortunes of Israel.

Thus we have to beware not to assume that the polarisation between visionaries and priests and the concomitant ideologies is an adequate description of the situation. As Hanson rightly suggests in his study, it is quite likely that the ideology of the visionary group was utilised by opponents. Thus we may in fact be talking about an extensive shared ideology which is in fact the basis of conflict. He argues that the oracles in both Ezekiel 40ff. and Zechariah were the attempts by the hierarchy to use language and outlook shared with the visionary opposition in the service of the status quo.

Misleading Polarisation
There is another example of the way in which Jewish thought is polarised. In a very influential monograph, D. Rössler argued that there was a significant divergence of opinion over the part which history played in theology between the pharisaic-rabbinic tradition and the apocalyptic tradition. It was the latter, Rössler argued, that preserved that concern with the wider cosmic dimensions of salvation which are very much to the fore in the writings of the

prophets. In the pharisaic-rabbinic tradition the concerns were less with God's purposes in history and more with obedience to the Law in the present. In was, therefore, a pragmatic concern which predominated and not the wider speculative visions of the apocalyptic dreamers. It was dealing with reality: how to be a righteous Jew in difficult circumstances; not wishing (and even working for) the impossible.

It is easy to suppose that the apocalypses must be the repositories of the religious and political aspirations of the marginalised and disinherited. After all, we seem to come closer in these texts to what Marx called the sign of the oppressed, the opium of the people. Their drama of future redemption, visions of hope might be best construed as the writings of those, who had not hope in this age, and looked to God for divine vindication in the age to come.

Study of the apocalypses reveals that such an analysis is by no means adequate. For one thing it is not easy to suppose that we have adequately described the ideology of these works by speaking of them as eschatological fantasies. It is apparent when we examine them that a vast array of different subjects are treated in them – concern with the future purposes of God is set alongside astronomical mysteries, descriptions of heaven, angels and theodicy, to mention but a few of the subjects. It cannot be the case that such varied concerns indicate the ideology only of the marginalised disinherited in Israel's society. Recent study of the apocalypses indicates that some of the apocalypses in whole or part may well be the product of the learned élites within Israelite society.

Interpreting Apocalyptic
Apocalyptic visions can function in several ways. *Firstly,* they can offer a short-cut in the interpretation of scripture to those whose task it was to deal with the sacred texts. The evolution of elaborate exegetical methods meant that understanding the divine demand was not easily come by. Indeed, on occasion there may well be cases which it was not possible to resolve. The matters treated in the apocalypses concern in particular those issues about which scripture had little to say, or were matters which were normally beyond human perception.

Secondly, we find in apocalyptic that Jewish version of the irrational element in religion which has a particularly vital period in late antiquity. It has often been pointed out that at this time in a variety of cultures we find a greater preoccupation with the dream, oracle and attempts to ascertain more directly the spiritual world. This being the case, we can discern in apocalyptic a symptom of the influence on Judaism of wider religious and spiritual currents from the Hellenistic world.

Thirdly, it is apparent that the visions of the apocalypses did provide an escape from the unacceptable realities which confronted Jews at the time. This was done in two ways. The visions which communicated divine oracles about the future hope confirmed the people in their belief and practice despite the horrors of the world around them and the lack of evidence of their fulfilment. Secondly, if we take seriously that dimension of apocalyptic which sees it being concerned with the heavenly world and divine mysteries, we may perceive how knowledge of this world and the secrets of it could so easily become an end in itself and detract from the issues confronting the people of God in this world. The mystical dimension of the apocalyptic literature must not be underplayed. The similarities between the apocalypses of Judaism and certain of the later gnostic texts illustrate this. While the radical otherworldliness of gnosticism is never found in Jewish literature, the seeds of it are surely to be found.

Fourthly, occasionally apocalyptic functioned as a spur to action and change in this world. In this utopian type we may discern the way in which apocalyptic fantasies impelled the Jewish fighters for freedom to take up arms against the Romans and in desperate straits to believe that God would come to their aid with legions of angels. We cannot be sure how much influence the Jewish apocalypses which are now extant had on those who fought for freedom from Rome (indeed it should be noted that the extant apocalypses are singularly devoid of injunctions to engage in an armed struggle), but we may be sure that something like the beliefs contained in them impelled the rash actions about which Josephus tells us in his account of the Jewish War.

Fifthly, while it is now becoming more widely recognised that the apocalyptic tradition did not completely disappear even from rabbinic Judaism, it does appear to have been the case that the literary genre apocalypse rapidly became obsolete after the first century AD in both Judaism and Christianity. While apocalyptic characteristics emerge in the Hekaloth literature, the apocalyptic genre finds its way into gnosticism, becomes linked with interest in hell and the after life, and emerges in Montanist piety in Asia Minor at the end of the second century AD. Clearly the apocalypse proved to be an inadequate and outmoded vehicle of the doctrinal concerns and material needs of the emerging church and rabbinic Judaism. The story of the demise of the apocalypse and its relationship to the wider social matrix is one which still waits to be written, though in view of the importance of it in the Second Temple period, it is one whose significance for the Jewish and Christian traditions may be quite large.

Finally, one other fact needs to be noted. The fact that we now possess Jewish tradition in written form indicates also something of its origin. While it is arguable that some of the Jewish pseudepigrapha with their evidence of ongoing additions and alterations could well have been oral traditions committed to writing only at a later stage, many of the pseudepigrapha bear all the hallmarks of literary works deliberately written for particular purposes. In saying this we are at once compelled to recognise that the task of writing such a work (or even committing traditions to writing) was not a task for the uneducated. Certainly it may have been carried out by the marginalised as the Dead Sea Scrolls indicate. Nevertheless the sophisticated and articulate are just as likely to have been marginalised as the poor, particularly if they were once in a position to influence affairs. All the evidence suggests that, however much the poor may have shared the outlook and ideas which are to be found in the literature which has come down to us, particularly with regard to the eschatological hope, we have in the literature now extant the views of those who were sophisticated enough to write down their beliefs and practices. In the Dead Sea Scrolls it is apparent that we have the ideology of a group whose origin at least was among some of the most self-consciously élite members of Israelite society, the priests. Nowhere more than in the case of the priesthood was there a concern to make sure that the power was kept in the hands of that élite. It was precisely because that power was now usurped by those who the Qumran group thought had no right to exercise it that they went out into the desert. So on the margin of society they were; but their separation was not because they were economically impoverished or socially disadvantaged. It was because they had lost the power which they considered to have been their right, and as a result were compelled to take a subordinate position. They were not interested in sharing that power or leading a revolution which would establish the fortunes of the whole of Israel. Their vision of the future centred on a restored Zion in which the Temple would once again be populated by righteous priests and be a place where proper sacrifices at the appropriate times could once again be offered in Israel.

Conclusion
It has to be recognised that analysis of the pseudepigrapha and the ideologies contained in them is only at a very preliminary stage.

Nevertheless if we want to pierce behind the veil of the isolated textual phenomena to ascertain more about the totality of that world from which they have emerged, it is imperative that the delicate task of matching ideology and culture is pursued to the full. Herein lies a fruitful way forward to greater appreciation of the social formation which gave birth to both primitive Christianity and rabbinic Judaism.

FOR FURTHER READING

L. Finkelstein, *The Pharisees*, Phildelphia 1946.

S. Freyne, *Galilee from Alexander the Great to Hadrian*, Notre Dame 1980.

P. D. Hanson, *The Dawn of Apocalyptic*, Philadelphia 1975.

J. Neusner, *From Politics to Piety*, Englewood Cliffs 1973.

G. Nickelsburg, 'Social Aspects of Palestinian Apocalypticism', in D. Hellholm, *Apocalypticism in the Mediterranean World and the Near East*, Tübingen 1983.

O. Ploeger, *Theocracy and Eschatology*, Oxford 1968.

D. Rössler, *Gesetz und Geschichte*, Neukirchen 1960.

C. Rowland, *Christian Origins*, London 1985.

M. Stone, *Scriptures Sects and Visions*, Oxford 1982.

4

THE RELIGION AND LIFE OF SECOND TEMPLE JUDAISM: THE EVIDENCE OF THE INTER-TESTAMENTAL LITERATURE

It is all too easy for the student to expect that when we speak of Judaism in the ancient world, we are speaking of a religious outlook with clearly defined beliefs and practices. Certainly it would have been possible for a pagan to distinguish a Jew from other members of his society. For example, the rite of circumcision and the observance of the weekly sabbath both attracted attention from pagan critics; but when it came to seeing differences of emphasis within Judaism, it was by no means as easy (e.g. Acts 18:15). That there were vast varieties of interpretation of the ancestral laws is apparent from the collection of writings which we designate the rabbinic corpus. While it may well be the case that the point of view represented here derives, more or less, from one particular wing of Judaism, there can be little doubt that even within the narrow confines of this perspective there emerged a vast array of differing interpretations.

Thus it is peculiarly difficult to write a systematic account of the beliefs and practices of the inter-testamental literature as if they represented an easily systematised and monolithic unity. It is essential to recognise this point. If we do, and acknowledge the diversity of literary type and theological emphasis, we may than be in a position to discern the *general outlines* of belief and practice which merge here. If we write a systematic account of Jewish theology, we shall find immediately that many differing emphases will have to be excluded in favour of the overall presentation. That said, we can make the following comments about the basis of Jewish life and thought which is to be found in this literature.

191

1. MAIN FEATURES OF SECOND TEMPLE JUDAISM

The Torah

The first and most obvious thing to say about the Jewish theology presupposed by this literature is the acceptance of the Torah as the normative basis for all Jewish life and thought. In addition, we may suppose that at this time most groups regarded as authoritative the prophetic writings of the canon as well as some other writings. Thus from the Exile onwards it is apparent that there was gradually emerging a religion focused on a body of sacred scripture. The consequence of this was the need for interpretation. All the extra-canonical Jewish literature bears witness to the inspiration of a body of sacred literature as the explicit and implicit interpretations of this literature indicates. The common ground ends there, however. As soon as it became necessary to interpret the meaning of the text, there arose that variety of interpretation which is so characteristic of the use of tradition. Herein lies one of the reasons for sectarianism in Judaism. While it may be true that in certain areas there was a considerable degree of common belief and practice (e.g. with regard to the calendar, observance of the sabbath and the practice of circumcision) in most areas of life the scriptures offered the opportunity for dispute and hostility between differing interpretative traditions.

Within the scriptures much is made of God's special relationship with his people. God had called Abraham, the father of the Jewish nation, from his home in Mesopotamia and had made of him a mighty nation. The story of these origins of the nation are told in the pages of the Torah. That agreement or covenant between God and Abraham was reaffirmed at several points in Israel's history, particularly, so the traditions assert, after Israel had been delivered from its bondage in Egypt. The story of the covenant between God and the people centred on the Exodus experiences and the demands of God revealed to Moses at Sinai. The centrality of the covenant in Jewish literature is a point which needs to be stressed. Those who come to the rabbinic literature afresh may feel that the covenant ideology is completely lacking in this material. The preoccupation with legal minutiae may seem to indicate an abandonment of these ideas: the memory of the deliverance of God and his gracious acts on behalf of his people and the response of the people to those gracious acts. It would be mistaken to suppose that lack of reference to the covenant and the mighty acts which undergird it should be taken to indicate a diminution of its importance, as E. P. Sanders has rightly pointed out. What we find in the rabbinic legal traditions is the product of the glad response of the people of God to the story of God's gracious dealings with his people. At the heart of the rabbinic halakah is the conviction that the appropriate response of God's people is to do all in its power to ensure the fulfilment of what God requires both in avoiding transgression and attempting to specify what is necessary when the scriptures are unclear or silent.

The Cult

Like the conviction about election, the regulations for the worship of God in the cult are prominent within the tradition in the Torah. There was probably not a group in the first century which did not look to the Temple or the traditions connected with it as an inspiration. It is apparent that for all Jews the Temple in Jerusalem was a focus for Jewish religion. According to Deuteronomy 12, God had commanded that worship had to be centred in one shrine, the Temple in Jerusalem. Those who lived outside Palestine still looked to Jerusalem (Daniel 6:10) and were concerned if there were any threats to its sanctity. Even those groups who were most hostile to the Temple did not reject the type of religious activity it stood for (which was after all laid down in the Torah). Thus the community which produced the Dead Sea Scrolls seems to have been implacably opposed to the priestly regime which ran the Temple. In reaction to this they seem to have forsaken society in Jerusalem and set up a community on the banks of the Dead Sea, (just as in the second century BC Onias set up a rival cultic centre at Leontopolis in Egypt). While the rival party was in control of the Temple, the community interpreted its own life as a sacrificial community (IQS 8 cf. Romans 12:1 and 1 Corinthians 3:16). But this was a temporary expedient. It looked forward to a time when the Temple would be organised according to the community's view of orthopraxy.

Even after the destruction of the Temple in AD 70 the hope was kept alive of its rebuilding. This may not seem so surprising after the First Revolt but that hope was one which existed after the devastation caused by Bar Kochba's revolt in AD 132–5. Thus we find that not only in the ancient Jewish prayer (the Tefillah) is there a prayer for the rebuilding of the Temple, but that in the earliest collection of rabbinic legal material, the Mishnah, there is included a tractate (Middoth) which offers an inventory of the measurements of the Temple. While it may well be concluded that this was there for sentimental or even antiquarian interest, it is more likely that this is an accurate reflection of the central place which the Temple had in the thoughts of most Jews of the time.

The Future Hope

The other area of Jewish piety also has its origins in the Torah (e.g. Deuteronomy 18:15ff.; Numbers 29:17ff.) but received its impetus from the passages dealing with it in the writings of the prophets: the future hope. It is in certain of the non-canonical writings that we find the most extended versions of this hope, thought it emerges quite clearly in rabbinic literature also (e.g. b. Sanhedrin 95a ff.). It cannot be said that this is evident in all the material at our disposal; some of it has hardly anything to say about the subject at all. Absence of such material should not be taken to indicate that there was a split in ancient Judaism about the importance of the future hope. That there were differences of opinion about it cannot be doubted. But what is likely is that these differences of opinion do not reflect an acceptance of this doctrine by one group and rejection by another but *differences of emphasis with regard to it*. For all Jews the future hope was an article of faith, but it was not for all an impetus for action and a present influence on attitudes. While specific details of the future hope differed, what does appear to have been the case is that without exception round about the beginning of the Christian era, the future hope was very much centred on this world. That is not to deny that in some passages we have evidence of a doctrine of a future life in another world (perhaps as a temporary phenomenon) but such beliefs are not to be found to exclude the hope for the fulfilment of the divine promises in this world. It was that kind of eschatological climate which was abroad in the first century AD and in which the primitive Christian movement grew up.

Summary

To summarise the main features of Judaism of the Second Temple in this way must not blind us to the variety of nuance and emphasis, often of a profoundly significant kind, which characterised the various groups and led to varying degrees of hostility and separation between them. The last century of Second Temple Judaism might best be characterised as a situation in which various religious groups co-existed with varying degrees of tolerance. Neither orthodoxy nor orthopraxy can be spoken of at this stage and the possibility of wide parameters both of belief and practice was a fact of life.

FOR FURTHER READING

S. Safrai and M. Stern, *The Jewish people in the First Christian Century*, Assen 1974.

E. Schuerer, op. cit., especially vol. 2.

2. EXCLUSIVENESS AND HOLINESS

The Question of Orthodoxy

There is evidence that Judaism was in a better position to draw the lines between 'orthodox' and others more carefully after the fall of the Second Temple, so that deviant positions which were deemed a threat to the interpretation of Jewish tradition as laid down by the sages at Jamnia or Yavneh could be excluded. Yet such a process should not conceal the fact that variation and difference of opinion is something which is allowed for even within the rabbinic sources. Within the boundaries prescribed by the authority given to the recognised teacher we find a degree of flexibility. Yet such flexibility is denied to those who find themselves outside this charmed circle. The holders of deviant beliefs who found themselves excluded would not have their views represented in the traditions of the group, except in so far as they offered a foil to the expression of the proper opinion on an issue. Inevitably the question was raised whether those who held divergent opinions had any part in the promise made to the covenant people. There seems to be little doubt that the members of the Qumran community, as their views are represented in the Dead Sea Scrolls, came very close to regarding Jews who did not subscribe to their way of thinking as apostates and subject to the judgement of God. Indeed, even transgression by a member against the strict rules of the community might lead to expulsion from the community and a life of spiritual deprivation and uncertainty (e.g. IQS 7.1).

If Mishnah Sanhedrin 10:1 is to be believed, the issue of the ultimate salvation of Jews did not depend on membership of a pharisaic haburah, but assent to some very basic propositions:

All Israelites have a share in the world to come, for it is written, Thy people also shall be righteous, they shall inherit the land for ever; the branch of my planting, the work of my hands that I may be glorified. And these are they that have no share in the world to come: he that says that there is no resurrection in the dead prescribed in the Law, and he that says that the Law is not from heaven, and an Epicurean. R. Akiba says: Also he that reads heretical books, or that utters charms over a wound.

The major limitation on entry into the world to come in the eyes of the rabbis, therefore, concerns one's attitude to the Torah and one particular interpretation of it. The exclusion of those who deny that the Law is from heaven probably refers to those antinomian gnostics who deny that the origin of the Torah lies with the supreme divine or to those who maintained that the oral interpretation of Torah was a human contribution, and the reference to the resurrection from the dead is a rejection of the Sadducean approach (cf. Acts 23:2). Nothing whatever, it may be noted, is said in this passage about the position of the ordinary Jew (*am-ha-aretz*). There are many derogatory references to this group in the rabbinic texts, but it would be wrong to suppose that such references necessarily imply exclusion from the righteous community. Indeed, the evidence such as it is would lead us to the conclusion that the rabbinic tradition took a very open-minded approach to the question of salvation. Membership of the pharisaic fellowship (*haburoth*) may well have guaranteed that the practice of holiness which God demanded of his people was fulfilled, but refusal to attend to this obligation was not of itself a reason for exclusion from the eschatological people of God. Yet in the decades after 70 it became necessary to delineate precisely between those in and those out. Already in M. San. 10 we see Akiba adding a reference to the reading of heretical books. When taken in conjunction with the curse on the minim (= heretics) in the edictions (*Shemoneh Esreh*), this indicates how it became necessary to confine the range of opinion which would be regarded as acceptable if one wanted to be a community rabbi.

Varieties of Jewish Identity
In speaking of the growth of sectarianism, therefore, one must bear in mind the fact that the various groups characterised their own identity in very different ways.

The reasons for this are not difficult to seek. The nature of Jewish religion, centred as it was on the written word, meant that interpretation of that sacred corpus of writings had become both a unifying and dividing factor for Judaism. Whereas all acknowledged the supremacy of the Torah, the interpretation of the meaning of the various demands contained within these texts was by no means unambiguous and the variety of interpretations offered was an inevitable cause of friction and sectarian grouping. Thus, while for the pharisees it was possible to see how the texts within the Torah could be made to yield evidence about the doctrine of the resurrection from the dead, such sentiments were certainly not shared by the Sadducees who would have considered much of the pharisaic justification of this belief on the basis of the Torah alone little better than special pleading (Acts 23:6). Some indication of the way in which the doctrine of the resurrection was supported from the Torah can be gleaned from Jesus' debate with the Sadducees in Mark 12:26. It is not our concern at this point to adjudicate between the two interpretations. What it does indicate is that without a rigorously applied control by some central body, it would be impossible to achieve any kind of uniformity in belief and practice. This was only likely within the smaller groups whose discipline could be applied more easily on its members.

The Question of Holiness
Preoccupation with boundaries between authentic devotees and those whose position seems more dubious is a feature of many, if not most, religious groups. Certainly it was true of Judaism. The need to mark a separation between those inside and those outside was an issue of considerable significance because holiness was such a central feature of Judaism. The basic documents of the Jewish religion showed a great concern with the demand of God to reflect his holiness: 'You shall be holy, even as I am holy' (Leviticus 19:2). Indeed, it could be argued that this preoccupation with holiness and the practical outworking of this demand forms one of the central features of religious debate in our period. How was Israel to maintain its identity as a nation precious to God? How were those Jews who regularly came into contact with the profane, whether through their work or their normal pattern of social intercourse, to seek to apply this rigorous demand? The answers to such questions were many and varied. On the one hand we find that the Dead Sea community concerned itself with the demand to be holy by removing its whole existence from the defilements which it saw going on even among fellow Jews into a place of seclusion where the risk of offence to the all holy God was minimised. On the other hand the Pharisees, equally concerned as they were about the need to preserve Israel as a holy nation, had before them a vision of a society which did not allow them to live with ideals only but to confront realities, which meant that those who would wish to take seriously the demands of God had also to make a living and to exist in a world where there

were considerable obstacles to the easy fulfilment of the divine
demands.

Holiness at Qumran
The discoveries in caves near the Dead Sea just after the Second
World War have certainly had a profound effect on our understanding of Judaism. The discoveries revealed the existence of a
strict community, in all likelihood living in the buildings at Khirbet
Qumran, whose communal life manifested a fanatical zeal for holiness. From the Scrolls themselves we get the impression of a group
whose priestly element is dominant. Not only does the priestly
messiah have precedence at the eschaton (IQSa) but the priests
have a particularly important place within the community and its
hierarchy. The priestly background of the group had a profound
effect on its theology. As in the New Testament we find that cultic
terms are spiritualised and applied to the life of the community (e.g.
IQS 9). What is more, the community clearly thought of its pattern
of life as a reflection of the heavenly order (IQS 2). The organisation
of the Community thus reflects the eternal pattern of things in
heaven. Any move away from his pattern will be an offence against
God who has planned things in such a way. The establishment of
such a pattern in the holy community and the correct fulfilment of
the everlasting design enabled the community to be an extension of
the heavenly world and to share the lot of the holy ones (IQS 11
cf. 1 QH 3.20). It is difficult to resist the conclusion that some
cultic influence is at work here. The priest who by virtue of his
office came into the closest possible contact in the shrine with
the divine presence on earth was particularly privileged. What the
Qumran community claims for itself is akin to the priestly privilege.
Its common life manifests that same kind of affinity with the holy
God vouchsafed to the priests. Inevitably such a belief depended on
the assumption that the common life must be free from any defile-
ment which might infringe the celestial character of their existence.
Complete separation is an understandable concomitant of such a
belief. Any contact with a profane world might affect the privilege
of the community to share in the lot of the holy ones and all possible
attempts had to be made to guard against such a possibility.

Pharisaism
A similar concern with holiness undergirds the concerns of pharisiasm and the later rabbinic tradition. Indeed, it can be said with
some degree of conviction that pharisaism was concerned to democ-
ratise the priestly demands for holiness and apply them to the whole

of the people of God. The vision of pharisiasm was of a holy nation, a priesthood of *all* believers in which all the people stood before God, fulfilling the commandment 'You shall be holy, even as I am holy'. Unlike the Qumran community, however, the Pharisees achieved this holiness not by complete separation from the world but by ensuring that those who sought such holiness managed to avoid unnecessary contact with the profane in their normal existence. The means of achieving this goal was to set up a fence around the Torah, to guarantee that there was no possibility of accidental infringement of the demands of the Torah. Also, it became necessary to specify exactly what constituted an infringement against the rules of holiness, so that in every possible situation the righteous man might know what was and what was not permissible for him. The rabbinic *halakah* manifests this minute concern with practical problems confronting an approach to holiness which takes seriously the need for a man to engage in ordinary activity and maintain the demands of the Torah. The complexities of business and normal existence, when seen in the light of the stringent demands of the Torah, required a sensitive and detailed explanation which might enable a complete understanding of the impact of the divine demands on the vagaries of human existence. It is easy to misunderstand the function of the *halakah* and to assume that it signified a retreat from the insights of the Torah to the bondage of a religion of works. Nothing could be further from the truth. However academic its discussion might have been, the issues which occupy the attention of the rabbis are those which might confront the Jew in his attempt to put into practice the commandments of God. It is indicative of the underlying concern of the *halakah* that it took seriously the need to resist the temptation to remain content with repetition of the written word, so that a move towards the immediate concerns of the individual interacting with the biblical prescriptions might yield a mode of obedience which would be appropriate to the changed circumstances of the observers of the commandments.

Holiness in the New Testament
The preoccupation with holiness was something which was just as important for early Christian theology as it was for contemporary Judaism. It has often been pointed out that Paul's favourite title for individual Christians is *hagioi*, holy ones, or saints (1 Corinthians 1:2; 6:11; Hebrews 10:22; Revelation 1:6; 1 Peter 2:5, 9). To be holy is one of the consequences of the new life in Christ which enabled the believer to enter that new relationship with God which the coming of Jesus Christ made possible. The means whereby this

holiness was extended to the Gentiles as well as the Jews and the ways in which it could be maintained within the life of the Christian community and in dealings with those who were outside the Church is one of the major concerns of the Pauline correspondence. The concept of a holy people offering the spiritual sacrifice of their lives before God (Romans 12:1) is one which is deeply rooted in Pauline thought. For Paul, holiness was the characteristic of every Christian. To be in Christ meant possession of the Spirit (Romans 8:9), and that Spirit was a holy Spirit (Romans 1:3). The Christians who were indwelt by the Spirit were themselves a living temple, a holy place where God's holy presence, the Holy Spirit, dwelt (1 Corinthians 3:16; 6:19).

Summary

In Pharisaism, the Dead Sea Scrolls and early Christianity, the concern to have a relationship with the holy God meant the extension of cultic language into the sphere of individual or community life. The God whose presence dwelt in the most holy place, into which nothing defiled could enter, was believed by all three groups to be a present reality in their own experience. The book of Revelation looks forward to the dwelling of the all holy God in the new Jerusalem, itself modelled on the pattern of the Temple. What we see happening is an extension of that area of holiness from the Temple to the group and in some cases the individual. There is what one recent writer has termed a sacred space around the individual or the group in which the divine holiness is manifested.

3. APOCALYPTIC: THE QUEST FOR HIGHER WISDOM THROUGH REVELATION

Clarifying the Issues

Much has been written in the last decade or so on the subject of apocalyptic in Judaism and Christianity at the beginning of the Christian era. Of course, one would not need to know much about contemporary scholarly debate to realise that the word 'apocalyptic' has passed into common parlance and can often be found in discussions of contemporary, economic, social and political affairs.

There has been much confusion in the discussion of apocalyptic, in particular its relationship to eschatology. In writing on both subjects it can appear that the two are closely related and can be used virtually interchangably. In writing on Paul's doctrine, for example, J. C. Beker can speak of Paul's apocalyptic gospel. In speaking as he does, he finds a close link between apocalyptic and eschatology but wants to distinguish the former from the latter:

> My reasons for using apocalyptic are two-fold: first of all the term apocalyptic guards against the multivalent and often chaotic use of the concept eschatology in modern times. Eschatology refers to last things, but in modern use last things often refers not to things that come at the end of a series but to things that are final and ultimate. In other words the use of the term apocalyptic clarifies the future – temporal character of Paul's gospel. Second, apocalyptic denotes an end-time occurrence that is both cosmic, universal and definitive. Paul expects the future to be an apocalyptic closure-event in time and space embracing the whole of God's created order. Thus the term 'apocalyptic' refers more clearly than the general term 'eschatology' to the specificity of the end-time occurrence.

In this quotation it is apparent that in using the terms apocalyptic and eschatology we are dealing with roughly equivalent subjects of discourse. This view is widespread and found in many of the most influential text-books.

The fact that apocalyptic can signify to most of us a particular set of categories, even when we know little about the religious origins of the word, may suggest that those who have written on the place of apocalyptic in antiquity are also likely to take a unified approach in their discussions of the subject. But this is far from being the case. Indeed, in one of the most frequently read books on the subject, the German professor, Klaus Koch, summarised the bewilderment which people felt in dealing with apocalyptic. But if the connections are so easily made by us all between certain contemporary affairs and the descriptions in the book of Revelation, why is it that there is a sense of bewilderment and confusion as a result of contemporary discussion? There are three reasons which spring to mind, which may go some way towards explaining why there is the sense of bewilderment.

Since the end of the last century, commentators on early Christian doctrine have had to reckon with the possibility of the pervasive influence on early Christianity of Jewish beliefs derived from the apocalypses concerning the hope for the future. Few would deny that the hope for a glorious new age in which sorrow and sighing would flee away, loosely referred to as eschatology, has a significant part to play either explicitly or implicitly in the presentation of the early Christian message. What is more, in the pages of the New

Testament it is evident that many Christians thought that the arrival of this new age was imminent (e.g. Mark 9:1; Revelation 22:20). While admitting that the word 'eschatology' itself has been, and continues to be, a source of confusion, the relationship between apocalyptic and eschatology is frequently left unexplained. Several distinguished scholars have used the word 'apocalyptic' to describe the beliefs concerning the arrival of a new age and see apocalyptic merely as a form of eschatology. This is an area of confusion where some clarification is needed both with regard to the antecedents of the apocalyptic movement and the best way of characterising it.

Origins

In the discussion of apocalyptic in the last thirty years or so, there has been a significant difference of opinion about its origins. Two accounts of its background call for some consideration, as they demonstrate the way in which assumptions are made about its character and place in the Biblical tradition.

On the one hand (and this view is the majority opinion at present) there are those who consider that apocalyptic is the successor to the prophetic movement, and particularly to the future of hope of the prophets. The concern with human history and the vindication of Israel's hopes is said to represent the formulation of the prophetic hope in the changed circumstances of another age. Those who take this line (among them may be named Rowley, Russell and Hanson) all stress the close links with prophecy but also point out the subtle change which has taken place in the form of that hope in apocalyptic. H. H. Rowley's often quoted contrast between the future hope in the prophets and in apocalyptic literature, sums up this approach:

> The prophets foretold the future that should arise out of the present, while the apocalyptists foretold the future that should break into the present . . .

This point of view has been very influential, because it has seemed to many that in the apocalyptic literature written round about the beginning of the Christian era, the future hope has been placed on another plane. Its stress from first to last is on the supernatural and other-worldly, just as in Revelation 21 the seer looks forward to a new heaven and new earth with the old creation having passed away.

While this view has been most influential, it has not gone unchallenged. Somewhat surprisingly, in view of the contents of the books concerned, it has been suggested that it is the Wisdom tradition of the Old Testament with its interest in understanding the cosmos

and the ways of the world which was the real antecedent of apocalyptic, and not the prophetic movement. In his Old Testament
Theology, the distinguished German interpreter Gerhard von Rad
(whose views are discussed by Koch), argued that it is in the
Wisdom tradition that we must look for the origin of apocalyptic.
We noted some points of contact between the apocalypses and the
Wisdom books, particularly the fact that apocalyptic is concerned
with knowledge, not only of the age to come but also things in
heaven and the mysteries of human existence. Such a preoccupation
seems to be akin to features of the wisdom literature. Von Rad's
interpretation has met with severe criticism, however. It has been
pointed out that the concern with the destiny of Israel, so evident
in parts of certain apocalypses, is hardly to be found in works like
Ecclesiastes and Ecclesiasticus, both of which seem to discourage
such speculative activity. In one respect, however, von Rad's suggestion has been taken up and refined. Rather than concentrating on
Proverbs and Ecclesiastes, with their practical wisdom applicable to
everyday life, it has been suggested that we should note that the
activities of certain wise men in antiquity were not at all dissimilar
from the concerns of the writers of the apocalypses. This is 'Mantic
Wisdom', which includes the interpretation of dreams, oracles,
astrology and the ability to divine mysteries concerning future
events. There is some trace of the role of such figures in the Old
Testament, e.g., in the Joseph stories in Genesis, but particularly
in the stories about Daniel, the Jewish seer who interprets the
dreams of Nebuchadnezzar and is regarded as a sage superior to all
those in the King's court. Dreams, visions and the like are all typical
features of the apocalypses, and it is now recognised that this aspect
of the Wisdom tradition may indeed provide an important contribution to our understanding of apocalyptic origins. It will be seen
how very different these two approaches to apocalyptic are: on the
one hand we have a description of it as a phenomenon whose primary
concern is with the future, derived from the prophetic hope, and
on the other we find an account of it which concentrates on its quest
for knowledge in its totality, of which interest in the future is only
a part, however significant.

Defining Terms
It will have been noted that I have used the word apocalyptic in
two ways. Besides using it as an adjective in phrases like 'apocalyptic
literature', apocalyptic or as it is sometimes referred to now, apocalypticism, is very frequently used to describe a cluster of ideas found
in Jewish texts written round about the beginning of the Christian

era. Some of these ideas, but by no means all, are to be found in apocalypses. Thus the word 'apocalyptic' is used to speak of a particular movement of thought with clearly defined characteristics, some of which may be said to be similar to certain ideas found in the book of Revelation.

In all discussions of apocalyptic, a clear distinction is made between apocalyptic (or apocalypticism) and the apocalypse. The latter is a particular literary type found in the literature of ancient Judaism, which is characterised by its claims to offer visions or other disclosures of divine mysteries concerning a variety of subjects. Usually such information is given to a Biblical hero like Enoch, Abraham, Isaiah or Ezra, so that pseudonymity is a characteristic of these writings. The apocalypse, of which the books of Daniel and Revelation are the two canonical examples, is to be distinguished from apocalyptic, which is usually viewed as a cluster of mainly eschatological ideas which impinged generally on the theology of Judaism. The distinction between the apocalypse and apocalyptic is an important one, as it is presupposed in most modern discussions. It must be recognised that there is not necessarily any overlap between the apocalypse and apocalyptic. Apocalyptic may be found in a variety of texts which are not revelatory in form. Indeed, in the opinion of some, the apocalypses themselves are not the best examples of apocalyptic. So it can be seen that in using the word, we have to exercise a great deal of care. In the New Testament, the Book of Revelation is an obvious example of an apocalypse. But many would argue that passages like Mark 13, when Jesus speaks of the future, I Thessalonians 4:16 and the like, are examples of apocalyptic, with their descriptions of the irruption of the Redeemer in to history, and, in the case of Mark 13, the cosmic catastrophes which must precede the coming of the heavenly Son of Man.

The distinction between apocalyptic and the apocalypse has been a source of exasperation to several recent commentators. One writer, whose knowledge of the literature is paralleled by very few, Michael Stone, has asked whether we should perhaps abandon the use of the word apocalyptic altogether, as its continued use will, he believes, confuse our discussions. That may be an extreme measure. But surely he is right to point out that something is going amiss when the critical examination of the Jewish and Christian apocalypses reveals that the apocalypses themselves contain very little of what is considered to be characteristic of apocalyptic thought, as usually defined. He is also right to say that unless we try to formulate another definition of the essence of apocalyptic which does justice to the apocalypses and their contents, the continued use of the word is going to remain ambiguous and misleading.

Apocalyptic as a Type of Eschatology

But what is the cluster of ideas labelled apocalyptic which has just been discussed? One of the most influential attempts to define apocalyptic has been that by Philip Vielhauer in his article on apocalyptic in the second volume of Hennecke's *New Testament Apocrypha*. Drawing on views which have been widely held for a long time, he asserts that the main interest of apocalyptic does not lie in cosmology but in eschatology:

> We may designate apocalyptic as a special expression of the Jewish eschatology which existed alongside the national eschatology represented by the rabbis. It is linked with the latter by many ideas, but is differentiated from it by a quite different understanding of God, the world, and man.

While he recognises that the world of ideas is far from uniform, he lists the following as characteristic features:

> (i) a contrast between the present age, which is perishable and temporary, and a new age, which is still to come, and which is imperishable and eternal; (ii) a belief that the new age is of a transcendent kind, which breaks in from beyond through divine intervention and without human activity; (iii) a wider concern than merely the destiny of Israel; (iv) an interest in the totality of world history; (v) the belief that God has foreordained everything and that the history of the world has been divided into epochs; and finally, (vi) an imminent expectation that the present unsatisfactory state of affairs will only be short lived.

Two things stand out in his treatment of apocalyptic: the belief that the future hope of a particular kind, viz. transcendent eschatology, is the key to our understanding of the thought-world of apocalyptic, and that there is sufficient cohesion in the ideas contained in the apocalypses to distil from them an outline of the essential features of apocalyptic.

Apocalyptic: Divine Wisdom through Revelation

Throughout his presentation, and many others like it, there runs a consistent thread which asserts that there existed in Judaism two types of future hope: a national eschatology found principally in the rabbinic texts, and other-worldly eschatology found principally in the apocalypses. The evidence from the apocalypses themselves however, indicates that such a dichotomy cannot be easily substantiated. Apart from a handful of passages which are always cited as examples of other-worldly eschatology, the doctrine of the future hope as it is found in the apocalypses seems to be remarkably consistent with the expectation found in other Jewish sources. Then, the selection of material which is used to offer the outline of the apocalyptic, such as is found in Vielhauer's essay, is not representative of the material in the apocalypses as a whole but is built up on the basis of several key passages. This has been pointed out by several commentators. *If* the point of departure from our understanding of the pattern of thought which we call apocalyptic, is the apocalypses, and *all* the apocalypses, not just Daniel and Revelation, then we shall have to admit that Vielhauer's description of apocalyptic is inadequate as a distillation of the essence of these works. Most current definitions of apocalyptic fail to do justice to the variety of material in the apocalypses and frequently work with a view of apocalyptic which is only loosely related to the apocalypses. It is as a result of this that apocalyptic can be seen as an ideology which may in fact have little or nothing to do with the apocalypses. The beliefs which we have outlined as being characteristic of apocalyptic can certainly be found scattered around various pieces of Jewish literature written round about the beginning of the Christian era. It must be said, however, that only a few texts are made to bear the brunt of supporting the existence of the distinct religious phenomenon, pieced together as it is from a wide variety of works from different backgrounds and dates and of differing literary types. If there is any unifying principle at all, it is that many of the features in Vielhauer's definition correspond with some concepts found in the Book of Revelation (though in the case of Revelation also, justice is not done to its main theme if we concentrate solely on eschatological matters).

The Revelation of John

In the space available it is impossible to look at Revelation as a whole and subject its various parts to examination. But it seems to me that we are able to understand its disparate elements if we see the underlying theme to be one which derives from the initial statement 'The Revelation of Jesus Christ' (Revelation 1:1) rather than from the eschatological message which runs through much of the rest of the book. Revelation is not merely an eschatological tract satisfying the curiosity of those who wanted to know what would happen in the future. Though it contains much teaching about 'What must happen after this' its purpose is to reveal *something hidden* which will enable the readers to view their present situation from a completely different perspective. When seen in this way, the significance of many of the visions in the Apocalypse fall into place: the Letters to the Churches offer an assessment of their churches' worth from a heavenly perspective; the vision of the divine throne-room in Revelation 4 enables the churches to recognise the dominion of their God; in Revelation 5, the death and exaltation of Christ is shown to mark the inauguration of the new age; and in chapters 13 and 17 the true identity of the Roman emperors and the City of Rome is divulged. Revelation is a text which seeks to summon to repentance and to give reassurance by showing – by means of direct revelation from God – that there is a heavenly dimension to exist-ence, which could be, and was being, ignored by the churches of Asia Minor.

The Meaning of Apocalyptic

Looked at in this light we can begin to see why Martin Hengel should have suggested that apocalyptic might be better understood as part of a much wider religious phenomenon in late antiquity; what he called 'higher wisdom through revelation'. He points to many parallels between the quest for knowledge through revelation in the apocalypses and non-Jewish material, as well as stressing the widespread trend in antiquity towards the irrational and the mysterious, so that revelation of what was hidden with God became an indispensable means of giving meaning and purpose to human existence.

If we think of apocalyptic in this way, we shall be able to see now the claim of the apocalypses to reveal mysteries about the future, the movements of the stars, the heavenly dwelling of God, angelology, the course of human history and the mystery of the human plight *all* fall within the category of the mysteries which can only be solved by higher wisdom through revelation. Such a quest makes sense of the piety manifested in the apocalypses, *including* the Book of Revelation. Indeed, the impact of the message of the latter depends very much on its claim to be a direct revelation from heaven, rather than the mere opinion of humankind.

Apocalyptic and Other Religious Currents

If such an approach to apocalyptic is accepted, it becomes much easier to understand the relationship between apocalyptic and other religious currents at the period. Two in particular call for mention:

gnosticism and early Jewish mysticism. Thirty years ago Professor C. K. Barrett made the following perceptive comment:

> The secrets in which apocalyptic deal are not simply secrets of the future; they include secrets of the present state of the heavenly world. . . . The contrast between this world and the other heavenly world is often loosely described as Platonic and to be quite foreign to Judaism; but this is not so. It is difficult to draw a sharp line between apocalyptic and gnosticism – a fact with large consequences.

Professor Barrett here is persuading us to move away from a view of apocalyptic which concentrates solely on eschatology to one which recognises its preoccupation with the world above and its secrets. When von Rad called apocalyptic 'a great cosmological gnosis', he was not far from the mark in indicating the similarity of apocalyptic to gnostic religion, with its revealed knowledge of God and the origin and destiny of man, by means of which an individual could gain redemption. The presence of apocalypses among the gnostic texts discovered at Nag Hammadi adds force to the arguments of those who see a link between the two. As far as one can see, apocalyptic did not reach a stage where its revelation was of itself salvific, but at times it comes very close to being so.

The second area which has attracted much attention recently, is the subject of early Jewish mysticism. Not only have the links between it and apocalyptic been suggested, but also exploration of the contribution of it to the understanding of the New Testament is beginning to gain momentum. There has been a tendency to suppose that the religion of the rabbis was far removed from that of the apocalyptists. The paucity of references to eschatological matters in early rabbinic literature should not lead us to suppose, however, that the rabbis were not interested in the higher wisdom. The rabbinic material is not easy to evaluate, but what can be said is that during the period of the Second Temple and immediately after its destruction in AD 70, there existed a mystical tradition among several prominent rabbis which was based on the startling description of the throne-chariot in the first chapter of Ezekiel and the account of Creation in Genesis 1. It is likely that some of the rabbis who occupied themselves in the study of texts like Ezekiel 1 actually experienced esctatic ascents to heaven to behold the divine throne-chariot similar to that described by John in Revelation 4. While it has to be said that there still much uncertainty on this subject, there can be little doubt that the study of the relationship between rabbinic mysticism and apocalyptic is an area where study is likely to bear much fruit in the future for our understanding of Judaism in antiquity.

Apocalyptic and Christianity
But where does early Christianity fit into this world of thought? Once we turn to the New Testament we have to ask ourselves which writings or passages indicate affinity with apocalyptic. In the past the answer has quickly been given by referring to Mark 13 and 1 Thessalonians 4:16, but such passages fall into the category of apocalyptic only if we see it primarily as a matter of a particular type of eschatology. It is true that scholars like Ernst Käsemann, who have argued that apocalyptic was the cornerstone of early Christian theology, mean by that the imminent expectation of the irruption of God into the present world-order to establish a kingdom of a transcendent kind. Thus talk of apocalyptic in early Christianity is usually limited to discussion of eschatological material. If however we separate apocalyptic from the future hope and characterise it as primarily concerned with higher wisdom through revelation, does this mean that apocalyptic was not after all a component of early Christian belief? To attempt to answer this question I want to explore two areas briefly : a) accounts of visions and revelations in the New Testament, and b) the impact of apocalyptic thought, particularly the cosmological dimension in New Testament theology and the relationship between apocalyptic and christology.

Visions and Revelations
In many strands of the New Testament, reference is made to the importance of visions and revelations. While due account must be taken of the fact that in the apocalyptic literature, these visions are pseudonymously attributed to a Biblical figure, there can be no denying the affinities which exist between the form and content of the visionary reports in the New Testament and those found in the apocalypses. Take the accounts of Jesus' baptism and the conversion of Paul for example. In the former, we have, particularly in its Marcan form, the personal vision reminiscent of the apocalypses and the call-visions of the prophets, and in the reference to the open heaven, a typical feature of visionary accounts. Whatever our views may be about the authenticity of this account, it stands at the beginning of Mark's gospel as the decisive moment when Jesus of Nazareth was called by God and anointed with the Spirit to preach the good news of the Kingdom of God. Similarly, at the start of Paul's ministry as an apostle of Jesus Christ there stands the

Damascus experience. Galatians 1:12 and 16 indicate that Paul felt impelled to describe his call in language derived from the prophetic commissions of the Old Testament (Jeremiah 1:5 and Isaiah 49:1) and, what is more, to use words which speak of the disclosure or revelation of God's Son to him: 'For I did not receive the gospel from man, nor was I taught it, but it came through a revelation of Jesus Christ' (1:12); 'God was pleased to reveal his son to me, in order that I might preach him among the Gentiles' (1:16). We may not want to assert that Paul, like his rabbinic contemporaries, was meditating on the first chapter of Ezekiel when he had his vision of the risen Christ, but it is difficult to ignore the links which exist between the account of Paul's conversion and the visions in the apocalypses. Such a connection is also apparent in the tantalisingly brief account he gives of visions and revelations in 2 Corinthians 12:2ff.:

But I will go on to visions and revelations of the Lord. I know a man in Christ who fourteen years ago was caught up to the third heaven – whether in the body or out of the body, I do not know, God knows. And I know that this man was caught up to Paradise – whether in the body or out of the body, I do not know, God knows, and he heard things which cannot be told, which man may not utter.

Here are all the hallmarks of the apocalyptic literature – the heavenly ascent, the secret revelatory pronouncement and a cosmology in which the heavenly world is divided up into different compartments. The passage presents us with clear evidence of the place which apocalyptic categories continued to play within the Apostle's spirituality.

Elsewhere in the New Testament it is specifically the account of Luke on the origins of the church which has most of the accounts of visions. Even allowing for Luke's special interest in the divine guidance of the church and its mission, the vision of the tongues of fire at Pentecost, the martyr Stephen's vision of the heavenly Son of Man, the decisive vision of the sheet descending from heaven which preceded Peter's preaching to Cornelius, and the thrice told account of Paul's conversion, all indicate to us the importance which Luke attached to visions and revelations in the life of the early church. Among other passages which might be considered, special mention should be made of the fact that the polemic of Paul against false teachers at Colossae indicates that they may have had an interest in visions, specifically of the activity of the angels in heaven

(2:18). Of course, the story of the extent of such influence does not end with the New Testament. Outside the New Testament, figures like Elchesai, Cerinthus and the Shepherd of Hermas as well as the Montanus movement may be mentioned.

It would however, be a mistake to confine the influence of apocalyptic to accounts of visions and revelations only. Obviously related to them are the beliefs which abound in the New Testament that with the return of the prophetic spirit, God was communicating to his people through his prophets, inspiring them with the tongues of angels and revealing mysteries through the Spirit which had long been hidden. Here we have a pattern of beliefs which has clear affinities with that quest for higher wisdom through revelation which was characteristic of apocalyptic.

Apocalyptic Cosmology
But let us turn briefly to other areas, namely the apocalyptic cosmology, and the relationship between the quest for authentic revelation of God and the revelation of God in Christ.

In 2 Corinthians 12:2ff. we have already seen that Paul speaks of an ascent to the third heaven. Spatial categories form an important part of apocalyptic thought. Heaven, the world above, is separated from the world below by the firmament. Above, there is a series of heavens, populated by angels, in the highest of which is God, enthroned in glory. Such spatial categories are presupposed by several New Testament writers and indeed form part of the argument of one or two documents. In Ephesians, for example, the author speaks of a heavenly dimension to the church's existence, by his use of the phrase 'in the heavenly places' he links the church with the exalted Christ (2:6 'God raised us up with Christ and made us sit with him in the heavenly places in Christ').

In the Letter to the Hebrews an important part of the argument concerns the belief that the superiority of Christ's sacrifice is that his offering of himself enabled him to enter not the earthly shrine but heaven itself, to the very presence of God. It is likely that the cosmology of Hebrews owes its origin to the apocalyptic literature of Judaism rather than any contact with Philo of Alexandria, though one should be careful not to polarise Philo's Hellenistic Judaism and apocalyptic thought too much. The contrast between the world below and the world above is very much a feature of the cosmology of the apocalypses. Without this framework, the force of the writer's argument is lessened. Christ the heavenly pioneer has entered into the inner shrine, behind the veil. He has entered not into a sanctuary made with hands, a copy of the true one, but into heaven itself, to appear in the presence of God on behalf of his people (6:19 ff., cf. 9:24).

The Gospel of John and Revelation

But it is what appears to be the least apocalyptic document in the New Testament that must be considered. The Gospel of John has frequently been regarded as an example of that type of Christianity which firmly rejected apocalyptic. What many mean when they say that apocalyptic is not characteristic of the Gospel of John is that there is no imminent expectation of the end but rather the 'necessity of preparation for an unexpected and uncertain future'. Given that exegetes tend to equate apocalyptic with the imminent expectation of the end, it is not surprising that they view the Gospel as a reaction against apocalyptic. It must be questioned whether we can see the relationship between the Gospel of John and apocalyptic in a new light if we approach it in the way suggested already: how does the Gospel of John fit in with apocalyptic as the quest for higher wisdom through revelation? When viewed from this perspective, the main thrust of its message appears to have a remarkable affinity with apocalyptic, even if we have to admit that the *mode* of revelation stressed in the Gospel differs from that outlined in the apocalypses. If we are right to assume that the goal of apocalyptic is the attainment of knowledge of the divine mysteries, and in particular the mysteries of God himself, then it can be seen that much of what the Fourth Gospel says relates to this theme. Jesus proclaims himself as the revelation of the hidden God. He tells Philip 'He who has seen me has seen the Father' (14:8) and at the conclusion of the Prologue, the Evangelist speaks of the Son in the following way: 'No one has ever seen God; the only Son, who is in the bosom of the Father, he has made him known' (1:18). The vision of God, the heart of the call-experiences of Isaiah and Ezekiel and the goal of the heavenly ascents of the apocalyptic seers and rabbinic mystics, is in the Fourth Gospel related to the revelation of God in Jesus. All claims to have seen God in the past are repudiated; the Jews have 'neither heard God's voice nor seen his form' (5:37). Even when, as in Isaiah's case, Scripture teaches that a prophet glimpsed God enthroned in glory, this vision is interpreted in the Gospel as a vision of the pre-existent Christ (12:41). No one has seen God except the one who is from God; he has seen the Father (6:46). The vision of God reserved in the Book of Revelation for the fortunate seer (4:1) and for the inhabitants of the 'new Jerusalem' who will see him face to face (22:4) is found, according to the fourth Evangelist, in the person of Jesus of Nazareth. Possibly an attempt is made to repudiate the claims of those apocalyptists who gained divine knowledge by means of heavenly ascents to God's throne when Jesus says to Nicodemus: 'No one has ascended into heaven but he who descended from heaven, the Son of Man' (3:13). For the Fourth Evangelist, the quest for the highest wisdom of all, the knowledge of God, comes not through the information disclosed in visions and revelations but through the Word become flesh, Jesus of Nazareth. Thus while the fourth Evangelist sets himself resolutely against any claim to revelation except through Christ, he presupposes and uses the basic framework of apocalyptic for his own christological ends. Thus in the major strands of early Christian literature we find manifested that same concern as had preoccupied the writers of the apocalypses: the quest for higher wisdom through revelation. Not only will a greater appreciation of this dimension of apocalyptic thought equip us to assess more accurately the nature of Judaism at the beginning of the Christian era, but also it will enable us to see the extent of the continuity between early Christian thought and contemporary Judaism.

To understand apocalyptic it is important to distinguish it satisfactorily from related concepts like gnosticism and eschatology. While it cannot be doubted that it is closely related to them both, any attempt to speak of it as if it were synonymous with either fails to do justice to the specifics of the religious current manifest in the apocalypses. Whereas in the past it has been customary to regard apocalyptic as a particular form of the ancient Jewish eschatological hope, it seems preferable to abandon a definition of it in which eschatology is a key characteristic. Rather we should see apocalyptic as that specifically Jewish manifestation of the quest for higher wisdom through revelation, that wisdom which seers longed to be shown. The future hope is one component of this quest. Thus, far from being merely a component of the variety of Jewish eschatology, apocalyptic is a means of revelation by which subjects like eschatology could be disclosed. The content of apocalyptic could, therefore, be eschatological (and often was).

FOR FURTHER READING

C. K. Barrett, 'New Testament Eschatology', *Scottish Journal of Theology* vol. 6 (1953) pp. 136ff.

J. C. Baker, *Paul's Apocalyptic Gospel*, Philadelphia 1982.

M. Hengel, *Judaism and Hellenism*, London 1974.

K. Koch, *The Rediscovery of Apocalyptic*, London 1972.

C. Rowland, *The Open Heaven*, London 1982.

H. H. Rowley, *The Relevance of Apocalyptic*, London 1947.

P. Vielhauer, 'Apocalyptic in Early Christianity', in Hennecke-Schnee-melcher, *New Testament Apocrypha* vol. 2, London 1965, pp. 608ff.

5

THE INTER-TESTAMENTAL LITERATURE AND THE NEW TESTAMENT: THE WITNESS TO ANCIENT JUDAISM'S ESCHATOLOGY

1. TOWARDS A BETTER UNDERSTANDING OF ANCIENT JUDAISM AND EARLY CHRISTIANITY

One of the most powerful motivations for research on Jewish literature has been the desire to locate the New Testament writings within the contemporary religious environment. Unfortunately, this orientation of the research on the Jewish texts has tended to distort the treatment of the Jewish literature. It cannot be said that interest in these texts has been across their whole range. Perhaps inevitably when the exposition of the New Testament is dominant, it is the interpretation of those passages of particular interest to the New Testament interpreter which are of most importance. The problem is that for many students of the New Testament, knowledge of the inter-testamental literature is confined either to those passages which seem to have closest contact with New Testament concepts or to the choice of material in commentaries which is mentioned to illustrate particular New Testament verses. As a result, it is all too easy to have an impression of Judaism which is partial and vague. The overall thrust of the documents and the Jewish communities which produced them are neglected.

The Relevance of the Jewish Material
The extent to which the New Testament scholar should take account of the Jewish material has been a matter of debate. In the first place there was a phase of New Testament scholarship when it was not the Jewish documents which were thought to have provided the soil

for the growth of Christian doctrine and religion. Rather it was the texts of the gnostics and the Hellenistic world which were used. The conviction that there was a myth of a descending redeemer and a gnostic religion already in existence at the beginning of the Christian era led many exegetes to suppose that it was to this world that the scholar should look for the elucidation of key New Testament theological ideas.

Secondly, there is the vexed question of the extent to which early Christian doctrine was an innovatory departure from Jewish ideas. This is an issue of continuing debate in scholarly circles. There is clearly a difference of opinion between those who think that the essential features of Christian doctrine and practice were inherited with little alteration from Judaism and those who would argue that key doctrinal concepts like the Incarnation and the Trinity were in fact the unique contribution of early Christian reflection on the Christ-event.

Thirdly, much reserve has been expressed in some quarters about the indiscriminate use of Jewish material to illustrate the New Testament. A frequently used source book of Jewish material is the collection put together by Paul Billerbeck. In this, many verses from the New Testament are illuminated by the use of a wide range of material, mainly (but not exclusively) from the rabbinic sources. Some New Testament scholars have protested about the inclusion of material from widely differing dates and provenances. Thus, it is asked whether ideas which are found in texts which may well have been written several centuries later than the New Testament can really be regarded as examples of background material; could it not have been, it is argued, that the New Testament itself might have provided the origin of the idea which is found in the Jewish text? This has meant that the indiscriminate use of Jewish material of widely different dates and provenances would not find ready acceptance in some quarters.

The question of the date of the various sources is one that looms large in discussions of the relationship between the early Christian movement and Judaism. Clearly, the debt in the use of ideas need not have been one way only; the fact that we so easily assume that the Christian movement must have been the debtor and never the contributor is testimony in itself to the conviction that is widespread that Judaism rejected Christianity from the very beginning and had no truck with its doctrine and practice. In addition, we have to beware that we are not guilty of wanting to safeguard the uniqueness of Christianity to such an extent that we refuse to countenance the possibility that the major doctrine did not already exist in one form or other in ancient Jewish religion. Sometimes one wonders whether the discarding of the relevance of Jewish sources on account of date may be simply an excuse to avoid taking their implications into account.

Jewish-Christian Interaction

Much study of the New Testament rests on the assumption that there was a clear demarcation between Judaism and Christianity from the very start. The historian of religions must not jump to such a conclusion, however. Our knowledge of both ancient Judaism and primitive Christianity has been filtered down to us through the authoritative, canonical collections. It is now not always easy to detect the vast amount of common ground which once existed between the two groups, not merely in the common inheritance of the Jewish scripture but also a common inheritance of ideas. These are not always evident, at least on a superficial reading of the Jewish sources. New Testament scholars are now recognising that the New Testament writings themselves reflect that painful process of Christian 'self-definition' which was consequent upon particular developments within Judaism and the interpretation of the Jewish traditions which were offered by the followers of Jesus of Nazareth, and that differences in form and emphasis may derive from the different concerns of early Christian as compared with rabbinic texts.

What has emerged in the revival of interest in the study of ancient Judaism in the last thirty years is a view of Judaism which has made *stark* contrast between Judaism and early Christianity in the first century out of the question. As had already been noted, the discovery of the Dead Sea Scrolls has had a remarkable impact. While it would be wrong to pretend that this eccentric group in the desert was typical of the thought of any but a small fraction of Jews, the impact of the Scrolls on the consideration of ancient Judaism has been enormous. It has now become such a commonplace of Jewish studies to hear that there was no such thing as orthodoxy (and orthopraxy) in first century Judaism, that one needs to be reminded that it was widely assumed, before the discovery of the Scrolls, that the rabbinic texts were the texts of Jewish orthodoxy. Of course, this is absolutely true, provided that we remember that when we talk of such an orthodoxy, we are thinking of a later period after the destruction of the Temple in Jerusalem in AD 70 and the triumph of the pharisaic rabbinic tradition. What few scholars now are prepared to support however, is the view that already in the period of the Second Temple, it was the piety of these texts which were regarded as normative by all Jews. Indeed, the indications are that during this period this particular religious outlook also was the property of only a tiny minority of Jews in Palestine.

Thus it has become much more difficult to speak of Judaism during the period of the Second Temple as if it were a monolithic entity with a norm of doctrine and practice, deviation from which was easily punished. No doubt there were those within first century Judaism who found the beliefs and practices of the primitive Christians highly offensive and controversial. What we are not in a position to assert is that the rejection of 'Christian' interpretations of the common traditions by one or more Jewish groups, necessarily meant that this was to be understood as a rejection of Christianity by Judaism. It is the use of Judaism and Christianity when speaking of first century conflicts which is anachronistic. Christianity was a Jewish movement, and its key figures thought of themselves as Jews albeit with a distinctive approach to the Jewish traditions. They at least did not believe that this led them into positions which were necessarily contrary to the Jewish tradition though, of course, there were certainly other Jews who thought the opposite. When one asserts that early Christianity should be regarded as a sect of Judaism, this seems to be so self-evident that it might be wondered what is so significant about such a statement. The fact is that acceptance of primitive Christianity in this light as part of the complex of religious and social development of first century Judaism in Palestine and the Diaspora is still difficult for many Christian commentators to handle.

There is no doubt that this recognition involves a painful acceptance by both Jew and Christian about their respective religions. It is tempting for some Jews to argue that early Christianity, at least in its Pauline form (Jesus is frequently rehabilitated as being more on the side of Judaism than of Christianity), was from the very start something alien to Judaism. Its repudiation of circumcision and observance of the Law of Moses seems to be incompatible with Judaism, and there was never any other possibility than that Judaism would exclude its illegitmate offspring. What is more, the hostile attitude taken towards Jesus and the Christians in the later rabbinic traditions has persuaded scholars to assume that from the very start Judaism repudiated Christianity and was never influenced by it. The stories which we possess (whatever their authenticity) concerning Eliezer ben Hyracanus (a contemporary of Rabban Yohanan ben Zakkai) and his knowledge of a tradition associated with Jesus should make us a little wary of assuming that there was neither a two way dialogue nor a similarity of ideological outlook between Christians and other Jews. Even if we make due allowances for the apologetic aim in Justin's *Dialogue with Trypho* (mid-second century AD), the drift of the argument is that there is more common ground between Judaism and Christianity than both ancient and modern commentators allow for.

The Distinctiveness of Christianity?

On the Christian side the problem has centred on central theological conviction that 'there is no other name under heaven by which you can be saved than Jesus'. This has imperceptibly led also to the conclusion that, because the early Christians were convinced that there had been a unique and decisive revelation of the divine purpose (Hebrews 1:1ff.), the doctrine which they used to speak of that theological datum must also have been unique. But the distinctiveness of the early Christian conviction that God had spoken decisively through his Son should not be confused with the view that a transcendence of Jewish categories must have taken place in order to speak of this. We cannot be certain (the evidence is not at our disposal), but it seems very likely amidst the social and religious turmoil of the first century that there were many other claims that the last days had arrived and the Kingdom of God was near. To make such claims and explore the consequences of them, therefore, was not of itself particularly distinctive; the doctrine that a new age would come and would be inaugurated by some messianic agent was after all the common property of many Jews. The fact that some of the doctrinal formulations most familiar to Christians such as the Trinity find no parallel in the Old Testament or in the rabbinic (and other Jewish) literature, might lead us to suppose that here after all is the unique contribution of the Christian theology, in taking the beliefs it inherited from Judaism and moulding them into something very different. That change and refinement went on cannot be doubted: that was a constant feature of Jewish interpretation. Nevertheless, the essential framework of ideas was in all probability inherited with little alteration from contemporary Jewish ideology.

FOR FURTHER READING

P. Henry, *New Directions in New Testament Study*, London 1979.

C. Rowland, *Christian Origins*, London 1985.

E. P. Sanders ed., *Jewish and Christian Self-Definition*, 3 vol. London 1981–3.

E. P. Sanders, *Paul and Palestinian Judaism*, London 1977.

M. Stone, op. cit.

2. THE ESCHATOLOGICAL MATRIX OF PRIMITIVE CHRISTIANITY

The Eschatological Horizon of the New Testament

With the publication of works like 1 Enoch there was growing interest throughout the second half of the nineteenth century in the implications of the ideology of such works for the understanding of the New Testament. Here, it seemed, was the milieu out of which the early Christian movement grew. The work of Johannes Weiss and Albert Schweitzer on the message of Jesus, and the latter on Paul, are a monument to this growing realisation that out of the eschatological stream of Judaism and the apocalyptic/visionary mentality of the apocalypses emerged the leading figures of Christianity. To say that New Testament studies have never been the same since Weiss and Schweitzer is something of an understatement. While it is clear that Schweitzer himself thought that the eschatological message died with Jesus, it is apparent that the effect of its rediscovery on biblical scholarship has been far reaching, however contorted the attempts may have been both to de-eschatologise and de-apocalyptise Jesus. The fact is that, however reluctantly, New Testament scholarship is reckoning that far from being on the periphery of early Christian experience, the future hope and the apocalyptic imagination provided the vehicle for the eschatological enthusiasm. That is not to deny that there have been a succession of studies in which attempts have been made to understand traditions in the New Testament in the light of the rabbinic tradition, and, in particular, to relate the teaching of Jesus to the rabbinic academics. Yet, however enlightening these have been for our understanding of the particular issues involved, the picture of Jesus in the gospels stubbornly refuses to be fitted into that of the conventional rabbi or for that matter, the zealot revolutionary.

Not only Jesus, but Paul and other New Testament writers also must be seen as imbued with this particular religious enthusiasm. The evidence for this is overwhelming. We only need to consider how many of the major themes of the New Testament are firmly woven in the fabric of the eschatological belief of Judaism: not just christological categories like Messiah and Son of Man, but central beliefs like the resurrection and the doctrine of the Spirit. None of these can be adequately understood without reference to the future hope of Judaism; indeed, so thoroughly did this world of ideas provide the atmosphere for early Christian understanding of reality that even when the transition to a more thoroughly hellenistic culture took place, and the thought-forms of Jewish Christianity proved to be either embarrassing or inadequate, the edifice of belief constructed with the building bricks of Jewish messianism and millennialism could not be completely demolished. However much the superstructure of the later Christian soteriology seemed to cast its shadow over Christian doctrine, the resurrection of Jesus and the resurrection of the body at the last day, the latter a central facet of the pharisaic-rabbinic tradition (M. Sanhedrin 10:1), stubbornly remained in the creeds of Christendom.

The Book of Revelation

To recognise the importance of eschatology for the understanding of early Christianity is to demand a reconsideration of the importance of Revelation. Throughout the history of the church the book of Revelation has provided problems of interpretation and doctrine for Christian thinkers. Its association with fringe movements from Corinthians and the Montanists, to Joachim of Fiore and the eschatological enthusiasts who have looked to him, has added to the suspicion which Christians have felt towards this work. Bultmann's assessment of Revelation as a 'weakly Christianised Judaism' would be a view held by many. The fact that it is on the periphery of the New Testament canon is an accurate reflection of the place it has, and had, within New Testament theology and its impact on the developing theology of the Church. Eschatology, like the book of Revelation itself, is indeed a matter to which one turns last of all after other doctrinal issues have been fully explored. Perhaps it takes the extravagant claims of someone standing outside the Church to remind us of the importance of Revelation. It was Friedrich Engels writing at the end of the last century who argued that, far from being peripheral for our understanding of early Christianity, it should be regarded as characteristic of the beliefs of the earliest phase of Christian thought. Clearly Engels was working with a chronology of the New Testament writings which would not be acceptable to us today (in this he was much influenced by Bruno Bauer), but his assertion about the priority of Revelation as a guide to the essence of the earliest phase of Christian thought is a salutary reminder of the centrality of eschatology for our understanding of the rise of Christianity.

While the book of Revelation may be a product of the Jewish-Christianity piety of Asia Minor, there is much in it which suggests that it also accurately reflects the beliefs of other branches of the tradition of the earliest church. The central theme of its presentation of the eschatological drama is the conviction that the death of Christ and his exaltation to the throne of God marks the decisive moment of change in the relationship between heaven and earth (Revelation

5). It was seen that this was the view which was adhered to by Paul in particular. But what of the other, less palatable features of the theology of Revelation? How do we assess the position of the doctrine of the millennium, the overthrow of the hostile powers and the use of apocalyptic imagery? Were they also part of the framework of early Christian thought?

Eschatological Themes in the New Testament
The presentation of the main features of early Christian hopes for the future is no easy task. For one thing, nowhere do we find a systematic presentation of the various facets of these beliefs. Rather we have various hints in contexts which usually are dealing with some other subject. What is more, the interpretation of the eschatological passages in the mainstream New Testament texts, particularly the gospels and the letters of Paul, are inevitably coloured by other doctrinal concerns. There can be little doubt of the centrality of the belief in an imminent coming of Christ in glory. It is a feature of most of the New Testament writings. The consequences of this descent of the exalted Christ from heaven to earth are by no means clear. In one of the most extended passages dealing with the climax of history in 1 Corinthians 15 (cf. 1 Thessalonians 4:15ff.) we find that the material concerning the reign of Christ is set out in the most general terms. Nothing whatever is said about the lot of the saints in the new age, save that at the last trump the dead will be raised and the righteous will be changed. Whether the resurrection was to be to a life on earth or in some supra-terrestrial realm is not spelt out. Thus we have to face the fact that in trying to elucidate the different facets of early Christian eschatological belief, we have to make the most of the hints available to us and to assess their import in the light of what is known to us from contemporary beliefs concerning the future.

Without probing too deeply the authenticity of the items of traditions in the gospels, it would be fair to say that they do suggest a prima facie case for assuming that a form of the millennial belief was accepted by the early church. In the Beatitudes we find that a promise is made to the meek that 'they will inherit the earth' (Matthew 5:5). In the parallel version in Luke similar sentiments appear. There is the promise that the hungry will be filled (6:21) and the poor will inherit the kingdom of God (6:20). With regard to the last promise it cannot be assumed without further argument that the inheritance of the kingdom of heaven refers to participation in a restored creation rather than a transcendent realm. It is very difficult, however, without excessive spiritualisation of these verses to suppose that the filling of the hungry and the inheritance of the earth refer to events in a world any different from our own, when a new age would bring about a reversal of values (Luke 6:24ff.). When one adds to these sayings the vow which Jesus made at the last supper not to taste of the fruit of the vine until he drank it new in the kingdom of God (Mark 14:25ff.) there does appear to be evidence to suggest that Jesus did indeed look forward to a day when the reign of God would be established on earth. Similarly, in the Pauline corpus, the classic statement of Paul's eschatological beliefs in Romans 8 includes a belief that the whole of creation is moving towards the birth of a new age. It is a movement which is centred in this world and concerns this creation and not some other realm. The distaste expressed by many early Christian writers for chiliastic or millennial beliefs, (e.g. Eusebius of Caesarea's reproach of Papias in EH iii, 39,13) should not blind us to the possibility that they may well be firmly rooted in the gospel tradition and the letters of Paul. It is certainly the case that there are not signs in either the gospels or the epistles that an earthly kingdom, whatever the duration, was countenanced (such a belief was by no means common in Judaism in any case). What is of much more interest is that the conviction that the reign of God *on earth*, which was the main component of Jewish eschatology, is an idea which is echoed in the foundation documents of the Christian church. This should not surprise us as the prevalence of chiliastic beliefs in the first two centuries of the Christian era is well attested.

There is a saying attributed to Jesus by Papias in Irenaeus (Adv. Haer. V.33:3f.) which evinces some of the characteristics of messianic oracles like Isaiah 11 with the emphasis on the harmony of creation and the perfection of its produce (cf. Syriac Baruch 29). In its present form one would doubt whether this saying could go back to Jesus, but the fact that it circulated under his name in the early church and was connected with Papias, who had a great concern for tradition, suggests that there may have not been too much that was incongruous in linking such an idea with Jesus of Nazareth.

Thus certain hints from the New Testament indicate that the expectation of a messianic kingdom set up on earth as in Revelation 20 may have been a central feature of mainstream Christian tradition in the first century. Even if there is evidence to suggest that both Paul (1 Corinthians 15) and Jesus (Mark 12:25ff.) expected that, at the resurrection, the righteous would inherit new bodies, there would appear to be nothing to suggest that the life of the resurrected would be lived in heaven but rather in a renewed earth.

God and Caesar

The hostility towards the Roman state and the rejection of its claims and power as seen in the book of Revelation contrast with the somewhat blander attitudes towards the state in Romans 13 (cf. 1 Peter 2:13–17; Titus 3:1). Nevertheless, the conviction that all that was opposed to God would ultimately be uprooted and destroyed, so graphically portrayed in Revelation (e.g. 17–20) is at least implicitly and often explicitly stated elsewhere in the New Testament. In the much disputed passages in 2 Thessalonians 2:3ff., we find Paul using the imagery of apocalyptic literature to speak of the ultimate expression of hostility to God which would be overcome by Christ at his coming. Similarly, in the gospels the traditional features of Jewish estchatology, the messianic woes and other cosmic catastrophes, are set out in full in Mark 13. Nothing is said in this chapter or its parallels about the overcoming of the forces of darkness and their destruction, though this seems to be implied in the process of judgement outlined in Matthew 25:31ff. As it stands, Mark 13 seems to be a torso of the traditional Jewish eschatological pattern. It mentions the messianic woes and the attendant features which would indicate the coming of the climax to the eschatological process. It speaks of the setting up of the abomination of desolation and the crisis for those in Judaea and the persecution of the elect. But after the coming of the Son of Man and his angels to save the elect, nothing whatever is said of the rest of creation. The chapter seems to give the impression that the redemption of the elect is a redemption out of a world fast sinking to destruction. One can only assume that the reason for this truncated version is that the fate of the elect, their tribulation followed by their triumph, covers the concerns of the author. Whether Mark 9:1 gives hints of a much larger eschatological portrait no longer reflected in the tradition we cannot be sure. Nevertheless implicit within the emphasis of Jesus on the coming of the kingdom is the belief that the powers of darkness (i.e. everything opposed to God) was being overthrown (e.g. Mark 3:22). In so far as the might of Rome stood in the way of the establishment of the reign of peace and justice, it must have been the case that the continuation of Roman sovereignty within the dominion of God would have been impossible. However guarded Jesus' remarks may have been on the subject of the relationship between the kingdom of God and the kingdom of Caesar (Mark 12:17) ultimately it has to be said that the two could not co-exist indefinitely.

In the Pauline corpus the overthrow of the hostile powers is clearly enunciated. In 1 Corinthians 15:24ff. the subjection of the principalities and powers (and by that Paul includes angelic and human potentates) to Christ is a feature of the eschatological process. Nothing is said explicitly here about Rome, but it would be a mistake to suppose that the quietist remarks in Romans 13:1 necessarily reveal a conviction that the status quo would remain. As in 1 Enoch 89:59ff., it is likely that there lies behind this verse the belief that God had allowed the powers in earth and heaven free reign for a certain period (cf. Revelation 12:12 and 13:5). Ultimately, however, as with the angelic representatives of the nations in 1 Enoch, the powers are judged and made subservient to the authority of Christ (15:28) and in some cases destroyed (1 Corinthians 15:24).

Conclusion

What the inter-testamental literature has enabled us to do is to see how texts which proclaim the messiahship of Jesus are firmly rooted in an era when hopes for deliverance from the bondage of the principalities and powers of the present evil age were rife. Even the rabbinic tradition, so often supposed to be devoid of such concerns, manifests the concern with that hope in the rabbinic corpus as well as in the liturgical material that it produced. The inter-testamental literature offers us the matrix of Christianity from which those Jews and Gentiles who believed that the hopes of the Bible had found their fulfilment in his activity began to fashion their ways of looking at the world in the light of that earnest conviction. This heterogeneous collection from many different times and places enables us to glimpse the way in which the Jewish tradition was developed and borne witness to in the Greco-Roman world in which Jesus was born.

FOR FURTHER READING

E. P. Sanders, *Jesus and Judaism*, London 1985.
A. Schweitzer, *The Quest of the Historial Jesus*, London 1910.
A. Schweitzer, *The Mysticism of Paul the Apostle*, London 1931.
G. Vermes, *Jesus the Jew*, London 1975.
J. Weiss, *Jesus' Proclamation of the Kingdom of God*, London 1971.

PART III

THE NEW TESTAMENT

1

THE FORMATION OF THE NEW TESTAMENT

1. THE BEGINNINGS OF CHRISTIAN LITERATURE

Christianity began with the life and teaching of Jesus Christ. The Church, consisting of his band of disciples, was not consciously separate from Judaism. Rather, Christianity was a movement within Judaism, carrying on the work which Jesus had begun to prepare the nation for God's kingdom. The Church had its Scriptures, but these were the same as the Scriptures of the Jews as a whole. So the sacred books of the first Christians were the books of the Old Testament, and no doubt they used and valued other Jewish writings at the time, classified today as Apocrypha and Pseudepigrapha. But the New Testament did not exist.

The central point in the Church's preaching (kerygma) was the heavenly lordship of Jesus Christ. He had been put to death without seeing the fulfilment of his message of the coming of God to set up his kingdom. But if he died as Messiah, he was also raised as Messiah (1 Corinthians 15:3–4), ready at God's right hand to be the agent of his kingdom. Thus the renewal of the preaching of Jesus after his crucifixion carried with it a statement concerning his own person and function; and acceptance of the message entailed acknowledgment of Jesus as the exalted Lord and allegiance to him. This had literary consequences.

Old Testament Exegesis
The Church's message carried with it a distinct attitude to Scripture, i.e. the Old Testament. This has been shown in Chapter 1 of Part I above. Not only were prophecies of the Messiah held to be fulfilled in Jesus, but the Scriptures were exploited more widely to support the kerygma, so that it is not too much to say that the whole of the Old Testament was regarded as prophetic of the events in which Jesus was the chief actor. This attitude to Scripture is comparable

to that of the Dead Sea Scrolls, in which all Scriptures are held to be prophetic of the Sect itself. It can also be compared with the updating technique of the Targums (Aramaic paraphrases of the Old Testament) whereby the Hebrew text is paraphrased in such a way as to make it applicable to the Targumist's own times. So what is distinct about the Church's use of Scripture is not the method but the application. All Scriptures are referred to Jesus as the Messiah or Christ.

Within the New Testament there are many quotations of the Old Testament which are used in this way. Some of them appear in several different New Testament books. It has therefore been suggested that the earliest Christian writing was a collection of proof-texts (the *Testimonia* theory of Rendel Harris). Though it may be doubted whether there was a single document of this kind in circulation, rather than a common work of exegesis, which was passed on orally in the course of the apostolic preaching, we can recognise in this exegetical work an activity which is leading in the direction of a distinctively Christian literature.

The Pattern of the Kerygma
The kerygma was passed on orally by the apostles (missionaries), but naturally followed a relatively fixed pattern. This has left literary traces in the New Testament in three ways.

Firstly, there are various passages which give the impression of being based on *credal forms*, e.g. Romans 1:3-4:

> . . . the gospel concerning his Son, who was descended from David according to the flesh, and designated Son of God in power according to the Spirit of holiness by his resurrection from the dead.

Paul also appears to be indebted to credal forms elsewhere in Romans, e.g. 'He who did not spare his own Son but gave him up for us all' (8:32); ' . . . Christ Jesus, who died, yes, who was raised from the dead, who is at the right hand of God' (8:34). It is notable that in this last passage Paul alludes to one of the Old Testament quotations just mentioned:

> The Lord says to my lord:
> 'Sit at my right hand,
> till I make your enemies your footstool.

This is quoted a number of times in the New Testament (Matthew

22:24; Acts 2:34–5; Hebrews 1:13), and must be regarded as one of the foundation texts of the primitive kerygma. The risen and exalted status of Jesus was expressed in the words of this psalm from the very beginning, and these words survive in the Christian creeds to this day.

Secondly, Paul furnishes evidence for *official statements* in connection with crucial items of Christian teaching. In 1 Corinthians 11:23–5 he reproduces a formal tradition concerning the Last Supper, which he uses as the basis of regulations for the celebration of the eucharist at Corinth. Almost the same form, but with some later modifications, is given in Mark's account of the Last Supper (Mark 14:22–4). Then in 1 Corinthians 15:3–8 Paul gives a formal statement of the death and resurrection of Jesus, with a list of the resurrection appearances. There is good reason to believe that this is the official tradition of the Jerusalem church, which Paul received on his visit to Jerusalem to consult Peter three years after his conversion (Galatians 1:18). Statements of this kind put into writing distinctive features of Christian faith, and thus form one of the initiatives making for a specifically Christian literature.

Thirdly, one feature of all four Gospels is the disproportionately lengthy Passion Narrative. It has long been recognised that this is likely to have originated from a custom of reciting the Passion story at Christian celebrations of the Passover. For the Passover consisted not only of a solemn meal, but also of the Haggadah, i.e. the recital of the story of the exodus of Israel from Egypt which the feast celebrates. By including the Passion story, Christians could recall the death of Jesus at Passover time, and interpret it in the light of the Passover as God's new act of redemption (cf. 1 Corinthians 5:7). This recital at the Christian Passover has kerygmatic significance, because it indicates the meaning of the death of Jesus proclaimed in the apostolic preaching. It is conjectured that this Christian form of the Passover Haggadah has provided the framework of the Passion Narratives in the Gospels.

Traditions of Jesus
Besides the kerygma, the Church needed moral and other teaching in its internal life, and this also forms a starting point for Christian literature. The converts needed guidance concerning the kind of behaviour that is appropriate to allegiance to Christ. This was best provided from the remembered teaching of Jesus himself. Paul in 1 Corinthians 7:10 clearly distinguishes between the teaching of 'the Lord' and his own directions. This implies that some sort of collection of Jesus' teaching was available. Significantly, the matter under

discussion (marriage and divorce) is found in the Gospels in both Mark and Q (= material common to Matthew and Luke, but not included in Mark). The Q material may have come from a written collection of sayings of Jesus. Whether the Q hypothesis (which will be discussed in a later chapter) is correct or not, it is altogether probable that the remembered sayings of Jesus were formed into collections which circulated at an early date to meet the needs of the expanding Church.

It is obvious that, in addition to direct moral instruction, illustrative stories about Jesus would be valued for teaching and exhortation. Many of the gospel episodes appear to have been preserved because of their usefulness for teaching in this way. There are some indications in the Gospels that short collections of particular types of material were made: parables, miracles, and controversy stories in which Jesus worsts the scribes and Pharisees. These were the materials, some perhaps oral and some written, which were available to the evangelists at a later stage.

Letters
As the Church grew and the apostolic missionaries went further afield, there was bound to be a need to keep contact and to consult the mother church. These practical concerns could be met by sending letters, and so the internal life of the Church soon includes written correspondence. Paul's letters (epistles) are the oldest that have come down to us. Naturally, at the time when they were written there was no thought of collecting them together and preserving them for posterity. The impetus for that came later, when not many were still extant. We can be sure that many letters of Paul and others have been lost. The attempt to make a collection of them can be regarded as the first step in the formation of the New Testament. But that happened long after Paul's death.

In these ways the Church began to produce a literature of its own in relation to the needs that arose in the course of the apostolic task. When Paul wrote his letters, there were no Christian books to refer to. His library was the Old Testament and some of the inter-testamental literature. At this stage there was no thought of a New Testament alongside the Old. When Paul speaks of himself and his co-workers as 'able ministers of the new testament' (2 Corinthians 3:6, AV), he is not referring to a collection of Christian writings, even though there is explicit contrast with the Law of Moses, which is the essence of the Old Testament. He means the gospel, the kerygma, of Jesus Christ, the fact that through Christ, God has established the new covenant promised by Jeremiah (31:31–4; cf. 1

Corinthians 11:25). Thus the Church, with its gospel of salvation, came into being before the formation of the New Testament. The Christian literature which now begins to appear is part of the process whereby the Church developed its self-understanding and worked out the theological implications of the gospel. As the oldest collection of Christian literature, the New Testament reflects and bears witness to this process. As such it is part of the tradition of the Church, a facet of its continuing life. This must be borne in mind when we come to the later history of the use and interpretation of the New Testament. We shall find that an artificial distinction is made between Scripture and tradition, which was an important factor in the conflict of the Reformation.

2. WRITINGS, READINGS AND HOMILIES

Synagogue Practice

In the worship of the synagogue it was customary for the Scripture readings to be followed by a homily or sermon. Jesus is depicted as giving the homily in the synagogue at Nazareth in Luke 4:20. In Acts 13:15 Paul is invited by the superintendent of the synagogue at Pisidian Antioch to give a homily after the reading of the Law and the Prophets. This seems to refer to the scheme of synagogue lessons, consisting of the *sēder* from the Pentateuch and the *haphtārāh* from the prophetical books. Paul's speech is an exposition of the Scriptures in relation to the fulfilment in Christ.

Christian worship most probably followed the synagogue pattern, and at first differed only in having a specifically Christian homily after the readings. But it would seem probable that this, or some other suitable point in the assembly for worship, was used as the occasion for reading messages to the whole congregation. There are indications in some of Paul's letters (e.g. 1 Corinthians 16:20; Colossians 4:16) that he expects them to be read to the assembled company in this way.

Public Reading of the Epistles and Gospels

There is thus a tendency for letters and homilies to overlap. Paul's letters conform to epistolary conventions with significant differences, because for the most part they are designed to be read to the whole assembly and not just addressed to individuals. The Epistle of James has a general address ('to the twelve tribes in the Dispersion'). If this is a genuine part of the original composition, it suggests that the letter was intended to be read at a number of churches (cf.

also 1 Peter 1:1). The Book of Revelation is addressed to the churches of the Roman province of Asia, specifying seven of them, but it is very unlikely that the seven letters of Revelation 2–3 were ever sent separately, so that circulation of the whole book seems more likely. It has been conjectured that the seven churches were on an ancient postal route in the province.

The question then arises whether the Gospels were composed for reading in the Christian assembly. Justin Martyr, writing about AD 155, describes the liturgy used in his day, and includes within it the reading of the 'memoirs' (*hupomnēmata*) of the apostles (*First Apology* 67). This is probably a reference to the Gospels. This is the first evidence for a Christian reading in addition to the Old Testament lections as a regular feature of Christian worship. Perhaps this was originally the introduction to the sermon, in which the Old Testament lections were expounded in relation to an aspect of gospel teaching. There is a possible example of this in the Gospel of John itself, for the great discourse on the Bread of Life in John 6:25–59 appears to be based on synagogue lections, the *sēder* Exodus 16 on the manna miracle and the *haphtārāh* Isaiah 54:9–55:5 on spiritual nourishment. But it is preceded by the gospel miracles of feeding the multitude and walking on water (John 6:1–24), which could well be taken from a collection of 'memoirs of the apostles' available at John's church. If this is correct, the practice of including a Christian lection was established during the first century, and the formation of the Gospel of John is to some extent indebted to it.

If, then, gospel readings were used as a bridge between Old Testament lessons and sermon, were the Gospels actually composed for this purpose? This theory has been put forward by several scholars in recent years, but the arguments are not convincing. It is one thing to take a book and divide it into sections for use as a lectionary. It is quite another to compose a book with this in mind. If this were the case, we should expect the form and structure of the book to be suited to the purpose, containing relatively self-contained units of roughly equal length. A glance at the four Gospels shows that none of them has this structure. They each have their own plan of composition, which shows them to be conceived as a whole without any consideration for lectionary purposes. Matthew in particular alternates blocks of narrative and blocks of teaching, which give his Gospel its own well articulated structure.

Origins of the Gospels

We thus have to look for a different origin of the Gospels. Some idea of the underlying traditions which the evangelists used as sources has been given in the last section. The needs there described also account for the impetus to collect together the traditions to form a biography of Jesus. Only one further ingredient is required, and that is public demand to satisfy curiosity about Jesus. This was bound to arise as the Church moved out, first from the circle of those who had actually known Jesus, then to those who had heard of him by repute, and eventually to those to whom the name (and the title Christ) meant nothing. As the living memory faded and the number of eye-witnesses diminished, there would be an increasing need to record what was known of the life of Jesus before it was too late. Luke 1:1–4 tells how 'many have undertaken' to do this, and explains that his own Gospel is intended to give a reliable account of the facts. His Gospel does in fact draw heavily on at least one of these predecessors, as it incorporates a great deal of Mark. Whether Luke knew and used Matthew is disputed (for the postulated Q source see above).

The motive of pious curiosity also accounts for some of the sources used by the evangelists. The Infancy narratives of Matthew 1–2 and Luke 1–2, which appear to be independent of each other, rely on traditions of the birth and childhood of Jesus which would never have circulated if Jesus had not become a cult figure after his death. They differ in style from the main bulk of these Gospels, because they are continuous narratives, whereas the rest is formed from carefully assembled units of tradition, apart from the Passion Narrative, which we have already considered.

Dating the Gospels

The Gospels evidently belong to a fairly developed stage of primitive Christianity, but it is difficult to date them accurately. A date after the Letters of Paul (written between AD 47 and 60) seems to be required. Mark 13 reflects fears of persecution which go beyond anything suggested by Paul. Accordingly Mark is generally dated in the mid sixties or even at the time of the fall of Jerusalem (AD 70) or a little later. If Matthew and Luke are dependent on Mark, they must be dated later still. Matthew's Gospel apparently stems from a Jewish Christian church which was at loggerheads with Rabbinic Judaism, represented by the Pharisees. This would suit the conditions of growing estrangement between Church and synagogue after the fall of Jerusalem, which came to a climax around 85–90. Luke's Gospel shows the clearest signs of awareness that the fall of

Jerusalem is a thing of the past, and should be dated at about the same time as Matthew, or a little later. John refers to the exclusion of Christians from the synagogue (John 9:22; 12:42; 16:2) in a way that suggests the conditions of the late eighties or nineties.

These suggested dates for the composition of the Gospels have been challenged by J. A. T. Robinson (*Redating the New Testament*, 1976) on the grounds that allusions to the fall of Jerusalem are few and uncertain, and the Gospels and other New Testament books fail to reflect the shattering impact of this event upon the Jews. He therefore proposed dates rather earlier in the century. As this would narrow the gap between the time of Jesus and the writing of the Gospels, it has consequences for the question of their historical reliability. For this reason Robinson's theory has been welcomed by many people, though it has not won much support from scholars. The debate on this issue continues.

Lost Gospels
It seems probable that other Gospels were coming into existence at the same time. Papias, a writer of the early second century, shows that the oral tradition continued and was valued after the Gospels were written (see next chapter). It is thus possible that good items of tradition, which bypassed the canonical Gospels, were included in other Gospels which are now lost. The best example is the story of the woman taken in adultery, which has been incorporated in the later manuscripts of the Fourth Gospel (John 7:53–8:11). It clearly formed no part of John originally, and is now generally printed separately, in a footnote or at the end, in modern translations of the Bible (e.g. RSV, NEB). The story evidently comes from a longer work, because it starts with the conclusion of another story. It has the character of the Synoptic Gospels rather than John, though there is nothing in them quite like it. A number of modern scholars accept it as a genuine memory of the ministry of Jesus, preserved in a lost Gospel.

In a rather similar way a fragment of a lost Gospel which has been discovered in modern times (*Pap. Ox.* 840) has the end of a warning about evildoing and then an episode in the temple at Jerusalem, in which Jesus and the disciples are accused of omitting the ceremonial purification. Jesus defends this on the grounds that inner purification is the true cleansing (cf. Mark 7:1–23; Matthew 23:27–8).

In view of this evidence it would be a mistake to suppose that the four Gospels are the only ones written in the first century, or even the oldest. More books were written in this early period than have come down to us. The others are lost because a conscious choice was made at some point to accept some and exclude others. This decision was not made easily or suddenly. But it was the kind of decision which eventually produced the canon of scripture of the New Testament.

Form and Character of the Gospels
Before leaving this subject, we need to consider a little further the form and character of the Gospels. All four have a common pattern, beginning with the preaching of John the Baptist (preceded by the Infancy Narratives in Matthew and Luke and by a Prologue in John 1:1–18), and ending with the Passion Narrative and a few Resurrection traditions. It is possible that Mark originated this pattern, to give a coherent structure to what would otherwise be only a collection of sayings and stories. If so, the lost Gospels, if not dependent on Mark, might have had a very different arrangement. But it must be also be pointed out that Mark's plan is not only biographical but also kerygmatic. It is a presentation of the Jesus traditions in such a way as to promote faith in Jesus as the Son of God, according to the apostolic kerygma. The same is true of John (explicitly in John 20:31). It can thus be argued that the Gospels are not even intended to be biographical, so that it is a mistake to treat them in any sense as history. However, it has been shown that biography in the ancient world is generally slanted to promote a particular interpretation of the subject. The Gospels should, then, be accepted as biographies with an evangelistic slant.

Luke certainly appears, from his opening remarks to Theophilus, to intend to write as a historian. Luke not only perceived the need for a definitive life of Jesus, but also saw that this was not a sufficient explanation of the phenomenon of Christianity in his own day, when the Church had spread widely through the Greco-Roman world, and had become predominantly Gentile in membership and estranged from the parent Jewish community. Though a number of different theories have been advanced for Luke's decision to write a second volume, the Acts of the Apostles, the best explanation is that he undertook it as a historian, and as such he can be compared with the contemporary Jewish historian Josephus. Deficiencies in his history are due simply to the scarcity of sources when he was writing, probably near the end of the first century. As in the Gospel, Luke has clear evangelistic and apologetic aims in the composition of Acts. It is no accident that the story concentrates more and more on the life of Paul, and ends with his arrival in Rome. Whether any further accounts of the apostles were written during the first century is unknown. But fictitious examples soon appear in the second century, in which the impetus to satisfy popular curiosity is evident.

Other writings in the first century were mainly letters, homilies or treatises, such as Hebrews, James and 1 Peter, which tend to have a common form because they were intended for reading at the Christian assembly. It can be assumed that only a fraction of such writings has survived. Letters are often ephemeral, and the decision to preserve them and make copies depends upon exceptional circumstances. The only substantial book of the first century which falls outside these categories is Revelation. This is generally held to have been written in the nineties, though a date much earlier is accepted by some scholars on account of veiled references to the emperor Nero (reigned AD 54–68) and the lack of evidence for imperial persecution in the reign of Domitian (81–96). This is a Christian example of the contemporary genre of Jewish apocalyptic writings, and bears some resemblance to the Similitudes of Enoch (1 Enoch 37–71) and 2 Esdras. Whether other Christian apocalypses were written in this early date is unknown, but again we shall find further examples in the second century. Christian apocalyptic appears on a small scale in some of Paul's Letters (1 Corinthians 15:20–28; 1 Thessalonians 4:13–5:11; 2 Thessalonians 2:1–12) and in the arrangement of Mark 13 (often called the Little Apocalypse, cf. Matthew 24 and Luke 21).

3. THE MAKING OF THE NEW TESTAMENT CANON

Criteria of Canonicity
Most of the books of the New Testament were in circulation by the end of the first century, but we cannot be sure that this was true of all of them. A date well into the second century is very widely accepted for 2 Peter on the grounds that it appears to know of the collection of the Letters of Paul (3:15–16). Also, a second century date should possibly be assigned to the Pastoral Epistles (1 and 2 Timothy and Titus), if they were not written by Paul.

This at once raises two points. Firstly, we have other Christian writings belonging to this period which were not eventually included in the canon of the New Testament. Chapter 2 of Part I has referred to the Apostolic Fathers, and they will be considered further in the next chapter. Here it need only be pointed out that 1 Clement certainly overlaps the New Testament, even if the early date (AD 69–79) favoured by some modern scholars is rejected and the traditional date (AD 96) is adhered to. Writing to the Corinthians,

Clement shows familiarity with Paul's letters to the Corinthians and with Romans, and possibly alludes also to Ephesians. Hence his letter gives evidence for the collection and publication of the Pauline Epistles. If an early date is assigned to the *Didache*, it must also be considered earlier than some of the New Testament books. The Letters of Ignatius (written AD 107–8, or perhaps a little later) and the *Epistle of Barnabas* (if that is dated early) may also overlap the New Testament. This shows that the canon was not formed simply by selecting the earliest Christian works, and of course the existence of other books now lost must not be forgotten in this connection.

Secondly, the late dates proposed for the Pastoral Epistles and 2 Peter necessarily entail the view that these are pseudepigraphical work, or, to put it more baldly, forgeries. This raises the question of the authenticity of other New Testament books. As all the books suspected of being forgeries are attributed to apostles, it can be deduced that apostolic authorship was felt to be desirable or necessary in order to win acceptance in the Church. In fact apostolic authorship became one of the standard criteria for canonicity in the second century, with the result that more forgeries were produced.

The second century thus opens with a number of Christian writings in circulation, but no Christian canon of Scripture. It is obvious that some books would be more popular or highly valued than others, so that to that extent it is possible to speak of an unofficial canon of general acceptance.

Epistles and Gospels

The first step towards the formation of the canon can be regarded as the collection of Paul's Letters. As Luke apparently did not have access to them in writing Acts, it is necessary to date the collection towards the end of the first century. It is possible that the opposition to Paul, clearly attested in his Letters, did not end at his death, so that his reputation was eclipsed for a while. Later in the century, when the position of Gentile Christianity was assured, there was a revival of interest, which can be seen in the enthusiastic Letter to the Ephesians (probably written in his name by an ardent admirer) and the importance attached to Paul in Acts. The Pastoral Epistles give evidence of a continuing desire to claim his authority at a later date. In these circumstances there would be a demand for his surviving Letters. There is some evidence that Romans was prepared for general publication before a collection was made. For the destination 'in Rome' is missing from some manuscripts in Romans 1:7 and 15, and the final chapter 16, consisting only of personal messages, is also omitted, or its omission is implied, in part of the manuscript tradition. Obviously, when several letters to different places were assembled, these features would be restored. It has been suggested that Ephesians, which also lacks the destination in some manuscripts, was composed as a 'covering note' for the collection, but this seems scarcely likely from the contents. Once more, circulation individually is a better explanation. The collection originally contained only the letters to churches, those to individuals (Philemon and the Pastorals) being added later. Hebrews, which is certainly not by Paul, was probably not added to the collection until the later part of the second century. It does not count as a forgery, for it is not written in the name of Paul.

Meanwhile the Gospels circulated separately. The quotations in the Apostolic Fathers perhaps give evidence that Matthew was the most widely used (see next chapter). It is not known whether Luke and Acts ever circulated together. John took much longer to achieve general recognition, partly because of its late date and partly because it was favoured by the Gnostic heretics, and so was suspected of being heretical.

Apocryphal Gospels
By this time there were certainly other gospels in circulation. The *Fragments of an Unknown Gospel* (*Pap. Egerton* 2) seems to be a blend of the canonical gospels, including John. Part of the spurious *Gospel of Peter* survives, dealing with the trial, death and resurrection of Jesus. It shows the growing tendency towards legendary embellishment and anti-Judaic polemic which is characteristic of popular Christianity of the time. It has been regarded as tainted with the heresy of Docetism (the teaching, first mentioned in Ignatius, that Jesus only seemed to be human and to die, Gr. *dokeō* = seem). But this is not a deliberate slant on the part of the author, but a consequence of unthinking preoccupation with building up miraculous details at the expense of the natural. All through the second century the problem posed to those of Greek education and pagan presuppositions by the Church's faith in Jesus as the Son of God was a factor in Christian self-understanding, and the line between orthodoxy and heresy was by no means clear.

Another gospel, which may have been entirely orthodox in its original form, but has survived only in a form adapted to Gnostic thought, is the *Gospel of Thomas*. This had been known from Greek fragments, but the complete text in a Coptic version came to light in the discovery of Gnostic texts at Nag Hammadi in 1945. It is not a narrative gospel, but a collection of sayings of Jesus, including many parables, mostly with parallels in the Synoptic Gospels. It is thus very similar to what the postulated Q source might have been. On the other hand, two features are characteristic of second century heretical texts. Firstly, the preface makes it out to be a collection of the 'secret words which the living Jesus spoke, and which Didymus Judas Thomas wrote'. This is probably intended to be a revelation given after the resurrection, which goes beyond the teaching available in the generally accepted gospels. This device, whereby the risen Jesus is made to be the mouthpiece of the author's teaching, is frequently used by Gnostic teachers, so as to claim the authority of Jesus for their views. Secondly, the reinterpretation of gospel sayings, though slight, is unmistakably Gnostic. The spiritual quest is for the saving knowledge, and salvation is achieved by the transcending of sex, whereby the conditions of mortality are surmounted.

The *Gospel of Thomas* is to be distinguished from the *Infancy Story of Thomas*, which is a collection of legends of Jesus as a child between his birth and the finding of him in the temple (Luke 2:41-51), which is reproduced as the conclusion. The *Protevangelium of James* gives the history of the birth and childhood of the Virgin Mary, and remained popular for centuries. Both books are replete with fantastic miracles. Other heretical gospels, known only from patristic quotations, are the *Gospel of the Ebionites*, the *Gospel of the Hebrews*, and the *Gospel of the Nazareans*, all of which are Jewish-Christian works possibly based on Matthew, and the *Gospel of the Egyptians*, which (like *Thomas*) identifies salvation with the transcending of sex. The device of placing a work on the lips of the risen Christ is employed in the *Epistula Apostolorum*, which is aimed at *opposing* heretical writers, but shows the tendency of the day by failing to give an orthodox alternative to the heretical views, in spite of the writer's good intentions. The Valentinian *Gospel of Truth* uses the word gospel simply to indicate the author's own teaching, and makes no pretence of connecting it with Jesus. The *Gospel of Philip*, another work from the Valentinian sect, shows the élitism of this class of literature, whereby the truly spiritual people (i.e. those who embrace the sect's teaching) are differentiated from the mass of simple believers.

Other Apocryphal Literature
Besides the proliferation of gospels in this period, there were other works which achieved varying degrees of popularity in the Church. The *Shepherd of Hermas* is included in the Apostolic Fathers as an orthodox work which might easily have been included in the New Testament canon, and is indeed included at the end of the Codex

Sinaiticus along with the *Epistle of Barnabas*. The *Shepherd* gives long allegories of the spiritual life, and was much valued for spiritual guidance. The example of the Acts of the Apostles was followed by the *Acts of Paul*. A Jewish-Christian romance of Peter is contained in the *Clementine Recognitions* (one of several spurious works attributed to Clement of Rome). The imaginative appeal of the Book of Revelation was continued by the *Apocalypse of Peter*, which gives a description of rewards and punishments in the afterlife, and thus is a precursor of Dante's *Divine Comedy*. It is, of course, one item in a long tradition, stretching back to pre-Christian models, and it exercised a continuing influence in later centuries.

With these and other works that could be mentioned, the Church in the second century had a sizeable library, and problems began to arise in connection with official approval for public and private reading. Controversy between various Christian groups had already begun. The bishops of the long established churches were anxious to prevent books that were tainted with heresy from falling into the hands of the faithful. Thus the formation of the canon is largely a matter of exclusion of books considered unsuitable for reading in church.

Marcion

However, the second decisive step towards the formation of the canon came, not from the orthodox bishops, but from the heretic Marcion (treated more fully in Part I, chapter 2). Marcion illustrates precisely the difficulty of the Jewish heritage of the Old Testament for many people of Greek culture and education, but in his case it was not a matter of Gnostic speculation. He was an ardent but misguided follower of Paul, accepting Paul's teaching that the Law has been superseded by faith in Christ, but drawing the false conclusion that the God and Father of Christ could not be the same God as the God of the Old Testament, who gave the Law to Moses, and whom Marcion calls the Demiurge. He therefore opposed the use of the Old Testament in worship, and wished to discourage reading of Christian books in which the Law is prominent, like the Gospel of Matthew. He drew up a list of books which he considered suitable for reading in worship. This consisted of the Letters of Paul and the Gospel of Luke only. This is the first 'canon' (= measuring rod, standard, or rule) of the New Testament in the sense of an approved list.

Marcion's text of Luke was to some extent edited to remove what he found offensive. The choice of Luke would seem obvious, as it is the most congenial to his views, but it is possible that he was not familiar with the other Gospels. His list of Pauline Epistles does not include the Pastorals, but these, as we have seen, may not have been included in the collection at this date (AD 140). He does, however, have Philemon, so that the collection is not confined to letters to churches. Instead of Ephesians he has a letter to the Laodiceans (cf. Colossians 4:16), but this may in fact have been the same letter, as apparently it had first circulated without the name Ephesus, as we have seen. Similarly his copy of Romans did not include chapter 16, or apparently even chapter 15, which he may have removed on account of the references to the Law in 15:1–9.

The importance of Marcion is that he led the way in defining a canon by means of exclusion of books considered unsuitable. Moreover, by rejecting the Old Testament altogether, he encouraged the idea of a New Testament to replace it, and so opened up the concept of a bipartite canon. By this time Rabbinic Judaism had made further progress in defining the canon of Hebrew scriptures, and this was bound to have its effect on the Church's attitude to Scripture. In the time of Jesus, the Pentateuch (the Law) and the Prophets (including the historical books from Joshua to 2 Kings) and the Psalms were universally accepted by Jews, but the status of many other books remained uncertain (see Part II above on the Apocrypha). But decisions made by the Rabbis at the academy of Jamnia towards the end of the first century led to the exclusion of various books, such as Ecclesiasticus (Sirach) and the Wisdom of Solomon, which were much valued by Christians. So in this period there were disputes between Jews and Christians concerning the limits of the Old Testament itself. We shall see that this is reflected in the earliest lists of the canon of the New Testament.

Tatian

A further factor at this time is the *Diatessaron* (= harmony) of Tatian. This is the first evidence for a collection of the Gospels. Tatian, a Syrian who later lapsed into heresy, was converted in Rome about AD 160, or a little earlier, and there compiled a harmony of the four Gospels so as to form a single continuous text. Though this is now lost, quotations in the Fathers and the Commentary of St. Ephrem on the Diatessaron (known completely only in an Armenian version) show that he used all four Gospels, but probably no others. Hence all four were in use in Rome at this time. Later, after expulsion for his heretical teaching, he returned to Syria and made a Syriac version of the Diatessaron. This was so successful that it ousted the separate Gospels for more than two centuries in the Syrian Church (the claim of some modern scholars that the Syriac Diatessaron is the earliest Syriac version of the Gospels, however, is incorrect). Copies were eventually destroyed, when a new Syriac version of the separate Gospels was produced on the authority of Rabbula, Archbishop of Edessa, at the end of the fifth century. The importance of the Diatessaron for our purpose is that it shows that, though the four Gospels were now generally accepted in the Church, the concept of the canon was not so rigid as to prevent some freedom in handling the text.

The Muratorian Canon

The state of the canon around AD 200 can be deduced from references in the Church Fathers (Tertullian, Clement of Alexandria, Irenaeus) of the time, and is graphically illustrated in the Muratorian Canon, discovered in 1740 by L. A. Muratori. It is a Latin text in an eighth century manuscript, but internal evidence suggests that it has been translated from a Greek original composed in Rome about AD 200 (A. C. Sundberg's arguments for a later date are not convincing).

The list is damaged at the beginning, but there can be no doubt that it began with Matthew. At the point where it opens it is passing from Mark to Luke. In the section on John stress is laid on its different character from the other Gospels, which suggests that John was still the subject of hesitation in some quarters. At this point words are quoted from the beginning of 1 John. Acts is mentioned and all the Epistles of Paul, including the Pastorals, but not Hebrews. Then come Jude, 'two of John', the Wisdom of Solomon and the Book of Revelation. To these are added two books which may be accepted for private reading, but do not have canonical status, the *Apocalypse of Peter* and the *Shepherd of Hermas*. The reason for the lower status of the *Shepherd* is that it was not written by an apostle. The list also explicitly rejects two forged letters of Paul, one to the Laodiceans (evidently not Ephesians, which has been included earlier), and the other to the Alexandrians (otherwise unknown, but significantly attributed to the Marcionite heretics). The canon also excludes the writings of Arsinous, Valentinus, Miltiades and Basilides, who were all second century heretics. The inclusion of Wisdom reflects the disputes concerning the limits of the Old Testament canon mentioned above.

It is important to notice the omissions from this list: Hebrews, James, 1 and 2 Peter, and possibly 3 John. There is other evidence that Hebrews was not widely known in the west at this date. Its acceptance into the canon was assured only by the fact that it was added to the Pauline Epistles in the east (Clement of Alexandria is the first to attribute Hebrews to Paul). The omission of 1 Peter is surprising, and has not been satisfactorily explained. James, 2 Peter and 3 John are not mentioned by the Latin Father Tertullian, and so may not have been in use in Rome at this time. On the other hand, 'two of John' may be intended to refer, not to 1 and 2 John, but to 2 and 3 John, seeing that 1 John has been mentioned earlier in connection with the Gospel. But this seems unlikely. As 3 John is a personal letter, its status was not so secure as 1 and 2 John, which are letters to a church and closely related in subject. What these omissions do show is that the Catholic Epistles (i.e. those not attributed to Paul) did not comprise a distinct collection at this period. Their status was far less secure than that of the four Gospels, Acts and the Pauline Epistles, which by now were accepted everywhere.

It is clear that the Muratorian Canon is concerned with the needs of the Church in the second century, and it can be regarded as an official attempt to regulate the situation.

The Closing of the Canon

During the following century there is little change. Origen, writing about the middle of the third century, has three categories. First there are the *received* books, comprising the four Gospels, Acts, Pauline Epistles (including Hebrews), 1 Peter, 1 John and Revelation. Secondly there are the *doubtful* or disputed books, listed as James, 2 Peter, 2 and 3 John, Jude, the *Shepherd*, and some others. Thirdly there are the *spurious* books, and a few examples are given, including the *Gospel according to the Egyptians*, the *Gospel of the Twelve* and the *Gospel of Basilides*. The doubtfulness attaching to the second category stems from the difficulty of establishing their genuineness. There were so many forged works of apostles, and these books had never achieved the wide acceptance of the first category, largely because they are not such significant writings.

A new factor, however, entered the situation, just after this time. In AD 265 Dionysius of Alexandria, anxious to curb the spread of millenarianism (based on Revelation 20) in his diocese, discredited the Book of Revelation by showing that it cannot be attributed to the same author as the Gospel of John, and therefore is not an apostolic writing. As a result, Revelation was excluded as a forgery in the eastern churches. This is reflected in the fourth century historian Eusebius, who took over Origen's three categories, but transferred Revelation to the doubtful books, and made it plain that he thought it ought really to be amongst the spurious books.

The continuing uncertainties demanded a decision. In the west the tendency was to accept all works attributed to apostles. Thus a fourth century catalogue included in the sixth century Codex Claromontanus excludes Hebrews from the Pauline Epistles, but has all the Catholic Epistles. Then follow *Epistle of Barnabas* (perhaps meaning Hebrews, as the two books are sometimes confused in the west), Revelation, Acts (not previously mentioned), the *Shepherd*, *Acts of Paul* and *Apocalypse of Peter*. In the east the great fourth century Codex Sinaiticus, which originally contained the whole Bible in Greek, though much of the Old Testament is lost, has the complete New Testament, including Revelation, but also adds the *Shepherd* and *Epistle of Barnabas*. The general tendency in the east, however, was to be cautious about the doubtful books. Revelation virtually ceased to be used. The Syrian Church rejected this and 2 Peter, 2 and 3 John, and Jude as well.

Athanasius

In the end the decision was provided by St. Athanasius, the hero of the Council of Nicaea. Responding to a request for guidance on the question of the canon, in his thirty-ninth Paschal Letter of AD 367 he gave a complete list of the books of the Bible. The list shows the influence of disputes with Jews as far as the Old Testament is concerned, as it gives only those accepted in the Hebrew Canon, apart from Baruch and the Letter of Jeremiah, which are tacked on to Jeremiah, and Esther is omitted. Then follows the New Testament as we know it, except that the Catholic Epistles are listed between Acts and the Pauline Epistles. This in fact remained the usual order in the east, and is reflected in the manuscripts. Finally, Athanasius has a list of books of secondary status as follows: Wisdom of Solomon, Ecclesiasticus (Sirach), Esther, Judith, Tobit, *Didache*, *Shepherd*. There is no mention of 1 and 2 Esdras (3 and 4 Ezra) and of 1 and 2 Maccabees.

The immense prestige of Athanasius at once settled the question of the Canon of the New Testament for the Greek-speaking east. In the Latin west his decisions were promoted by Jerome and accepted by Augustine later in the century. Morever his clear distinction between canonical and deutero-canonical books in the Old Testament had lasting consequences. On the other hand the Syriac-speaking church of Syria did not respond so readily, and continued to omit the minor Catholic Epistles and Revelation. Though these were restored to the Syriac New Testament in the sixth century in the West Syrian (Jacobite) Church, they have never been accepted by the East Syrian (Nestorian) Church. Even in the

Greek Orthodox Churches Revelation is not normally read in public worship.

Summary

Looking back, we can see that the status of the New Testament books has changed since the period when they were coming into existence. At first they were written in relation to particular circumstances, especially the Letters, and their survival was to some extent a matter of chance. But they no doubt gained a wider circulation and were longer lasting than the many other books because of their intrinsic merit. Though apostolic authorship was regarded as the proper criterion for acceptance in the second century, this was really too uncertain to be the deciding factor in practice. Long use in the main churches of ancient foundation and absence of obviously heretical teaching were the two real criteria. By the time of Athanasius, Origen and others had already written commentaries on the gospels and other New Testament books. They were used regularly in worship in addition to the Old Testament lections. Schemes for dividing them up for lectionary purposes had been devised, and these have survived in many of the old manuscripts. The concept of a canon, comparable to the Old Testament, was universally accepted. Uncertainty attached only to the 'disputed' books, and this was removed by the authoritative decision of Athanasius.

Problems of the Canon

The closing of the canon had the effect of placing the New Testament on a different level from other Christian writings. It has tended to attract a supernatural aura, as if it were directly inspired in a way that is not true of other literature. But it is clear that the New Testament did not drop down from heaven. The most that can be said is that the intrinsic merits of these books and the process of their selection to form a canon can be traced to divine guidance. In fact, even from a completely secular point of view, the New Testament can be valued as an indispensable archive of the earliest Christian literature and as the primary source for the history of Christian origins. For the Christian believer, it is the record of the action of God in Jesus Christ and the saving message of the gospel. But it must also be recognised that for historical reconstruction of New Testament times and for fuller appreciation of the teaching of Jesus in its original setting, it is necessary to take into account all available sources and to treat them with equally scholarly integrity. The New Testament cannot be regarded as immune from critical inquiry from this point of view. The history of the study and interpretation of the New Testament is to some extent a history of emancipation from an uncritical, and therefore unrealistic, attitude towards it, whereby its meaning was obscured and its probative value for faith was misunderstood. The most important aspect of criticism is self-criticism, so that the critic may be fully aware of what he or she is doing and alive to the dangers of self-deception. In particular, any claim to possess the New Testament faith is liable to disregard the diversity of doctrinal statement that is contained within the New Testament itself, and rests on a false identification of part of the New Testament witness with the whole. The classic example of this is Martin Luther, who, in spite of all his greatness, made the doctrine of justification by faith the criterion for promoting some parts of the New Testament (especially Romans) to the exclusion of others (especially James).

It has to be granted that the critical approach to the New Testament has led to greater difficulties than the earlier critics ever imagined. If there is indeed variety within the New Testament, that affects its value as the primary witness of faith, and the nature of biblical faith has to be thought out afresh. There is, too, a tension involved in treating the New Testament like other ancient sources for the purposes of historical enquiry and retaining it as a collection of sacred books for use in worship and private meditation. There is a grave gap between the biblical scholars and the pastoral ministers, who often find the work of biblical scholarship wholly negative and unrelated to the religious needs of the people. Finally, the nature of Holy Scripture as the inspired Word of God has been called in question by the critical approach. These issues will necessarily be before us as we trace the story of the study of the New Testament in the following chapters.

FOR FURTHER READING

The Cambridge History of the Bible 1: From the Beginning to Jerome, edited by P. R. Ackroyd and C. F. Evans, CUP, Cambridge 1970.

Barrett, C. K., *The New Testament Background: Selected Documents*, SPCK, London 1956, rev. 1987.

Cartlidge, D. R. and D. L. Dungan, *Documents for the Study of the Gospels*, Collins, New York and London 1980.

Grant, R. M., *The Formation of the New Testament*, Harper and Row, New York 1965.

Kümmel, W. G., *Introduction to the New Testament*, Abingdon, Nashville, and SCM, London 1975.

Moule, C. F. D., *The Birth of the New Testament*, 3rd ed. rev., A. & C. Black, London, and Harper and Row, San Francisco 1981.

von Campenhausen, H., *The Formation of the Christian Bible*, A. & C. Black, London 1972.

2

THE MORAL USE OF THE NEW TESTAMENT IN THE PATRISTIC AGE

The formation of the New Testament is part of a larger process of the beginnings of Christian literature. The separation of the New Testament books from the rest to form the canon took place gradually. But their growing prestige as widely accepted apostolic writings gave them a leading position as documents for reference in the ongoing life of the Church. In this chapter we shall look at some of the ways in which they are referred to in the patristic period. As we should expect, they were valued primarily in connection with moral instruction, so that they were appealed to for guidance in the practical application of Christian life. This means that they were used in a direct and straightforward way for the most part, without the complications which we have seen in the Christian use of the Old Testament. However, from the end of the first century the problem of heretical teachers became more prominent in Christian writings. False teachings had to be rebutted by appeal to the authentic tradition. For this purpose the New Testament books were specially important. We can thus trace a separate class of references to the New Testament, concerned with matters of doctrinal controversy. The next chapter will be devoted to this development. Thirdly, as the canonical status of the New Testament enhanced the authority of the books, and made them the subject of close study, difficulties such as discrepancies or manifest errors were bound to come to light. Consequently some of the issues which have come to the fore in modern critical study were felt from quite early times. This will be referred to briefly at the end of the next chapter.

1. THE APOSTOLIC FATHERS

The circumstances which produced the books of the New Testament were the teaching needs of the Church, and they were valued precisely for the help that they gave. The Gospels preserved the teaching of Jesus, and the Epistles provided advice and inspiration in living the Christian life. At first there was bound to be considerable overlap with the continuing oral tradition of teaching in the Church, or other written collections, now lost. In the Apostolic Fathers it is often quite difficult to distinguish between references to the canonical Gospels and references to these other traditions. There is some evidence to suggest that, even when the written Gospels were widely available, the oral tradition was valued more highly. According to Irenaeus (*Adv. Haer.* V. 33:4) Papias had heard John speak, and was a friend of Polycarp. A fragment of Papias' lost *Exegesis of the Oracles of the Lord* shows how he placed oral witness above written accounts:

> If anyone came who was a direct follower of the elders, I would enquire about the words of the elders, what Andrew or Peter said, or Philip or Thomas or James or John or Matthew or any other of the disciples of the Lord, and what Aristion and the elder John, who were disciples of the Lord, say. For I considered that what was in books would not benefit me so much as what came from the living and continuing voice (fragment in Eusebius, *H. E.* III. 39:4).

Clement of Rome

This emphasis on oral continuity needs to be borne in mind as we look briefly at *1 Clement*, the earliest of the Apostolic Fathers. Clement's letter to the Corinthians is in a sense a continuation of Paul's correspondence with Corinth, though after a considerable interval. This remains true, even if the generally accepted date for the letter (AD 96) is rejected in favour of an earlier date (about AD 70), as advocated by some modern scholars. Clement knows 1 Corinthians, referring to it explicitly as 'the epistle of blessed Paul the Apostle' (47:1). This need not imply that the collection of Paul's Letters was already in circulation, as Clement was Bishop of Rome and personally concerned in the affairs at Corinth. Even so, his references to 1 Corinthians are confined to the opening chapters on divisions (47:3) and the famous chapter on love (1 Corinthians 13), which is the model for 49:5. Also, there are abbreviated quotations from Hebrews 1 in 36:2–5, and slight allusions elsewhere, not in any way suggesting that Hebrews is the work of Paul, but reflecting the fact that Hebrews was well known in the church at Rome.

On the other hand, Clement's very sparse references to the gospel tradition do not seem to be taken directly from any of the Gospels as we have them. 1 Clement 13:2 has a cluster of sayings from the Sermon on the Mount: 'Have mercy, that you may receive mercy. Forgive, that it may be forgiven to you. As you do, so it will be done to you. As you give, so will it be given to you. As you judge, so will you be judged. As you show kindness, so will kindness be shown to you. By what measure you measure, by that it will be measured to you.' These sayings are scattered throughout Matthew 5–7, and some appear together in Luke 6:31–8, but the text is never quite the same. Clement refers briefly to the Parable of the Sower in 24:5, but the quotation ('The sower went out'), though the same in all three Synoptic Gospels, is not sufficient to establish direct dependence. In 46:7–8 he refers to Jesus' words on causing offence, apparently conflating Matthew 26:24 (Mark 14:21) and Matthew 18:6–7 (Mark 9:42): 'Woe to that man. It were good for him if he had not been born, rather than that he should offend one of my elect ones. It were better for him that a mill-stone should be put round him and that he should be cast into the sea, than that he should pervert one of my elect ones.' Thus the 'little ones' of Matthew 18 have become the 'elect ones', which suggests interpretation in terms of members of the Church. The best explanation of all these references is that Clement is dependent on the continuing oral tradition, or parallel written tradition, and not quoting from one of the canonical gospels.

Barnabas

Clement's sparse use of New Testament traditions contrasts sharply with his numerous references to the Old Testament. Exactly the same is true of the very different *Epistle of Barnabas*. This anti-Judaic tract makes elaborate use of the Alexandrian style of allegorical interpretation of the Old Testament. Many of the quotations are the same as those used in the New Testament, though always with variations of text and a different application. Actual allusions to the New Testament are very few indeed, though the use of the same Old Testament quotations and some very small similarities of phrase suggest that the author may have read Romans. Gospel allusions are confined to a few well known aphorisms, such as 'Many called, but few chosen' (4:14). But these are not sufficient to prove direct use of the Gospels rather than parallel tradition.

The Didache

The *Didache*, however, presents a much more difficult problem. The book is composite, and begins with a Christianised version of a Jewish moral homily on the Two Ways (the way of life and the way of death, 1–6). In fact a short version of this document, without the Christian additions, is also included in Barnabas 19–20. Then chapters 7–15 give a series of regulations on church order and worship, which are notable for the large number of quotations from the gospel tradition, including the Lord's Prayer in a form almost identical with Matthew 6:9–13. Most of these are sayings of Jesus found in both Matthew and Luke, and so could have been drawn from the sayings source Q rather than the canonical Gospels. They are usually closer in form to Matthew than to Luke, but not always. The same is true of the sayings included in the Christian part of the Two Ways in chapters 1–2. The writer frequently introduces them with a reference to 'the gospel', but this means the tradition of the teaching of Jesus, and does not necessarily mean one of the Gospels or even a written source. The practical application of the sayings illustrates the circumstances which helped to preserve them. Thus Matthew 7:6, 'Do not give what is holy to dogs,' is quoted exactly in Didache 9:5, but used to justify the exclusion of unbaptised persons from the eucharist. The final chapter (16) is an eschatological warning with many points in common with Matthew 24 and the parallels in Mark and Luke. If the Didache stems from the same region as Matthew (probably Syria), it is not difficult to imagine that the author could use the same traditions as were collected together in Q and used by Matthew without actually being dependent on Matthew. On this view the Didache gives evidence for the diffusion of these traditions in the region, and their preservation in several different works.

Ignatius
To this region also belongs Ignatius, bishop of Antioch, the capital of Syria. Early in the second century he wrote letters of encouragement to churches in Asia Minor, while journeying under guard to Rome to suffer the death penalty for his faith. Here we find clearer evidence for the use of the actual New Testament books. It appears that the Letters of Paul are now available as a collection, as he speaks of 'every letter' of Paul (Ign. Eph. 12:2). Though actual quotations are few, Ignatius shares to some extent the thought and diction of Paul. Gospel references are also allusive, so that it is possible to argue that Ignatius prefers the oral tradition. But a few allusions to special features of Matthew suggests that he did make use of the written Gospel. Speaking of the baptism of Jesus in Smyrnaeans 1:1, he says it was 'that all righteousness might be fulfilled' (cf. Matthew 3:15). In his letter to the Ephesians 5.2 he

254   THE HISTORY OF CHRISTIAN THEOLOGY

mentions 'the prayer of one or two' (cf. Matthew 18:19–20). In Ephesians 18:2 he refers to the virgin birth of Jesus in connection with descent from David. In the next chapter he reproduces the story of the star and the magi, presumably deriving it from Matthew 2. Here there is a delightful detail: the sun and the moon and the rest of the stars form a chorus to welcome the new bright star, rather like Joseph's dream in Genesis 37:9–10. But the story is interpreted as the public manifestation of the meaning of Christ's coming for salvation, because the magic arts of the magi and all others like them were expelled by their acknowledgement that God's act had begun in him, and 'the abolishing of death was taken in hand' (19:3).

Ignatius is also the first writer to show what appears to be the influence of John, e.g. Magnesians 7:1, 'As the Lord did nothing without the Father', and 8:2, 'Jesus Christ his Son, who is his Word that proceeded from silence, who in all things was well-pleasing to him who sent him.' Both passages show a debt to John 8:28–9, and the second presupposes the Logos (Word) christology of John 1:1–14. Once more, it is impossible to be sure whether Ignatius knew the Gospel of John, or was familiar with the thought and diction of Johannine Christianity from which it sprang.

Polycarp

Polycarp, Bishop of Smyrna, was a friend of Ignatius, though it was many years later that he was martyred after a long life (traditionally AD 155). A letter of his to the Philippians survives, apparently written shortly after the death of Ignatius (perhaps AD 107). It is now widely held, however, that the main body of the letter (chapters 1–12) was written much later, about AD 140, and the paragraph about Ignatius (chapter 13) has been tacked on at the end. The dating is important, because chapters 1–12 are rich in New Testament quotations and allusions, and this is more readily explained if these chapters belong to the later date. They are concerned with moral exhortation, especially on the responsibilities of those who hold office in the church. There are allusions to several Pauline Epistles, including the Pastorals, and also to 1 Peter. In 7:1 there is an important quotation from 1 John: 'For every one who shall not confess that Jesus Christ is come in the flesh is antichrist; and whoever will not confess the testimony of the cross is of the devil' (cf. 1 John 4:2; 3:8; 2 John 7). Gospel references are mostly to the Sermon on the Mount, and the use of Matthew, rather than oral tradition or other sources, seems probable. There are no certain allusions to the Gospel of John.

2 Clement
It thus seems that, by the middle of the second century, reference is made increasingly to the canonical books of the New Testament, rather than to parallel traditions, whether written or oral. So also the spurious *2 Clement*, which is really a homily by an unknown author, has several allusions to the Gospels and Epistles. As these are always paraphrastic it is difficult to tell whether they are reminiscences of the canonical text, or based on other traditions. It is, however, the considered opinion of recent scholarship that the canonical books have exercised the main influence on the author, even if his quotations have also been affected by other parallel traditions.

Shepherd of Hermas
Similarly the *Shepherd of Hermas* reflects the transition to more explicit reference to the canonical books. The book is a series of moral allegories in the form of 'Visions', 'Mandates' (instructions) and 'Similitudes'. It seems that the original 'Visions' were received by Hermas before the death of Clement (Vis. 2:4), the rest being added later by the same author until the whole was completed some time after AD 140. It is notable that allusions to New Testament books become more common in the Mandates and Similitudes. Here it is at least probable that Hermas used Matthew, and possibly Mark and Ephesians. In particular, there is a striking new version of gospel parables, whereby the scenario of the Wicked Tenants (Matthew 21:33–43) is combined with the theme of the Talents (Matthew 25:14–30) to produce an entirely new allegorical story of the rewards of good service (Sim. 5:2).

2. MARCION

Christianity in the second century made its way very largely as a religion of moral uprightness rather than a gospel of salvation. It was experienced primarily in terms of the good life under the heavenly lordship of the risen and exalted Christ. The divinity of Christ was presupposed, and in his exalted state he was not clearly differentiated from God. The Christian tradition of life and worship was now sufficiently well established to support a recognisably Christian character and moral aim. It is thus a moralistic and legalistic outlook which characterises the Church at this time.

The Attraction of Marcion's Teaching
The inadequacy of this tendency explains the success of Marcion, who promoted a very one-sided version of Christianity wholly based on Paul. Some account of Marcion has been given in Chapter 2 of Part I, but a few further points may be added. Firstly, his achievement of winning a large following throughout the Mediterranean world was due to various factors, but these certainly include his appeal to New Testament books as the basis of his teaching. These were only the Letters of Paul and the Gospel of Luke, all heavily expurgated, as we have seen, but at least they were books with which Christians were now very familiar, unlike the exotic and esoteric works of the Gnostic teachers. Secondly, his idea that Jesus was the representative and revealer of the God of Love, wholly distinct from the harsh God of the Old Testament (the Demiurge), removed at a stroke the legalism of much contemporary teaching. Instead, his system offered release from the burdens of human life and the prospect of a new mode of existence in response to faith. This made for a simplified form of Christianity, which superficially made Paul's teaching on justification by faith intelligible, though it in no sense penetrated Paul's teaching. In fact, as an other-worldly religion, it encouraged asceticism and disparagement of the present world. This suited the climate of moral opinion of the second century, in which sexual continence was held up as the highest virtue by many teachers. This was especially true of the Gnostics, whose aim was to provide a way of life in which the spiritual replaces the material. Marcion was able to do this in a way that could be accessible to everyone, and not confined to a privileged élite, because he did not make his system rest on an elaborate and unbiblical cosmology.

Dualism in Marcion
Marcion presented his ideas with immense conviction and enthusiasm, but he paid a high price for his position. He had to propose an absolute dualism, in which the God of Love and Jesus his Son belong to a totally different order of being from the God of the Old Testament and his creation. Thus Jesus is presented in docetic terms: he only *seemed* to be human, and he only *seemed* to die. Humans, however, belong to the created order, so that their salvation consists in a change to a new nature, leaving their former nature behind. Consequently there is no concept of a good, but fallen, human nature that is capable of being redeemed. The death of Christ on the cross was a matter of paying the penalty of human

obligation to the Demiurge, thus releasing mankind from the curse of the Law.

The redemptive meaning of the crucifixion is clearly a casualty of Marcion's system, and it figures hardly at all in the Apostolic Fathers whom we have considered. It was, however, kept before the eyes of Christians in the eucharistic liturgy, and was stoutly maintained in the anti-Judaic literature of the period. Thus the necessity of Christ's death is maintained, using Old Testament passages, in Barnabas 11–12 and in the works of Justin (*First Apology* 48–50; *Dialogue with Trypho* 89–91).

Melito of Sardis

The sacrifice of Christ is also the subject of the *Homily on the Pasch* of Melito of Sardis. Dated about AD 170, it is the oldest known sermon for the Christian Passover, which was not yet separated into the two commemorations of Good Friday and Easter Day. This eloquent composition includes elaborate comparison between the exodus from Egypt and the crucifixion of Christ, and is clearly directly based on the Jewish Passover Haggadah in which the exodus was commemorated. Melito imagines the Jews keeping the Passover festival at the same time as Jesus suffers on the cross, and accordingly makes subtle contrasts between details of the festival and aspects of the crucifixion. He draws his references for the death of Christ from the canonical Gospels, especially John, whose dating of the Last Supper on the eve of Passover is followed, so that the death of Christ coincides with the slaughter of the Passover lambs. But he also makes allusion to the non-canonical *Gospel of Peter*, which he treats as a further source of information. In a characteristically anti-Judaic passage he says, 'Bitter for you Herod whom you followed, bitter for you Caiaphas whom you trusted,' thus making Herod equal to Caiaphas as an instigator of hostility to Jesus, as in *Gospel of Peter* 1:1–2. Melito takes the Old Testament seriously as real history, which has come to its climax in the historic person of Jesus. It is very probable that he was directly concerned to combat the influence of Marcion and Gnostic teachers who similarly repudiated the Old Testament and proposed a docetic Christ.

3. LATER WRITERS

Tertullian

Though many of the writings of the Church Fathers are refutations of heresies and treatises on doctrinal questions, numerous sermons and commentaries have survived which show the continuing and increasing use of the New Testament for purposes of moral instruction. Thus the North African writer Tertullian (AD 160–225), who is the first of the great Latin Fathers, wrote a large number of controversial books between AD 195 and 220, including his great work *Against Marcion*. But his writings include homiletic works. As a representative of these we may mention his short treatise *On Prayer*. This begins with an exposition of the Lord's Prayer as the model for Christian prayer, and then proceeds to discuss practical matters such as posture and dress. There are frequent references to points in the Gospels and Epistles, including in chapter 28 a slightly altered quotation of John 4:23–4: 'The hour is coming when the true worshippers will worship the Father in spirit and in truth. God is Spirit and thus requires his worshippers to be such.'

Clement of Alexandria
Another important example of the homiletic use of the New Testament is to be found in Tertullian's contemporary, Clement of Alexandria (AD 150–215). Clement is the first great Christian representative of the allegorical method of exegesis, but his homily, *Who is the Rich Man that is Saved?*, is an exposition of Mark 10:17–31, addressed to wealthy people who are alarmed at the demand of Jesus that his true disciples should give up all they possess. Clement argues that what is at stake is attachment to riches, and that this must be seen in relation to a broader understanding of the ethics of Jesus. The homily is entirely free from allegorical interpretation, and holds to the actual meaning of the text. It can be objected that Clement has relativised the text, and so evaded its true meaning. But it is an honest and straightforward attempt to apply the teaching of Jesus to the conditions of society in his own time.

Here it may be mentioned that the moral application of the parables of Jesus was by this time universally achieved by allegorising the details. Thus, in his *Stromateis* VI. 14, Clement applies the thirtyfold, sixtyfold and hundredfold yield in the Parable of the Sower (Matthew 13:8) to different degrees of reward in heaven.

Origen
Devotion to the literal meaning of the New Testament by an even greater exponent of allegorical exegesis can be seen in Origen (AD 185–253), Clement's successor in the school for catechumens in Alexandria. Though his adoption of allegorical method affected his work on the New Testament, this did not mean repudiation of the literal meaning wherever this was clear. He endeavoured to model

his life on the literal sense of the Gospels, taking seriously the hard sayings of Jesus to a degree that Clement's audience could not face, even 'making himself a eunuch for the sake of the kingdom of heaven' (Matthew 19:12) by emasculation (according to Eusebius, *H. E.* VI 8:1–3). It is thus not surprising that the beginnings of the monastic life towards the end of the third century are associated with literal acceptance of the hard sayings in the midst of a wealthy society that sought to evade them. According to Athanasius (*Life of Antony* 2), the young Antony (AD 251–356), the founder of Christian monasticism, discovered his vocation through hearing the words which troubled Clement's audience: 'If you would be perfect, go, sell what you possess and give to the poor, and you will have treasure in heaven; and come, follow me' (Matthew 9:21). He at once began a life of extreme simplicity, and some years later withdrew to the solitude of the desert.

Chrysostom

Finally, mention must be made of the vast homiletic output of John Chrysostom (AD 347–407), one of the great representatives of the Antiochene school of exegesis. As a follower of this school, he was opposed to the indiscriminate use of allegorical exegesis. His treatment of the New Testament in his sermons is always realistic. He had a great capacity to expose the meaning of Scripture and to give it practical application. He, too, exemplified his understanding of the gospel by his ascetic life-style, even though he held high office as Bishop of Antioch and later as Patriarch of Constantinople. Moreover he pressed home his criticism of luxury and vice without fear or favour, with the result that he created enemies at court, and was finally banished. His surviving homilies include series on Matthew, John and many of the Pauline Epistles. But he also has left a series on Acts, which, he says, to many people 'is so little known that they are not even aware that there is such a book in existence.' Obviously the Gospels and Epistles were chiefly used for instruction in doctrine and morals, and Acts was read, if at all, for pleasure, along with the spurious acts referred to above. (*For further reading, see end of next chapter.*)

3

THE THEOLOGICAL USE OF THE NEW TESTAMENT IN THE PATRISTIC AGE

1. THE GNOSTIC TEACHERS

At the same time as the books of the New Testament were winning acceptance as the basis of Christian teaching and practice, the Church was forced to clarify its theology in the face of the mounting confusion concerning doctrine. Anxiety about false teachers is expressed within the New Testament itself, especially in its later strands (e.g. Acts 20:29–30; 1 Timothy 1:6–7; 2 John 7). Different teachers attracted groups of disciples, thus forming a sect, like the Valentinians who followed the teaching of Valentinus. It seems likely that some of these groups were genuinely trying to understand the new faith and were not in intention unorthodox, but their presuppositions led them to false conclusions. They tended to be intellectuals, concerned with the inner life, very different from the practical allegiance to Christ and preparation for his second coming which formed the main concerns of the primitive Church. The divide between Gnosticism and Christianity is not always clearcut, especially as second century Christianity was still unsure of the philosophical basis of its doctrine. Philosophy was confused with spirituality, so that Clement of Alexandria distinguished between the ordinary literal-minded Christian and the 'spiritual' (really, intellectual) Christian, whom he actually refers to as the true Gnostic (*Strom.* II. 52:7). Gnosticism thus tends to be élitist and dualistic, and is closely allied to the ascetical tendency of the time.

The Gospel of Thomas
Not unnaturally, such heretical teachers read their own ideas into the Christian writings, and also adopted them in support of their particular doctrines. Though their works are largely lost, as they were banned by ecclesiastical authority, a spectacular find of thirteen

scrolls at Nag Hammadi in Egypt in 1945 revealed fifty-two tractates of varying lengths written in Coptic, but translated from Greek, and emanating apparently from the Valentinian sect. The tractates include the full text of the *Gospel of Thomas*, which is a collection of the sayings of Jesus, comparable to the postulated document Q. Many of them are almost identical with the sayings in the Synoptic Gospels, and show no Gnostic features. The following example, however, based on Jesus's sayings about children (cf. Matthew 18:3; 19:14), gives an expanded text, incorporating the idea of transcending the sexes. There may be allusion to Paul's assertion that in Christ there is 'neither male nor female' (Galatians 3:28), and to Jesus' saying on cutting off the hand or foot or eye that causes offence (Matthew 17:7–9).

Jesus saw children that were being suckled. He said to his disciples: 'These children being suckled are like those who enter the kingdom'. They said to him, 'If we are children, shall we enter the kingdom?' Jesus said to them: 'When you make the two one, and make the inside like the outside, and the outside like the inside, the upper side like the underside, and when you make the male and the female into a single one, so that the male will not be male and the female will not be female; when you make eyes in the place of an eye, a hand in place of a hand, and a foot in place of a foot, an image in place of an image, then you shall enter [the kingdom]' (*Thomas* 22).

Thus physical organs are to be replaced by spiritual organs for the wholly spiritual experience of the kingdom.

The emphasis on transcending sex also appears in fragments of the *Gospel of the Egyptians*, preserved in quotations in the writings of Clement of Alexandria. The denigration of sex arises from the Gnostic presupposition that matter is inherently evil, and Clement completely rejects this idea. However, he wants to defend the value of the *Gospel of the Egyptians*, which he claims is not really Gnostic, but has been misunderstood. Thus he twice quotes the following text: 'When Salome asked "How long will death flourish?", the Lord replied, "So long as you women give birth." ' But he insists that this does not really mean that childbearing is a hindrance to salvation, but that it is a way of saying that death is experienced in human life as a matter of cause and effect in the created order, or alternatively that it is a simile for the lusts of the mind which hinder progress towards eternal life (*Strom.* III. 45 and 64).

Sexual Licence?

Clement also, it appears, defended the *Secret Gospel of Mark*, according to a recently discovered letter attributed to him. This was an expanded version of Mark, preserved in a single copy in the library at Alexandria, and made available only to 'spiritual' persons, because of the risk of misunderstanding if read by the common people. Clement claims that this work has been pirated by the Carpocratians, a libertine sect which encouraged sexual licence as an expression of the love command, which of course Clement thoroughly disapproves. The book included a story, inserted after Mark 10:34, in which Jesus raises a young man from a tomb, and subsequently 'the youth comes to him, wearing a cloth over [his] naked [body]. And he remained with him that night, for Jesus taught him the mystery of the kingdom of God'. Clement absolutely denies the suggestion of the Carpocratians that a homosexual relationship is implied, but he regards the story as authentic. But it seems rather to be a version of the Lazarus story in John 11:1–44, correlated with the mysterious man who fled away naked in Mark 14:51–2. A further fragment in the letter refers to Salome as one of the followers of Jesus, which brings the work into the same orbit as the *Gospel of the Egyptians*. It is most unlikely that these additions belonged to the original form of Mark, in spite of the arguments of Morton Smith, the discoverer of Clement's letter.

Gnostic Use of John

The heretical use of John begins with *Basilides*, a second century teacher at Alexandria. Accounts of his teaching vary, but according to Hippolytus his system of cosmology presupposed successive emanations of spiritual beings from the uncreated God, and he claimed that this was done by means of a principle of divine generation of a seed which is identified with the word of God in creation: 'The seed of the cosmic system was . . . the word which was spoken, "Let there be light" (Genesis 1:3). And this, he says, is that which has been stated in the Gospels, "He was the true light, which lightens every man who comes into the world" ' (John 1:9, cf. Hipp. *Ref*. VII. 10).

Amongst the Valentinians, *Ptolemaeus* owes a debt to John in his cosmology of a series of emanations in four pairs (the Ogdoad), which include Word (Logos), Life, Truth and Man (cf. John 1:1–4), but surprisingly not Light. Another follower of Valentinus, *Heracleon*, has the distinction of being the first person to write a commentary on John. His work is lost, but is frequently referred to by Origen in his own commentary. Commenting on John 1:3–4,

Heracleon asserted that the Logos 'provided them (i.e. enlightened, or spiritual, men, mentioned in verse 4) with their first form at their birth, carrying further and making manifest what had been sown by another (i.e. the Demiurge), into form and into illumination and into an outline of its own'. He can claim that the spiritual person has a special capacity derived from God through the Logos in addition to the human nature derived from the creator of the natural world (the Demiurge – like Marcion, Heracleon will not identify God and the Demiurge, because spirit and matter cannot be mixed).

Besides these examples, some of the newly recovered tractates from Nag Hammadi show the influence of John, especially the *Trimorphic Protennoia* (= the three forms of the primeval idea). The third of these three forms is the Son, or Logos, and in this section there are numerous echoes of John's Prologue. It is disputed whether this is a Gnostic Christianisation of an originally entirely non-Christian work, or is a new composition by a Gnostic Christian.

The attempts of these and other teachers to provide an intellectual basis for their understanding of Christian faith were no doubt well meant, but had to be firmly resisted. The absolute dualism, allowing no relationship between the divine and created orders, normally encouraged moral asceticism and denigration of marriage. They were also necessarily docetic, denying the real humanity of Jesus. Moreover, they made faith subordinate to an intellectual rationalisation, available only to a spiritual élite, and so destroyed the gospel for the common people.

2. THE ORTHODOX RESPONSE

Irenaeus
Those who sought to correct these errors, and to prevent Christianity from disintegrating into a mass of opposed sects, had to do more than refute mistaken opinions. They also had to construct for themselves a sound intellectual framework for Christian doctrine. This work was begun by Irenaeus (AD 130–200) in the later part of the second century. Following the same presuppositions as Melito, he set out to recall the Church to the biblical foundations of its faith, so that his constructive teaching is firmly based on the Old Testament and almost the complete range of New Testament books. He shows a great debt to Paul, and especially to the Letter to the Ephesians, which is the basis of his doctrine of the recapitulation of human history in Christ. He thus gave full value to the human nature of Christ. At the same time, his refutation of the

Gnostics led him to turn to the Gospel of John for elucidation of the cosmic position of Christ, and he boldly claimed John for orthodoxy. A careful reading of John, he maintains, is the best way to refute the heretics who make such free use of John (*Adv. Haer.* III. 11:1–7). For John supports neither the separation of God from the Demiurge nor the separation of the impassible Christ from Jesus who was crucified:

> John, the disciple of the Lord, preaches this faith, and seeks, by the proclamation of the Gospel to . . . persuade them that there is but one God, who made all things by his Word; and not, as they allege, that the creator was one, but the Father of the Lord another; and that the Son of the creator was, indeed, one, but the Christ from above another, who also continued impassible (i.e. not subject to suffering), descending upon Jesus, the Son of the creator, and flew back again into his pleroma (i.e. the heavenly sphere of all spiritual beings).

Incidentally, Irenaeus supports his use of John by asserting that there must be *four* Gospels and *only* four (thus excluding the noncanonical gospels), on the grounds that there are four winds and that there are four cherubim around the throne of God with different faces – a lion, an ox, a man and an eagle (Revelation 4:7). Later writers amended the order to correspond with Ezekiel 1:10, thus producing the conventional symbols of the evangelists – Matthew the man (or angel), Mark the lion, Luke the ox, and John the eagle.

Irenaeus had a stronger sense of history than most theologians of his day. Like Melito, he saw the Old Testament as prophetic of Christ, so that Christ sums up, or recapitulates, the past. Similarly Christ sums up the future, so that the meaning of Christ is worked out historically in the Church. Thus Irenaeus uses typological exegesis, which can be distinguished from the allegorical exegesis of Alexandria, which is concerned with timeless truths in the life of the soul. On the other hand a degree of allegorism remains, as illustrated in the application of the cherubim to the four Gospels.

Origen
There are really three main interests in this period, and these are united in Origen, who succeeded Clement in the school at Alexandria at a very young age. Firstly, he was an ardent biblicist, and could use the moral teaching of the New Testament in a straightforward way, as we have already seen. Secondly, he continued Clement's exposition of the spiritual life, using allegorical exegesis, in

which the personalities of the Bible are identified with virtues and vices in the soul. Thirdly, he felt the same need as the Gnostics to explain the Christian revelation in philosophical terms of the relationship between God and the created order.

Because of his interests and general approach to the Bible, Origen frequently treats the New Testament in exactly the same way as the Old. He tends to regard the literal (or historical) meaning as the wrong interpretation. Thus he points to the discrepancy between John and the Synoptics concerning the timing of the Cleansing of the Temple to prove that these accounts were never intended to be taken literally. When they are interpreted allegorically, however, they can be brought into a 'harmony' (*Comm. on John* X. 16). Here he gives a typological interpretation like Irenaeus and a spiritual interpretation like Clement.

> We may regard these ocurrences as a symbol of the fact that the service of that temple was not any longer to be carried on by the priests in the way of material sacrifices, and that the time was coming when the law could no longer be observed, however much the Jews according to the flesh desired it, . . . the kingdom of God being taken away from the Jews and given to a nation bringing forth the fruits of it (Matt. 21.43).
>
> But it may also be the case that the natural temple is the soul skilled in reason, which, because of its inborn reason, is higher than the body; to which Jesus ascends from Capernaum (John 2.12), the lower-lying place of less dignity, in which, before Jesus' discipline is applied to it, are found qualities which are earthly and dangerous, . . . which are driven away by Jesus with his word plaited out of doctrines of demonstration and rebuke, to the end that his Father's house may no longer be a house of merchandise.

Origen then compares the accounts in the other Gospels, which have the Cleansing directly after the Entry into Jerusalem. Here he has his well known explanation of the colt and the ass, which it was obviously impossible for Jesus to bestride literally (Matthew 21:1–11). He decides that the ass is the Old Testament and the colt the New, both together being bearers of the Word of God. But the important thing is that, whatever is made of his exegesis, Origen is seriously trying to give full value to the actual words of Scripture.

However, it must be admitted that Origen's interpretations are often far-fetched and fanciful, and that his conviction that the allegorical sense is the key to the true meaning is fraught with danger of wild subjectivism. Among the Latin Fathers Tertullian complained that it is the way of the heretics, who want to evade the plain meaning of the text. In fact both Origen and Tertullian in their different ways were guided by their loyalty to the Rule of Faith, that is, the common faith shared by the main body of Christians, which was later to be crystallized in the creeds. But whereas Irenaeus and Tertullian were cautious in speculation concerning the philosophical basis of faith, Origen was brilliant and constructive. Without intending to undermine orthodoxy, his theories about the Trinity, the pre-existence of human souls, and the spiritual nature of the resurrection body, were too daring to win general acceptance, and accordingly his theology was condemned.

Theological Response
However, the theological problems demanded solution. Because the Gnostic systems made Christ an intermediary, as something less than God and yet fundamentally different from mankind, the implications of the Rule of Faith had to be drawn out with clearer exposition. Matters came to a head in the late third and early fourth century, when *Lucian of Antioch* founded the Antiochene school of exegesis in conscious opposition to the excesses of Origenism. The biblical realism of this school tended to think of Jesus in historic terms, and therefore as subordinate to God, his father, though his heavenly origin was not denied. At this time *Arius*, who may have been a pupil of Lucian, attempted to maintain monotheism by asserting that Jesus, as God's Son, is in a lower category than God the Father, and indeed owes his existence to the Father's decision to produce the created order. This led to the Arian controversy, in which John 14:28, 'The Father is greater than I', became a key text. Though Arianism was condemned at the Council of Nicaea (AD 352), the controversy continued through the century until its final resolution at the Council of Constantinople (AD 381).

The point at issue can be viewed in terms of scriptual interpretation. For the subordinationist view of Jesus' sonship arises from the attempt to make theological statements on the basis of a literal understanding of particular texts, such as John 14:28. On the other hand *Athanasius* (AD 296–373), the leading opponent of Arius, though he had to wrestle hard with the contradictions of the New Testament texts, which could only with difficulty be brought to bear on the questions at issue, did at least recognise that talk about the nature of God can proceed only by way of analogy, so that it is not possible to construct theology by taking Scripture literally. The crucial term in the debate was the adjective *homoousios* (= of one substance), which allowed a proper differentation between Jesus and the Father without necessitating subordinationism. But the word was disapproved, on the grounds that it was unscriptural, tainted by previous use in some of the Gnostic systems, and capable of being interpreted in a way that might fail to do justice to the distinctions between Father, Son and Holy Spirit in the Godhead.

3. AFTER NICAEA

Athanasius

The subsequent debate thus paid special attention to the meaning of words. To this end Athanasius drew attention in his *Letter on the Decrees of Nicaea* to the importance of ascertaining the *meaning* of Scripture. Thus he supports 'of one substance' (*homoousios*) as a word, which, though not found in Scripture, conveys the meaning of Scripture, by citing John 1:18; 6:46; 8:42; 10:30; 14:10.

Cyril of Alexandria

This insistence on the meaning of Scripture meant that the scope of allegorisation for doctrinal statement was curtailed. Though the allegorical method continued to be used for the Old Testament, its value was seen to be in the prefiguring of truths of the New Testament. But these truths must be deduced from the New Testament by the application of reason. Cyril of Alexandria (died AD 444) in his commentary on John paid special attention to the ways in which it supports the orthodox faith. In his doctrinal work he broke new ground by placing the consensus of patristic teaching alongside Scripture as the test of theological orthodoxy. Thus Scripture and tradition support each other, and the weakness of exclusive reliance on Scripture, which can be made to mean anything, is overcome.

Theodore of Mopsuestia

In the school of Antioch the emphasis on literal interpretation of Scripture opened up new dangers in the post-Nicene period. The greatest of the Antiochenes was Theodore of Mopsuestia (AD 350–428), whose work of exposition paid particular attention to passages disputed in the doctrinal controversies. This had an unfortunate effect, because, in dealing with the Gospels (notably in his commentary on John), he attempted to distinguish between Christ's humanity and his divinity in relation to his deeds and words. This laid him open to the charge of what later became known as Nestorianism, i.e. the doctrine that there are two separate persons in Christ, one divine and the other human. It is clear, however, from his writings as a whole, that he did not really hold this view. What he was trying to do was to account for the fact that Jesus in the Gospels does not always speak and act as a recognisably divine person. Thus he was aware of the problem of reconciling a dogmatic view of the divinity of Christ with the impression that is given when the Gospels are treated as historical documents. His difficulties were partly due to an over-literal approach. This literalism can be observed when he tries to elucidate John 5:25, 'the hour is coming, and now is, when the dead will hear the voice of the Son of God, and those who hear will live.' He assumes that the phrase 'and now is' must refer to actual events in the present: the widow's son (Luke 7:11–17), the daughter of the ruler of the synagogue (Mark 5:21–43), pre-eminently Lazarus (John 11:1–44). Nevertheless Theodore's attention to the literal meaning, care for textual points, and attempt to see the New Testament writings in historical focus, have earned for him the reputation of being a precursor of modern historico-critical study of the New Testament. The above example shows that this can be claimed only with considerable reservations.

Jerome

In the Latin west Jerome (AD 331–420) stands out as the greatest scholar of this period. His knowledge of Greek and Hebrew, acquired in his long years in the east, fitted him to undertake the revision of the Old Latin version of the Bible, which had become urgently necessary in view of the multiplicity of variant readings and discrepancies from the Greek. In 383, at the request of the aged Pope Damasus (died AD 384), he began to revise the text of the Gospels, thus producing the first books of the Latin Vulgate. The scholarly skills required for this undertaking gave him an outstanding capacity to deal with problems and difficulties of the text. This can be seen in his commentary on Matthew, written much too hurriedly in 398 in response to the request of a friend for a plain commentary on the text. Thus, commenting on the petition, 'Give us today our daily bread', in the Lord's Prayer, he points out the difficulty of understanding the true meaning of the extremely rare Greek word, *epiousion*, generally translated 'daily'. He says:

In the so-called Gospel according to the Hebrews instead of bread 'necessary for existence' I found *maar*, which means 'of tomorrow', so that the sense is: 'Give us today our bread of tomorrow, i.e. of the future' (*Comm. on Matt.* 6:11).

The gospel referred to was probably an Aramaic translation of Matthew, used in the Aramaic-speaking Christian communities of Syria. Thus *maar* (properly *māhār*) is a translation of *epiousion*. On the other hand it could go behind the written Gospel to continuous oral tradition in the liturgy. If so, it might well be the original Aramaic used by Jesus, as has been strongly argued by J. Jeremias. However, Jerome did not accept it for his own translation.

In spite of much scholarly care, Jerome still shows the tendency to use allegorical interpretations under the influence of Origen. This appears, along with another very interesting reference to the Aramaic gospel just mentioned, in his commentary on Matthew 12:13 (the man with a withered hand):

> In the gospel which the Nazarenes and Ebionites use, which we have recently translated from Hebrew into Greek, and which is called by most people the authentic Gospel of Matthew, the man who had a withered hand is described as a mason, who asked for help with these words: 'I was a mason earning my living with my hands; I pray you, Jesus, to restore my health so that I may not shamefully beg for food.' Until the coming of the Saviour there was in the synagogue of the Jews a withered hand, and the works of God were not done there; after he came to earth, the right hand was given back to the apostles who believe and restored to its original function.

The final allegorising comment is in line with Jerome's retention of Origen's explanation of the ass and the colt in Matthew 21:1–11 as the Old and New Testaments. Similarly he interprets the Parable of the Mustard Seed (Matthew 13:31–2) in terms of the Gospel, which is smaller than all other philosophies, but has the greatest capacity to issue in the totality of the faith.

In his commentaries on Galatians, Ephesians and Titus, Jerome is naturally more concerned with the literal meaning of the text, but in fact his work is again largely derivative, and includes fanciful explanations of details. He has no use at all for his older contemporary *Marius Victorinus Afer*, who wrote practical commentaries on the Pauline Epistles without attention to the work of other writers, or for the much more important commentaries of *Ambrosiaster* (a name coined by Erasmus for an unknown writer, whose commentaries had been attributed to Ambrose until Erasmus proved this to be false). The latter continued the tradition of Latin writers from Tertullian onwards, and penetrated Paul's meaning more successfully than other commentators of the period.

Augustine

Finally, Augustine (AD 354–430) was converted in 386, partly as a result of the example of Victorinus Afer, and ten years later became bishop of Hippo in North Africa, where he produced a vast output of writings. Though he never wrote the great commentary on Romans which he intended, the decisive impact of Romans on his own understanding of his conversion makes it central to many of his theological writings. From it he developed his doctrines of predestination and original sin and the need for prevenient grace, which had immense influence on the subsequent history of theology in the west.

In this connection he found a key text in Romans 5:12, 'Therefore as sin came into the world through one man and death through sin, and so death spread to all men because (Latin *in quo*) all men sinned,' and he refers to it many times in his writings. But he took *in quo* to mean 'in whom', referring back to 'one man' earlier in the verse, i.e. Adam. This suggests that everyone is born a sinner simply as a result of descent from Adam. Augustine derived this interpretation from the commentary of Ambrosiaster on this verse: 'Thus he said "in whom", though he was speaking about the sin of the woman (i.e. Eve), because he referred not to the species but to the race. And so it is clear that in Adam all have sinned in a lump; for he was corrupted through sin himself, and all those whom he has begotten are born under sin'. Augustine thought that this commentary was by the great theologian Hilary (died AD 367), though it was later attributed to Ambrose. He simply assumed on the strength of this authority that it gave the correct meaning of the text. It is doubtful if he ever consulted the Greek, where he would have seen that 'because' is the true meaning. On the other hand he did consider the possibility that 'death' or 'sin' might be the antecedent of *in quo*. Though he rightly rejected these alternatives, his refusal to adopt 'because' prevented him from reaching the real meaning of the verse. There was perhaps some obtuseness in this, because his theological opponents in the Pelagian controversy, who denied Augustine's doctrine of original sin, stoutly maintained that 'because' was correct.

Augustine also considered the principles of biblical interpretation in his book *On the Teaching of the Christians*. Here he makes it clear that the literal sense should be sought first. But when this fails to yield a satisfactory meaning, various devices may be employed. He quotes the opening words of St. John's Gospel to show that the verse is open to different interpretations according to the way in which it is punctuated. Significantly he decides that only one punctuation is consistent with the Rule of Faith, so this must be adopted. He also recommends the *Rules of Tyconius*, a manual of exegesis for dealing with obscure passages in the Bible, which had been published in 382 and became widely influential. One was the rule that expressions of time may give the part for the whole, and on this basis he resolves the disagreement between six days (Matthew 17:1; Mark 9:2) and eight days (Luke 9.28) in the accounts of the transfiguration of Jesus. Elsewhere he suggests that doubtful passages should be interpreted by comparing other passages where the same words are used in a less ambiguous manner, so that Scripture interprets Scripture. Anything that might be dishonouring to God must be interpreted figuratively, because the words of Scripture are the expression of eternal truth. Similarly the tradition of allegorical interpretation is to be retained to explain meaningless details. On this basis he allegorises every detail in the story of the Wedding at Cana (John 2:1–11), the six waterpots becoming the six ages from Adam to Christ, and the two or three measures indicating all humanity (two measures: the circumcision and uncircumcision; three measures: the three sons of Noah, the ancestors of the human race).

4. NEW TESTAMENT PROBLEMS

Augustine, and Jerome before him, are clearly aware of the problems which confront every serious student of the Bible, and it is instructive to see how some of the concerns of modern biblical scholarship were already felt in the age of the Fathers.

The Four Gospels

The most obvious difficulty confronting students of the New Testament is the relationship between the Gospels. The Gospel of John presented a problem from the first. Clement of Alexandria defended it on the grounds that it has a different purpose from the rest: 'But last of all, John perceiving that the external facts had been made plain in the Gospel, being urged by his friends and inspired by the Spirit, composed a spiritual Gospel' (quoted by Eusebius, *H. E.* VI.14.7). The difference is thus explained by contemporary needs. The common people want the plain facts, and try to live by the moral teaching of Jesus. The educated élite, like Clement himself, want a gospel that will elevate their minds to higher realities, freed from the cares of daily living. This explanation of the Fourth Gospel is not satisfactory, because it does not cover the discrepancies. Consequently Jerome (*On Illustrious Men* 9) suggested that the ministry of Jesus in John belongs to the time between the baptism of Jesus and the imprisonment of the Baptist, omitting the events between the imprisonment and Jesus' entry into Jerusalem, whereas the Synoptic Gospels cover the part which John has omitted. Thus Jerome can argue that there is no fundamental discrepancy between John and the Synoptics as they cover different periods. Of course he has to assume that Jesus cleansed the temple twice.

Discrepancies between the Synoptic Gospels were usually dealt with by harmonising the accounts. Augustine, however, in his *Agreement of the Evangelists* 2 faced the fact that the real problem is not the discrepancies, but the exceptional degree of agreement, which makes it impossible to regard them as written independently. He points out that they are often word for word the same. He therefore suggests that Mark, as Matthew's 'attendant and epitomiser', deliberately abbreviated Matthew. Augustine is thus aware of the Synoptic Problem, which has figured so prominently in modern study. His solution is inadequate, because he makes no attempt to follow it up in detail, and the position of Luke is left unclear. He is not really interested in the question. It is simply a difficulty to be disposed of before starting his exposition of the Gospels.

Problems of Translation

Meanwhile the commentaries of Jerome, as already indicated, are notable for their attention to difficulties arising from his observations as a translator. Commenting on Matthew 2:23, he notes that the quotation, 'He shall be called a Nazarene', is not attributed to a particular prophet, but to the prophets in general. Thus it is not to be regarded as a direct quotation, but as a statement that accords with the broad meaning of prophecy. However, he also points out that it may allude to Isaiah 11:1, which foretells a 'branch' from the root of Jesse, because the Hebrew for 'branch' is a word that might be construed as 'Nazarene'. In the prefaces which Jerome provided for his Vulgate translation of the Bible, he also shows knowledge of debates on authorship and canonical status of the books. Moreover he was keenly aware of the problem of variant readings. In translating the New Testament he frequently introduced Alexandrian readings in preference to the Western readings found in the Old Latin version which the Vulgate was designed to replace (see p. 331

below on textual criticism). Looking ahead to the period of our next chapter, we may here observe that the Vulgate in its turn became corrupted, partly through the influence of the Old Latin, which continued in use for some time, and an important work of revision was undertaken by *Alcuin* (AD 735–804), the brilliant scholar from York in the court of Charlemagne. Further efforts at revising the Vulgate text were made at various times throughout the Middle Ages.

FOR FURTHER READING

The Cambridge History of the Bible 1.

Hennecke, E., *New Testament Apocrypha*, 2 vols., SCM, London 1973–4.

Lake, Kirsopp, *The Apostolic Fathers* (Loeb Classical Library), 2 vols. , Heinemann, London 1912–3.

Quasten, J., *Patrology*, 3 vols., Spectrum, Utrecht 1950–60.

Wiles, M. F., *The Spiritual Gospel: the Interpretation of the Fourth Gospel in the Early Church*, CUP, Cambridge 1960.

——, *The Divine Apostle: the Interpretation of St Paul's Epistles in the Early Church*, CUP, Cambridge 1967.

4

THE NEW TESTAMENT IN
THE MIDDLE AGES

1. GREGORY AND BEDE

From East to West

Our story began in the east, with the rise of the New Testament in the Greek-speaking world of the eastern Roman empire. We have seen the New Testament in process of formation as the collection of those Christian writings which acquired special status as canonical scripture. These books thus became the Church's most important deposit of literature. It was the chief source and point of reference for moral and spiritual life and for establishing the truth of doctrine in the age of the great controversies. The fourth of the fully ecumenical councils was the Council of Chalcedon (AD 451). This approved the Chalcedonian definition of the divine and human natures in Christ, which has remained the formal basis of the doctrine of the person of Christ in both eastern and western Christendom ever since. Thereafter the political and cultural division of the Greek east and the Latin west led increasingly to misunderstanding, lack of co-operation, and eventually complete estrangement. From this point the history of the Church in the west must be considered in separation from that of the Church in the east.

As far as the Bible is concerned, it is in the west that the crucial developments took place. The basic understanding and methods of interpretation already laid down in the age of the Fathers continued in both east and west. But in the east there is little change for many centuries. Only in modern times has the critical approach to the Bible, developed in the west, had some impact on the eastern churches. Consequently the story from this point onwards will be devoted to western Christianity, and the present chapter will take us to the dawn of the Reformation. The central position which the Bible holds in the Reformation cannot be understood except in the light of the history of the Bible in the Middle Ages.

The Bible and the Spiritual Life

The fundamental point to bear in mind is that the aim of biblical study was to promote the spiritual life. The Alexandrian tradition of allegorical exegesis had been developed for this purpose. It was presupposed that the sacred text must have a spiritual meaning. This could not always be found by a plain reading of the text, because the literal meaning is only occasionally directly relevant to the spiritual life of the individual. Rules of interpretation were needed to enable the reader to unlock the treasures of the Scriptures, such as the rules of Tyconius. Inevitably the expertise required to read the Scriptures profitably was confined to the educated. The common people were not only unable to read the Bible, but had little equipment to interpret it when they heard it read. This explains the resistance to vernacular translations of the Bible, which we shall meet in our study of the mediaeval period. This was not a conspiracy on the part of powerful ecclesiastics to withhold the truth from the common people, but a concern for what was felt to be the proper use of sacred Scripture. Not surprisingly, Jesus' admonition not to cast pearls before swine (Matthew 7:6) was quoted in this connection (in Knighton's *Chronicle* against Wycliffe's translation, early fifteenth century).

With such a spiritual aim, the scholars of the time continued the traditions of exegesis which had been passed on from Origen to the west by Hilary and Ambrose, and especially by Jerome and Augustine. With the decline of classical culture, the study of Scripture was centred mainly in the monasteries to begin with, before the rise of the cathedral schools and eventually the mediaeval universities. The monastic tradition of spiritual reading (*divina lectio*) was maintained specifically for the edification of the soul in contemplation and discipleship. The four senses of Scripture (literal, moral, typical of Christ, and anagogical = applied to ultimate salvation) had already been established in the teaching of the Desert Fathers, so that there was no tension between scholarship and monastic spirituality.

Those who could not read the Bible were made aware of its teaching through liturgy and art. Everyone was familiar with the basic gospel stories. The patriarchs and other familiar characters of the Old Testament were known from childhood almost as personal friends. Certain stories, such as the sacrifice of Isaac in Genesis 22, were universally understood to be the types of gospel events, in this case the sacrifice of Christ. The manna in the wilderness (Exodus 16) was similarly related to the eucharist. Such references were provided in the liturgy, partly by the choice of lections (which might be the subject of a homily), and partly by the antiphons and responses which decorated different parts of the liturgy. The same passages were favourite subjects for sculpture, painting and stained glass. Thus popular imagination was nourished by vivid stories and even more vivid artistic representations of them, which conveyed symbolically the nature of human life in relation to God's plan of salvation. The line between symbol and reality was not easily drawn. Ideas of heaven and hell were shaped by the apocalyptic pictures of Revelation. These were supplemented from non-canonical sources, as many books not accepted into the canon continued to be popular for centuries. The *Apocalypse of Peter* and *Apocalypse of Paul* added horrific details to the common ideas of hell. Devotion to the Virgin Mary led to widespread use of the legends of the childhood of the Virgin in the *Protevangelium of James*. Later in the Middle Ages books of devotion were produced, such as the *Liber Pauperum*, in which a picture of a gospel scene is supported by two Old Testament types, provided with a brief explanation, and decorated with verses from psalms and prophets. The reader would thereby be encouraged to explore in meditation wider aspects of the gospel episode for the benefit of the spiritual life.

Gregory the Great

At the beginning of the period the outstanding biblical scholar is Gregory the Great (540–604), the wealthy aristocrat who gave away his riches to embrace the monastic life, and eventually became Pope of Rome. Much of his writing is devoted to the needs of the clergy, whose education he was deeply concerned to improve. He was also a celebrated preacher, drawing large crowds to hear his sermons. Forty of his *Homilies on the Gospels* have survived. These show both great eloquence and practical realism. He deals with the literal sense and gives some attention to allegorical interpretations, but it is the moral sense which is his real aim.

In general Gregory thinks of the Bible as a school for training in the love of God and of one's neighbour. The literal sense may help, especially in the Gospels. But the harder and seemingly less relevant passages should be studied carefully to discover the wisdom which they contain for the Christian life. This especially applies to the Old Testament (Gregory's treatment of Job along these lines has been shown above in Part I, chapter 5).

Naturally Gregory draws on the work of his predecessors, especially Jerome and Augustine, selecting what he finds useful and discarding the rest. In particular, interpretations relating to the doctrinal controversies which concerned us in the last chapter, are no longer retained. His work laid the foundation for the mediaeval exegesis, which shows a remarkable homogeneity throughout the period. The study of the Bible is intended primarily to appeal to the heart and will of the reader, with the practical aim of promoting love of God and care for humanity. But the clergy also require training in theology, and from this point of view the Bible is the book of the faith. As the era of doctrinal conflict belongs to the past, the Bible is not quarried for texts to support a particular point of view. The basis of faith is the accepted tradition of dogmatic statement in the creeds and other formularies agreed by the councils. The work of theology is, then, the exposition of Scripture in the light of the Rule of Faith. It must be shown how scriptural statements relate to the dogmatic formulae of the Church (we have already seen an example of this in Augustine's comment on the punctuation of John 1.1). There is no single way in which this can be done. The reader has to seek for the higher truths in the Bible, using such means of exegesis as are available to him. These will include the methods recommended by Augustine and the contemporary understanding of grammar and logic.

The Venerable Bede

For this purpose the voluminous writings of the Venerable Bede (673–735) had lasting value. Drawing on the work of Augustine and Gregory, and also on the *Etymologiae* (a sort of encyclopedia of grammar, rhetoric and theology) of Isidore of Seville (560–636), Bede produced commentaries on many books of the Bible and also treatises to assist his fellow monks in the interpretation of it, like *De Schematis et Tropis* on figures of speech. The following excerpts from his commentary on Mark, dealing with Mark 5:21–43, illustrate his approach to biblical exegesis, and show the kind of interpretation which continued throughout the Middle Ages:

> In this reading the ruler of the synagogue begs for the salvation of his daughter, but while the Lord is coming to his house a woman who has a flow of blood catches his attention first and anticipates the healing. Then the daughter of the ruler of the synagogue reaches the desired healing, being recalled indeed from death to life. In this reading the salvation of the human race is displayed, which was dispensed when the Lord came in the flesh in such a way that first some people out of Israel came to faith, then 'the full number of the Gentiles came in, and so all Israel might be saved' (Romans 11:25–6). As for the ruler of the synagogue, and why he came to the Lord to ask on behalf of his

daughter, who is he understood to be better than Moses himself? For this reason he is aptly named Jairus, i.e. one who enlightens, or who is enlightened, because he received words of life to give to us. Thus through them he enlightens others, and was himself enlightened by the Holy Spirit, whereby he was able to write or teach the life-giving precepts . . . The careful reader will ask why the evangelist, in explaining the words of the Saviour (i.e. 'Talitha cumi', Mark 5.41), inserted on his own initiative 'I say to you.' For in the Syriac (i.e. Aramaic) saying which he has quoted no more is said than 'Little girl, arise.' Perhaps he thought that this ought to be done so as to express the force of the Lord's command. He was thus taking care to convey to his readers the meaning of the speaker rather than the actual words. For it is also customary in references to Old Testament testimonies for evangelists and apostles to take care to give the meaning of the prophecy rather than the words. So, then, taking the little girl by the hand, the Lord revived her, because, unless the hands of the Jews, defiled with blood, are first washed, their synagogue is dead and will not arise (Migne, *P.L.* (92, col. 179, 183)).

There are several interesting points here, which have a wider bearing. Firstly, Bede presupposes that the literal or historical meaning is not of any particular interest to the reader, so that he at once proposes a theological interpretation which will bring it to life as a valuable spiritual lesson. He sees it, then, as a story that can shed light on the Christian Gospel of universal salvation. Secondly, the synagogue points to the Jews, and this, coupled with the subsidiary story of the woman who had a flow of blood, suggests the two stages of the preaching of the gospel, to the Jews first and afterwards to the Gentiles. Thus the story is a model of the stages of salvation history, elucidated with an apt quotation from Romans. The same general approach, including the Romans quotation, is given in Jerome's Commentary on the corresponding story in Matthew 9.18–26. Thirdly, though no attempt is made to provide a unified interpretation along these lines and the story is tackled piecemeal, further details fit the general scheme and enhance its effect. The name of Jairus is said to mean enlightening or enlightened, and this suggests that he is a figure of Moses, the giver of the Law and chief representative of the Jewish religion. We may note the positive attitude to Moses, who is regarded as an inspired prophet, who prepared the way for Christ. Fourthly, the explanation of the name is a typical case of fanciful etymology based on a real Hebrew word (*yā'īr* = he enlightens). This naturally comes from

Jerome, who himself followed the older commentators on the meaning of names. The technique of deriving a meaning for a biblical name from its supposed etymology goes back into Jewish tradition, and is frequently found in Philo. Fifthly, the same appeal to Semitic language is made in the second excerpt, where Bede explains the addition of 'I say to you'. Again, we must presuppose dependence on previous writers. Here we may also note Bede's expectation that the careful reader will feel the need for this kind of explanation of a difficulty, and the way in which his appeal to the Old Testament quotations in both Gospels and Epistles recalls Jerome's comment on Matthew 2.23 (referred to above, p. 272). Finally, the mention of the girl's hand has suggested a harsh comment on the Jews, which sadly represents Christian anti-Jewish polemic over many centuries. But the interesting thing is that it is no new thought on the part of Bede, because here he has reproduced Jerome's comment on Matthew 9.25 almost word for word. This kind of interpretation has already been mentioned in connection with Bede's work on the Old Testament in Part I.

This example from Bede can be taken as typical of exegesis for many centuries after this time. The rule of faith is the guide to interpretation, but the precise application of any particular passage has often been determined in advance in the work of older commentators. Difficulties in the text are noted, and these are explained with the aid of literary and grammatical rules, and also of the compendia of information such as that provided by Isidore of Seville. As the object of Bible study is not to open up new lines of interpretation, but to distil what is considered best in a continuous tradition of exegesis, the words of predecessors are incorporated in the work of later writers, sometimes without acknowledgement.

2. THE MEDIAEVAL SCHOOLS

During the Dark Ages the torch of learning was kept alight mostly in the monasteries. Since the time of Charlemagne, however, cathedrals were required to maintain schools for the education of the clergy. The development of these schools encouraged a more systematic approach, with greater emphasis on theology. The monastic schools continued to flourish in the early part of this period, and the commentaries of *Rabanus Maurus* (died 856) have the leisurely style which is characteristic of the older monastic tradition. As already indicated in connection with his Old Testament work, his commentaries are largely quotations from his predecessors. Ambrosiaster, Jerome, Augustine and Bede figure frequently as his sources, but he also quotes from Theodore of Mopsuestia and John Chrysostom, the leading figures of the Antiochene school of exegesis, whose writings were available in the west in Latin translation (Chrysostom in a Latin paraphrase made by Alcuin).

Lanfranc

A more concise style is presented by the commentaries of Lanfranc (1010–89). His name is best known as an outstanding Archbishop of Canterbury, summoned from the abbey of Caen in France by William the Conqueror in 1070. But before that he had established a considerable reputation as a scholar, being proficient not only in theology but also in the 'liberal arts', i.e. grammar, logic and rhetoric, based on the classical tradition of education. His commentary on the Epistles of Paul is again largely derivative. In fact it has been shown that much of his commentary is an abridgement of a manuscript of the commentary of Ambrosiaster. This applies to Romans and Corinthians, but from Galatians onwards his manuscript contained the Latin version of Theodore (a ninth-century manuscript which changes from the one writer to the other at precisely this point has actually been discovered in modern times). In both cases, Lanfranc follows his sources very closely. For Hebrews, however, which was not available in the other sources, he has used the Alcuin version of Chrysostom.

With such a slavish following of earlier writers, it may be asked whether Lanfranc has anything to offer of significance for our purpose. There are, in fact, two features that are of interest. One is that he is more willing than his predecessors to use his knowledge of the liberal arts to elucidate the actual meaning of the text. Commenting on Romans 6.20–1 ('When you were slaves of sin, you were free in regard to righteousness. But then what return did you get from the things of which you are now ashamed?'), he seeks to elucidate the logic of Paul's statement by means of a syllogism:

Reason why they ought to be slaves of righteousness.
It is necessary to be slaves of either righteousness or sin.
But when one is enslaved to sin, one is absent from righteousness.
The return is obtained from what one is ashamed of.
This is unsuitable (i.e. to one's purpose).
Therefore it is righteousness that should be served.

Similarly he notes from his knowledge of rhetoric that in Romans 15:14 ('I am satisfied about you, my brethren, that you yourselves are full of goodness . . .') Paul is using the device of *captatio benevo-lentiae* (capturing the good will of the readers). This attention to rhetorical aspects of Paul's writing will reappear in modern study of the New Testament.

The other point is that Lanfranc is not merely a commentator. He is much more a teacher. So, for the benefit of his readers he inserts brief summaries at the end of Paul's involved arguments to make the whole point clear. For example, at the end of a string of quotations in Romans 3:9–18 he says: 'So the meaning is: the above psalm verses apply to you also, you Jews!'

The Gloss
This interest in teaching method can be connected with the development of the Gloss, which was already well established by Lanfranc's time. This, as we have seen in connection with the Old Testament, consisted of the biblical text with exegetical notes, written either between the lines or in the margins. Where both methods are used, they form virtually two different commentaries, being derived from different sources. Obviously they have to be given in very abbreviated form. They are the sort of notes that a student might write into the text, or a master might use to aid his memory when lecturing on the continuous text. But in this period the Gloss began to become a definitive commentary, as the leading scholars compiled glosses as distillations of their study of the earlier commentators. Lanfranc is one of the scholars responsible for this development, which reaches its classic form in the *Glossa Ordinaria* of Anselm of Laon in the twelfth century. Anselm himself compiled the gloss on the Letters of Paul and the Gospel of John.

It is no accident that this development began at the same time as increasing attention was being given to the study of law. Since the time of Charlemagne the ancient Roman traditions of law had been taken up into Christian statecraft, and a body of jurisprudence, based on the laws of Justinian, had grown up, along with the development of canon law on the basis of the canons issued by the ecumenical councils of the Church. These required collections of comments and opinions, so that the fundamental texts were glossed with relevant quotations from notable jurists.

Disputed Questions
A further factor, which is also reflected in Lanfranc's approach, is the method of disputation in teaching. Students were encouraged to ask questions for elucidation. Some of the teachers provided the questions themselves in order to engage the pupils' attention and

sharpen their critical powers. This is the real feature which distinguishes between the monastic *divina lectio*, which was allied to contemplation, and the teaching in the cathedral schools, which was aimed at training in theology. *John Scotus Erigena* (810–77), who was a philosopher well read in the Greek philosophical and theological tradition, wrote a commentary on the Gospel of John which is notable for the raising of questions in this way. Anselm drew on it for his *Glossa Ordinaria*. Anselm's work was followed up by *Peter Lombard* (1100–60), who taught at the cathedral school in Paris. He revised and expanded the Gloss on the Psalms and the Pauline Epistles. This revision virtually replaced the other for these books, and is sometimes referred to as the *Magna Glosatura*. In this and other developments of the Gloss the points for disputation receive fuller treatment, corresponding with the practice of teachers to expand particular points when lecturing on the Gloss. It was an obvious next step to take these points separately, so that a commentary might be reduced to a series of *Quaestiones* excerpted from the Gloss. Peter Lombard went a stage further, and in his famous *Sentences* arranged the Questions, not haphazardly as they arose in connection with the biblical text, but in order of subjects as a basis for systematic discussion. These were collected in four books, published in the years 1155–8. The arrangement is significant, for it marks the change from biblical study to systematic theology: (1) the Trinity, (2) Creation and Sin, (3) Incarnation and Virtues, (4) Sacraments, Final Judgment and Eternal Life. Subsequently the *Glossa Ordinaria*, the *Sentences* of Peter Lombard and the *Scholastic History* of Peter Comestor (published in Paris in 1169) became the standard set texts for study and comment in the schools. Comestor's *History* runs from the Creation to the end of the Acts of the Apostles, and incorporates many fanciful details and explanations. It served as a general introduction to the Bible as a whole.

The effect of these developments was to detach theology from the direct study of Scripture, although the Bible remained the official basis of all theological teaching. The transition is matched by the further evolution of the scholastic system, whereby the cathedral and monastic schools gave way to the new concept of independent universities. The disputes between *Bernard of Clairvaux* (1090–1153) and *Peter Abelard* (1079–1142) still show the tension between monastic and scholarly ideals. Bernard insisted that the study of Scripture was to be undertaken for the sake of the love of God, and the Bible was to be interpreted to this end on the basis of the Rule of Faith. Abelard, himself a monk teaching at the monastic school of St. Geneviève in Paris, was primarily a philosopher with a brilliant and subtle mind. He followed up the prevailing method of the Questions for disputation, and pointed out that the connection between biblical statements and Church doctrines is not always obvious, and has to be reached by a process of reason. His treatise *Sic et Non* ('Yes and No') presented a series of statements in the Bible, which demanded the greatest ingenuity to bring them into line with the received faith of the Church. His aim was to show that the use of logic is indispensable to arrive at the truth of the biblical revelation. Thus the text of Scripture is treated as a divinely inspired formula requiring special expertise for its elucidation. The subjects handled in *Sic et Non* vary from great doctrinal matters, such as the interpretation of statements which have a bearing on the Trinity and the Incarnation, to small points of detail, such as the question whether the woman who anointed the head of Jesus was the same as the woman who anointed his feet, and the question whether the author of the Letter of James was James the Lord's brother or James son of Zebedee and brother of John.

The Abbey of St. Victor
The foundation of the Abbey of St. Victor in Paris (see Part I, Chapter 6) was an attempt to hold together the monastic and scholastic traditions in an institution which taught theology alongside the cathedral school at the same time as maintaining the spirituality of the monastic life. The important contacts with Jewish scholars, which influenced the work of the Victorines towards a closer grasp of the literal sense, has already been shown in connection with the Old Testament. There could be no comparable influence to encourage the study of Greek in the way that Hebrew was now being studied, though Abelard advised Héloïse and her sisters of the Convent of the Paraclete to learn both languages. Serious study of Greek had to wait another century for the remarkable achievement of Robert Grosseteste in Greek studies.

At the same time the Vulgate text of the Bible, as used in the schools in Paris, was provided with numbered chapter divisions for ease of reference. This had never been done before, reference being made by the use of incipits (opening words) of a passage or some other suitable heading (thus Jesus in Mark 12:26 says, 'Have you never read in the book of Moses concerning the bush?', i.e. in the passage about the burning bush). Though there were some variations to the system, these divisions eventually became fixed in the form that is now universally used in Bibles. The numbering of verses was a further refinement, introduced a little later. This enabled the production of concordances and other works of reference on a much more systematic basis.

In this atmosphere of more intense and more accurate study of Scripture, *Hugh of St. Victor* (died 1142) made a notable plea for attention to the literal sense in his treatises *On the Scriptures* and *Didascalicon*. However, the establishing of the literal sense is only the first step in biblical study, which should proceed to meditation (making use of the rich tradition of allegorical exegesis) and so to contemplation, as Bernard had insisted. Gillian Evans quotes Hugh's advice to the novices of his community: 'You brothers, who have now enterd the school of discipline, ought first to seek in holy reading what may instruct you in virtuous behaviour, rather than what will make you sharp-witted, and you should seek rather to be informed by Scripture's precepts than to be impeded by questions'. Nevertheless the questions have to be asked, and must be answered sensibly. In dealing with the Gospel of John, Hugh showed how two apparently contradictory statements can be reconciled. In John 5:22 Jesus says, 'The Father . . . has given all judgment to the Son,' but in 8:15 he says, 'I judge no one'. The solution is to be found in the different senses of judgment. In this case the context shows that the first saying refers to the eschatological judgment, whereas the second is concerned with passing judgment in this present life.

Hugh's work shows a change in the direction of greater expertise in handling Scripture, but the fundamental aim has more in common with Bernard than Abelard. It was the latter's interest in philosophical and theological questions which won the day. Paris was by this time attracting both masters and students from far and wide, who set up their own schools alongside the cathedral school. In fact the Abbey of St. Victor itself can be seen as an example of this tendency. Gradually these schools created a common organisation and before the end of the twelfth century had formed a university (in those days known as a *studium generale*). The long training in the liberal arts, which was founded on the ancient classical tradition and always preceded the study of the Bible (or 'sacred page', as it was called), prepared students to exercise their intellectual abilities on the Questions rather than the substance of Scripture, though that was not the real aim. However, disputations concerning theology, conducted, as we have seen, on the basis, first, of the Questions, and, secondly, of the Sentences, attracted the greatest interest, especially as it was also a time of intellectual ferment with regard to the philosophical basis of faith. Bernard clung to the Platonic 'Realism', which had been the basis of thought in the west from Augustine onwards. According to this view, abstract concepts (known as 'universals') have real existence apart from the individual things or persons ('particulars') in which they are embodied. From this point of view the world of experience is only a shadow of eternal reality. God's truth is made known in symbols, and these can be discarded when reality is reached. So in the Bible, when the literal meaning appears to say nothing that is useful, the truth must lie in the reality which it symbolises. This is the justification for allegorical exegesis, though the method is so subjective that it is always in danger of 'collapsing into fantasy' (to use Beryl Smalley's phrase).

The influence of the work of Aristotle at this time, however, gave rise to a different tendency, followed to some extent by Abelard, which came to be known as 'nominalism'. This asserts that reality is located in the things themselves, and universal concepts (including the knowledge of God) can be reached only by logical deduction from the given phenomena. However, the tradition of allegorical exegesis in relation to doctrine was so strong, being enshrined in the great cumulative work of the Gloss, that it was not discredited by this new philosophical approach. Instead, it continued to be used as the means of logical deduction from the given word of Scripture to reach the theological truths which were sought in the exposition of Questions and Sentences. But the overall effect of the controversy was to draw interest away from the study of Scripture for its own sake.

Dominicans and Franciscans

At the same time a new factor entered the biblical scene as a result of the rise of the orders of friars. St. Francis and St. Dominic were almost contemporaries. Both founded orders primarily concerned with preaching in the early part of the thirteenth century. St. Francis himself was deeply opposed to the scholastic ideals of the time, disapproving of the pride in the possession of books, and the rivalry of different teachers, and the neglect of the simple ideals of the gospel. His own preaching was a very simple exposition based on a literal understanding of the Gospels. As the Franciscan order began to grow, the demand for education for the sake of preaching soon brought the friars to the universities, in spite of Francis' grave objections to this development. At the same time most of the popular preaching was in the hands of self-appointed teachers, following various heretical movements, and it was to oppose these that St. Dominic founded his Order of Preachers, originally to combat the spread of the Albigensians in Languedoc. Systematic theological education was seen to be essential from the first. Thus both orders set up houses of study in Paris and elswhere. The Dominicans had a house in Oxford as early as 1220, and the Franciscans followed very soon after their first arrival in England in 1224. Robert Grosseteste, who had been trained in Paris, at once perceived the value of the Franciscan order for reform of the Church, and undertook to teach theology at their Oxford school.

Surprisingly the emphasis on the need for popular preaching did not lead to any movement to make the Scriptures available in the vernacular. Already some translations had been made of parts of the Bible, especially by the Waldensian sect in Italy, which had begun as a popular reforming movement similar to the ideals of Francis, but had broken with the authority of the Church. The Dominicans held that the simple Gospel, available without interpretation, would encourage further heresy. Even possession of a book of the Bible in the vernacular was regarded as an indication of heresy. Thus the object of the education of the friars was to train them to handle the Scriptures with knowledge of its true religious meaning, rather than the literal sense alone. For this purpose the Gloss as well as the sacred text was indispensable.

The rise of the mendicant orders brought two developments in biblical study. In the first place, the emphasis on the literal sense, which we have seen in Hugh of St. Victor, combined with the needs of preaching, encouraged the collection of further information. Discrepancies between the Vulgate and the Greek New Testament, so far as they were known from patristic comments, were noted and attempts were made to explain them. First steps were taken to prepare dictionaries and concordances of biblical words. The use of the Bible for moral exhortation was given special attention. The new information was collected in a new section of the Gloss, usually written in blocks interrupting the continuous biblical text, and known as *postilla* (a word which perhaps means 'additions'). In the second place, the problems of interpreting Scripture received fresh assistance from the logical works of Aristotle, which were now becoming available from the Latin translations of writings that had survived in Arabic versions but not formerly been known in the west. These refined the understanding of the nature of literary composition, making a more accurate assessment of an author's intentions possible, and also improved the methods of argument whereby logical deductions could be made for the benefit of theology.

Aquinas

The influence of these works can be seen in the two great Dominicans of the thirteenth century, Albert the Great (1200–1280) and

Thomas Aquinas (1225–1274). Albert produced notable commentaries on the new Aristotelian writings. With regard to the Bible, he dismissed the mass of allegorical interpretation as logically absurd, and insisted on the importance of the literal sense in order to establish the intention of the author. Only when this has been established can the allegorical sense be discovered by logical inference. Thomas, as we have seen in connection with the Old Testament, clarified the distinction between the senses of Scripture by showing that allegories, metaphors and similes which belong to an author's intention belong to the literal sense, which is quite a different matter from allegorising what is fundamentally something else. Very frequently the moral sense is the literal sense. God is the real author of Scripture, but he makes his will known through the writings of men. It can thus be presupposed that Scripture will accord with the doctrinal teaching of the Church. But the task of showing this accord, and of advancing theology further, must be done by logically sound deductions from the literal sense which expresses the intentions of the writer. Thomas allowed the traditions of allegorical exegesis only for devotional purposes, as an aid to stirring the imagination and the will. These depend upon the unity of Scripture, in which the symbolic connections between one part of scripture and another are observed, e.g. Christ as the paschal lamb. His *Catena Aurea* (golden chain) on the Gospels is thus an enlargement of the Gloss, in which the comments of the Fathers are strung together. The number of authors cited is astonishing, including Greek as well as Latin Fathers, both ancient and modern (e.g. the eleventh century Greek commentator Theophylact, who continued the moral emphasis of Chrysostom). When dealing with the raising of Jairus' daughter in Mark 5:21– 43, Thomas has many of the same points as we saw in Bede, such as the quotation of Romans 11:25–6 and the meaning given to the name Jairus (here properly attributed to Jerome).

Bonaventure

It is, nevertheless, evident that, in spite of Thomas's defence of the traditional allegorical exegesis, its creative value was running out. The real interest of the schoolmen lay in the problems of logic and theology, for which the interpretation of the Bible was a necessary tool, but not an end in itself. The Franciscan scholar Bonaventure (1217–74) clung to the traditional Platonic philosophy, and so continued the allegorical method in which the Scriptures are a repository of symbols of the faith. But his exegesis, attempting to carry forward that of his predecessors, only succeeded in becoming even more fanciful. But it should be remembered that behind it was a powerful conviction that God is known by love rather than by reason, so that the purpose of Scripture is to open the mind to the mystical knowledge of God rather than to form the basis of a process of logical deduction.

The difference between Bonaventure and Thomas Aquinas reflects the difference between their two orders. The Dominicans were dedicated to oppose heresy and to uphold the teaching of the Church. The Franciscans always retained a regard for the religion of the heart as well as of the mind, as can be seen in the strongly devotional character of the works of Bonaventure. Their ministry of preaching among the common people was coupled with a concern for the spiritual renewal of the Church, which stemmed from Francis' literal acceptance of the gospel. With these intentions they were a prey to the attraction of *Joachimism*, which flourished in the late thirteenth century.

Joachim of Fiore

Joachimism constituted an independent method of biblical interpretation, which had an immense influence in subsequent history. It is indeed a new form of apocalypticism, in which the present evil time is regarded as the prelude to the glorious future, and represents Joachim's sincere attempt to discover the will of God for his own age. Joachim, abbot of Flora (1132–1202), used the symbolism of names and numbers to try to discover the pattern of God's dealings with mankind. He recognised the fundamental distinction between the two dispensations of the Old and New Testaments, but cutting across this he saw three overlapping stages in the history of humanity, which he referred to as the three 'states of the world'. The first of these 'began with Adam, flowered from Abraham, and was consummated in Christ'. It is the age of the Father, when the married state is the norm of life under the Law. The second 'began with Uzziah (cf. Matthew 1:8), flowered from Zachariah, the father of John the Baptist, and will receive its consummation in these times' (i.e. Joachim's own time). This is the age of the Son, consisting of forty-two generations (i.e. 1260 years), marked by the clerical state, or order of the clergy, who by Joachim's day had to be celibate. The third 'state', which is the Age of the Holy Spirit, 'beginning from St. Benedict, began to bear fruit in the twenty-second generation (i.e. 660), and is to be consummated in the consummation of the world' (quotations from the *Book of Agreement of the Old and New Testament*, f. 19r). The characteristic of this coming age, which is already indicated by the reference to Benedict, is that it will have a new and better order of celibate monks in whom the life of the spirit will reach its perfection. It is 'the very order which Jesus planned' (*Exposition of the Apocalypse*, f. 83v).

Joachim evidently has the mentality which sees significance in numbers and patterns of names and ideas, and is impressed by coincidence. Even those of a very different cast of mind may well feel that such findings cannot be lightly dismissed. The Franciscans regarded themselves as the new order of the age of the Spirit, especially the 'Spirituals', i.e. the group who were trying to retain Francis' ideal of absolute poverty against the tendency towards a less rigid observance. But even some of the Dominicans felt they were the new order. Successive groups made the same claim, including the Jesuits after their foundation in the sixteenth century. The great missionary expansion of the era of Spanish colonisation of the Americas was also inspired by Joachimite ideals. Joachim's treatment of the Book of Revelation as a coded prophecy of present and future events has had endless followers. Nevertheless Joachimism could not make much impact in intellectual circles, because it is basically irrational and impossible to control. But it marks an important departure in the history of biblical exegesis, because the biblical text was made to signify, not the teaching of the Church as already universally accepted, but supposed future events with implicit criticism of the Church in its present state. In its peculiar way it set the Church under the judgment of the gospel.

3. WYCLIFFE'S BIBLE

Bible or Church?
Joachimism was an extreme case, but the movement expressed a dissatisfaction with the present state of the Church which was to become more acute in the following century. The consistent premiss that the truth of the Bible is identical with the faith of the Church applied equally to those like Bonaventure who retained the traditional allegorical interpretation, and to those like Aquinas who sought to interpret it on the basis of logical deduction from the literal sense. Thus scholarship tended to uphold the power of the Church at a time when the power of the papacy was reaching its height. Nevertheless the desire for reform was bound to draw attention to the discrepancy between the gospel and the increasing corruption of the Church. The claim that the truth of the Bible and the teaching of the Church are identical was in danger of becoming untenable. The first sign of this has been attributed to Henry of

Ghent (died 1293), an Augustinian who attempted to combine the older tradition of interpretation with the new ideas based on Aristotle. He noted that the tradition of the Church exists alongside the Bible, and suggested the theoretical possibility that they could differ. Then William of Ockham (1285–1347) from an entirely different point of view developed a form of Nominalism (cf. p. 285 above) in which he denied the proposition that theological truth can be reached by logical deduction from the statements of Scripture, so that the faith has no other support than the tradition of the Church. These theories assisted the canonists to treat papal Decretals as a source of authority independent of Scripture, and so to increase the centralisation of the Church under the power of the Pope. Thus the conflict between biblical authority and ecclesiastical tradition, which came to a head in the Reformation, has its roots in this period.

This conflict can also be expressed in terms of the interpretation of Scripture. Those who wish to reform the Church need look no further than the literal sense of the Gospels. In spite of the concentration of interest in philosophy and theology in the universities, the tendency in Bible study was to increase the means of establishing the literal sense. Nicolas of Lyre (1270–1340) made a very notable advance in his *postilla* to the Old Testament, as we have seen. His contributions to the New Testament were less acute, as he did not know Greek, but were also aimed at clarifying the literal meaning. His commentary on the whole Bible achieved wide acceptance, and was the first biblical commentary to be printed (Rome, 1471–2). Thus the tools were at hand to set the literal meaning of the Bible against the ecclesiastical tradition enshrined in the various forms of spiritual interpretation.

Wycliffe
However, the time for this had not yet come. John Wycliffe (1330–84) shows both the urgent need for reform and also the limitations of what was then possible. Wycliffe reacted strongly against the corruption and worldliness of the Church of his time, and wished to restore it to its primitive purity. At the same time he was disenchanted with developments in philosophy, represented by such teachers as Ockham, which separated theology from its grounding in Scripture. He therefore favoured the older Platonic tradition, stemming from Augustine, and belonging (in his view) to an age when the Church was less corrupt. The older commentators had deduced all their teaching from Scripture, so that the primacy of Scripture as the source of true doctrine and the guide to authentic

Christian life was clearly the genuine Christian tradition, which had been thoroughly corrupted in his own day. Fired with reforming zeal on this basis, Wycliffe proceeded to propound his views with enormous vigour and without fear or favour, and of course aroused strenuous opposition from the authorities.

Two things are specially relevant to our purpose. In the first place, Wycliffe's insistence on the primacy of Scripture makes his position very similar to Reformation Protestantism, in which *sola scriptura* (the Bible only) is set against the authority of the Church. From this point of view Wycliffe was a precursor of the Reformation, and many of the arguments used in his battles with the ecclesiastical authorities were to reappear then. But the central point at issue was quite different. For, whereas Luther found in the Bible the doctrine of justification by faith in contrast with the legalism which he saw in the Church, Wycliffe saw the Bible, in particular the New Testament, as the revelation of God's law. He took the idea of the kingdom of God quite literally, and wanted to see all secular rulers model their statecraft on the Gospel. The Church is likewise under obedience to the Gospel, though it has erred grievously in departing from the letter of Scripture. For this reason Wycliffe will not allow that the Church is the essential organ to mediate the faith to the people. Every person, he holds, can work out his own salvation from the Gospel, and the religious orders (which are bitterly attacked for their hypocrisy and laxity) have no monopoly of authentic Christian living. Moreover Wycliffe's philosophical realism made him think of the truth of the Bible as a heavenly reality set out in symbols, so that his central understanding of the Christian message is supported by allegorical interpretation to bring the entire Scriptures into a unity. Thus the healing of the paralysed man in Mark 2:1–12 is thoroughly allegorised in line with the patristic tradition. The sick man is the Jewish people coming to Christ for spiritual healing. The four bearers of his pallet are the patriarchs, Abraham, Isaac, Jacob and David. They ascend to the roof of the house because the thoughts of the faithful are directed heavenwards. In a sermon, preached in 1376, in which he used the same exegetical material, he compares the house with its roof opened in the centre to a cloister, which is open to the sky above, but closed to the world on its four sides, 'so as to signify (if only it were true!) how the conversation and affections of the inhabitants should be in the heavens, and that the four affections of the soul, i.e. joy, sorrow, hope and fear, should be closed towards temporal things'.

Translation of the Bible
In the second place, Wycliffe's public claim that every person can find saving truth in the gospel encouraged the growing demand for translation of the Bible. There had been various attempts at Bible translation in England, and the making of a vernacular version had never been formally proscribed. This had been largely connected with the Old Testament in the light of the growing interest in Hebrew studies. The most recent example had been the English Psalter by the mystic Richard Rolle (died 1349). Significantly this was done, not for general use, but for a particular person, the recluse Margaret Kirkby, who shared Rolle's spiritual ideas. Wycliffe's Bible was the first attempt to produce the whole Bible in English for the benefit of the common people. Wycliffe organised rather than undertook the project, which was completed and then thoroughly revised after his death by members of his group of followers, who came to be known as the Lollards. Other translations of the Sunday epistles and gospels were also produced as a result of his influence at around the same time. All these translations were taken from the Latin Vulgate. The revised form of Wycliffe's Bible achieved wide popularity, and was used alike by those who were loyal to the Church and by groups of reforming spirits among the common people who can be regarded as the ancestors of Puritans and Dissenters in England. But official opposition was strong. The old suspicion, that vernacular Scriptures tend to lead people into heresy, seemed to be confirmed by Wycliffe, because his translation was a direct consequence of his attack on the authority of the Church. The opposition of the scholars, who numbered many members of the Franciscans and Dominicans, was also aroused by his vigorous hostility to the religious orders. Private initiatives towards translation were forbidden for the first time in England at the Council of Oxford of 1407. Consequently Wycliffe's Bible was never printed, when printing became available later in the fifteenth century. Leading Lollards, expelled from England, took refuge in Bohemia, where they influenced the reformer John Huss.

Towards the Reformation
Other factors were also paving the way for the Reformation at this time. Firstly, in spite of attempted prohibitions, vernacular Bibles were beginning to make their way on the continent of Europe, and were being printed in Germany by the late fifteenth century. These were bought by the rising middle class of comparatively prosperous people who did not know Latin.

Secondly, Gerard de Groote, a contemporary of Wycliffe in

Holland, promoted the *devotio moderna*, a form of meditation on the Gospels as the basis of personal spirituality. The *Imitation of Christ* by Thomas à Kempis is a fruit of this approach. It is a spirituality which uses the literal sense of the New Testament, and is notable for its psychological and moral realism and rejection of abstract speculation. The movement was much indebted to the writings of Augustine and Bernard of Clairvaux.

Thirdly, there was a growing reaction against the domination of Aristotelian philosophy in the schools. Wycliffe is just one example of this. But it has to be seen from the broader perspective of the Italian Renaissance of this time. The scholastic method had detached intellectual study from contemplation and made study an end in itself. This favoured the recovery of ancient learning. At the same time classical literature and art were capturing the attention of scholars and the wealthy patrons of the arts. For some, this encouraged a new humanism, detached from the traditions of the Church. For others, like *Erasmus of Rotterdam* (1469–1536), who had been trained in the spirituality of the *devotio moderna*, it included a fresh appreciation of the Church Fathers, and through that a return to Platonist philosophy in direct opposition to the schools.

Fourthly, the philological work on the text of Scripture continued throughout this period. Hitherto this had been largely a matter of Hebrew studies, aided by the Jewish rabbis, but the interests of the Renaissance made recovery of Greek in connection with the New Testament only a matter of time. *Lorenzo Valla* (1406–57) wrote a dialogue, comparing Christian, Stoic and Epicurean views *On Pleasure* and a number of controversial books against the schoolmen and the establishment of the Church. The most damaging was his proof that the so-called *Donation of Constantine*, a document which had long been held to support the primacy of the papacy, was a forgery. But he also wrote a collection of *Annotations on the New Testament*, in which he made use of his knowledge of Greek to show that many of the opinions of the schoolmen depended on faults in the Vulgate text. The strictly philological approach of these notes, entirely unlike any commentaries of the New Testament known at the time, marks the beginning of a whole new era in the study of the New Testament.

Conclusion

Thus the Middle Ages close with the real possibility that the New Testament can be studied for what it is in itself, instead of being regarded as the book of the Church's doctrine in coded form. Mediaeval scholasticism has run its course. There is at least some advance in historical understanding, and the literal meaning has been clarified over against the figurative senses. Though allegorical interpretation is not repudiated, but is rather encouraged by the recovery of patristic learning, there are factors which favour appreciation of the literal sense. Amongst these we may count the *devotio moderna* and the sheer impact of the New Testament when read in the vernacular by intelligent but untrained readers. The linguistic skill for close study of the New Testament text is at last being acquired. At the same time the conviction that the revelation of God is given in the Bible remained unassailed. Finally, those who were discovering the Bible through the new translations found in it a source of comfort and illumination which could not be had from the scholastic approach of the clergy. A new generation was arising which matched love of Jesus with love of the Gospels in which his words are preserved. The Bible was thus set to become a focus of devotion without the intervention of sacraments and priestly ministration. It is not surprising that the way is opening for a new contention, that the Bible contains all that is necessary for salvation. That will be one of the issues of the Reformation.

FOR FURTHER READING

The Cambridge History of the Bible 2: The West from the Fathers to the Reformation, edited by G. W. H. Lampe, CUP, Cambridge 1969.

Deanesly, Margaret, *The Lollard Bible*, CUP, Cambridge 1920.

Evans, Gillian R., *The Language and Logic of the Bible: the Earlier Middle Ages*, CUP, Cambridge 1984.

——, *The Language and Logic of the Bible: the Road to Reformation*, CUP, Cambridge 1985.

Reeves, Marjorie, *The Influence of Prophecy in the Later Middle Ages: a Study in Joachimism*, OUP, Oxford 1969.

Smalley, Beryl, *The Study of the Bible in the Middle Ages*, rev. ed., Blackwell, Oxford, 1952 and University of Notre Dame Press, Notre Dame 1964.

5

RENAISSANCE AND REFORMATION

Emergence of a Theological Dilemma

Renaissance and Reformation must be taken together, because they represent two opposite sides of the transition from the mediaeval to the modern era, and thereby set up a conflict in the understanding of the Bible which has persisted to the present day. The Renaissance began a process of liberation of the mind, both from inherited superstitions and prejudices and from the domination of thoughts and ideas imposed by authority, which opened the way to objective evaluation of the Bible. The Reformation owed much to the Renaissance, but moved the Bible to the central position of religious authority on account of the break with the authority of the Church. This invested the Bible with a quality of absolute authority in matters of religion which put it above critical assessment. Thus the tools for a critical approach were being provided at the same time as the Bible was acquiring a position of immunity from criticism. Modern critical study of the Bible has its roots in the freedom of enquiry characteristic of the Renaissance, and typified by the work of Lorenzo Valla before the Reformation had begun. Later developments put limits to free enquiry, because the Bible, as the word of God, was held to be inerrant. In the long run this led to a Protestant neo-scholasticism, based on the absolute authority of Scripture itself. Thus, though Reformation attitudes to the Bible depended on the liberation of the mind associated with the Renaissance, they turned into a new captivity. It was not until the Enlightenment, beginning in England in the late seventeenth century, and flowering in Germany in the eighteenth, that the restraints were lifted and critical study could begin. There followed a long battle between the critics and those who opposed criticism and feared where it might lead. The central issue was the nature of biblical authority in religion. This issue still remains unresolved today.

The Contribution of Renaissance Humanism
The contribution of the humanism of the Renaissance is twofold. In the first place it enlarged the concept of the literal sense of Scripture, which had already been reached by Thomas Aquinas, that the literal sense is to be identified with the intention of the author, whether this consists of historic narrative, metaphors, parables or moral exhortation. The object is to expose the meaning of the text. This approach provided encouragement to private judgment in evaluating Scripture, over against the authority of the tradition of exegesis.

John Colet (1466–1519) commented on the Epistles of Paul without reference to the opinions collected in the Gloss. He uses straightforward exposition for the most part, though he digresses from time to time to enlarge on matters touching spirituality in the light of his interest in neo-Platonic thought. But Paul's letters are not treated as a textbook of theology.

In the second place, the new learning promoted serious study of the Greek text of the New Testament. A start had been made by Valla, as we have seen. *Desiderius Erasmus* (1469–1536) had heard Colet's lectures in Oxford, and although Colet made no use of the Greek text in his lectures, he was encouraged by him to pursue the study of the New Testament and determined to do so in Greek. He thus has the distinction of being the first person to publish a printed edition of the Greek text of the New Testament, besides the publication of important collections of the works of Greek and Latin Fathers. His admiration for the Fathers inclined him to retain a form of allegorical interpretation in dealing with the Old Testament. Though, like Colet and Sir Thomas More, and many others who were imbued with the new learning, he wished for the reform of the Church and wrote a satire against corruption in the Church and the decadence of the monasteries called *The Praise of Folly*, he drew back from participation in Reformation controversy as this developed under *Martin Luther* (1483–1546). Luther, too, shows the influence of the Renaissance in his knowledge of the classics, his attention to the Greek text of the New Testament, and his insistence on the right of private judgment in the interpretation of Scripture. Erasmus, however, felt bound to oppose the principle of private judgment in view of the way the Reformation developed, and wrote a tract on the subject against Luther.

Erasmus can be taken as the starting point for all the main developments in the study of the New Testament in this period. In this chapter we shall look at these under the four headings of text, translation, interpretation and authority.

1. TEXT

Erasmus' Greek New Testament
Erasmus published his Greek text of the New Testament at Basle in 1516, the same year as More's *Utopia*, when he was widely acknowledged to be the leading scholar in Europe. He was not the first person to have it printed, however, because Cardinal Ximénes had already included it in the *Complutensian Polyglot*. Both projects reflect the impact of Valla's *Annotations on the New Testament*, which Erasmus had discovered while in Italy in 1504 and published under this title (Valla called it a *Collation*). Cardinal Ximénes (1436–1517) had founded a Christian university at Alcalá (Complutum), which was a centre of Jewish scholarship in Spain, specifically for the study of Hebrew, Greek and Latin. The Polyglot, with its provision of grammatical and lexical aids as well as ancient versions of the Scriptures, was intended to assist reform by presenting the true text of the Bible, and to oppose Jewish criticism of the Vulgate Old Testament by a comprehensive presentation of the evidence. The New Testament, forming volume five of the massive six-volume work, was the first volume to be printed in 1514, but was not bound and published until 1520, when the Pope's authority was at last received after a long delay. During the interval John Froben, a printer in Basle noted for his scholarly accuracy, persuaded Erasmus, who was known to be preparing a Greek text, to complete it quickly, which he did on the basis of a few manuscripts available in Basle, and the text was published in 1516 in parallel with a revised text of the Vulgate. Though he had been long occupied with study of the Greek text, and so his work was founded on notes made from many other manuscripts elsewhere, his edition was in fact based on inferior manuscripts, and this had its effect on the translation of the New Testament in the Reformation period. It took nearly three centuries for the necessary labour of textual criticism to be put on a scientific basis, and it is not until modern times that Bible translations have been produced on a sound text-critical foundation. So another aspect of today's conflict on the authority of the Bible here comes to the surface, for modern translations have to vie with strong popular attachment to the Authorised, or King James, Version (AV), which is based on poor texts.

The importance of achieving a reliable Greek text is very simply illustrated by one feature of Erasmus' text of 1516. He omitted the so-called Johannine Comma (italicised in the following quotation) from 1 John 5:7–8, because it was not included in any Greek manuscript known to him:

> [6]This is he that came by water and blood, even Jesus Christ; not by water only, but by water and blood. [7]And it is the Spirit that beareth witness, because the Spirit is truth. For there are three that bear record *in heaven, the Father, the Word, and the Holy Ghost: and these three are one.* [8]*And there are three that bear witness in earth,* the Spirit, and the water, and the blood, and these three agree in One (1 John 5:6–8, AV).

The earliest authority for these words is a Latin writing by a follower of the Spanish heretic Priscillianus (died AD 386). They are not found in any of Augustine's many writings or any earlier Latin Fathers. They are totally unknown in the east. It is probable that they were a marginal gloss which had become incorporated in the text of 1 John used by this writer. Later the Johannine Comma became widely diffused in Latin manuscripts, and was accepted as an official part of the Vulgate text. By the Middle Ages it was valued as a fundamental biblical testimony to the doctrine of the Trinity, and was accepted as such by Thomas Aquinas. Astonishingly, Valla makes no mention of the addition in his *Annotations*, though he comments on a small point of difference between the Greek and the Vulgate at the end of verse 8. Perhaps he did not dare to dispute it, in spite of his boldness in other matters. But Erasmus would not insert it into his printed Greek text for the entirely proper reason that it did not exist in the Greek manuscripts. In spite of the predictable outcry, he maintained his position in the second edition of his text (1519), which embodied corrections and some better readings resulting from further study. But for the third edition (1522) he reluctantly inserted it on the strength of a Greek manuscript containing it which had been sent to him as evidence. It is for this reason that the Johannine Comma was retained in the numerous later editions of the Greek text in the sixteenth century, and so came to be included in AV (1611). There was added support for it from the Complutensian Polyglot, which included it in the Greek text. This, however, had not been done on the evidence of Greek manuscript, but was an editorial judgment that the Vulgate text was superior to the Greek and therefore the original Greek must have had it. Hence the Comma was translated from the Latin without any textual support.

Erasmus suspected that the manuscript which he had received was a copy created by his opponents, who had had the Comma

included by translation from the Vulgate, as it is in the Complutensian text. Modern study has confirmed this suspicion, as it was
certainly copied during this period. The Comma has been added as
a variant reading in the margin of some older manuscripts, but
always by a late hand. Though we can hardly excuse Erasmus'
opponents of cheating, we have to remember their very deep conviction that the Vulgate in its familiar form was the true text, so that
they took it for granted that the Greek texts which were in process
of being examined must be wrong. Even Erasmus was guilty of
something similar in another passage. In desperate haste to complete
the preparation of the text for Froben, he discovered that only one
of the manuscripts available in Basle included Revelation, and that
was defective at the end. So he retranslated the last six verses from
the Vulgate in order to complete the book. For the fourth edition
(1527) he substituted the text of these verses as printed in the
Complutensian Polyglot on the basis of manuscripts which cannot
now be identified.

For the 1519 edition Erasmus printed his own new Latin translation, made from the Greek, in place of the Vulgate. This was a
matter of great importance to him, because he earnestly wished to
have the best text universally available. But this also produced an
outcry, because his very careful renderings often disagreed with
highly valued traditions. For instance the Greek *presbuteros* (=
'elder') was translated *senior* instead of the Vulgate's *presbyter*, which
was generally regarded as meaning 'priest' in the technical sense.
He also insisted, following Valla, that Greek *metanoein* refers to a
change of heart, hence 'repent', against the Vulgate 'do penance',
which was applied to the sacrament of penance. For the rest of his
life Erasmus continued to collect textual information, and compiled
his own *Annotations*, following the example of Valla. He was a far
better textual critic than has often been realised. Jerry Bentley has
shown that he had grasped one of the cardinal principles of textual
criticism, that variant readings in a given passage must always be
explained, and that usually the hardest reading is to be regarded as
original, as corruption is likely to come about through different
attempts to cope with the difficulty.

Other scholars quickly followed the lead of Erasmus. In 1518 the
prestigious Aldine Press at Venice printed the whole Bible in Greek
(another 'first', as the Polyglot was still not yet published), and the
text of Erasmus was used for the New Testament. In 1534 Simon
de Colines of Paris published a text based on comparison of Erasmus
and the Polygot, but also including important readings from further
manuscripts. Unfortunately his manuscript sources are not known.

This ought to have instigated a more scientific approach, beginning with careful collation of all known manuscripts, in order to arrive at the best possible text. The search for manuscripts in the monastic libraries of Europe was well under way. Though the Vatican refused to allow publication of Codex Vaticanus (code letter B), the best of all ancient manuscripts of the whole Bible in Greek, made in the fourth century, some of its readings were becoming known, and Erasmus knew that it did not include the Johannine Comma.

Codex Bezae

During this time the Calvinist reformer Theodore Beza acquired a remarkable fifth century manuscript (now known as Codex Bezae; code letter D). This contains the Gospels and Acts in Greek and Latin on opposite pages, and came from the very ancient and originally bilingual monastery of St. Irenaeus at Lyons. It has many far-reaching differences from the text as printed by Erasmus, and, on its Latin side, from the text of the Vulgate. Some of its unique readings were incorporated by Colines' step-son Robert Estienne (Stephanus) in the third edition of his Greek New Testament (1550; previous editions 1546 and 1549). Estienne's son Henri had collated several manuscripts, including D. Not all Henri's work was included, and Beza availed himself of it for his own edition of 1565, for which he also used the sixth century bilingual Codex Claromontanus for the Pauline Epistles. However, this is not a truly critical edition, because the listing of variant readings is very selective. Indeed Beza seems to have been afraid to make much use of these two important manuscripts. His text is mainly that of Erasmus. It went through many editions, culminating in the popular reprint by the brothers Elzevir at Leyden in 1624. When this was printed again in 1633 the publishers' preface presented it as 'the text received by everyone', and so gave the name *Textus Receptus* for this text. Thus Erasmus' third edition of 1522, as modified by Beza in 1565, became the standard text, and the impetus towards a proper critical text ceased. Like the Authorized Version in English, which is based on the same Greek text, the *Textus Receptus* remained unchallenged until comparatively recent times. The reasons why it is to be regarded as an inferior text, only partly indicated above, will be explained in a later chapter.

One reason for Beza's reluctance to change Erasmus' text was his own theological position. As a Calvinist he depended on the authority of the Bible, and the variants which were coming to light threatened to undermine it. Consequently in his exegetical notes he even resorted to conjectural emendation of the text to support his views on some occasions (e.g. he felt 'those who were being saved', Acts 2:47, ought to be 'those who were to be saved', to accord with the doctrine of election).

Status of the Vulgate

It may seem as if the Reformers had taken over the task, originally associated with the humanists, of recovering the Greek text of the New Testament. But the Catholics could not disregard it. The bitter strife of the Reformation had already led to schism. The Latin Vulgate was under attack. The authority of the Catholic Church could not be maintained without clarifying it in relation to Scripture. The Council of Trent (Tridentum) was called in 1546 to deal with this and other issues of the Reformation, in fact to promote reform of the Church from within (which is what Erasmus and many others had wanted). To the embarrassment of the Council, Estienne produced at the same time a de luxe edition of his critical edition of the Vulgate, based on his own work on the Latin manuscripts in relation to the Hebrew and Greek text, which he had already published in 1540 after preliminary editions. The Tridentine fathers took note of the critical problems. They acknowledged that the Johannine Comma did not belong to the Greek textual tradition. They also observed that Codex Vaticanus (B) did not contain the story of the woman taken in adultery (*pericope de adultera*) in John 7:53–8:11, and that it concluded the Gospel of Mark at 16:8. But they reaffirmed the Vulgate as currently printed as reliable for the faith of the people. Without a genuinely critical edition of the Greek text, and knowing that Erasmus' edition was based on inferior manuscripts, they could claim that nothing had as yet happened to shake confidence in the Vulgate. It was not associated with heresy, unlike the vernacular translations made from the Hebrew and Greek in use among the Protestants, which were made by heretics. Grave doubts were expressed about permitting the use of the Scriptures in the vernacular, but the need could not be denied. It was decreed that approved translations must always be furnished with explanatory notes. Biblical lectureships were encouraged. Later, seminaries for priests were established. Though the aim was to encourage confidence in the Vulgate as currently used, and so no new edition was ordered by the Council, the need of revision was undeniable. This was met eventually in the Sixtine Edition (ordered by Pope Sixtus V in 1590, but found to be unsatisfactory) and the Clementine Edition (by Pope Clement VIII in 1592).

The Syriac New Testament

A minor sensation was caused by the first publication of the Syriac (Peshitta) version of the New Testament by Widmanstadt at Vienna in 1555. This had been brought to the west by a delegation of Maronite Christians from Syria some forty years earlier, seeking to place their church under the jurisdiction of Rome. But it was a long time before this unknown language was sufficiently understood to make preparation of a printed edition possible. Syriac is a later form of Aramaic, and so it was assumed to be the actual language underlying the Greek of the Gospels. So it was claimed that the actual words of Jesus himself had been found. The version was also included in the *Antwerp Polyglot*, ordered by Philip II of Spain and printed in Antwerp in 1569–72 with a transliteration in Hebrew-Aramaic script for the benefit of those unfamiliar with the Syriac script. Naturally those books of the New Testament which we have seen were not accepted by the Syrian Church (2 Peter, 2 and 3 John, Jude and Revelation) were not included. As the text followed the Greek very closely, agreeing with it in omitting the Johannine Comma, it was not felt to contribute anything further to the controversy over the relative merits of the Latin and Greek texts, and interest in it soon lapsed.

2. TRANSLATIONS

Erasmus and Luther

We have come a long way from Erasmus, but must return to his time to take up a second project which he had at heart, and for which the study of the Greek text was but a preliminary, the provision of reliable translations for the benefit of the people. Erasmus had been trained in the biblical spirituality of the *devotio moderna*, and he wished to promote the knowledge and love of Jesus as the centre of the biblical message. In this he was influenced by the friendship of Sir Thomas More. His new Latin translation (1519) was a step in this direction.

Vernacular translation from the original texts begins with Martin Luther, who shared this aim, and had already used the Greek text as the basis for his lectures on Romans and other books in Wittenberg before his break with Rome in 1517. Soon after this he formed the intention of making a new German translation of the whole Bible. The New Testament was done first on the basis of Erasmus' text, and appeared in 1522. The huge demand necessitated a succession of reprintings, which allowed opportunity for many corrections. It is a masterly translation, because it combines natural, idiomatic German with accuracy and fidelity to the original. Hence it established itself as the German 'authorised version' for centuries, and had an equally profound effect on language and culture in Germany as the Authorised Version in England. Luther was not alone in the work of Bible translation in Germany, but his version largely superseded others. In Switzerland the Reformers were naturally equally active, and the Zürich Bible, completed in 1530, is a German version based on Luther, though using separate translations of the Old Testament books which were still not available in Luther's version. Luther's version was so successful that it is the real basis of the Catholic German translations of the period (Emser, 1527; Eck, 1537), which were designed to follow the Vulgate more closely for the sake of Catholic teaching and to prevent Catholics from resorting to Luther's translation. Emser's version established itself as the normal translation for Catholics for nearly three centuries. But it owed its quality to its reproduction of what Luther had already achieved.

French Translations

At Geneva the French-speaking Calvinists took up the translation of the Catholic humanist Jacques Lefèvre, whose New Testament was published by Colines at Paris in 1523. This was largely made from the Vulgate, but at Geneva Pierre Robert Olivetan, a kinsman of Calvin, improved it in relation to the Greek and also in its literary quality, to form the Neuchâtel Bible of 1535, and after many revisions this became the standard Bible of Geneva of 1588. At the same time the Louvain Bible was produced by Catholics also on the basis of Lefèvre, and was subsequently revised with increasing debt to the Geneva revisions. However the vernacular Bible has never had the influence on the language of the French people as it had in Germany and England.

Tyndale

England already had the complete Bible in Wycliffe's version, which continued to be widely used in spite of having been proscribed a century earlier. But the ferment surrounding Erasmus and the work already in hand on the continent inevitably created a demand amongst those of reforming sympathies for a new version based on the original languages. William Tyndale (1494–1536) determined to do this, but could get no official approval for the project, and took refuge among the Reformers on the continent. After much difficulty he managed to get his New Testament printed at Worms, and sent copies to England in 1526. But every effort was made by the authorities to seize and burn it. However, further printings were done in Holland, the final edition in 1535. Tyndale did not live to complete the Old Testament, though he published part of it. His work was a notable achievement, comparable to Luther's in its quality. The translation was made completely independently of Wycliffe's version, using a more colloquial English, avoiding Latinisms, which made for easy reading by the common people. It is, in fact, more colloquial than AV, which nevertheless is deeply indebted to it. The relationship between them can be appreciated from the following quotation of Hebrews 1:1–4 from Tyndale's first edition of 1526 and a modern printing of AV:

God in tyme past diversly	God, who at sundry times and in
and many wayes spake unto	divers manners spake in time past unto
the fathers by prophets: but in	the fathers by the prophets, hath in
these last dayes he hath spoken	these last days spoken
unto us by hys sonne, whom he	unto us by his Son, whom he
hath made heyre of all things:	hath appointed heir of all things,
by whom also he made the worlde.	by whom also he made the worlds;
Which sonne, beyng the brightnes	who being the brightness
of his glory, and very ymage off	of his glory, and the express image of
his substance, bearynge uppe all thyngs with the worde of his power,	his person, and upholding all things by the word of his power,
hath in his awne person pourged	when he had by himself purged
oure synnes and is sytten on the right	our sins sat down on the right
honde of the maiestie on hye,	hand of the majesty on high;
and is more excellent then the angels,	being made so much better than the angels,
in as moche as he hath by inheritance	as he hath by inheritance
obteyned an excellenter name then have they.	obtained a more excellent name than they.

Unfortunately Tyndale was unashamedly Lutheran in his sympathy.

He borrowed the prefaces and many exegetical notes from Luther. He also followed him in translating *metanoein* 'repent' (which Luther had derived from Erasmus), and used 'senior' or 'elder' for *presbuteros* like Erasmus. Hence his version could not be approved by those, including King Henry VIII, who were striving to prevent the spread of Reformation teaching in England.

Coverdale

Nevertheless the need for translation had to be met, and Thomas Cranmer, the Archbishop of Canterbury, persuaded the king to allow appropriate action. His first initiative failed, and so he turned to the work of Miles Coverdale, who had given some help to Tyndale, and in spite of not having his linguistic ability had produced a version of the complete Bible at Zürich in 1535. This was based on Tyndale, the continental versions and the Vulgate. Though obviously unsatisfactory, Coverdale's version is notable, because the rendering of the Psalms, at times obscure, but always beautifully phrased, came via the Great Bible into the first English Prayer Book of 1549, and was retained in the Book of Common Prayer of 1662, and is still used in Anglican worship today. Finding that it was not made directly from the original languages, Cranmer promoted a translation ascribed to Thomas Matthew (actually a composite work edited by John Rogers), in which the New Testament is the 1535 edition of Tyndale. But this did not satisfy those who objected to Tyndale. So then Coverdale, abandoning his own version apart from the poetical books, made a light revision of 'Matthew', using Erasmus' notes for the text of the New Testament, and this version, which came to be known as the Great Bible, was now at last (1539) the first English Bible to be published with the sanction of the king and the bishops. This version, improved in a second edition of 1540, remained the standard Bible of the English people for the next twenty-five years.

The Geneva Bible

By this time the return of England to the jurisdiction of Rome under Mary I had driven the reformed bishops into exile at Geneva. This provided the impetus to revise the Great Bible with the resources available there, and so the Geneva Bible came into being (1560). It is marked by more careful scholarship than any previous version, and the Calvinism of the environment in which it was produced is not unduly prominent, though it appears in prefaces and notes. This version came to England with the return of the exiles on the accession of Elizabeth I, and achieved considerable popularity. But again the course of the English Reformation was too complex to allow the two versions, the Great Bible and the Geneva Bible, to be used side by side. The Geneva Bible was valued for its accuracy, but feared for its Calvinism. So in 1568 the Bishops' Bible was produced as a compromise, and revised in 1572. It is mainly the Great Bible, with all controversial matter excluded and devoid of the offensive prefaces and notes.

An English Roman Catholic Version
Meanwhile it was essential for the hard-pressed English Roman Catholics to have a vernacular Bible, and this had to be suitable for response to Protestant claims. The Rheims-Douai version (NT printed at Rheims, 1582; OT at Douai, 1609, conformed to the Clementine Vulgate of 1592) is thus a very careful translation, supplied with copious notes on disputed topics. Naturally ecclesiastical words are given in Latin form. But the laboured accuracy, use of the Vulgate as main base, and numerous Latinisms, often specially coined for the purpose, make it very stilted, and it must have been difficult for the average lay person to understand properly. Nevertheless it survived, and contributed fine points of grammar and some Latinisms to the AV.

The Authorised Version
All these English Bibles came to a magnificent conclusion in the Authorised Version, ordered by King James I and published in 1611. The Bishops' Bible had failed to establish itself as the national version. The Great Bible still provided epistles and gospels in the Prayer Book, but most people preferred the Geneva Bible for private reading. In 1604 the king was approached to order a fresh translation which would end these discrepancies as part of the process of accommodating the strongly Calvinist Puritans in the national Church. It has been suggested that the real aim was to secure the Geneva Bible as the sole approved version. But King James saw that this would not solve the problem, and insisted on a new version which would gather up the best in the existing versions in the light of good scholarship, and also forbade the inclusion of interpretative prefaces and notes. A team of scholars was recruited. The Bishops' Bible was to be the basis, but the other versions were to be preferred when accuracy demanded it, and the use of controversial translations of ecclesiastical terms was to be avoided. The whole Bible was divided into six groups of books, each having its own set of scholars to deal with it. But consultation between the scholars was arranged, and a review committee was formed to correlate the results. The

new translation gained from the greater accuracy of the Geneva and Rheims versions. The influence of the latter can be seen in a greater use of Latinisms in the New Testament, which gives to it a greater stateliness compared with Tyndale. The lack of a sound textual basis, however, is still apparent in the inclusion of the *pericope de adultera* and the Johannine Comma. The AV was given a privileged position from the first, as the printing of all other versions in the folio size required for public reading from a lectern was forbidden. But it gradually ousted the Geneva Bible for private reading (last printed in 1644), and this was due to its own merits as a fine version capable of satisfying all parties.

The achievement of a single universally accepted version, at a time when Tudor English was giving way to modern English, had a creative effect upon English literature and culture, just as Luther's Bible had in Germany. Phrases from the AV, read in every household, became part of everyday speech in all walks of life. This is true, in spite of the fact that, retaining so much of Tyndale, it was to some extent archaic in style even when first published. Bible-based sects in England and America have often retained the language of AV within their own group in distinction from current usage right up to modern times.

3. INTERPRETATION

Luther: Sola Fide

Erasmus wanted the Bible to be available to all people, so that they might be familiar with Jesus Christ, and discover in him the key to understanding the whole of the biblical revelation. This was to be the means of reform, for a truly devout hierarchy and secular government would have clear ideals to guide their decisions and would work for the good of all people in the realm. Luther shared the humanist ideals, but his character and personal experience led him to direct confrontation with the ecclesiastical authorities. First, his famous 'tower experience', when he was wrestling with the meaning of Paul's Letter to the Romans, solved his agonising doubts about the possibility of salvation by his sudden realisation that the justification of sinful humanity in the sight of God is a matter of faith alone. Paul was arguing against the Judaisers, who were insisting on imposing the Jewish Law on Gentile converts. But Luther saw a parallel between the works of the Law and the institutions of the church, including the priesthood and sacraments and the rules of the religious order to which he belonged. These now seemed to him to be barriers rather than aids to salvation, because they stood in the way of the individual's personal acceptance of salvation through the act of faith alone. Justification by faith alone became the foundation of all his subsequent teaching. It entails the view that human nature, corrupted by sin, has no power of achieving eternal salvation, which is entirely the work of God. Luther drew from Augustine his emphasis on the innate sinfulness of human nature, and from the fourteenth-century German mystic Johann Tauler the concept of the direct knowledge of God in the soul, which gives assurance of salvation without any need for action.

Luther thus began to put forward these views in his lectures at Wittenberg. Then matters came to a head in 1517 when J. Tetzel preached indulgences to the souls in purgatory merely for the payment of a fee, in order to raise funds on behalf of the Pope's building plans. Luther was so enraged that he made a public protest by attaching ninety-five theses to the door of the Schlosskirche in Wittenberg. And so the Reformation began.

Luther's objection to Tetzel's preaching struck at the whole mediaeval system of penance. It was viewed as a transaction, in which divine forgiveness was conditional on the performance of an act of punishment or by paying the appropriate penalty. But Luther's doctrine of justification could not allow this, because all that is necessary for salvation has been accomplished in the death of Jesus. The forgiveness of God cannot be earned or bought. It can only be received in faith. Luther found support for his teaching from his study of the Greek of the New Testament, when he discovered from the writings of Erasmus (and through him from Valla) that *metanoein* means 'repent', against the Vulgate equivalent 'do penance'.

Luther: Sola Scriptura

Luther's protest set the Bible and the tradition of the Church in direct opposition to one another, in a way that Erasmus and those of a similar mind were most anxious to avoid. Besides attacking manifest abuses, it posed a serious question against the authority of the Church in matters of faith and order. For Luther would not surrender his position in deference to the demands of his superiors, because the authority of the Scriptures is above that of the Church. The point at issue is the idea of the sources of Christian doctrine. The Bible had always been regarded as the revelation of God, and therefore the primary source of doctrine. The two were kept together by the practice of interpreting the Bible in agreement with the Rule of Faith from the Patristic period to the end of the Middle Ages. Only at the end of the mediaeval period was the concept of two sources of doctrine, Bible and Church, developed, as we saw in the last chapter. In denying that the tradition of the Church is above Scripture, Luther could claim the support of Augustine and the Fathers, who knew no such distinction, against the scholasticism of his own day. He thus moved from *sola fide* ('by faith alone'), which was his initial insight into the nature of the Christian message, to *sola scriptura* ('the Scripture alone'), which is the contention that the Bible contains all that is necessary for salvation. This notion of the sufficiency of Scripture was to become the hall-mark of the Reformation. Having denounced various practices and doctrines in a series of three controversial writings, on the grounds that they were not supported by Scripture, Luther refused to withdraw his positions precisely on this issue at the Diet of Worms in 1521. It is here that, according to tradition, he uttered his famous words, 'Here I stand. I can no other. May God help me. Amen'.

Luther: Private Judgment

However, it was not enough to claim the sufficiency of Scripture, because it could be replied that the Church, in particular its chief representative the Pope, has authority over the interpretation of Scripture. Luther maintained on the contrary that the Bible is self-authenticating. Those who read it in faith will discover its truth, and will have the light of the Holy Spirit to guide their understanding. He therefore insisted on the right to private judgment over against submission to the judgment of the Church. He ridiculed the idea that one man, the Pope, should be regarded as having a monopoly of biblical interpretation.

Luther's concept of private judgment was opposed, but also misunderstood, by Erasmus. For Luther the foundation of faith was God's act in Christ, which justifies the sinner. This act of justification must be received in faith, because human beings have no power of themselves to effect their own salvation. In so far as the act of God is a message of salvation – God's verdict of acquittal – it is God's Word, and the Word of God continues to speak through the Scriptures. Thus Luther distinguished between the Word of God and the Scriptures through which it is conveyed. The Word can obviously be apprehended more clearly in some parts of Scripture than in others. Besides the Letters of Paul, Luther valued especially the Gospel of John and 1 Peter, which he used frequently in his lectures. But, when the heart is warmed by the message of the gospel, the reader of the Bible is rendered capable of discovering Christ in other parts of Scripture, and the enlightening of the Holy Spirit guides the interpretation. So the Scriptures are spiritual, because they lead the reader to God. In this way no authoritative guidance outside the Scripture is required, for the Scripture interprets itself (*scriptura scripturae interpres*). Erasmus, on the other hand, was influenced by Neoplatonic philosophy to value the interpretations of the ancient Fathers, and indeed began a programme for publication of them in printed editions, so that their interpretations might be appreciated in context, instead of in the isolated quotations of the Gloss. He would not deny that the Fathers were truly spiritual men. He thus could not agree with Luther's opposition to the allegorical sense, nor did he grasp Luther's concept of the Christian interpretation of the Old Testament which occupied our attention in Part I. By contrast for Luther, or at least for his more ardent followers, the Fathers were not spiritual and remained unenlightened, because they failed to hear the Word of God which is contained in Scripture.

Consequences of Reformation Principles

Several further points follow from this controversy. In the *first* place, Luther's concept of the Word of God has special importance for the value which he placed on preaching, which has had a permanent effect on Lutheran Christianity. Gillian Evans quotes the following dialogue from Luther's *Table Talk* (no. 5177):

> Somebody asked, 'Doctor, is the word that Christ spoke when he was on earth the same in fact and effect as the Word preached by a minister?'
>
> Luther replied, 'Yes, because he said, "He who hears you hears me" (Luke 10:16). And Paul calls the Word "the power of God" ' (Romans 1:16).
>
> Then the inquirer asked, 'Doctor, isn't there a difference between the Word that became flesh (John 1:14) and the Word that is proclaimed by Christ or by a minister?'
>
> 'By all means!' he replied. 'The former is the incarnate Word, who was true God from the beginning, and the latter is the Word that's proclaimed. The former Word is in substance God; the latter Word is in its effect the power of God, but it isn't God in substance, for it has a man's nature, whether it's spoken by Christ or by a minister.'

A *second* point is that we can now see why Luther is really very selective in his use of the Bible, including the New Testament. In the preface to his translation of 1522 he called James 'an epistle of straw' (*ein recht strohen Epistel*). But this was a relative judgment.

By comparison with other books it has no evangelical skill in its composition. The Word is what matters, and this comes through more clearly in some parts of Scripture than in others.

Thirdly, in spite of Luther's antagonism to ecclesiastical institutions not supported by Scripture, he did not depreciate the outward expressions of worship, especially the two sacraments of the gospel, baptism and eucharist. The Neoplatonic outlook of Erasmus led him to regard the outward institutions as merely concessionary to human weakness. The truly spiritual person does not need them, because salvation takes place in the mind. This was quite different from Luther's view, as he could see public worship, especially the sacraments, as authorised by Scripture and as functioning in the same way as preaching to enable people to apprehend the Word of God. Though he rejected the doctrine of transubstantiation as an explanation of the eucharistic elements, he held that the eucharistic words of Jesus should not be spiritualised away, because the elements are a real means of communion with Christ. Other reformers, however, shared Erasmus' Neoplatonic presuppositions, notably Ulrich Zwingli at Zürich. There thus enters into the Reformation movement a strong current of opposition to the sacraments, based on contrasting what is outward and material with what is inward and real.

Fourthly, Luther's stand on *sola scriptura* found a ready response among other reforming groups of the period, who did not necessarily share his special focus on justification by faith. What has been called the left wing of the Reformation, the Anabaptist movement, represents a popular tendency akin to the *devotio moderna*, in which discipleship rather than redemption is the chief concern. For such groups the doctrine of *sola scriptura* gave freedom from allegiance to the hierarchical Church, and the opportunity to create a form of Christian life entirely based on the New Testament. Though baptism was used as a rite of initiation (re-baptism in most cases, as they rejected infant baptism), they mostly dispensed with outward forms of worship.

Finally, Luther's stand carried with it the negative corollary, shared by nearly all the reformers, that what is not contained in Scripture is not to be required of the Christian. This was difficult to press absolutely, because (as was pointed out at the time) certain aspects of the faith, including even the doctrine of the Trinity, were presupposed by the reformers, though they are not clearly stated in Scripture. Anabaptists, however, were prepared to surrender even these in the attempt to live by the Scripture alone. At the end of the century F. P. Socinus (1539–1604) caused consternation in the established Protestant churches by denying everything, both doctrinal and ecclesiastical, that could not be directly proved from Scripture.

Calvin

Meanwhile John Calvin (1509–64) represents the continuation of the learned humanism of the age of Erasmus within the Reformation camp. He was convinced on both of Luther's main positions of *sola fide* and *sola scriptura*, and he worked on this basis with intellectual rigour and sound common sense. Using Reformation principles he made a constructive synthesis of biblical teaching for a new policy of church and state in his *Institutes of the Christian Religion* (first edition, 1536). He regarded the Scriptures as God's word, dictated by the Holy Spirit, though not in a slavishly literal sense. He was aware of the human limitations of the biblical authors. But behind them is the utterance of God through the Spirit, and this can be perceived and acknowledged by the Christian through the internal testimony of the Spirit in the believer. In his commentaries, which cover all books of the New Testament except 2 and 3 John and Revelation, he aims to give the sense of the text as clearly as possible, making careful distinctions in the light of his linguistic knowledge. His ideas on the secular state are derived mainly from the Old Testament, carefully distinguishing what should be considered obsolete with the coming of Christ from what has permanent value. His ideas on the Church are based mainly on the New Testament, from which he drew the presbyterian form of government. However, he does not work exclusively from the Bible, and takes careful note of the teaching of the early Fathers. He defends infant baptism against the Anabaptists, though it cannot be proved directly from Scripture, on the grounds of ancient practice attested by the Fathers. But his main argument is that baptism corresponds with Jewish circumcision, which was done in infancy (*Institutes* IV. 16, 1559 edition). This illustrates his idea that the Christian church is the community of the new covenant, corresponding with, but superseding, the community of the old covenant, so that the New Testament matches the Old at a higher level.

Calvin shared with Luther the conviction that only Christians have the possibility of eternal salvation. The concepts of election and predestination, based on Paul's teaching in Romans 9, play a central part in his thinking. Behind this lies Luther's insistence on justification by faith alone, but with new emphasis on the fact that the saving death of Christ is God's sovereign act of mercy. Those who believe do so because they are predestined to do so.

Commenting on Romans 9:22, Calvin says, 'He (i.e. Paul) does not give a reason for the election of God in such a way as to show the cause why this person is chosen, and that rejected; for it was not fitting to expose those things which belong to the secret counsel of God to human judgment, and also it was a mystery that cannot be analysed; he therefore restrains us from enquiring curiously into what surpasses human understanding'. Thus Calvin stands in the tradition of Augustine, but with added care to preserve the absolute sovereignty of God.

Reformation Confessions of Faith

Calvin's treatment of ecclesiastical institutions gives the primacy to the New Testament, but inevitably he tends to treat the New Testament as law. Thus, in spite of Luther's contrast between law and gospel, the concept of a divine law constantly reappears in Reformation thinking. Reformed bodies produced confessional statements, like the Augsburg Confession of the Lutherans (1530; accepted in a much revised form by certain Calvinist churches, 1540), and the Thirty-Nine Articles of the Church of England (1563). These were statements of agreement for common life and mutual recognition, rendered necessary by the rejection of the central authority of the Roman Catholic Church, but they tended to become doctrinal tests and to promote the legalistic outlook. So also there appeared systematisations of the teaching of Luther at a later stage, which amounted to a neo-scholasticism, like the *Key of Holy Scripture* of Flacius Illyricus (1567), which makes the Scripture say what Luther made it say. Thus the 'confessions' replace the Rule of Faith as the real basis of interpretation.

4. INSPIRATION AND AUTHORITY

The success of the Reformation claim of the sufficiency of Scripture depended on the conviction that the Bible is divinely inspired. This was accepted on both sides in the conflict. But the repudiation of the Church's claim to be the interpreter of Scripture necessarily enhanced the importance of the idea of the inspiration and authority of the Bible.

Verbal Inerrancy?

In the first place, general acceptance of the truth of the Bible carried with it the idea of verbal inerrancy. But the discrepancies are far too numerous, even in the New Testament alone, to be simply disregarded. There are also clear mistakes, and in the Old Testament much that is offensive to Christian ideas about God. In the hands of Origen these problems could be accepted as pointers to the real truth, which was to be found by allegorical interpretation. Obviously such an expedient was no longer possible with the new emphasis on the literal sense. In fact a great deal of the mediaeval exegesis was taken up with solving problems of this kind. But the Catholic position, making the Church the guardian of interpretation, allows for some confusion at the same time as insistence on the general reliability of Scripture. Luther also refused to be thrown off balance by the discrepancies or mistakes of Scripture because of his distinction between the Word of God and the Scriptures in which it is expressed. Calvin, as we have just seen, could speak of the books of the Bible as dictated by the Holy Spirit, but at the same time he made allowances for the limitations imposed on the sacred writers by the conditions of the time in which they lived.

Nevertheless the necessity of arguing on the basis of Scripture, as the only agreed authority in the unending doctrinal disputes of the period, forced the protagonists to rely on the exact words of Scripture to maintain their views. The scholars could attach divine inspiration to the original Hebrew and Greek, but this soon applied more generally to the vernacular translations. We have seen that the Council of Trent, without supporting verbal inerrancy, was under pressure to uphold the reliability of the Vulgate. But in Protestant circles, where a simple vernacular translation was established as the Bible in common use, as happened in Germany and England, there has always been a tendency to apply the notion of verbal inerrancy to the translation, just as if it were the original text.

The desire to uphold verbal inerrancy soon produced efforts at harmonisation, to explain away the discrepancies of Scripture. Thus Andreas Osiander published a *Harmony of the Gospels* (1545), in which he employed the simple device of assigning discrepant accounts of the same episode to different occasions. He had a precedent in the work of Jerome, who had been forced to hold that Jesus cleansed the temple twice, once at the beginning of his public ministry and once at the end, in order to explain the relationship between John and the Synoptics, as we have seen above.

The Witness of the Spirit

The point of insisting on verbal inerrancy was to preserve the authority of the Bible as something that inheres in the Bible itself, without the need of any external authority. This is, of course, the presupposition of the claim of the sufficiency of Scripture, but it can scarcely be denied that the Bible requires interpretation to make it usable as the foundation of religion. Unfortunately, those who refuse all external authorities never agree among themselves, as Erasmus pointed out in his dispute with Luther. Though Luther and Calvin avoided the difficulty by their attitudes to inspiration mentioned above, both retained a large debt to the tradition of the Church in practice which prevented an absolute break with the past and the consequent dissensions and splits which characterise the Anabaptist and similar groups. But as the sixteenth century wore on, and the Bible-based wrangles between different groups showed only too clearly the limitations of appeal to the Bible as the sole authority, there was a tendency to emphasise Calvin's notion of the internal testimony of the Spirit in terms of direct illumination which would cut through the contention. This applied particularly to the controversies concerning predestination and free-will, which came to a head in the disputes between Calvinists and Arminians in Holland late in the century. As the Bible was the only authority to appeal to, the arguments always turned on the method of handling it. As it became clear that the problems were insoluble by rational argument based on biblical texts, there was an increasing tendency among the Calvinists to split into sects, each with a distinctive interpretation based on the testimony of the Spirit in the heart. This tendency reaches its climax with the Inner Light doctrine of George Fox and the Quakers in the seventeenth century.

New Testament Prophecy

The doctrine of verbal inspiration also affected the handling of New Testament texts which refer to the future, such as Mark 13, 2 Thessalonians 2 and Revelation. How far are they already fulfilled, and how far are they still awaiting fulfilment in the future? The temptation to identify the scarlet woman of Revelation 17 with the Church of Rome was irresistible in the heated controversies of the age, and quickly became established as the accepted interpretation among Protestants. *Theodorus Bibliander* (1504–64), a follower of Zwingli, identified the 'lawless one' of 2 Thessalonians 2:8 with the Pope, but correctly saw that the reference in Revelation 13 is to the emperor Nero. Catholic exegetes were inclined to see Revelation fulfilled in the downfall of the Roman Empire and the triumph of the Church. On the other side the success of the Reformation suggested to some exegetes that their own time was the period referred to in Revelation. This, with the new emphasis on the experience of the Spirit, suggested further the beginning of a third era, comparable to the expectations generated by Joachimism. It is thus not surprising that the Anabaptists and similar sects paid much attention to the interpretation of apocalyptic texts. The use of the Bible more generally for purposes of prediction, with imminent expectation of the Second Coming of Jesus determined by plotting out correspondences between current events and the 'wars and rumours of wars' of Mark 13, is another persistent feature of biblicist groups, based on verbal inerrancy, which shows no sign of abating.

These attitudes are peripheral to the major importance of the period of Renaissance and Reformation. Three things were achieved which constitute a breakthrough in the use and understanding of the New Testament: the recovery of the Greek text; the wide diffusion of vernacular translations, made possible by the invention of printing; and the liberation of interpretation from the rigid control of ecclesiastical authority. The Catholics were, of course, correct in their fear that possession of the Scriptures and freedom of interpretation would lead to chaos and heresy. The Reformation churches did not escape the tendency to impose ecclesiastical authority of another kind. But perhaps the mistakes and bitter controversies of the Reformation period were necessary to create the conditions in which the New Testament could be viewed objectively and its problems faced without preconceived answers.

FOR FURTHER READING

The Cambridge History of the Bible 3: The West from the Reformation to the Present Day, edited by S. L. Greenslade, CUP, Cambridge 1963.

Bentley, J. H., *Humanists and Holy Writ: New Testament Scholarship in the Renaissance*, Princeton University Press, Princeton 1983.

Bruce, F. F., *The English Bible: a History of Translations*, third edition, Lutterworth, Guildford and London, 1979 = *History of the Bible in English*, OUP, New York 1978.

Forstman, H. J., *Word and Spirit: Calvin's Doctrine of Biblical Authority*, Stanford 1962.

Grant, R. M. with D. Tracy, *A Short History of the Interpretation of the Bible*, rev. ed., Fortress, Philadelphia 1984.

Harbison, E. H., *The Christian Scholar in the Age of Reformation*, Eerdmans, Grand Rapids ²1983.

Wood, A. S., *Captive to the Word: Martin Luther, Doctor of Sacred Scripture*, Paternoster, Exeter 1969.

6

THE RISE OF MODERN CRITICISM

The Enlightenment of the late seventeenth century is chiefly associated with the beginnings of experimental science and the discovery of natural laws which suggested that the universe had its own autonomy, and was not subject to manipulation by supernatural forces. The astronomical calculations of Copernicus (1473–1543) and Galileo (1564–1642) had dethroned the earth from the central place in the universe by demonstrating the solar system. These developments of knowledge were bound to affect the way people understood the nature of reality and to call in question the teachings of religion and the authority of the Bible. It is out of the Deist attacks on the Bible in this period that the critical approach to the Bible was formed.

1. THE APPEAL TO REASON

After the Reformation

As a result of the Reformation the Bible had immense authority throughout northern Europe during the seventeenth century. It was not only the foundation of theology and religious practice, but also of social organisation and the state. In Lutheran lands (Scandinavia and Germany) the systematisation of Luther's teaching put a brake on the tendency to turn the Bible itself into a code of law. Where Calvinism prevailed this tendency had far-reaching consequences. The Reformation in England took a particular course which had its effect on the understanding of the Bible and paved the way for the Enlightenment. For in England great efforts were made during the reign of Elizabeth I (1559–1603) to contain the different religious groups in a single national church, comprising not only those influenced by the Reformation but also those who wished to retain Catholic worship and sacramental doctrine. In the controversies between the Anglicans, who wished to achieve this, and the Puritans, who tended to separatist and extremist forms of Calvinism, the Anglicans argued for retention of ancient customs as far as possible, and valued the contribution of the Fathers to the formation of Christian life and doctrine. The Puritans rejected everything that was not directly provable from the Bible, and regarded the rest as 'popery'. There were, indeed, grounds for real fear that England might return to the papal jurisdiction once more.

The Appeal to Reason

In the controversies of the time appeal to reason was made by both sides. Richard Hooker (1554–1600), whose treatise on *The Laws of Ecclesiastical Polity* is the classic apology for the Anglican position at the time, points out that reason cannot be dispensed with in the effort to derive a Christian polity from Scripture. In the confusion of arguments, not only with the Anglicans, but also between Puritans and Independents and other Calvinist groups among themselves, natural law tends to become the final arbiter, because the problems at issue cannot be resolved by appeal to Scripture alone. The influence of humanism in education ensured the teaching of classical learning in the grammar schools, many of which were founded in this period, so that the idea of natural law received support from the study of Cicero and the Stoics. In this way a strong Calvinist like John Milton (1608–74), who was bitterly opposed to the Anglican retention of mediaeval priesthood and episcopate and canon law, could even argue in favour of divorce against the apparent meaning of Matthew 19:3–9. Though this raised a storm of protest, and led to his separation from the Presbyterians with whom he had been associated, it is significant as an example of the tendency to make room for freedom of conscience, and of course continues the reformed tradition of private judgment. On this issue he contrives to save the teaching of Jesus by ingenious interpretation, but the real concern is to preserve moral justice following the failure of his own marriage. Thus morality is the focus of religion, and when there is conflict it is the Bible that has to give way.

The moralism of English religion, which appears in Milton, was bound to renew objections to the Bible on moral grounds, especially on the part of those who were trained in philosophy as a separate discipline from theology. There were some radical thinkers, like Matthew Hamond, who was burned at the stake in 1579, because he 'denied Christ' and said 'that the New Testament and gospel of Christ are but mere foolishness, a story of men, or rather a fable.'

The distinguished humanist, *Lord Herbert of Cherbury* (1583–1648), anticipated the Deists by isolating five constants of religion, all amenable to reason, which lie behind all religions, though religions always tend to be corrupted by priests and theologians. Hence the claim of revelation is unnecessary, and religion must be judged by reason and morality. Herbert explicitly includes moral criticism of the barbarities of the Old Testament.

The World of Experience

At the same time the consistent opposition to outward forms and ceremonies on the part of the Puritans led to concentration on the inward spiritual experience, which can be related fairly easily to a philosophical account of the nature of reality, whereas the historical character of the Bible and of the action of God in Christ is more difficult to accommodate. This shift of emphasis is characteristic of those, like Milton, who followed the Platonist tendency in philosophy. Among the Cambridge Platonists towards the end of the century there was an absolute confidence in the power of reason, coupled with great interest in the advances in natural science that were being made. It was becoming apparent that the world of experience and the world of the Bible were splitting apart. Many of the Cambridge scholars retained their religious faith only by adopting Deism, which allows for creation by God, but reduces the possibility of divine intervention in the world. This obviously poses a fundamental question to biblical revelation. So the attack extended beyond the barbarities of the Old Testament to the notion of miracles within the New Testament too.

Thus at the end of the seventeenth century the appeal to reason was needed on at least two counts. Politically, it was needed to secure religious toleration (enacted by Act of Parliament in 1689) after years of strife. It is no accident that the Latitudinarians (Anglicans who supported toleration) included the Cambridge Platonists and others among the Deists. Intellectually, reason was the mainspring of the Deist position. Those who attacked the biblical revelation on grounds of reason had to be answered with rational arguments.

Rational Defence and Attack

A notable deistic thinker who defended revelation at the same time as promoting toleration and intellectual freedom was John Locke (1632–1704). In his *Essay Concerning Human Understanding* he suggested that revelation should be considered continuous with nature rather than opposed to it. From this point of view supernatural occurrences should be regarded as having an ultimate explanation in terms of natural causation which is not yet available. Revelation is necessary, however, because mankind cannot attain to truly moral living without its aid. Nevertheless Locke reduced the content of revelation to the barest minimum for Christian faith. In his view Jesus was the Messiah who rose from the dead, and whose teaching was confirmed by miracles, but the theological superstructure of christology was unnecessary. In work on Paul, published after his death, he insisted that Paul's letters should not be used as a basis for theology, but be recognised for what they are, occasional pieces written in particular circumstances which can be deduced only from the internal evidence of the letters themselves. It is interesting to observe how this approach takes up Colet's wish to read Paul in context and also the historical concerns of Spinoza (see Part I, chapter 7).

So the Bible itself, instead of being the absolute authority which it had been for Protestants for the past century and a half, has now become dependent on reason for its defence, and reason is parsimonious in the amount of truth she will allow to it. Other writers of the early eighteenth century were far less generous than Locke. There were attacks on the concept of messianic prophecies (Anthony Collins), on the folly of taking the gospel miracles literally, including the resurrection of Jesus, rather than in an allegorical sense (Thomas Woolston), and on the need for a special revelation when natural religion provides everything that is worth while in the gospel (Matthew Tindal). Collins showed that the New Testament application of prophetic passages differed from that of the actual prophets. Following Locke's contention that the true meaning can only be that of the original author, he claimed that the New Testament applications were simply false. Though his view may be regarded as an oversimplification, it constitutes an important point, which laid a foundation for the development of historico-critical method. The counterattack by Joseph Butler in his famous *Analogy of Religion* (1736) showed that, once it is granted that reason permits the existence of natural religion, it follows that revealed religion is reasonable by analogy. Consequently the miracles of the gospel, though unprovable, are to be accepted as probable. Like Locke, he claimed that natural religion alone is not sufficient for moral living as understood by Christians. But by making the biblical concepts of divine action in miracles and revelation separate from the category of natural religion, Butler prepared the ground for the much more sceptical David Hume to dismiss the biblical record as superstitious constructs of the human imagination. At the end of the eighteenth

century Tom Paine's *The Age of Reason* (1795) dismissed the Bible
as a web of barbarous ideas of no moral value, even the New
Testament being nothing but 'absurdities, contradictions and false-
hoods'. It is evident that the appeal to reason was forcing a radical
reappraisal of the Bible. This was to be the effect of Deism in
Germany in the later part of the eighteenth century. But first other
factors of the period must be taken into consideration.

2. CRITICAL METHOD

Advances in Philology
The critical work of Valla and Erasmus in the Renaissance period
was continued all through the later time of the Reformation by
scholars who preferred to keep out of controversy for the most part.
The characteristic preference for the literal sense was beginning to
show fruit in commentaries which had a better grasp of the Bible
as a product of historical circumstances, instead of regarding it
virtually as something that dropped down from heaven. The printed
Greek texts, which, as we have seen, were in great demand all
through the period, enabled commentators to pay more attention to
matters of grammar and philology. The moderate Lutheran *Joachim
Camerarius* (1500–74), who had helped to draw up the Augsburg
Confession, paid special regard to such questions in his commentary
on the Gospels, published shortly before his death. In the seventeenth century *Hugo Grotius* (1583–1645), a Dutch lawyer and
scholar, who sided with the Arminians against the extreme Calvinist
sects in Holland, and like the English Latitudinarians worked hard
for toleration, published *Notes on the New Testament* (1641) which
are remarkable not only for detailed philological comments, but also
for his prefaces to the individual books of the New Testament.
These deal with questions of authorship and historical setting in a
manner that anticipates the introductions to biblical books in
modern commentaries. His work on the Old Testament has been
described in Part I above.

It seems desirable to mention *Benedict (Baruch) Spinoza* (1632–77)
at this point, though his work was concerned with the Old Testament, and has been dealt with in Part I. He also, as a free-thinking
Jew of Christian sympathies, laboured for toleration in Holland,
and is to be counted among the early Deists. He pointed out in his
Tractatus Theologico-Politicus that the Bible is not concerned with
philosophical problems or the question of miracles as such, but with
obedience to God. But as the use of reason can also reach the

same concept of submission to the will of God, the Bible is really dispensable by the intelligent person. Having thus deprived the Bible of any theological value, Spinoza can only recommend it to study for its historical and antiquarian interest. He is thus led to enunciate the kind of questions which may suitably be addressed to the text. They concern the language of the book, its contents, difficult passages, historical setting, and the use made of the book in history, and how it has become part of the canon. This again anticipates the agenda for historical study of the Bible, which was not taken up until the work of J. G. Eichhorn more than a century later.

In England the Anglican *John Lightfoot* (1602–75) realised that many of the problems of the New Testament might be solved if the Jewish background were better understood. He was an outstanding rabbinic scholar, and was the first person to attempt to sketch the historical and cultural conditions in the time of Christ on the basis of Jewish sources. His six volumes of *Horae Hebraicae et Talmudicae*, published intermittently between 1658 and 1678, and written in English in spite of the Latin title, made rich use of the Talmud and Midrash and the mediaeval Jewish commentaries now available in the printed rabbinic Bible, and laid the foundation for all subsequent work of this kind. One observation that has become well known is that Jesus' use of Aramaic *abba* (father) in prayer (Mark 14:36, cf. Romans 8:15; Galatians 4:6) was not a normal mode of addressing God in Jewish prayers.

Textual Criticism

At the same time textual criticism of both Old and New Testaments was advanced by the publication of Brian Walton's *Biblia Sacra Polyglotta*, generally referred to as the London Polyglot, in 1657. It is the last of the great polyglot Bibles. Though Walton, who was assisted by Lightfoot, reproduced texts with Latin translations which had already appeared in previous publications, he saw that the value of the texts for comparative purposes lay in the assembly of information. He not only produced the best and most comprehensive layout of the various versions, including the Ethiopic version of the New Testament and Persian for the Gospels, in addition to the Syriac and Arabic versions, but he also added an appendix of variant readings, making use of the work of Stephanus which was referred to in the last chapter. Moreover he included at the foot of the page throughout the text of the New Testament variant readings from the newly discovered Codex Alexandrinus (code letter A). This is the great fifth century manuscript of the whole Bible in Greek, third in importance only to Codex Vaticanus, which was not generally available to scholars as we have seen, and to Codex Sinaiticus, which was not discovered until the nineteenth century. It had been offered for political reasons to King James I by the Patriarch of Alexandria, though it did not actually reach London until 1627, in the reign of Charles I. Examination of it quickly showed the inferior quality of the *textus receptus*, and this could now be readily appreciated by readers of the London Polyglot. Walton's bold insertion of these variants thus made it plain that the *textus receptus* could no longer be regarded as satisfactory.

Meanwhile the French Oratorian *Richard Simon* (1638–1712), besides pioneering work on the criticism of the Old Testament referred to in Part I, opposed excessive reliance on the New Testament on the part of Protestants by pointing to the uncertainties of the text. He thus set out to establish the facts about the New Testament as a preliminary to assessing its worth, and published a series of books between 1689 and 1695 on the Greek text of the New Testament, the ancient versions of it, and the evidence of quotations in the Fathers. These books are remarkable for their objectivity and perceptiveness in matters of detail. Simon is generally claimed to be a critical scholar far in advance of his time.

Simon's work had some influence in England, where several scholars were convinced of the need to construct a critical Greek text of the New Testament to replace the discredited *textus receptus*, which continued to enjoy exaggerated regard among those who believed in verbal inerrancy. A start was made by John Mill (or Mills), who published in 1707 the *textus receptus* with a critical apparatus listing variant readings from nearly a hundred manuscripts. At the same time the great classical textual scholar Richard Bentley announced a programme for a new critical edition of the Greek and Latin texts of the New Testament, based on principles of textual criticism which he had worked out in dealing with classical authors. However he died before much of the work had been done, and the project was abandoned. He had in any case been anticipated by a new text and translation of the New Testament by Daniel Mace, which was published anonymously in 1729. Though he made good use of the textual information provided by Mill, his work was marred by bold conjectures, which laid it open to criticism. With the rather eccentric and colloquial translation, many people regarded the work as bordering on blasphemy.

Advances in Germany

The next real advance took place in Germany. Here the Pietist movement, which encouraged personal devotion to Christ on the basis of Scripture, had an ardent representative in *J. A. Bengel* (1687–1752). His confidence was shattered by Mill's presentation of the evidence for textual variation in the New Testament. The result was that he produced his own critical edition on the basis of readings already in print, and this was published in 1734. Though the text was still the *textus receptus*, he introduced a system of signs to indicate the different worth of the variants, clearly showing which should be preferred to those given in the text. But the importance of this edition was his explanation of the principles of textual criticism by which such decisions may be reached. These include recognition of the grouping of manuscripts, which may give help in tracing the history of a particular reading; the need to explain the relationship between two or more variants, so as to decide which is likely to be original and to see how the erroneous readings occurred; and the rule already observed by Erasmus, that normally the shorter reading is to be preferred to the longer one, because of the tendency of ancient scribes to clarify the text by expanding it. Having thus restored his confidence in the Greek text, and made a notable contribution to textual study in the process, Bengel published in 1742 his *Gnomon of the New Testament*, in which he set out to elucidate the New Testament as a guide to life with commentary based on sound philology. This is a work of sound judgment, which was much used by John Wesley, and is still referred to by modern scholars.

The two aims of a more reliable Greek text (Bengel) and of a better understanding of the Jewish background to the New Testament (Lightfoot) come together in *J. J. Wettstein* (1693–1754), with whom we may conclude this section. His large two-volume edition of the Greek New Testament was published at Amsterdam in 1751–2 after years of toil. Having been grossly unfairly treated in his young days for attempting to publish a critical text, he now presented, like all his predecessors, the *textus receptus*, but printed beneath it a scientifically planned critical apparatus which clearly indicated the readings to be preferred. For this purpose he used code letters (A for Alexandrinus, B for Vaticanus, etc.) for the earlier uncial manuscripts and numerals for the later minuscules, thus devising the system which is still in use today. Almost equally lasting has been his rich assembly of parallels from classical and rabbinic sources to illustrate words and phrases, which are placed at the foot of the page. Even more important, he added an essay on interpretation, in which he insisted that 'since we read with the same eyes the sacred books and the laws given by decree of the princes, as well as all ancient and modern books, so also the same rules are to be applied in the interpretation of the former as we use for understanding the latter.' The critical tools which he provided in this great edition help to make this possible by assisting the imaginative effort required to enter the world of the ancient writers, and so to share their mind and outlook. Here at last the New Testament is viewed objectively without the imposition of a preconceived theological interpretation.

3. HISTORICAL METHOD

The philological work on the New Testament which we have just reviewed was thus preparing the ground for a realistic understanding of it in context, in which the aims and methods of the authors are assessed objectively, and attention is given to what they actually say. But this still does not provide the means to assess the value of the New Testament books for history. To take an obvious example from the debates of the time, what is the status of a miracle story? Is it a factual account of something that happened in New Testament times, even though such things rarely, if ever, happen now? Or is it to be denied outright, on the grounds that the world is so ordered that miracles are excluded (the position of most of the Deists)? If, then, it is not a factual account, but nevertheless is contained in a work which claims to be reliable, can some other explanation be found? The answer to such questions is the province of 'higher criticism', which refers to a further stage of investigation after the foundation of textual study, or 'lower criticism', has been established (it is thus not higher in a moral or aesthetic sense). For this purpose it is not enough to shake off the traditional interpretation, guided by dogmatic preconceptions. It is necessary to be aware of one's own presuppositions, and to take steps to avoid being influenced by them unduly. A Deist can be just as dogmatic in approach to the sacred text as a traditionalist. So, though the next step forward in biblical interpretation received its impetus from the Deists, it achieved only the hope and intention of objectivity, and the claim to have reached a truly historical account of the biblical record was largely illusory. But it set the wheels in motion for genuine advance through drawing attention to historical method and making the first attempts to use it.

Semler

The move towards a historical understanding of the New Testament first clearly appears in J. S. Semler (1725–91), who was Professor of Theology at Halle from 1752, and had been influenced by the ideas of the English Deists and by the work of Simon and Wettstein. His outlook is apparent in the title of the best known of his numerous writings, *Treatise on the Free Investigation of the Canon*. This freedom has already been referred to in connection with his attitude to the Old Testament above. Though, as was there pointed out, he claimed to be faithful to Luther in distinguishing between the Word of God and the Scriptures in which it is contained, he made the distinction on the grounds of reason rather than theology. He was thus able to avoid the necessity of attributing divine inspiration to every word of Scripture. The critic is then free to view the various books historically. The Old Testament can be detached from the New Testament, and within the New Testament the books are not all on the same level. The variety of Christian life and teaching which they attest can be given full value so as to gain a stereoscopic view of earliest Christianity with the aim of constructing a primitive history. In this way Semler deduced the different character of the Jewish-Christian church of Jerusalem by comparison with the Gentile churches founded by Paul. He thus put on a sounder footing a distinction that had already been made by the controversial Irish Deist John Toland in his *Nazarenus* (1718), who had pointed to the Ebionites (Jewish Christians of the second century) as the survivors of Christianity in its original form.

Semler also undertook research into the text of the New Testament, and was the first person to allocate the groups of manuscripts distinguished by Bengel to different geographical areas. He found four ancient groups, Western, Egyptian, Palestinian, and texts stemming from the work of Origen. All these are distinct from the later Eastern texts which form the basis of the *textus receptus*. These groupings have had to be modified by subsequent research, but roughly accord with later findings.

Michaelis

Semler's historical approach to the New Testament was carried forward by J. D. Michaelis (1717–91) at Göttingen. His *Introduction to the New Testament*, originally based on the work of Simon and published in 1750, and greatly enlarged for the fourth edition of 1788, addressed the historical evaluation of the books, especially in relation to authorship. Assuming, as so many assumed from the second century onwards, that apostolic authorship is the essential criterion for inclusion in the canon as an inspired writing, he downgraded those books which could not be attributed to apostles in the light of historico-critical examination. The Synoptic Gospels and Acts are secondhand in the sense that they do not come from eyewitnesses (he regarded Matthew as an adaptation from an Aramaic original). On the other hand the genuine Letters of Paul have first-rate importance as evidence for earliest Christianity. We can see here the dilemma of a scholar who wishes to retain a traditional idea of the reliability of the Bible, but is constrained by the claims of historical method, which can no longer be disregarded in the study of the Bible. Michaelis' pupil, *J. G. Eichhorn* (1752–1827), however, welcomed his work, because he found in it a critical tool to pierce through the written Gospels to the real Jesus of history. He was prepared to look steadily at the biblical writers as authors, who mould oral or written sources. This marks the beginning of a real application of historical method. It was in connection with this approach to study that Eichhorn coined the phrase 'higher criticism'.

Reimarus

Finally, mention must be made of the sensation caused by the *Wolfenbüttel Fragments*, published by G. E. Lessing at intervals in 1774–8. These were excerpts from the work of H. S. Reimarus (1694–1768), though the author's identity was not disclosed until 1813. Reimarus was a sceptical Deist, and the book from which the fragments were taken was not intended for publication, but was an attempt to work out the truth of Christian origins for himself from his rationalist standpoint. Thus his aim is similar to that of Eichhorn, though the presuppositions are entirely different. In the last of the fragments, Reimarus declares his conclusion that Jesus had no new revelation to give, but preached the coming of the Messiah (not identified with himself) in terms of an earthly ruler. When he died, and the Messiah still had not come, his disciples stole the body (as suggested in Matthew 28:13) and invented the resurrection so as to renew the preaching in terms of a universal redeemer, thus making a bid for power for themselves. This carries forward a favourite theme of the English Deists, derived from the Puritans, that priests are always frauds, corrupting by their self-interest the pure original religion. But instead of directing the accusation against Roman Catholics or establishment Anglicans, Reimarus directed it against the original disciples themselves. It is a telling example of the way in which the claim to objectivity, which is the aim of historical method, may be vitiated by unexamined presuppositions.

The *Fragments* caused a storm of protest, because it made historical criticism appear dangerous and destructive, and this fear has arisen again and again in the subsequent history of study of the Bible. Though Reimarus' reconstruction is untenable and really had little positive influence, it was taken by Albert Schweitzer as the starting point for his famous *The Quest of the Historical Jesus* (1910), which will claim our attention later. Schweitzer saw that the real significance of Reimarus is that he pointed to the character of Jesus' preaching as the proclamation of an eschatological message rather than the enunciation of timeless truths of religion.

FOR FURTHER READING

The Cambridge History of the Bible 3
Frei, H. W., *The Eclipse of Biblical Narrative: a Study in Eighteenth and Nineteenth Century Hermeneutics*, Yale University Press, New Haven 1974.
Kümmel, W. G., *The New Testament: the History of the Investigation of its Problems*, Abingdon, Nashville, 1972, and SCM, London 1973.
Reventlow, H. G., *The Authority of the Bible and the Rise of the Modern World*, SCM, London 1983.
Richardson, Alan, *The Bible in the Age of Science*, SCM, London 1961.

7

MAJOR CONCERNS OF CRITICISM: THE NINETEENTH CENTURY

By the end of the eighteenth century the historico-critical method of studying the Bible had begun to emerge as the way forward for the future. First in Germany, and later in England and America, great advances were made in understanding the history of the books of the Bible in relation to the literature and culture of the ancient world. But the process was painful, because of the tension involved in treating a book which had enjoyed a privileged position for centuries as if it were no different from other books of its time. This new objective approach threatened the central conviction that the Bible is the Word of God in a special sense, conveying God's revelation of himself to his people. The critical method had been forged largely by those who shared the rationalist spirit of the Deists, who had no use for the concept of a special revelation. Consequently the newer methods of study encountered great resistance from those who felt that the basis of faith was being undermined by them. If faith depends on the Bible alone (*sola Scriptura*), there is nothing left if that is taken away.

Thus, just as the Reformation period was an era of conflict, in which the central issue was the relation between Bible and Church, and this dictated the problems that were perceived and the ways in which they were tackled, so the nineteenth century reopens conflict in a new way, and the major concerns which we shall survey in this chapter arise directly from the new issue which has come to the fore as a result of the Enlightenment. This is the relation between the Bible and the threat to the claim of supernatural religion. In the Old Testament the major debate centres on the status of the biblical accounts of creation. In the New Testament the person of Jesus is the most sensitive topic. Before coming to this, however, we shall begin our survey with textual criticism. This is an area of study which lies outside the conflicts of the time, but has its own fascination as a story of discovery.

1. TEXTUAL CRITICISM

The Status of the Textus Receptus

The real foundation for textual work in the nineteenth century was laid by *J. J. Griesbach* (1745–1812). who had been a pupil of Semler and followed up his observations. He produced a critical edition of the New Testament (1774–5 and later editions), which was the first to depart significantly from the *textus receptus* (though this was still used as base) and contained much information on variant readings from the work of Mill and Wettstein. His edition is important, however, for the principles which he laid down for establishing the text of the New Testament, and which were only partially carried out in the text which he printed.

Griesbach took from Semler the geographical grouping of texts, but he reduced them to three, which he called Alexandrian, Western and Constantinopolitan (or Byzantine). The high standard of accuracy of the biblical school in Alexandria in ancient times makes the identification of a specifically Alexandrian type of text very important, and this has been confirmed by later investigation. In spite of its name, Codex Alexandrinus (A), does not give the Alexandrian text in the four Gospels, but an early form of the Byzantine text. Elsewhere, however, it is a valuable witness to the Alexandrian texts. The best representatives of this text are Vaticanus (B) and Sinaiticus (‫א‬), though the former was still not readily accessible to scholars, and the latter was still undiscovered in Griesbach's time. The Western text refers to variants which are found especially in the Old Latin version (i.e. before the Vulgate) and in Greek manuscripts copied in the west. The most famous of these is the bilingual Codex Bezae (D), referred to in chapter 5. The Western text is characterised by alterations and explanatory additions. Many of these can now be proved to go back into the second century, when the books of the New Testament were becoming widely diffused, but the lack of canonical status meant that there was little control over the copying process. It is now known that this text was not just a product of western Christianity, but was generally spread in the east as well, though it is chiefly in the western manuscript tradition that it has survived. So the title Western is still used, but students of textual criticism have to be wary of drawing false conclusions from it. The Byzantine text, called Constantinopolitan by Griesbach and often referred to today as the Koiné (= common), was correctly estimated by Griesbach as an inferior text. This is because the majority of manuscripts of this group reflect an unsatisfactory revision by Lucian of Antioch (died 312), which was aimed more at improving the Greek style than at preserving the original text. As the use of the Greek language shrank to Greece itself with the collapse of the Roman Empire, the Byzantine text became predominant, because it continued to be used in Greek churches, whereas elsewhere the Greek text fell out of use and ceased to be copied. This is the reason why the great majority of later manuscripts (known as minuscules on account of the style of writing) contain the Byzantine text, and this explains why it was the inevitable basis for the *textus receptus*.

It would seem to be obvious that the Alexandrian text is superior to the rest, but this fact should not be taken uncritically, as in any particular case the true reading may be preserved in a manuscript of a different type. Griesbach therefore worked out rules of textual criticism, as a guide to probability in evaluating variant readings. Here he was building on the work of Bengel, and did it so well that his rules have remained the accepted basis of textual criticism.

Amongst the followers of Griesbach *Karl Lachmann* (1793–1851) deserves special mention. He was the first to abandon the *textus receptus* altogether and to publish a critical edition of the Greek New Testament on the basis of the ancient manuscripts (1831; second edition with full critical apparatus, 1842–50). He aimed to reconstruct the text as it was known in the fourth century by eliminating the variants which cannot be traced back as early as this. But this was really an impossible aim. The available information was still too limited, though the number of uncial (i.e. pre-minuscule) manuscripts had been increased by further research. But, more importantly, even a late manuscript can preserve a very ancient reading, if it has been copied from a very ancient exemplar, so that the actual age of a manuscript does not indicate its value as a witness to the original text.

By this time the search for ancient biblical manuscripts was being pursued in the libraries of the monasteries of the eastern Mediterranean. In 1858 William Cureton published a manuscript of the four Gospels in Syriac, which was not the common Syriac version (the Peshitta), but a much older version not previously known. A further manuscript of the same version came to light at the monastery of St. Catharine on Mount Sinai towards the end of the century. This Old Syriac version, which seems to have been ousted by the success of Tatian's *Diatessaron* in the Syrian Church, has proved to be very important, because it shares many of the same readings as the so-called Western text.

Codex Sinaiticus

The monastery of St. Catharine on Sinai had already yielded the famous Codex Sinaiticus, the great fourth century manuscript of the whole Bible, which includes the *Epistle of Barnabas*, and *Shepherd of Hermas*, though much of the Old Testament is missing. *C. Tischendorf* (1815–74) had discovered a few Old Testament pages in the waste-paper basket on his first visit to the monastery in 1844, and acquired further pages on subsequent visits, but did not gain access to the main manuscript until 1859. After complex negotiations he bought it on behalf of the Tsar of Russia, who had financed his expedition. After the Russian revolution it was purchased for the British Museum by public subscription in 1933. The code letter for New Testament reference is the Hebrew letter aleph (א), thus starting the alphabetical list, so that its close connection with A (Alexandrinus) and B (Vaticanus) can be kept in view. Tischendorf had already published successive editions of the Greek New Testament, beginning in 1841. The eighth edition (1864–72) made full use of the newly discovered manuscript, and also had the fullest apparatus of textual evidence so far produced. He was also the first scholar to obtain permission to incorporate the evidence of B. At the same time a British scholar, *S. P. Tregelles* (1813–75), completed in 1872 an edition which was the fruit of a lifetime's research. This is notable for his careful corrections to previously published lists of variants and the use of quotations of the New Testament in the Fathers, and marks another break with the *textus receptus*.

Westcott and Hort

The climax came with the text of *B. F. Westcott* (1825–1901) and *F. J. A. Hort* (1828–92). Their text, published in 1881, is based primarily on א and B, which they regarded as most nearly preserving the 'neutral' text. By this term they distinguished between these two finest examples of the Alexandrian text (often supported by the even more ancient papyrus fragments from Egypt, which have subsequently come to light) and the rest of the Alexandrian group, which show a greater degree of grammatical improvement and literary polish. But the designation 'neutral' also implies that it is virtually the original text, unspoilt either by attempts at improvement or by contamination from Western readings. This was really too optimistic, and was not borne out by their own observation that there are some important omissions in the Western text (in spite of its tendency to incorporate additions), which should be accepted against the evidence of ℵ and B. They called these 'Western non-interpolations', implying that the additional matter has been interpolated into the text that lies behind the other groups. The best known of these, which readers of modern translations such as RSV find rather disturbing, are the omission of part of the words of Jesus at the Last Supper in Luke 22:19b–20, and the omission of Luke 24:12 in the resurrection accounts. Both of these, however, have been reconsidered by recent scholars and accepted as true to the original text, on the grounds that other factors better explain their loss from the Western text. Westcott and Hort also published a very full treatise on the methods of textual criticism. Their work finally broke the dominance of the *textus receptus* and influenced the Revised Version of the Bible of 1881 and many subsequent translations.

2. THE SYNOPTIC PROBLEM

The question of the relationship between the three Synoptic Gospels came to the fore in the period under review as a direct result of the observations of textual criticism. The discrepancies between them were a matter of discomfort to verbal inspirationists, and an easy target for sceptical critics. Textual criticism, with its attention to exact words and variants, was beginning to reveal a constant tendency among scribes to assimilate one Gospel to another, so that the real similarities and differences between them could not be established with precision. However, it was also abundantly clear from study of the Greek text that there must be a literary relationship between them. We have already seen that this was the conclusion of Augustine, who thought that Mark was derived from Matthew, with Luke presumably dependent on both, though Augustine leaves the position of Luke open.

Griesbach's Synopsis

The problem of Gospel relationships had been raised by an Englishman, H. Owen, in 1764, in a short treatise on their relative value as history. But the first person to look at the problem scientifically was Griesbach, who regarded his textual work as a preliminary to a fresh appraisal of the New Testament. In 1776 he published his *Synopsis* of the Greek text, in which the common material of Matthew, Mark and Luke, and also of John where appropriate, are set out in parallel columns to enable exact comparisons to be made by a synoptic view of the text. It is this pioneering work which has given the name Synoptic Gospels as an easy reference to the first three Gospels. In his analysis of the evidence, Griesbach upheld the priority of Matthew in accordance with tradition, which assigned it priority as the work of an eyewitness, the apostle Matthew. But against Augustine he argued that Luke was the second Gospel to be written, and that Mark came third, being excerpted from both Matthew and Luke. This theory raised very acutely the question of the ending of Mark, as textual criticism had established beyond any doubt that Mark 16:9–end is a spurious addition, and if Mark knew both Matthew and Luke his abrupt ending at 16:8 is incomprehensible. Griesbach's solution was to propose a 'lost ending' of Mark, cut off before the general diffusion of the Gospel. This theory has been constantly repeated in subsequent study, even when Marcan dependence on the other two Gospels is abandoned. Griesbach also explained the absence from Mark of the teaching of Jesus, which features so prominently in Matthew and Luke, by supposing that Mark omitted it deliberately for the sake of a shorter narrative. This is perhaps just credible, but it does not explain the *longer* form of the narrative material which Mark does use. Moreover, as comparison of the Greek texts shows that Mark is sometimes closer to Matthew and sometimes to Luke, we have to think of him as arbitrarily switching from one to the other in a very odd manner. The obvious difficulty involved in the view that Mark's fuller and more circumstantial narratives are the result of secondary editing led *G. C. Storr*, in a book *On the Aim of the Gospel History and the Letters of John* (1796), to suggest that Mark must lie behind Matthew and Luke rather than the other way round.

Lessing's Aramaic Gospel Theory

That Storr's view was not followed up immediately is due to the more speculative 'higher criticism' which stemmed from the Deist debates. Semler's idea of an original 'Nazarene' Church suggested to *G. E. Lessing* (the publisher of the Reimarus *Fragments*) that there was an original Aramaic Gospel, which was known and referred to by the early Fathers as the *Gospel of the Nazareans* (see chapter I above). Lessing identified this with Aramaic Matthew mentioned by Papias, and held that all three Synoptic Gospels were based on it independently. He thus broke through the theory of direct relationship between the Synoptics, as their common material is traced to this earlier source. This also had the effect of downgrading them from the point of view of verbal inspiration, as the Synoptic writers are seen as editors reworking this original gospel for the benefit of their Greek-speaking communities. Matthew is considered to be the earliest of the three on account of its more Jewish character. At the same time, though this might suggest that Matthew is to have the credit of greatest authenticity, Lessing praised the Gospel of John precisely for rescuing the Gospel from its Jewish origins and presenting it in a form more suitable to the religious mind. Ironically, the Jewish character of John has come to the fore in modern studies, as we shall see in the next chapter. But Lessing's opinion reflects the idealism which persisted in German religious thought from the eighteenth century onwards.

J. G. Eichhorn (whose *Introduction* has been mentioned above) approved of Lessing's suggestion of an original Aramaic gospel, but added a new and valuable observation that there must also have been a separate source or sources of sayings of Jesus, used by Matthew and Luke, but not by Mark. He thus anticipated the Q hypothesis.

Herder and Oral Tradition

Meanwhile J. G. Herder (1744–1803), in essays on the Gospels published in 1796–7, modified Lessing's view by suggesting that the underlying source was not a written gospel but a relatively fixed oral tradition, which has been most faithfully reproduced by Mark. Matthew adapted the tradition to show Jesus as the fulfilment of the messianic prophecies for the sake of a Jewish readership. Luke presented it in a form adapted to the needs of a Hellenistic audience. Herder thus paid attention to the literary character of the Gospels, and in doing so he recognised the variety of literary forms which they contain. Thus he singled out miracle stories, parables and long sayings as the items which in his view have the greatest stability in oral tradition, and this is why they show the closest similarity in the three Gospels. In fact, this similarity is really too great to be accounted for only by a common oral tradition, and Herder conceded that Luke must have known Matthew. Other proponents of an oral source, such as J. C. L. Gieseler and F. D. E. Schleiermacher, were no more successful in arriving at a plausible solution.

Formation of the Two Source Hypothesis

The crucial observations for a better answer to the problem were made by three German scholars, whose work all appeared at about the same time. In 1835 *K. Lachmann* published an essay on the order of material in the three Gospels, demonstrating that Matthew and Luke nearly always agree with the order of Mark, but never agree in their placing of non-Marcan material in relation to it. Without asserting that Matthew and Luke were dependent on Mark, he concluded that Mark follows most closely the original gospel used by all three. Contrary to Lessing, he did not identify the original with the work attributed to Matthew by Papias, but, following a suggestion of Schleiermacher, he regarded that as the sayings source used by Matthew and Luke. Then in 1838 *C. G. Wilke* showed from detailed textual comparisons that, if Mark best preserves the underlying tradition, Matthew and Luke are likely to be dependent on Mark itself, rather than on a source which bypassed Mark. If this is right, then the necessity of postulating an original gospel behind Mark drops out. In the same year *C. H. Weisse* reached the same view independently. Mark has the more primitive character. Matthew and Luke both abbreviate Mark, improving the Greek style and dropping Aramaic words which Mark occasionally includes. Like the argument from order, they agree together when they are following Mark's words, but hardly ever (Weisse says never) agree together when they depart from his words. Weisse also agrees that, if Mark is a major source for Matthew and Luke, it is also necessary to postulate a sayings source to account for the rest of their common material. In this way the 'two source' hypothesis was reached, in which Matthew and Luke are held to be primarily dependent on Mark and the sayings source (called 'Q' by later scholars). This theory soon made its way, and held the field for the rest of the nineteenth century. It was been challenged in more recent times, as we shall see, but by no means overthrown.

3. THE LIFE OF JESUS

Study of the life of Jesus became a central issue in the nineteenth century as a result of the Deist assault on revealed religion and the rise of historical criticism. The evaluation of the Synoptic Gospels, which we have just reviewed, was an essential element in the debate on this issue, and was usually undertaken in connection with it. Deism accepted Jesus only as a moral teacher, in line with the view that revealed religion cannot really be distinct from natural religion, which is primarily an inward and spiritual pursuit of the good life. Idealism added to this the myth of the 'noble savage' (Rousseau), in whom naturalness and spontaneity and poetic appreciation enlarge the concept of the human spirit beyond mere moralism. So Herder thought that Jesus was summing up the whole history of Israelite religion in the concept of an invisible and eternal kingdom.

He totally neglected the eschatological aspect of the preaching of Jesus, which had featured in Reimarus' *Fragments*. Thus the approach to the life of Jesus tends to be dictated by the kind of religion, moralistic and spiritualising, which is felt to be desirable by those who seek to defend the gospel. The objectivity which is required for a proper application of the historico-critical method constantly eludes the scholars of this period.

Jesus therefore appears as the herald of a new religion of the spirit. Another point which follows from this, and has already appeared in connection with Reimarus, is the tendency to ascribe to the disciples or the evangelists a fatal alteration of the original message, either deliberately or through misunderstanding. This continues a theme which is clear in English Deism and has its origins in the Puritan attitude to 'popery', in which the organised church is regarded as a creation of 'priestcraft', whereby a power-seeking clique imposes on the people a debased religion of externals and smothers the truly spiritual religion.

Rationalist Interpretations
These characteristics appear in the work of *H. E. G. Paulus* (1761–1851), a theologian of rationalist views, who laid out his presuppositions in a work on the Synoptic Gospels in 1802, and followed them up in a four-volume *Life of Jesus* in 1828. He regards the miracle stories of the Gospels as based on authentic memories, but rejects any supernatural interpretation of them, explaining them entirely in terms of natural causes (e.g. Lazarus was in a coma when buried, but had recovered when Jesus called him out of the tomb). In his view the disciples were deluded by their misunderstanding of Jesus' acts as miracles into supposing that Jesus was a divine person, though really Jesus was propounding a new religion of the spirit in conformity with the will of God. A similarly rationalist approach to the miracles appears in an early work of *K. A. Hase* (1800–90), his short life of Jesus for students, published in 1829. However, he overcomes the main difficulty of Paulus' reconstruction by introducing the theory of a change in the perception of Jesus himself. At first Jesus thought of the coming kingdom in political and messianic terms, and gathered together the disciples on this basis. Later he taught a more spiritual view of the kingdom, which the disciples largely failed to understand. Thus the apocalyptic outlook of earliest Christianity is mistaken, much of the material in the Synoptic Gospels has been wrongly apocalypticised, and only the Gospel of John has preserved the real teaching. Hase saw the turning point in the understanding of Jesus in the episode at

Caesarea Philippi (Mark 8:27–33). This idea of a turning point became a feature of all subsequent lives of Jesus.

F. D. E. Schleiermacher (1768–1834) also approached the life of Jesus with a rationalist view, but with a deeper religious feeling, derived from the Pietism of the Moravian settlement at Herrnhut. In lectures delivered shortly before his death, but not published until thirty years later, he interpreted the message of Jesus in line with his own philosophy, in which the reality of religion is identified with feeling and intuition. Miracle stories are only to be accepted as trustworthy in so far as they illustrate the power of mind over matter. Like Hase, Schleiermacher finds the truth of the gospel primarily in John.

Strauss
The climax of the rationalist lives of Jesus comes with D. F. Strauss (1808–74), one of the founders of the 'Tübingen school' of New Testament critics. He perceived that the attempt to find the religion of Jesus by stripping away the miraculous elements of the Gospels failed to do justice to the Gospels as historical narratives. If the old supernaturalist view can no longer be used to support the truth of the Gospels, and the rationalist view has failed to provide a satisfactory alternative, then only one further possibility remains open, and that is to see the Gospel story in terms of myth. With devastating throughness he showed how point after point in the Gospels cannot be taken literally because of discrepancies or inherent improbabilities. He allowed only the barest substratum of history to survive, that Jesus was a follower of John the Baptist, who went out on his own to preach the coming kingdom, with the expectation of the Messiah. After his death the disciples were convinced that he was himself the Messiah, and came to believe that he was risen and exalted to heaven. The Gospel narratives are told from this point of view, taking up themes from messianic prophecy and other aspects of the Old Testament to express their understanding of Jesus. Contrary to the prevailing opinion, the Gospel of John is the least reliable, presenting an even more mythicised picture of Jesus than the Synoptics. Strauss stated at the outset that his philosophical understanding of religion gave him the ability to stand back from the Bible and view it objectively in a way that his predecessors had failed to do. He held that Christian truth was independent of the historical value of the Gospels, and that the true significance of Jesus is that he became the focus for ideas of incarnation and exaltation which ideally can apply to every person. Naturally his *Life of Jesus* (first published 1835–6) created a storm of protest. The

category of myth was not new, as the primeval history in Genesis was already being explained in this way by the Old Testament critics. But the almost total scepticism which resulted when this was applied to the Gospels was more than most people could bear. Hengstenberg, the leader of the orthodox opposition, declared that Strauss had proved that rationalism inevitably leads to radical scepticism, so that there is really no half-way house between faith in the supernatural and total unbelief.

Idealist Interpretations
The work of Strauss also raised questions concerning the actual historical origins of a faith in Jesus which apparently so greatly misunderstood him. This point was taken up by *F. C. Baur* (1792–1860), his former tutor, who approached it from his interest in *Tendenzkritik*, i.e. establishing first the intention of the New Testament writers. From this point of view John could be excluded altogether from the search for the Jesus of history, because his intention was not to write history. For reasons which will appear in the next section Baur gives pride of place to Matthew as the most Jewish Gospel. His views were thus supported by the Griesbach hypothesis of the priority of Matthew, and fell with the rising popularity of the priority of Mark. But he made the valid point that part of the historical scepticism of Strauss arose from treating John and the Synoptics alike, as there is less need to question the Synoptics when the evidence of John is discounted. Even so, the theological motivations of the Synoptic writers need to be recognised. Baur's wish to present Jesus as a Jewish moralist, devoid of any theological significance, leads him to deny such distinctively Jewish features as the eschatology of Matthew. It may thus be asked, in view of the massive effect of the theological tendencies of the evangelists, whether their evidence for the life of Jesus can ever give assured results. A. Schwegler, another of the Tübingen scholars who came under Baur's influence, took the line that this was impossible.

With the growing success of the theory of Marcan priority after the mid-century, a new attempt could be made to get behind the tendencies of the evangelists to a stage nearer to the life of Jesus by following up the implications of the two-source hypothesis. *H. J. Holtzmann* (1832–1910), assuming that Mark was based on a lost earlier work, decided that this and the sayings source common to Matthew and Luke (not yet called Q) together formed a reliable basis for reconstruction. Following Hase, he made much of the Caesarea Philippi episode as a turning point in Jesus' career. But Holtzmann's ideas were still dominated by the idealistic view of the kingdom of God as an inward reality unrelated to history, so that the eschatological meaning of the preaching of Jesus continued to be arbitrarily excluded. Holtzmann rescued the life of Jesus from the myths of Strauss and the *Tendenzkritik* of Baur, but he set the fashion for a whole series of 'liberal' lives, in which the idealistic notion of Jesus as a teacher of inward religion continued unabated, and the emergence of the organised Church remained unexplained. Moreover the decisive significance of Jesus for salvation, seen by Paul, and proclaimed afresh by Luther, has no anchorage in the Jesus of history as presented in these reconstructions. Consequently *M. Kähler* (1835–1912), looking back over the century, argued that the Church must stand by the preached Christ, the Christ of faith, regardless of the current attempts to describe the Jesus of history, which in his view were just as speculative as the theological interpretations which they sought to replace. Thus Kähler in 1892 enunciated the classic problem of the gulf between the Jesus of history and the Christ of faith, which has come to the fore in more recent times (hence the publication of the English version of his work, *The So-Called Historical Jesus and the Historic Biblical Christ*, in 1964).

Challenge to the Liberal Portrait: Weiss and Schweitzer
Nevertheless the hold which the liberal portrait of Jesus had over German scholars – not to mention the phenomenal success of the rationalist and romantic *Life of Jesus* (1863) by E. Renan in France, with its local colour derived from travel in Palestine – continued to the very end of the century and beyond it in A. Harnack's *What is Christianity?* (1900) and in J. Wellhausen's *Introduction to the First Three Gospels* (1905), in which the Jewishness of Jesus receives ample recognition, but the eschatological expectations of Jewish thought of New Testament times is entirely overlooked. But by this time J. Weiss, in his *The Preaching of Jesus of the Kingdom of God* (1892), had perceived that Jesus' message could not be detached from the Jewish eschatology of the time, which was now considerably clarified as a result of more recent research into Jewish thought, of which more must be said later. This brought back the point which had been used polemically by Reimarus to discredit Jesus, and provided the cue for Albert Schweitzer (1875–1965) to find the solution to *The Quest of the Historical Jesus* (1906). This book is a summary of the work on the life of Jesus from Reimarus onwards. At the end of it Schweitzer states his own view, that, rightly or wrongly, Jesus expected a divine intervention in the near future which would end the present world order. So the liberal idea that

Jesus was introducing a new and more spiritual religion within the present order is false. Put thus bluntly, the dilemma of reconciling the Jesus of history and the Christ of faith is solved in favour of divine intervention, against the Deist and rationalist rejection of the action of God. But the expected intervention itself raises an even more acute problem. For it failed to materialise, and Jesus died with his hopes unfulfilled. So, in the end, Schweitzer has to leave Jesus in his own time, as one who can be understood only within the ideas of that time, and his value for later generations is confined to the inspirational power of his example. No one could be satisfied with Schweitzer's picture of a deluded Jesus, offering his life to force God's hand to bring in the kingdom which had failed to come. But the rigorous insistence on the eschatological frame of ideas could never again be set aside in research into the life of Jesus.

4. THE PRIMITIVE CHURCH

Baur's Dialectical Interpretation

We must now retrace our steps to F. C. Baur, the leader of the Tübingen school, which is chiefly associated with radical views on the history of earliest Christianity. The ground had already been prepared by various expressions of doubt concerning the authenticity of New Testament books, such as the Pastoral Epistles (Eichhorn and Schleiermacher), 1 Peter (H. H. Cludius), and Ephesians and 2 Thessalonians (W. M. L. de Wette). Semler, amongst others, had sharply differentiated the Jewish-Christian and Gentile Churches. A start had been made on the study of the ideas of Paul by L. Usteri in 1824, but he worked too much under the influence of Schleiermacher to avoid the characteristic idealism, so that Paul's doctrine of justification by faith is reduced to a mental attitude. Baur, on the other hand, approached Paul with historical realism, derived from his experience in classical studies. In 1831 he published an important article on 'The Christ Party in the Corinthian Church', in which he demonstrated from 1 Corinthians the internal oppositions of the Church in Paul's own day. He followed this up with a study of the Pastoral Epistles (1835), in which he detected an effort to cover up conflict in the Church in the time of the writer (not really Paul) in the early second century. So he identified the conflict in this case with the Church's struggle with Gnosticism. By this time he had been influenced by the philosophy of Hegel to look beyond conflict to a resulting higher synthesis. He found this in the emergence of the Catholic Church. On this basis he developed the theory of a lasting conflict, which appears first in Paul and continues into the second century. It is basically the conflict between Jewish Christianity and Pauline Christianity, which first comes to the surface in Paul's altercation with Peter referred to in Galatians 2. This continues in the opposition between Ebionites (known from second century sources) and Gentile Christianity, which has its own threat from the attraction of Gnosticism. Attempts at overcoming the strife appear in spurious letters written in the name of Peter and Paul, but really belonging to this later time. The Acts of the Apostles was written in the second century to heal the breach. Baur was thus driven, in his book on Paul published in 1845, to regard Acts not only as deliberately covering up the rift between Peter and Paul, but also as totally unreliable historically. One element in the conflict was the development of christology in the Pauline churches, which shows a tendency to move towards Gnosticism. This movement can actually be seen in the Gospel of John. It follows from this reconstruction that the Jewish and Ebionite teaching is considered to be more faithful to the Jesus of history precisely because of its lack of an articulated christology. Baur failed to recognise the eschatological element in the teaching of Jesus, as we have already seen.

The theory of Baur thus requires a late date for those books (the Pastoral and Catholic Epistles and Acts) which were considered to reflect later stages of the conflict. Some of his followers suggested dates far into the second century. Thus, in the hands of the Tübingen scholars, the New Testament began to dissolve into a maze of speculative reconstructions of early Church history.

Replies to Baur's Theories
Replies to Baur came from various quarters. *E. Reuss* (1804–91) took him to task for failing to see that, in Paul's struggle to gain recognition of the Gentile Church, there was also a moderate party, which actually included Peter and James (Galatians 2; Acts 15), in addition to the strict Judaizers. He also pointed out that opposition to such insistence on the Law goes back to the attitudes of Jesus himself, so that it is not an innovation with Paul. Moreover, it is a mistake to suppose that only one historic situation is reflected in the books of the New Testament, which belong to a variety of situations. Thus they do not need to be strung out along a straight line far into the second century. *A. Ritschl* (1822–89), who was one of Baur's followers in the Tübingen school, abandoned this position in the second edition (1857) of his book on *The Origin of the Ancient Catholic Church*, pointing out that the growth of the Church was a matter of developing local communities, and not the end product

of years of conflict, even though conflict may have been part of the process. Finally *C. Weizsäcker* (1822–99), who succeeded Baur in the chair of Church History at Tübingen, showed on the one hand that the tradition behind the Synoptic Gospels gives no indication of conflict in the pre-Pauline community, and on the other hand that the conflict which arose later never was healed, because Jewish Christianity, in so far as it survived beyond the first century, was not absorbed into the Catholic Church. Baur had correctly seen that the second-century Pseudo-Clementine writings, which show Peter in conflict with Simon Magus, are really using Simon as a cover-up for Paul (just as the anti-Christian Jewish literature of the period is violently hostile to Paul). This does show the later Jewish-Christian (Ebionite) opposition to the influence of Paul, but it was a mistake on Baur's part to connect this continuing conflict with the books of the New Testament.

Origins of the Ministry
One aspect of Baur's reconstruction was the question of the organisation and ministry of the primitive Church. Though bishops, presbyters and deacons are mentioned, it is not clear whether bishops (i.e. overseers) are identical with presbyters, as they are never mentioned together, or indeed how far these designations are titles of office-holders rather than merely functional descriptions. It is only in the Apostolic Fathers, particularly the letters of Ignatius, that the threefold ministry emerges clearly as the form of church government. Thus Baur's late date for New Testament books also required that these writings, too, should be regarded as spurious and assigned to an even later date.

Thus the dating of the Apostolic Fathers became a crucial factor in the debate. The greatest work in this connection was done by *J. B. Lightfoot* (1828–89), who, together with Westcott and Hort, whose work on the text of the New Testament has been mentioned above, formed a Cambridge school of exact scholarship, aimed at overturning the speculative Tübingen theories by ascertaining all the facts. The letter of Clement to the Corinthians (1 Clement) was confirmed as authentic, and assigned to about AD 96. 2 Clement, which has many New Testament allusions, was declared to be spurious and dated some forty years later, and the Pseudo-Clementines later still. The most difficult problem was the Letters of Ignatius. These existed in several different recensions, some containing more letters than others and longer forms of the text. *James Ussher* (1581–1656) in the seventeenth century had proved that, out of thirteen letters attributed to Ignatius, only seven were known to the ancient Fathers. Moreover the longer text of those seven was due to interpolations by the same hand as the six spurious letters, which should be dated in the fourth century. But then in 1845 a Syriac version, which had recently been discovered, was published, which contained only three of the seven letters which were claimed as genuine. Ritschl insisted that only these three could be accepted. Baur argued against the authenticity even of these. The conservative church historian *Theodor Zahn* (1838–1933) argued for the genuineness of all seven letters. This position was given its most complete demonstration by Lightfoot in three volumes of his great, but unhappily never finished, commentary on the Apostolic Fathers (1885).

Responding again to the challenge of Baur, Lightfoot also began a series of detailed commentaries on the Letters of Paul, which have particularly valuable discussions of details affecting the history of early Christianity. In this way historical criticism was turned against unsatisfactory historical reconstruction, and the history of the rise of Christianity was put on a surer footing. In Germany *H. A. W. Meyer* (1800–73) had begun a comparable series of commentaries with co-operation of other scholars in 1832, and the whole New Testament was completed by 1852. This series aimed at philological and historical accuracy from the start, and has been kept up to date by a succession of distinguished scholars in revised editions ever since.

5. INSPIRATION AND AUTHORITY

Preserving the Religious Value of the New Testament
The religious value of the New Testament was the real issue at stake in all these scholarly developments, and is the reason why the work of Baur and his colleagues aroused such enormous controversy. Their drastic treatment of the New Testament and early Christian literature appeared to undermine the integrity of the New Testament. It called in question the claim of a special revelation. It also destroyed the historic basis of Christianity, leaving it only as an idea. In fact a clear distinction had been made as early as 1787 by J. P. Gabler, who argued that the task of biblical theology is an historical description of the theology which the Bible contains, whereas dogmatic theology has the perennial task of enunciating the faith in a constructive and relevant way, which can be performed

only after the other task is done. Many of those who followed this contention sincerely believed that divine truth would be more accessible as a result. But at the same time their rationalist principles were driving them more and more into religious scepticism. There were those like Eichhorn, Schleiermacher, and especially Strauss, who attempted to overcome the dilemma by using the concept of myth. This was especially useful in dealing with the problem of miracles, as these need not be taken at face value but could be interpreted as mythical representations of spiritual truths. But this, like the traditional allegorical interpretation, really imposes on the text an 'acceptable' meaning which does not actually arise from it. Indeed, this method of dealing with miracles, in which they were made to yield moral truths as their 'real' meaning, is itself one of the forms of allegorical interpretation. Its popularity stemmed from the philosophy of *Immanuel Kant* (1724–1804), who used it to save the moral integrity of the Bible as the revelation of God. It is a valid way of deriving profit from Scripture, but not legitimate either for establishing the historical truth of the Bible or for exposing its character as divine revelation.

German Scholarship in England

The Tübingen theories, and the advance of biblical criticism in general, evoked a lively debate and a great stream of books in Germany, because of the large number of universities with theological chairs. Elsewhere conditions were very different. In France all theological study had been swept away by the Revolution, and this was only gradually reinstated later, and there were virtually no centres of theology at an academic level for the rest of the century. In Britain the universities were few, and tended to be isolated from continental developments. Any scholars who made use of the German approach to critical scholarship were regarded as liberals, whose views could lead only to radical scepticism. The idealism of Schleiermacher provided no solution, because it was regarded as rationalism. The mythic theory of miracles was anathema. *E. B. Pusey* (1800–82) studied Semitic languages in Germany in the years following 1825, and so came into contact with Eichhorn, Schleiermacher and others, but on his return to England he dissociated himself entirely from their critical methods. The poet *S. T. Coleridge* (1771–1834), who supported free enquiry, also visited Germany and absorbed some of the new tendencies. He maintained that no doctrine of the inspiration of Scripture was satisfactory, if it failed to take seriously the literary character of the individual books. He put forward a new interpretation of inspiration in terms of the power of Scripture to affect the human spirit through its message. He put the matter briefly: 'It finds me'. It is significant that Coleridge had associated with the group of Unitarians in Cambridge, who combined the notion of free enquiry, derived from the Deists, with a positive, though unorthodox, religious position. At the beginning of the nineteenth century they were among the few people to take a sympathetic interest in what was happening in Germany. Later, it was a convert to Unitarianism, *Mary Ann Evans* (1819–90), better known as the novelist *George Eliot*, who undertook the English translation of Strauss' *Life of Jesus*, published in 1848.

This was horrifying to British religious feeling at the time. In the country at large Deism had waned, and the rationalism of the late eighteenth century had been discredited by the excesses committed in the name of reason in the French Revolution. There were three principal religious influences at the time, all of them inclined to traditionalist views and deeply suspicious of German rationalism. There was the Low Church party in the Church of England, also called Evangelicals, who, along with the Methodists, had a view of personal religion comparable to that of the German Pietists, laying great stress on the atoning death of Christ. There was also the continuing hold of Calvinism in Scotland and in English sectarian religion, with its emphasis on the sufficiency of Scripture and its determination to order its faith and life by the Bible alone. Thirdly, the High Church party in the Church of England became the Anglo-Catholic movement after 1833, in which the main impetus was the restoration of the faith and worship of the ancient Church with great stress on the teaching of the Fathers. Pusey was one of the founders of the movement.

The Liberal Anglicans

Clearly there was not much scope for freedom of enquiry, but in Anglican circles there were some who wished to keep an open mind, and later formed a distinct group as the Broad Church party. A pioneer of this group was the educator *Thomas Arnold* (1795–1842) who published in 1832 his essay *On the Right Interpretation and Understanding of the Scriptures*, insisting that a clear distinction must be made between the religious value of the Bible and the historical and factual information which it contains. *H. H. Milman* (1791–1868) caused a stir by his comparatively liberal treatment of Israelite history in his *History of the Jews* (1829). He followed this up later with a *History of Christianity to the Abolition of Paganism in the Roman Empire* (1840), which made use of the historico-critical approach. Both works derived their method from the work of the

German classical historian, B. G. Niebuhr, who had used the category of myth to explain the legends of the foundation of Rome.

Essays and Reviews

Finally, a group of Broad Churchmen, headed by *Benjamin Jowett* (1817–93), the professor of Greek at Oxford, produced in 1860 *Essays and Reviews*, a collection which was aimed at giving a reasoned presentation of the new trends.

The storm which eventually broke over this publication was out of all proportion to its worth, for it was a haphazard collection hurriedly put together, and none of the essays had outstanding merit. Part of the trouble was that all the seven writers except one were clergy of the established Church of England, and the complaints against them reached Parliament. The book was formally condemned by the Convocation of Canterbury in 1864 as containing matter inconsistent with Anglican doctrine. There can be little doubt that it crystallised the growing fears of the mass of Anglicans and others at the spread of rationalism, which up to this point had been confined to individuals (mostly Unitarians), but now appeared in what seemed to be a manifesto from within the Establishment itself. Actually it was in no sense a manifesto, and any such intention was explicitly rejected in the preface to the book. However, it was clear that the writers supported an evolutionary theory, not only of creation, but of the development of religion in human history, which threatened the status of the Bible as divine revelation. The collection included no essay on the person of Christ, but the views of the writers, especially Jowett, came close to the presuppositions of the liberal lives of Jesus like that of Strauss. That Jesus was the Son of God, whose death atoned for the sins of the world, received no recognition. The text of Scripture was made subservient to the rationalist views of the essayists.

Reaction

There thus came about a hardening of the traditional view of the inspiration and authority of Scripture. Amongst Evangelicals and sectarians the old confidence in the truth of the Bible had to be bolstered up by a theory of verbal inspiration. The Bible is the Word of God, and God cannot lie. The verbal inerrancy of the Reformation period now becomes biblical fundamentalism. The difference between them is a matter of the attitude towards human knowledge. Verbal inerrancy could be held without contradicting knowledge gained from experience, because at that time such knowledge did not call in question the main statements of the Bible (the classic example is the pre-Copernican view that the earth goes round the sun), though there were always *some* contradictions to pose problems for the strict infallibilists. But in the mid-nineteenth century the accumulation of factual knowledge of both science and history created so many contradictions that the theory of verbal inerrancy could be maintained only by deliberate rejection of such knowledge, or by rigidly keeping the Bible and religion apart from the rest of human knowledge as a reserved and privileged area. Thus, those who wished to save the integrity of the Bible as traditionally understood had a problem to face with regard to their own integrity.

Roman Catholic Study
In the Roman Catholic Church the reaction to the results of the 'higher' criticism was equally negative, in spite of the work of such men as Richard Simon and, more recently, *Alexander Geddes* (1737–1802) on the Old Testament, because of the lack of education at university level already referred to. As the critical work on the Bible was promoted by Protestants of liberal and rationalist views, it did nothing to allay the suspicion among Catholics that private judgment leads to rationalism and eventually to atheism. This seemed to be confirmed by the radical theories of the Tübingen school. By the 1860s the papacy was increasing its power. It was the time of Ultramontanism, and the definition of papal infallibility was already under discussion. Thus a mood of triumphalist, but irrational, authoritarianism had taken hold, making the Church a bulwark against the inroads of atheist thought. Consequently Catholic scholars were discouraged from pursuing critical work on the Bible, and the Vatican Council in 1870 strongly asserted the plenary inspiration of Scripture and the Church's prerogative of interpretation.

The damage that was done by these negative reactions of church people of all persuasions has proved to be long-lasting. General acceptance of the critical approach to the Bible begins only in the twentieth century, but fundamentalism has retained an immense hold, especially in England and America.

Towards Acceptance of Critical Scholarship
Nevertheless the period following the publication of *Essays and Reviews* saw a gradual acceptance of biblical criticism on the part of scholars. This was due in the first instance to the scholars in Germany who modified the extreme positions of the Tübingen school. But it was also due to the patient and painstaking work of

British scholars such as J. B. Lightfoot who formed a middle ground of conservative and scrupulously honest scholarship, which exerted a moderating influence and helped to reconcile people to the inevitable march of historical criticism. Thus by the 1880s the main results of critical scholarship were widely accepted in the English-speaking world, and critical works appeared from the pens of Scottish, English and American scholars, as well as a steady stream of translations of German works. *F. W. Farrar* (1831–1903) delivered the Bampton Lectures at Oxford in 1885 on the history of the interpretation of the Bible, which presented biblical criticism as the climax. It is significant that he felt bound to admit that up to that date nothing of any real importance had yet emerged from British scholarship. The change of mood can be seen in the essays published by *Charles Gore* (1853–1932) under the title *Lux Mundi* (1889) as a kind of successor to *Essays and Reviews*. The book is a manifesto of the Anglo-Catholic party, asserting the conviction that traditional orthodoxy need not be threatened by biblical criticism, but rather needs its support in order to be viable in the age of science. At the same time the Methodist *A. S. Peake* (1865–1929) played a very active part in popularising biblical criticism as part of a programme of raising the educational standard of the ministry of the Methodist Church, and this had much wider influence in preparing the way for the acceptance of criticism in England. Moreover a slight lifting of the barrier to critical study in the Roman Catholic Church (though sadly soon to be reimposed) allowed the French Dominican scholar *M.-J. Lagrange* (1855–1938) to open a house of biblical studies in Jerusalem in 1890, which has remained a centre of advanced biblical scholarship ever since. Thus the nineteenth century ends on a more hopeful note, and the real limitations of the critical approach to the Bible, which have become apparent in the latter part of the twentieth century, were not yet perceived.

FOR FURTHER READING

The Cambridge History of the Bible 3.

Ellis, Ieuan, *Seven against Christ: a Study of 'Essays and Reviews'*, Brill, Leiden 1980.

Farrar, F. W., *History of Interpretation*, Macmillan, London, 1886; repr., Baker Book House, Grand Rapids 1961.

Kümmel, W. G., *The New Testament.*

Neill, Stephen, *The Interpretation of the New Testament, 1861–1961*, OUP, Oxford [2]1966.

Rogers, J. B. and D. K. McKim, *The Authority and Interpretation of the Bible*, Harper and Row, New York 1979.

Schweitzer, Albert, *The Quest of the Historical Jesus*, A. & C. Black, London, 1910, and Macmillan, New York 1948.

8

MAJOR CONCERNS OF CRITICISM: THE TWENTIETH CENTURY

One reason for the general acceptance of biblical criticism by the New Testament scholars of the late nineteenth century was the success of scientific method in all branches of study, especially in history and archaeology. It was impossible to disregard the new knowledge which was flooding in from all sides. Whereas the historical study of the Bible had been largely confined to the information available within the Bible itself, now there were new sources, not only for the ancient world of classical culture in which Christianity grew up, but also for the whole culture region of the Ancient Near East from Egypt to Mesopotamia, which lies behind the history of the Bible from start to finish. The Bible could no longer be treated in isolation from its historical background.

The new knowledge that was becoming available brought with it more than additional information, to be absorbed and integrated in the historico-critical study of the Bible. It also placed the Bible in the global context of the history of the human race and the phenomenon of religion. During the twentieth century Christianity has had to come to terms with other religions, and the Bible has had to take its place alongside other sacred books. The problems which faced our ancestors as a result of the Enlightenment have not gone away, but have become more acute. Historical criticism was expected to establish the truth about Jesus and the rise of Christianity in such a way as to confirm faith in the Bible as the record of a divine and saving revelation from God. But if the practitioners of criticism follow the scientific principle that observable phenomena are always to be explained in terms of cause and effect, little room is left for the idea of the direct action of God. Thus, while a global view removes the privileged position of the Bible, the accumulation of scientific knowledge threatens its claim to special revelation.

In this chapter we shall be chiefly concerned with the acquisition of knowledge about the New Testament and its world, and how this has affected the continuing study of the major concerns of criticism which occupied our attention in the last chapter. The question of inspiration and authority will be reserved for the final chapter, in which new approaches to the New Testament will be considered. This may point the way towards fresh confidence in the religious value of the Christian Scriptures.

1. NEW DISCOVERIES AND NEW TOOLS

The Jewish Background
The Old Testament is part of the background to the New Testament, because it is the collection of sacred books of the Jews, which achieved canonical status within the New Testament period itself. It thus has the greatest importance for the religion of the Jews at this time, and therefore for the primitive Church which sprang up within Judaism. But the Old Testament is not continuous with the New Testament from the point of view of historical documentation. It is important not to leap from one to the other, as if nothing happened in between. At the beginning of the twentieth century the chief sources for the Inter-testamental Period (200 BC to AD 100) were the Apocrypha and Pseudepigrapha and the writings of the Jewish historian Josephus (see Part II). Since the Apocrypha and Pseudepigrapha were not accepted into the Jewish canon of Scriptures, it should have been obvious that they did not represent mainstream Judaism at the time. It was thus a mistake to construct the picture of Judaism mainly from these sources, as was done by *W. Bousset* (1865–1920), whose book on *The Religion of Judaism in New Testament Times* (1903) long remained a standard work in Germany. The picture was to some extent corrected in the third edition of 1925, in which H. Gressmann added material from early rabbinic sources. In particular, the American scholar G.F. Moore made a major study of *Judaism in the First Centuries of the Christian Era* (3 vols., 1929–30), using these sources, whereby the picture of what has been termed 'normative' Judaism was reconstructed. Thus the work of John Lightfoot and Wettstein was now carried forward energetically by many scholars, including the liberal Jew *C.J.G. Montefiore* (1858–1938), who wrote a commentary on the Synoptic Gospels incorporating much rabbinic material. The great *Commentary on the New Testament from the Talmud and the Midrash* of H.L.

Strack and P. Billerbeck (4 vols., 1922–8) is the acknowledged successor to the work of Lightfoot and Wettstein.

The difficulty of using rabbinic material is that it is the product of the renewal of Judaism after the cataclysm of the fall of Jerusalem and the destruction of the temple, and represents mainly the traditions of the Pharisees who effected the renewal. Dating the material is often extremely difficult, so that its relevance to the New Testament is problematical. That there was no such thing as 'normative' Judaism in the time of Jesus has been shown by the sensational discovery of the Dead Sea Scrolls in 1947, which give direct evidence for another segment of Judaism at the time (probably the Essenes). As the Scrolls have been considered in Part II, here we need observe only some of the reasons why this major collection of Jewish material has special importance for the study of the New Testament. First we may note that the Scrolls share with earliest Christianity and with some of the Pseudepigrapha a vivid eschatological expectation, in which God is thought to be about to intervene in the very near future to establish the messianic kingdom. In this connection the Qumran concept of two Messiahs, one priestly and the other royal, though differing from the Christian proclamation, has very great importance for our understanding of the messiahship of Jesus in the thought of earliest Christianity. Secondly, the interpretation of the Hebrew Scriptures by the Qumran Sect has features which closely resemble the handling of it by New Testament writers, and significantly differs from rabbinic usage. Thirdly, the Qumran ideas of good and evil, truth and falsehood, and their relation to a dualistic belief in good and evil angelic powers, have numerous points of contact with statements in the New Testament, and have tended to vindicate the Jewish basis of early Christian theology over against the rival claim of direct influence of Hellenistic or early Gnostic thought. Finally, the Scrolls not only give a vast store of information about the Qumran Sect itself, but also fill out the picture of Judaism in New Testament times as a whole. They have thus made possible a more realistic assessment of the information which was already available before the discovery, so that a more convincing understanding of Judaism in the period is available.

The Hellenistic Background
At the same time as the recovery of the Pseudepigrapha was arousing much interest at the beginning of the century, studies in the field of ancient religion in Greece, Egypt, Syria and Mesopotamia were opening up new resources of comparative material in connection with Christian origins. Archaeologists had discovered quantitites of

papyrus documents, often very fragmentary, which had resisted the ravages of time on account of the exceptionally dry climate of Egypt, and the finds were constantly being increased by new accessions. These included social and commercial documents, and also magical and religious texts.

Hellenism refers to the diffusion of Greek culture over this whole region as a result of the spectacular conquests of Alexander the Great (died 323 BC). The Greek style and the Greek language were used everywhere among the ruling classes, including educated Jews. The debt of Philo, the Jew of Alexandria (20 BC – AD 50), to Greek philosophy was, of course, well known to scholars. But his work was related to contemporary currents of thought and literary styles of the Cynic-Stoic teachers by P. Wendland, in an article published in 1895, who thereby drew attention to the possibility of similar influences on the New Testament, especially on Paul.

The spread of Hellenism also had the reverse effect of bringing oriental religious ideas and cults into the Greek world. These found expression in the mystery religions, secret organisations which enjoyed immense popularity alongside the official cults of traditional religion. The most important mystery cults for a possible bearing on Christian origins are those of Attis in Asia Minor and Isis and Osiris in Egypt. F. Cumont, in his *Oriental Religions in Roman Paganism* (1907), made available much information on such cults, and also on Zoroastrianism, which had a large following throughout the fertile crescent from the fifth century BC onwards, and undoubtedly influenced Judaism in this period. At the same time R. Reitzenstein, who was working in the field of the mystery religions, drew attention to Greco-Egyptian texts relating to Hermes Trismegistos as the revealer-figure of a philosophical mysticism (*Poimandres*, 1904). Some of these texts, known as the *Hermetica*, show a striking similarity to the thought and diction of the Fourth Gospel. Moreover they show a blend of Egyptian religion (Hermes Trismegistos is the Egyptian god Thoth) and Greek philosophy (Platonic and Stoic), and also owe a debt to the Genesis creation accounts in connection with cosmology. Reitzenstein believed that the texts proved the existence of a widespread myth of a primal divine man (here identified with the revealer Hermes) which could have influenced christology in primitive Christianity.

The Jewish element in this very syncretistic religious literature reappears in the second century in Gnosticism. The Gnostic sects posed a grave threat to Christianity, as we have already seen. Though they are known only from the second century, the presence of Jewish features in their cosmological systems suggests that they originated in contact with diaspora Judaism apart from the rise of Christianity, and so might be much older. At the beginning of the twentieth century knowledge of Gnosticism had been almost entirely confined to the refutations of them by Irenaeus and other patristic writers, which were obviously biased against them. However information was beginning to become available about one Gnostic sect which still survives in Iraq and Iran, known as the Mandaeans. They claim to be descendants of followers of John the Baptist, who moved eastwards after the fall of Jerusalem, though this is historically doubtful, and the veneration of the Baptist is probably not an original element. The name Mandaeans comes from the title of a future saviour figure, *Manda de Hayyé*, an Aramaic expression for 'knowledge of life'. The use of Aramaic suggests that the sect originated in Syria, and does not exclude Jewish influence. Translations of the sacred books of the sect were made available by Reitzenstein, M. Lidzbarski and others, and so brought it to the attention of New Testament scholars in the years following the First World War.

The Mandaean texts are problematical, because they are the end-products of centuries, and have absorbed a variety of religious ideas, probably including some from Christianity. Thus they scarcely qualify as untouched Gnostic texts contemporary with Christian origins. This deficiency was dramatically made good by the discovery of the Nag Hammadi texts, already referred to in chapter 2. The texts contain Coptic translations of Greek tractates, composed at various times in the first few Christian centuries. Some may be pre-Christian works, which have been subsequently Christianised. Where knowledge of the Old Testament appears, Jewish influence on pre-Christian Gnosticism is to be suspected. The tractates are strange and difficult to understand, especially as they are often much damaged, leaving great gaps in the text. The one unifying factor is the Gnostic interest in the relation of the individual soul to the divine life. This suggests that they were valued for their esoteric and mystical teaching. Work on critical editions of these texts is proceeding under the auspices of the Nag Hammadi Research Project of the Claremont Graduate School in California. Though English translations of some of the tractates, especially the *Gospel of Thomas*, have been long available, the complete collection did not appear in English until 1977 (*The Nag Hammadi Library*).

Textual Criticism

The search for texts of the New Testament itself continued in the twentieth century, and many further manuscripts have come to light. This especially applies to papyrus texts from Egypt, which have yielded the oldest surviving copies of New Testament books. Only a few fragments were available at the end of the previous century. The first large collection of papyri is in the Chester Beatty museum in Dublin, acquired in 1930–1. Modern editors of the Greek New Testament use a Gothic P and raised numeral to designate the papyri, so that they are clearly distinguished from the uncials (capital letters) and minuscules (numerals). The most important items in the Chester Beatty collection are P^{45}, containing parts of the Gospels and Acts (early third century), P^{46}, containing the Letters of Paul and Hebrews, but excluding the Pastorals (AD 200), and P^{47}, containing part of Revelation (third century – but copied before the authorship of Revelation was thrown into doubt in the east by Dionysius of Alexandria).

The oldest copy of any New Testament book now in existence is P^{52}, a tiny fragment of the Gospel of John, dated between AD 135 and 150. It came to the John Rylands Library in Manchester in a collection acquired in 1921, but was not spotted until 1934. The early date shows that John was already diffused and being copied in Egypt in the early second century, and so precludes the late date proposed by the Tübingen school.

Since the Second World War further papyri have been published from the collection in the Bodmer Library in Geneva, the most important being P^{66}, containing most of John, and P^{75}, containing much of Luke and John, both dated about AD 200.

These finds have had to be integrated into the process of reconstructing the most reliable text of the New Testament. The work of Westcott and Hort was followed up in Germany by *Bernhard Weiss* (1827–1918), who published in 1894–1900 a critical text on rather different principles, but with similar results. Abandoning the effort to reach back to the 'neutral' text, he considered every passage in the light of internal probability and the characteristic causes of errors in copying by hand. He was in fact led to regard B (Vaticanus) as the manuscript most free from errors, and it is his preference for it which explains the similarity to Westcott and Hort's text. *Eberhard Nestle* (1851–1913) then produced a consensus edition, taking the best supported readings from the three texts of Tischendorf, Westcott and Hort, and Weiss. This edition, first published in 1898, has been constantly updated by its later editors, Erwin Nestle and Kurt Aland, and in the process the principles on which it is based have changed, as we shall see below.

At the same time *H.F. von Soden* (1852–1914) sought to place the text on a sounder footing by vastly increasing the collection of variant readings from previously unexamined manuscripts. His work, eventually published in two large volumes, has been described as monumental, but failed to make a real advance in textual criticism, because he wrongly supposed that the Koiné texts, to which most of his new material belonged, stemmed from a source of the same value as the Alexandrian texts, and so accepted Koiné readings too readily. In fact, as explained in the last chapter, the Koiné must be regarded as secondary and unreliable, being based on the stylistic revision of Lucian of Antioch in the fourth century.

Textual criticism was still dominated by the idea that manuscripts could be arranged in families deriving from a common ancestor, so that false readings could be eliminated by working back through the family tree. This was maintained by B.H. Streeter in his study of *The Four Gospels* (1924), who tried to connect groups of manuscripts with local texts at different church centres, from which each group is descended, though he allowed for cross fertilisation between them. In a few cases the derivation of a group of manuscripts from a common ancestor has been demonstrated. The Lake group (family 1) identified by Kirsopp Lake in 1902, and the Ferrar group (family 13) discovered by W.H. Ferrar in 1868 and subsequently enlarged by the identification of further members of the group, are the best examples. The latter also has special characteristics which Streeter connected with the local text of Caesarea.

These, however, are small groups of Koiné minuscules, and it has proved impossible to extend the genealogical method to embrace the important uncial manuscripts and papyri. We have to be content with observing the tendencies of broad groups of manuscripts, which fall into the three main categories of Alexandrian, Western and Koiné groups. These retain their value, however, because the different tendencies must always be taken into account when assessing a disputed reading. But because of the limitations of the genealogical method, textual criticism in the twentieth century has moved steadily towards the dominance of the eclectic method, in which each reading is assessed on its merits along the lines of B. Weiss, using the principles worked out much earlier by Griesbach. To establish what is likely to be the true text in any given instance, it is necessary to take all factors into account. So attention has to be paid to the author's style and vocabulary, the possibility of accidental errors in copying, the tendencies of certain groups to expand or improve the underlying text, and the possibility of assimilation of one Gospel to another in parallel passages.

The Nestle text, known as the Nestle-Aland text since the 26th edition of 1979, moved steadily towards an eclectic text in this way. Hence the printed text is not that of any one manuscript, but it is a reconstructed text, aimed at reproducing what is most likely to have been the original wording of the New Testament. The critical apparatus attempts to give the fullest information in the briefest form, and is a miracle of compression. This has been made possible by the great assembly of textual information at the Wurttemberg Bible Society, using modern methods of microfilm copies of texts and computer-based storage of information. The same text is also used for the special edition for translators of the New Testament, published by the United Bible Societies, which limits the textual information to passages where there are important variants, but gives fuller guidance to enable the translator to come to a decision on the evidence. There is, in fact, a tendency to abandon all other editions in favour of the Nestle-Aland text, because of the vast resources that lie behind it and the skill of its editors. But it has been criticised both for wrong choices of readings in the printed text and for defects in the presentation of textual information. There is still work to be done on the text of the New Testament.

The Language of the New Testament
The manuscript discoveries of modern times have not only supplied biblical texts and evidence for the cultural and religious background to the New Testament, but also have given new understanding of the Greek language of the New Testament. This differs from classical Greek and the better educated style of contemporary writers, and has more in common with the language of the Septuagint Greek version of the Old Testament and related Hellenistic Jewish literature. Thus it has sometimes been claimed that the New Testament was written in a distinctively 'biblical' Greek, developed among Greek-speaking Jews. But the vast quantity of contemporary material from the papyri has proved that it is really the simplified form of Greek commonly used in the whole culture region (hence it is referred to as the *koiné* = common). This was demonstrated by A. *Deissman* (1866–1937), whose collection of comparative material, *Light from the Ancient East* (1908), first made these findings generally accessible.

Greek, however, was not the normal language of Jesus and the disciples, even though they probably had some knowledge of it. It was often supposed that Jesus spoke Hebrew, but G. *Dalman* (1855–1941) proved that Aramaic was the language normally spoken in Galilee at the time, and proceeded to construct a grammar of the language from surviving Aramaic sources, and then attempted to reconstruct the original Aramaic form of *The Words of Jesus* (1898). This also has had long-lasting influence, as studies of the teaching of Jesus constantly look for indications of the underlying Aramaic, which can help towards establishing the authenticity of the sayings.

Thus authentic sayings of Jesus in the Gospels must be regarded as translations from Aramaic, and this raises the question whether the sources used by the evangelists were in Aramaic, or were already in Greek translation. It is quite widely held that the Q collection of sayings was originally in Aramaic, though it had evidently been put into Greek before it was used by Matthew and Luke. Moreover the evidence of Papias was adduced to suggest that the Gospel of Matthew was actually composed in Aramaic originally, though this must be regarded as very unlikely if Matthew is based on Mark. C.F. Burney made out an impressive case for *The Aramaic Origin of the Fourth Gospel* (1922), supposing it to have been first written in Aramaic; however, it seems better to think of the evangelist as one who wrote in Greek, though Aramaic was his first language. The Semitic features of the language of Revelation, which often make the Greek seem quite barbarous, are probably to be explained similarly.

Finally, attention has been given to the variations in the semantic range of particular words in their use in different cultural settings. Taking up a suggestion that biblical words have acquired special theological naunces, G. Kittel (1888–1948) embarked on his great *Theological Dictionary of the New Testament*, begun in 1933, and completed under the editorship of G. Friedrich in 1973. All significant words are included, and in each case there is treatment of the word in ancient classical Greek writings, in the *koiné*, in its usuage in the Septuagint and related Jewish literature and in early Christian writings. It is a mine of information, but is has been criticised for giving the impression that the etymology of a word can decide its meaning and for the idea that a particular theological meaning can attach to a word as a biblical word, quite apart from its actual usage. It is true that the exigencies of translation brought particular words into prominence in connection with theological ideas, which then became conventional in Hellenistic Jewish usage. The most obvious case is *doxa*, which means 'reputation' in secular Greek, but was selected as the translation for Hebrew *kābōd* ('glory'), which has no precise equivalent in Greek. On the other hand Paul's special use of 'righteousness' and 'faith' belong to his particular argument in Galatians and Romans. Similarly it has been noted that Hebrew thought is dynamic and active, whereas Greek tends to be more a matter of static concepts. But there is obvious danger in making too much of this kind of observation.

2. THE RISE OF CHRISTIANITY

The new material available for study opened much wider horizons, and one result was a fresh attempt to explain the rise of Christianity out of the narrow confines of Judaism and its ultimate success in dominating the Greco-Roman world. The crucial problem was to locate the decisive point where Christianity became a distinctive religion. Obviously it began within Judaism. But Judaism itself was much affected by external influences at this period, and Christianity could be regarded as a sect in which such influences were particularly strong. On the other hand an obvious break could be made with the opening of the Church to the Gentiles; in this case original Christianity need not be sharply distinguished from its Jewish background, and the decisive change would be due to Paul's adoption of Hellenistic ideas.

The History of Religions School

The investigation of the wider religious background to solve this problem gave rise to the history-of-religions school of New Testament scholars, which was dominant in the early part of the twentieth century. The presupposition of these scholars was that distinctive features in early Christianity were derived from influences outside Judaism. W. Bousset emphasised the Iranian features in the contemporary Jewish apocalyptic, and so suggested two stages of influence from the wider religious background. First, Jesus' preaching of the kingdom was identified with Jewish apocalyptic expectations, with the result that he was regarded as the Son of man of Daniel 7:13 (held by Bousset to be a Jewish version of a mythical man in the Zoroastrian system). Then, as a result of the expansion of the Church, Jesus was identified with Hellenistic notions of a deified man as Lord (hence the confession 'Christ is Lord', *Kyrios Christos*, Philippians 2:11). Thus catholic Christianity was regarded as the result of religious syncretism in the welter of religious cults of the Greco-Roman world.

Reitzenstein's work on the mystery religions, and later on the *Hermetica*, contributed further to this impression. Paul's concept of being 'in Christ' suggested a debt to Hellenistic mysticism, and the beginnings of Gnosticism appeared to lie behind Colossians 1:15–20. Similarities of language between John and the *Hermetica* suggested that John was indebted to this kind of religious writing. Reitzenstein's theory of a Hellenistic myth of a divine man also seemed to account for features in John's presentation of Jesus as the one sent from God. This was taken up by R. Bultmann, drawing on the

Mandaean texts for the concept of the man from heaven as the revealer of divine truth.

The Jewish Background: A Corrective Factor

All of these positions have been subjected to criticism. Similarity of language and ideas does not necessarily require influence to account for it, and is insufficient to establish such influence unless actual contact between the two sides can be demonstrated. Most of these scholars operated with an inadequate notion of Jesus as only a moral teacher, derived from the liberal tradition, to which the institutions, sacraments and dogmas of the Church seemed completely alien. Karl Holl, weighing up the work of the history-of-religions school in a lecture delivered in 1925, pointed out that the approach provided no explanation of the ultimate triumph of Christianity in the Greco-Roman world, if Christianity was always at the receiving end of syncretistic influence. It was thus necessary to reconsider the central importance of Jesus himself, and how far the subsequent developments were the result of the stimulation which he gave. In any case some corrections to these theories could be made from the studies of the Jewish background, which were advancing at the same time. Weiss and Schweitzer had already rung the death-knell on the liberal view of Jesus by strongly stressing the eschatological orientation of his preaching. It was agreed by all that after his death he was proclaimed as the risen one, with the result that he himself became the central feature of the apostolic preaching (or *kerygma*), and, in the famous phrase of Bultmann, 'the proclaimer became the proclaimed.' Thus death and resurrection were rooted in the experience of the first Christians, and influence from pagan mythology, if any, could only be marginal, and certainly not determinative of the beginning of Christianity. Bousset's idea that *Kyrios* (Lord) was derived from Hellenistic influence, could be answered on linguistic grounds, for Paul in 1 Corinthians 16.22 quotes the liturgical cry *Maranatha* (Our Lord, come!), which is clearly a formula of the Aramaic-speaking Christians before the expansion into the Hellenistic world. Similarly J. Jeremias has shown that the words of Jesus in the Last Supper accounts in the Gospels and Paul are too strongly Semitic in language to belong to this later time (*The Eucharistic Words of Jesus*, 1953). Consequently Paul cannot be said to introduce a new sacramentalism into the simpler meal of Jesus and the apostles. The eschatological orientation of the meal ('you proclaim the Lord's death until he comes,' 1 Corinthians 11:26) has its best parallel in the community meal at Qumran, which points forward to the messianic age.

The Dead Sea Scrolls have also helped to restore confidence in the Jewish character of the Fourth Gospel, as they reflect religious words and ideas which Reitzenstein supposed must derive from the influence of pagan Hellenistic thought. H. Odeberg, writing in 1929, had gathered parallels to John from many sources, including the Mandaean texts, but he added some from the Jewish mystical tradition, which had not previously been adduced. The publication of the Scrolls, however, has shown the currency of these ideas at a time contemporary with the New Testament, and so helps to root John in the Jewish religious aspirations of the time. The idea of the revealer from heaven, which was taken up enthusiastically by Bultmann, using the Mandaean material, remains only an inference for New Testament times, and has not been found in any actual Gnostic texts of the time. Nevertheless the more recent publication of the Nag Hammadi texts has reopened speculations that Gnosticism, or rather proto-Gnosticism, may have exerted some influence on John.

The Historical – Theological Approach

Thus the trend of New Testament study in the twentieth century has been away from the supposition of the history-of-religions school that influences from pagan forms of religion have had decisive effect on the rise of Christianity. Instead, the main thrust of scholarship has followed what may be called the historical-theological approach. This seeks to relate the rise of doctrine to the actual history of Jesus and the primitive Church, tracing the lines of development from the cradle of Christianity in Galilean Judaism to its emergence as an organised body with a complex belief structure in the age of the Fathers. A few salient features of this work may be indicated from the vast proliferation of relevant studies.

(a)*Study of the life and teaching of Jesus* has continued to show the seminal importance of the emphasis of Weiss and Schweitzer on the eschatological character of his message. The recovery of the Jewish background, especially in the light of the Scrolls, has confirmed the impression that devout Jews of the time were looking for divine action in the near future to restore the fortunes of Israel, often including in their expectations the hope of the Messiah. But this also raises the question whether such a hope was justified. If Jesus preached that God's kingdom was imminent, was he simply wrong, as Schweitzer maintained? It appears that the disciples, in identifying the risen Jesus with the coming Messiah, took his teaching literally. But then they had to revise their ideas, when the parousia (i.e. the coming of the Messiah as God's agent for the general resurrection and final judgment) failed to occur. If this is correct, it is necessary to assume a crisis in the early Church as a result of the delay of the parousia. Two possible approaches to these problems have been canvassed.

The first is generally referred to as *consistent eschatology*, i.e. that statements referring to the future are consistent in actually being intended to have a future reference. On this view Jesus was bound by the outlook of his time in giving his eschatological message. At first the disciples after the resurrection expected the parousia rapidly, and this is still the view of Paul (cf. 1 Corinthians 7:29). Whether the delay caused a major crisis or not, reinterpretation of the original message was necessary, and this is what appears in the later strands of the New Testament.

The second approach is *realised eschatology*, which suggests that Jesus claimed that the future act of God was already being realised in the present. On this view he need not have expected a future event at all, and the disciples were mistaken in supposing that this is what he meant. This approach was given what may be regarded as its classic formulation in C.H. Dodd's *The Parables of the Kingdom* (1935), in which the parables were shown to be assertions that the kingdom of God is already present, even if only in a small way, like a mustard seed. Thus Jesus is represented as reinterpreting eschatological expressions to point to the crisis that is always present when people are confronted with the reality of God. R. Bultmann went further, and claimed that, to reach the real meaning of Jesus, his words must be freed from their outward form of mythological language, for the real concern of Jesus was with the search for authentic existence. Thus the future statements of Jesus are really timeless on Bultmann's view. More will have to be said later about Bultmann's programme of demythologisation and existentialist interpretation of the New Testament.

More recently scholars have refused to regard these positions as mutually exclusive alternatives. Following the historical-theological approach, they have maintained that while the consistent eschatology of Jesus is to be taken seriously, elements of present fulfilment should also be recognised. Thus J.A.T. Robinson speaks of an 'inaugurated eschatology' (*Jesus and his Coming*, 1957). W.G. Kümmel has suggested that Jesus saw his own mission as the beginning of the coming age, so that christology has a point of origin in the significance which Jesus attached to his own person and mission (*Promise and Fulfilment*, 1945).

(b)*The value of the Fourth Gospel* for the study of Christian origins has been much disputed in relation to these issues. Bultmann, whose magisterial commentary appeared in 1941, not only used the history-of-religions approach, making much of the Mandaean parallels to the revelation-discourses in which the main teaching of Jesus is given, but also applied to it his existentialist theology to establish the evangelist's meaning. Thus the recurring demand of John to believe in Jesus becomes the demand for authentic existence. The historical value of the Gospel for the life and teaching of Jesus himself is reduced almost to vanishing point. It also follows from this assessment of John that the Johannine community, from which it and the three Letters of John emanate, is to be regarded as a heavily gnosticised form of Christianity.

The recovery of confidence in the Jewish background to John, however, has suggested other approaches. First, the possibility of a date much earlier than the traditional date (AD 90–100) has been explored by J.A.T. Robinson (finally worked out in *The Priority of John*, 1985) This led him to postulate greater historical accuracy on the part of John, which is often regarded by him as a better guide to historical facts in the life of Jesus than the Synoptic Gospels. It must be said, however, that few scholars are convinced by this theory. Secondly, J.L. Martyn observed that the topics under discussion in the discourses of John reflect, not the conflict between Jesus and the Pharisees as it appears in the Synoptics, but disputes between Christians and Jews later in the century, when the Church was becoming finally estranged from the Synagogue (*History and Theology in the Fourth Gospel*, 1968). This approach has the advantage that the content of the discourses is taken seriously, for they are all concerned with points in developing christology and Jewish objections to them. It has led further to a more convincing picture of the Johannine community within the spectrum of early Christianity, as a distinct group with its own tendency. Though the debate is with Jews, there is a speculative side to it which suggests that John and his opponents share some of the interests of proto-Gnosticism. Thus on this view John is not indebted to Gnosticism, but shows the tendency to lose sight of the real history of Jesus as the century draws to a close, and marks a step in the direction of the Gnostic forms of Christianity which appear in the second century.

(c) *The history of earliest Christianity* has also been seen in relation to the development of theology. Though the Tübingen theory of a very late date for Acts has long been abandoned, doubts about its historical value have continued. M. Dibelius, followed later by E. Haenchen in his *Meyer Commentary* on Acts (1946, but much revised in later editions), pointed to the variety of literary forms used by

Luke in Acts and the theological motivation of his narrative. In particular he cast doubt on the historical basis of the speeches, which can be compared with fictitious speeches in Greek historiography. The first part of Acts was in any case under suspicion on account of the total failure of Luke to say anything about the beginnings of the Church in Galilee, contrary to the implications of the resurrection stories in Matthew and Mark. Hence E. Lohmeyer (*Galilee and Jerusalem*, 1936) suggested that Luke had covered up a rift between two simultaneous beginnings, which ended with the triumph of James the Lord's brother and the Jerusalem church. Though Luke has a liking for miraculous detail, which gives a legendary impression, and his narrative lacks a firm grasp of the course of events until he reaches the story of Paul, he is clearly strongly motivated theologically. The progress of Christianity from Jerusalem to Rome, from the beginnings in Judaism to the capital of the Gentile world, is his theme. Hence there has been a tendency to deny that Luke is a real historian altogether, and to treat him as a theologian who is not interested in establishing the facts. This judgment has been challenged by M. Hengel, who has shown that Luke's aims and methods are not fundamentally different from those of the ancient historians of the time. Luke gives a slanted presentation, it is true, and he is limited by the inadequacy of the sources available to him, but he has made a genuine attempt to give an accurate picture. Thus the evidence of Acts is not to be simply set aside, though it must always be used with proper caution. It has to be recognised that we do not have the information to solve all the problems, and the origins of Christianity in Galilee must remain unknown, failing any other evidence.

Hengel has also given attention to the doctrinal development of earliest Christianity, showing (in a long article entitled 'Between Jesus and Paul') how the primitive proclamation (*kerygma*) of the lordship of Jesus as Messiah and designated agent of God for the coming judgment was filled out as further consequences were perceived. In particular, the converts among the Hellenist Jews of Jerusalem drew the conclusion that the sacrificial death of Christ rendered the sacrificial system of the temple obsolete. Thus the way was prepared for Paul's break with the Law, and for the independent handling of the theme of the atoning death of Christ in the Epistle to the Hebrews.

Paul thus appears to be less of an innovator than has often been claimed. In fact he takes up positions already reached by the Hellenists, and applies them vigorously to the crisis that befell his own great mission to the Gentiles. This was the Judaistic controversy, the question whether Gentile converts should be required to become Jews, and so members of the covenant people of God, before they could join in the fellowship of those baptised into the name of Christ, the members of the new covenant. It is recognised that this was not just a theoretical matter, but had practical consequences, as, for instance, table fellowship at the eucharist was affected by the Jewish laws for ceremonial purity.

(d)*The study of Paul* thus stresses the continuity between him and the primitive church, to which indeed he appeals when he quotes what appear to be official formularies of the Jerusalem church in 1 Corinthians 11:23–5 and 15:3–7, on the Lord's Supper and the resurrection respectively. But the German idealist tendency to make Paul the champion of true religion, derived from the central import- ance ascribed by Luther to the Pauline doctrine of justification by faith, has continued to give an erroneous assessment of Judaism as a legalistic and unspiritual religion. This was challenged by E.P. Sanders (*Paul and Palestinian Judaism*, 1977), who showed from a vast array of relevant Jewish sources the inadequacy of the popular stereotype of Pharisaism. K. Stendahl, in an essay published previously, had shown that the caricature of the guilt-ridden Pharisee, derived from Romans 7, misinterprets Paul and has no real foundation in the available evidence. Paul's objection to the Law is that it is not the decisive thing for salvation, for it has been superseded by God's new act of redemption in Christ. Thus Jews who keep the Law also need incorporation into Christ, which is a matter of faith. Gentiles, who have a standard of morality equivalent to the Law, need only incorporation into Christ, and should not be required to submit to the Law in addition. The Thanksgiving Hymns (1QH) of the Dead Sea Scrolls have given striking evidence for Jewish awareness that people cannot be justified before God by their own efforts alone, but require the cleansing that only God himself can give.

This correction of the understanding of Paul in relation to Judaism has also been extended to reasearch into the life of Jesus. Again the stereotype of the Pharisees in the Gospels has been shown to be partial and biased. A further work of E.P. Sanders (*Jesus and Judaism*, 1985) sums up a series of studies of this question. The crucial issue is seen to be, not legalism, but the direct authority from God which Jesus claimed for his message, which involved radical criticism of religious practice and brought him into sharp conflict with the various elements of the religious establishment.

(e) *Paul's devotion to the cause of Gentile Christianity* eventually triumphed. Meanwhile Jewish Christianity remained small, and after the fall of Jerusalem lacked a natural centre, so that the congregations became isolated, and tended to lapse into heresy or wither away. But the Johannine community appears to be a Jewish group, as suggested above. Recent work on the Gospel of Matthew has supported the idea that it stems from a group closer to mainstream Judaism, which gives a better idea of the nature of Jewish Christianity. This accepts the messiahship of Jesus and retains vivid expectation of his return for the judgment. The Law remains binding, but with considerable modifications of the rules of purity and repudiation of sacrifice. The same strand of Christianity can be seen in the *Didache*. A comprehensive account of *The Theology of Jewish Christianity* (1958) was made by J. Daniélou, using also the Clementine writings, which show bitter opposition to Paul. One feature of this literature is the reluctance to place the exalted Jesus on an equality with God, so that there are traces of an angel christology, in which he has the highest rank among the angels. We can see from this how difficult it was for those brought up in Judaism to accept the doctrinal development in the main Gentile church, in which the divinity of Christ was in process of formulation in relation to Greek philosophical ideas of cosmology. The Jewish background to ideas of an angel christology appears in 11Q *Melchizedek*, a Qumran fragment in which the archangel Michael (here called Melchizedek) is to be God's agent in the coming judgment. The Book of Revelation depicts the glorified Jesus (symbolically described as the Lamb) as sharing God's throne, but stops short of ascribing full divinity to him.

(f) Another component of early Christianity is referred to as *Early Catholicism*, which appears in the Pastoral Epistles and some other later strands of the New Testament. Here there is evident a more structured organisation, with grades of ordained ministers, and great emphasis on the need to preserve the deposit of faith. Thus Paul's dynamic concept of faith as a matter of relationship with God has given way to a preoccupation with dogmatic orthodoxy. The designation Early Catholicism is not altogether happy, as it represents the liberal German protestant objection to Roman Catholicism. But it is correct to see a tendency to preservation of the institution and loss of the original vision as Christianity moved into the second generation, and by the early second century the confusion of belief and the rise of heretical teachers presented serious problems.

(g) Whereas Acts seems to present the rise of Christianity along a straight line of development from Jerusalem to Rome, it should now be clear that it is necessary to think of different groups, in which *different doctrinal and practical forms* develop in response to varying circumstances. The conventional idea, that orthodoxy was the gift of the risen Christ to the Church, which was then threatened by heretics for selfish ends as the first century drew to a close, can no longer be maintained. An extreme reaction to this view appears in W. Bauer's *Orthodoxy and Heresy in Earliest Christianity* (1934), arguing that it is a mistake to suppose there was ever a single core of belief, but a multiplicity of tendencies. On this view orthodoxy is the tendency that eventually triumphed, and those that were regarded as heretical have an equal claim to be taken seriously as the authentic belief of Christendom. Bauer did not take his study back to the New Testament period, apart from later strands which can be seen in the second century. A collection of essays, *Trajectories through Early Christianity* (1971), edited by J.M. Robinson and H. Koester, pointed to lines of development which can be discerned within the New Testament, and become more prominent and distinct in the second century (e.g. a line can be drawn from the Dead Sea Scrolls through the Fourth Gospel to the rise of Gnosticism). But this implies that it is a mistake to think of a multiplicity of origins. The right model is a simple original statement of belief (the *kerygma*), stemming from the earliest community, and developing new features or at least distinctive emphases as the Church expands and becomes divided into a variety of groups. This has been explored by J.D.G. Dunn in *Unity and Diversity in the New Testament* (1977).

3. GOSPEL CRITICISM

The continuing 'quest of the historical Jesus' has in the twentieth century made use of new approaches to Gospel criticism. Some of these methods are applicable to other parts of the New Testament also. The basic problem is to assess the extent to which the Gospels can be regarded as historical documents. It is recognised that they depend on traditions of the life and teaching of Jesus that have been transmitted orally in the first instance, so that it is not enough to solve the Synoptic Problem with regard to written sources. Investigation of this question has led some scholars to extreme scepticism, as the real Jesus of history disappears behind what have been felt to be entirely unreliable traditions. Thus scholarship is often regarded as destructive of basic Christian faith. For this reason it is important to understand why and how scholars have reached such disturbing conclusions, and to what extent a more positive answer to the 'quest' may now be said to be available.

The Synoptic Problem

The priority of Mark was, broadly speaking, the agreed view of scholarship at the beginning of the century, except that a Vatican clamp-down on critical study (to be explained in a later section) very soon required Roman Catholic scholars to adhere to the traditional priority of Matthew. The designation Q for the source (*Quelle*) common to Matthew and Luke, coined perhaps by B. Weiss, was now an agreed convention. This two-source Synoptic theory was given full treatment in Streeter's *The Four Gospels* (1924), already mentioned in connection with textual criticism. Streeter attempted to show that the materials in Matthew and Luke not derived from Mark or Q came from two independent sources, which he designated M and L. He also put forward the Proto-Luke theory, that Luke was originally a complete gospel consisting of L and Q, and that this was combined with Mark to form the present Luke at a later stage. Though this remains an open possibility, it is now generally accepted that the material comprised under the symbols M and L is too varied to suggest that each was a single source. So we have to think of varied material which each evangelist put together along with his use of Mark and Q. Some of it may have been oral.

The priority of Matthew was upheld by various Roman Catholic scholars, especially J. Chapman, L. Vaganay and B.C. Butler, using often complex theories of the pre-history of the sources, whereby Matthew might be the earliest complete gospel, but Mark might preserve more primitive forms of the tradition. Since the withdrawal of restrictions following the Second Vatican Council, many Catholic scholars have openly sided with the consensus in favour of the priority of Mark. But the other view has retained adherents, and won new recruits on the Protestant side as a result of the energetic campaigning of W.R. Farmer (*The Synoptic Problem*, 1964). He advocated a return to the hypothesis of Griesbach, that Luke is dependent on Matthew, and Mark on both Matthew and Luke. The theory overcomes the problem caused by the minor agreements between Matthew and Luke against Mark, and also cuts out the need for the Q hypothesis, as Luke has in this view taken the sayings direct from Matthew. It is, however, open to a number of objections, which have been presented by C.M. Tuckett (*The Revival of the Griesbach Hypothesis*, 1983).

Two further theories were brought together by M.D. Goulder (*Midrash and Lection in Matthew*, 1974). Assuming the priority of Mark, he claimed that Matthew was wholly dependent on Mark, all the additional matter, including the sayings usually attributed to Q, being expansions by Matthew, often based on Old Testament models (rather like rabbinic *midrash*). Luke depended on both Mark and Matthew. Moreover both Matthew and Luke, in Goulder's view, were composed as lectionaries for reading in connection with the Old Testament calendar of lessons as used in the synagogue. Thus the connection between the Old Testament readings and the Gospel passages would be apparent to the congregation. It will be seen that this highly speculative theory drastically reduces the authenticity of the sayings of Jesus.

Form Criticism

The written sources of the Gospels are not the beginning of the process, but must have been collections of traditions which had been transmitted orally in the first place. H. Gunkel had drawn attention early in the century to work on folklore in relation to the traditions underlying the Old Testament. The idea was applied to the Gospels almost independently by K.L. Schmidt (*The Framework of the Story of Jesus*, 1919), M. Dibelius (*From Tradition to Gospel*, 1919), and R. Bultmann (*History of the Synoptic Tradition*, 1921). This method of study, which owes its inspiration in the first instance to the interests of the history-of-religions school, has proved to be extraordinarily fruitful. First the individual units of tradition are isolated (e.g. a miracle story, or a parable, or a proverb), and editorial matter (usually at the beginning or end, connecting it with the context) is stripped off. Then the unit is classified according to its form (a miracle story, etc.). The critic then tries to picture the setting in the life of the Church which is likely to have preserved the tradition (e.g. preaching, or the liturgy, or disputes with unbelievers). It may prove possible to distinguish between adaptation for new circumstances and what is likely to have been the original point in the teaching of Jesus. By this means it is hoped to reach behind the written traditions to Jesus himself.

Inevitably there is a large subjective element in the method, which depends on good judgment and to some extent on intuition. It is one thing to suggest a convincing life-setting (*Sitz im Leben*) for the preservation and currency of a unit, another to reach behind that to Jesus himself. The interpretation of the parables is notoriously difficult from this point of view, for the appeal of the story remains while the application may be changed drastically. The parable of the sower (Mark 4:3–8) has actually been supplied with an interpretation (4:14–20), which applies it to the experience of the Church's mission. It is very doubtful if this element goes back to Jesus himself, who probably told the parable for quite a different purpose. Sometimes the difficulty of going behind the setting in the Church is such that the critic is likely to suspect that the unit has actually been created within the Christian community, so that it is wrongly applied to Jesus in the Gospels. The question concerning David's Son (Mark 12:35–7) is widely held to be such a case. Käsemann suggested that certain 'sentences of holy law' (e.g. Mark 8:38) might be the work of Christian prophets, speaking in the name of the risen Christ. Thus the line between community formation and Jesus himself becomes blurred. The emphasis on the role of the community has led to radical scepticism on the part of some scholars, who hold that very little, if any, of the Gospel sayings and stories can be accepted as genuine. It seems that nothing attributed to Jesus in the Gospels is safe, once the form critics have got their hands on it.

This judgment is far too pessimistic. Form criticism must be undertaken with a completely open mind, but the method does not dictate the results. In view of what we know of the history of earliest Christianity and the gradual process of the formation of the Gospel traditions, it is intrinsically probable that a nucleus of authentic material has survived, which has nevertheless suffered from the accretion of extraneous matter to some extent. We should not expect to have the precise words of Jesus in every case, but rather the gist of what he said, but special value attaches to the very striking sayings which form the climax of the 'pronouncement-stories' (e.g. Mark 3:31–5). B. Gerhardsson (*Memory and Manuscript*, 1961) tried to prove that much of the sayings tradition goes back to a rabbinic style of dictation and memorisation on the part of Jesus and the disciples, but this theory has not won acceptance. On the other hand various tests increase the possibility of authenticity: Semitisms in the Greek, implying translation from Aramaic (e.g. 'speak a word against' in Luke 12:10 Q, against 'blaspheme' in Mark 3.28); double attestation (Luke 12:10 and Mark 3:28 are independent versions of the same saying, one preserved in Q and the other in Mark); dissimilarity from what the Church might be expected to wish to remember (e.g. Jesus' cry of dereliction on the cross, Mark 15:34), or from what would be a commonplace on the lips of a Jew (e.g. Mark 2:27 – it is recognised that this criterion must be used with great caution); congruity with the general thrust of Jesus' teaching. J. Jeremias devoted much of his life to determining the authentic style and content of the teaching of Jesus, and the results of his work, collected in his *Theology of the New Testament: the Proclamation of Jesus* (1971) provide a rich store of material, which shows the positive value of the form-critical method.

Redaction Criticism

The success of form criticism was considerable, but as it became apparent that there was a limit to what could be done by this method, scholars turned to the consideration of redaction criticism. This takes up the editorial matter, which is set aside when a unit is examined form-critically, and also examines the changes which each evangelist has made to his source-material, in order to discover the aims and tendencies of the evangelists themselves. Pioneering studies using this method include *The Theology of Luke* (1954) by H. Conzelmann and *Tradition and Interpretation in Matthew* by G. Bornkamm, G. Barth and H.J. Held (1960). The enormous overlap between the three Synoptic Gospels makes it possible to see exactly what Matthew (for example) has done with Mark (assuming Marcan priority). This then provides a basis for broader conclusions with regard to his methods of composition, aims and interests, and a comprehensive picture of his theology and the situation of his church within the spectrum of early Christianity can be built up.

Redaction criticism can also be used where we do not have the underlying source. The process is inevitably more subjective, but can still lead to useful results. Thus a knowledge of Mark's style and interests and vocabulary derived from his editorial characteristics can also help the critic to observe changes which Mark is likely to have made within the units of tradition themselves, so as to adapt them to the needs of his presentation of the gospel. Similarly signs of reworking and expansion have been observed in some of the material attributed to Q. It thus becomes possible to trace the tradition-history of a unit in relation to the changing needs of the life of the Church. In this way redaction criticism supplements form criticism.

Redaction criticism is also concerned with the theological aims of the evangelists. From this point of view it takes up and corrects the *Tendenzkritik* of the Tübingen school. An epoch-making book, which has come into its own with the rise of redaction criticism, was W. Wrede's *The Messianic Secret in the Gospels* (1901). Wrede explained the reticence of Jesus concerning his Messiahship, which is a notable feature of Mark, not in terms of gradual perception on the part of Jesus (the popular psychologising view of liberal lives of Jesus at the time), but as a deliberate ploy of the evangelist to cover up the fact that Jesus never actually claimed to be the Messiah, though that was the faith of the disciples after the resurrection. Hence Mark adds editorial comments to the tradition to the effect that Jesus warned those whom he cured to keep silence (e.g. Mark 1:34). Subsequent study has suggested that there may be some basis for this feature in the underlying tradition, in as much as Jesus may have been anxious to avoid any impression that he thought of himself as a political agitator, which is what acceptance of a popular claim to messiahship would mean. In any case, it is clear that Mark's life of Jesus has strong theological motivation, with a careful succession of confessions of faith (e.g. Peter, 8:29; Jesus himself, 14:62; the centurion, 15:39) and special emphasis on the necessity of the cross (8:31–3; 9:31–2; 10:32–4); and the recurring feature of the failure of the disciples to understand Jesus (e.g. 8:14–21) supports Wrede's thesis.

Interestingly, the theological position of Mark has striking similarities to that of John, who also makes much of the necessity of the cross, and indeed makes it the moment when the full truth of Jesus' relationship with God is disclosed to the eye of faith (cf. John 3:28). The recognition that John includes historical tradition comparable to the sources of the Synoptic Gospels has also made possible a redaction-critical approach, whereby John's style and diction may be separated from the underlying tradition to some extent. The Johannine style then stands out much more clearly in the discourses, which then appear to be Johannine compositions with only a limited basis in the sayings tradition. Accordingly the idea of Bultmann (*The Gospel of John*, 1941) that John used a proto-Gnostic source for the discourses is no longer widely held. Whether John made direct use of one or more of the Synoptic Gospels is still an open question.

The Titles of Jesus
The 'messianic secret' raises the question of the meaning of the titles applied to Jesus in christology. These have been studied in relation to the New Testament as a whole (e.g. O. Cullmann, *The Christology of the New Testament*, 1957; F. Hahn, *The Titles of Christ in Christology*, 1963), but their use in the Gospels has special problems. G. Vermes (*Jesus the Jew*, 1973) showed that titles like Christ (=Messiah), Lord and Son of God, which suggest divinity in the light of subsequent history of Christian doctrine, would not have had the same meaning to a contemporary Jewish audience. In fact, all three just mentioned are designations of the Messiah, thought of as God's human agent without any overtones of divinity. They thus acquired fresh significance in the light of the resurrection and in relation to the presuppositions of converts in the Hellenistic world beyond the confines of Judaism. The movement of thought has been traced in the small monograph by M. Hengel, *The Son of God* (1975).

It is also recognised that Jesus was popularly regarded as a prophet during his ministry. There is some evidence that he was identified with the eschatological prophet like Moses (Deuteronomy 18:15–18), who also figures in the expectations of the Qumran Sect (1QS 9:11). This never became a major title in christology.

The most problematical designation is Son of Man, and it has been the subject of endless debate throughout the century. The phrase appears as a title for Jesus only in the four Gospels (plus Acts 7.56), and then only in the sayings of Jesus himself, or references to them. The phrase obviously corresponds with Aramaic *bar (e)nash(a)* = Hebrew *ben adam*, meaning a member of the human species, or more loosely in Aramaic just a man. But it is often used as a title in the gospel sayings, especially when the context reflects Daniel 7:13 (e.g. Mark 13:26). Under the influence of the history-of-religions school a far-reaching theory was built up of an alternative messianism in the Judaism of New Testament times, which lies behind the Christian usage. According to this theory, the Zoroastrian myth of a primal man, who embraces all human souls, was taken up in apocalyptic circles as the basis of a concept of a future celestial Messiah, entirely distinct from the political and human Davidic Messiah of popular expectation. This figure makes his apperance in the 'one like a son of man' who receives dominion from the Ancient of Days in the vision of Daniel 7. Other Jewish sources appealed to by the proponents of this view were the Similitudes of Enoch (1 *Enoch* 37–71) and 2 Esdras 13. On this basis it was suggested that Jesus included the expectation of the Son of Man in his preaching of the kingdom of God, but he did not identify himself with this figure. That was done subsequently by the disciples in the light of the resurrection experience, and therefore the sayings of Jesus which appear to make the identification must be regarded as inauthentic, or at least adapted. Thus the Son of Man was current in earliest Christianity as a messianic title for Jesus, though it dropped out of use when the Church moved into a Greek-speaking setting. So it does not appear in Paul, though he shows the influence of the myth in his idea of Christ as the new Adam (cf. 1 Corinthians 15.45). A standard presentation of this (mainly German) view is *The Son of Man in the Synoptic Tradition* (1963), by H.E. Tödt.

British scholarship, well represented by M.D. Hooker's *The Son of Man in Mark* (1967), tends to discount the mythological background as a direct influence, though not excluding it from the sources of Daniel's vision, and takes the latter as the real basis of the usage in the Gospels. It is also generally assumed that a considerable number of the Son of Man sayings are authentic, so that Jesus really did identify himself with this future messianic figure. Though the Danielic Son of Man is mentioned only as the recipient of glory, he clearly represents the suffering Jews of the time of the Maccabean Revolt, who will be encouraged by this vision to expect a glorious future after their present trials. So it is argued that Jesus not only identified himself with this figure, but also understood his vocation to suffer in the light of it, and formed the expectation of vindication beyond suffering. Moreover he saw himself as the representative of all God's people, who are destined to share in the future glory. Attractive as this theory is, it raises an acute problem with regard to Jesus' reticence in claiming to be the Messiah, and indeed the phrase Son of Man has to be regarded as a covert way of making such a claim, not intended to be understood by everyone. Moreover some of the sayings refer to Jesus in the present without any future overtones (e.g. Matthew 8:20).

A lecture by Vermes in 1967 (summarised in *Jesus the Jew*) insisted that *Bar enasha* could not be recognised in Aramaic as a title (as Lietzmann had pointed out in 1896), but must mean just a man or the man. He therefore took Jesus' use of the phrase (especially in the present sayings, like Matthew 8:20) to be an idiomatic way of making a self-reference without any messianic implications. This view has been worked out more fully by B. Lindars (*Jesus Son of Man*, 1983), suggesting that Jesus used the phrase as an ironic self-reference, in accordance with normal Aramaic idiom, especially in contexts where his prophetic calling from God was denied (e.g. Matthew 11:19). The phrase, thus established as a style-feature of the sayings tradition, was later correlated with messianic application of Daniel 7:13 in the light of the resurrection and developing christology. On this view the phrase was never used as a title for Jesus outside the sayings tradition, and this explains why it does not appear in Paul.

All three views described above continue to have their protagonists, and so the debate continues.

4. THE THEOLOGY OF THE NEW TESTAMENT

Looking back over the above sections, we can see that there has been a vast expansion of New Testament studies in the twentieth century. Indeed, all that is written above is very selective, and many issues have had to be passed over in silence, and many great contemporary scholars are unmentioned. But perhaps enough has been said to justify the claim made at the outset, that the success of the critical method, established painfully during the nineteenth century, opened the way to a much richer knowledge of the history of the rise of Christianity and to new solutions to the literary problems of the New Testament.

One further result of the accession of new knowledge has been the development of the theology of the New Testament as a subject in its own right. For centuries the New Testament was used as the text-book for theology, but always on the assumption that the truth of Scripture was identical with the Rule of Faith, even if it required highly sophisticated methods of exegesis to bring them into line. Thus the New Testament was not really viewed historically, nor allowed to speak for itself. The beginnings of a changed view have been traced to *J.P. Gabler*, a pupil of Eichhorn, in a lecture delivered at Altdorf in 1787. He pointed out that the biblical writers were men of their own time, and must be understood in their own historical context before any general conclusions can be drawn from their writings with regard to unchanging truths of religion. During the nineteenth century this programme was largely understood in terms of an attempt to distil the essence of religion by discarding the contingent and ephemeral elements revealed by historical criticism. This aim explains the character of the liberal lives of Jesus.

Objectivity
However, the sheer intrinsic interest of historical study, coupled with the rise of the history-of-religions approach at the beginning of the twentieth century, led to a change of emphasis. Historical investigation of the New Testament includes the attempt to expose the theology implicit in the work of each writer and to place it in the spectrum of a reconstruction of the earliest history of Christian doctrine. This is primarily a phenomenological or descriptive task. The question of religious truth is set aside, on the grounds that it lies beyond the scope of historical enquiry. In fact the search for Hellenistic, Gnostic or oriental influences to explain the rise of Christianity implies that it cannot be explained solely in terms of divine action and the human response to it.

The phenomenological approach is thus a controversial matter, for it appears to be a case of opting out of the real issue of the religious truth of the Bible. At the beginning of the century this led to renewed opposition to critical study on the part of the Roman Catholic Church. The modernist Alfred Loisy (1857–1940) had attempted to answer the extreme reductionism of Harnack's *What is Christianity?* by asserting that the truth of Christianity does not depend on the intentions of Jesus himself, but is to be found in the development of the faith of the Church under the guidance of the Holy Spirit. Such a view only confirmed the suspicion that critical study leads inevitably to denial of the divine inspiration of Scripture. Loisy was excommunicated, and biblical study was placed under rigid control. The ban was lifted on the accession of Pope Pius XII in 1943, but later further restrictions were imposed, so that it was not until 1965 that full freedom was accorded to Roman Catholic scholars as a result of the Second Vatican Council.

Commitment

Meanwhile a resounding protest against the phenomenological approach had come from Karl Barth (1886–1968) in his commentary on Romans (1919). He insisted that the meaning of the New Testament requires the reader to accept Christ as God's sole and sufficient communication with humanity, and the task of New Testament theology is to make this plain. His trenchant criticism of the barrenness of critical study at the time exerted wide and lasting influence. In Germany it led to Bultmann's programme of demythologisation, whereby he sought to find the real meaning of the New Testament, including the message of Jesus himself, in the confrontation with existence, which, in his view, is the reality of religion when stripped of its mythical clothing in a pre-scientific culture. His *Theology of the New Testament* (1950–3) is explicitly concerned, not merely to describe the various facets with historical accuracy and fulness, but also to interpret the theology in this way. Bultmann has been criticised for the individualism of his position, which leaves little room for the corporate aspects of Christianity and its social implications.

Another response to Barth, more popular in Britain and America, is the biblical theology movement, which takes the traditional view that God makes himself known through historical events when they are interpreted in the light of faith. Thus Jesus is the culmination of divine disclosures which go back to the initial act of creation. This approach makes possible a theology which spans both Testaments, including a positive place for eschatology. Biblical theology can claim to accord with the actual teaching of the New Testament, in which the idea that God has taken action through Christ for the salvation of humanity is a central and recurring theme. Oscar Cullman's *Christ and Time* (1946) and *Salvation in History* (1965) pointed to the creative tension between the event of Christ in cross and resurrection and the final consummation. The Church thus looks both back to the past and forward to the future as it lives under the present lordship of Christ (cf. 1 Corinthians 11:26), and it is from this perspective that the New Testament addresses the reader in any time or place.

FOR FURTHER READING

Bultmann, Rudolf, *The History of the Synoptic Tradition*, Blackwell, Oxford, and Harper and Row, New York [2]1968.

Collins, R.F., *Introduction to the New Testament*, Doubleday, Garden City and SCM, London 1983.

Dunn, J.D.G., *Unity and Diversity in the New Testament*, SCM. London 1977.

Finegan, Jack, *Encountering New Testament Manuscripts: a Working Introduction* to *Textual Criticism*, Eerdmans, Grand Rapids 1974.

Jeremias, Joachim, *New Testament Theology 1: The Proclamation of Jesus*, SCM, London 1971.

Krentz, Edgar, *The Historical-Critical Method*, Foretress, Philadelphia 1975.

McKnight, E.V., *What is Form Criticism?*, Fortress, Philadelphia 1969.

Metzger, B.M. *The Text of the New Testament*, OUP, Oxford [2]1968.

Marshall, I.H. ed., *New Testament Interpretation*, Paternoster, Exeter 1977.

Perrin, Norman, *What is Redaction Criticism?*, Fortress, Philadelphia 1969.

Robinson, J.M. and H. Koester, *Trajectories through Early Christianity*, Fortress, Philadelphia 1971.

Vermes, Geza, *Jesus the Jew*, Collins, London 1973; Fontana, [3]1980.

9

INTERPRETING THE NEW TESTAMENT TODAY

Though historical criticism continues to be immensely productive, there is a feeling abroad that it has had its day, and that it has failed to deliver the goods. It was expected that scientific and impartial enquiry would not only clarify the Jesus of history and the original impetus of the Christian movement which stems from him, but also establish the truth of the Christian faith. But historical enquiry can only find answers to historical questions. The faith of the first Christians can be described, and some account of the events which were decisive for the form of their faith can be given. But the claim that God was at work in these events, that (to borrow Paul's phrase in 2 Corinthians 5.19) 'God was through Christ reconciling the world to himself', is the response of faith to these events, and cannot be established by historical enquiry alone. But it is precisely the character of the New Testament as writings written from faith to faith, which gives it its special significance. From this point of view the New Testament ranks as sacred literature, the class of literature which performs a sacred function. This observation opens up new perspectives which are being explored in various new approaches to the study of the New Testament.

In this chapter we shall be concerned with the more important aspects of the new approaches, which suggest directions for the future. We shall then return to the question of the inspiration and authority of the New Testament, and so bring this book to its close.

1. NEW APPROACHES: SOCIOLOGY AND STRUCTURALISM

The sacred function of the Bible has been clarified as a result of the recent interest in sociology. The pioneer in this field was E. Durkheim (1858–1917). He studied religion as a social phenomenon, and his observations include two fundamental points. In the first place religious texts and dramatic or symbolic rituals provide objective expression of mythical ideas of the nature of reality, and so touch on the deepest aspects of human life in a manageable form. In the second place organised religion sustains both the values and the practical rules of society, and so acts as a cohesive force, very frequently (but not always) allied to the maintenance of the *status quo*. When the Bible is viewed from these points of view, different questions are asked and new insights emerge.

The Sociological Approach

The sociology of earliest Christianity has naturally come to the fore in recent study. This uses the methods of historico-critical enquiry, but from a different standpoint. Whereas the history-of-religions school looked for religious influences which might have contributed to the formation and development of Christian faith, the sociologist looks for social and economic factors which would be likely to provide its sense of direction. It is recognised that there were conditioning factors which helped to shape and focus the religious aspirations of the time. The most obvious example is the unrest in Judaea under Roman rule, making for the opposite responses of quietism, withdrawal and other-worldliness on the one hand and of religiously inspired political activism on the other. Consequently there has been a great debate on the question whether Jesus was involved with the activist Zealot movement or not. The debate has been fully documented in *Jesus and the Politics of his Day* (ed. E. Bammel and C. F. D. Moule, 1984).

More broadly, the rise of Christianity can be seen as something that was made possible by the convergence of a number of different factors at the time. It is obvious that our greatly increased knowledge of Judaism in New Testament times has given fresh insights here. This, together with social, economic and political conditions, determined the form for any action which might be claimed as a divine act of universal salvation. This has been applied to the Jesus question by A. E. Harvey in his *Jesus and the Constraints of History* (1982). The sociology of earliest Christianity has been explored by G. Theissen, especially in *The First Followers of Jesus* (1977), and by W. A. Meeks in *The First Urban Christians: the Social World of the Apostle Paul* (1983).

All these are primarily historical studies, but the sociological approach to the New Testament is also interested in its value for the religious goals of Christianity today. The New Testament can be read in the light of modern understandings of society, regardless of the questions raised by historical criticism. This is what has happened in Latin America, where the Bible has been accepted more or less at face value as the book of the Church and interpreted in the light of current social (often Marxist) theory. In this way the New Testament serves the aims of liberation theology, in which Jesus' preaching of the gospel to the poor and outcast provides legitimation for the struggle to achieve peace and justice. Other issues, such as racialism and sexual discrimination, also suggest appeal to the New Testament to legitimate black theology and feminist theology. In particular, the place of women in earliest Christianity has become the focus of a great deal of study, especially in America. E. Schüssler Fiorenza has made a notable contribution to feminist theology on the basis of sound criticism of the New Testament (*In Memory of Her: a feminist theological reconstruction of Christian origins*, 1983).

The Structuralist Approach

The attempt to dispense with critical assessment of the Bible is partly motivated by the notion of the Bible as a sacred book, which gives it a timeless validity and an oracular quality. Most people are alive to the danger of taking a quotation out of context to back up a theological argument without regard to its real meaning. On the other hand the historical critic may well equally miss the real meaning out of concern to delve beneath the text in order to answer questions of historical origins. Various new approaches thus show a desire to reinstate the text for what it is in itself, and to apply methods of appreciation used in the study of general literature. There is even an anti-historicism which claims that historical criticism is an illegitimate way of handling the text. This extreme view, however, needs to be resisted, because it can lead to failure to reckon with the complexity of the Bible, as we shall see.

The most important new method under this heading is *structural analysis*. This is concerned, not with the formal structure of a poem or unit of tradition (which is a matter of artistic composition), but with the deeper structure of human self-expression. The method starts from two basic insights, associated with the social anthropology of C. Lévi-Strauss (*Structural Anthropology*, 1960) and the structural linguistics of F. de Saussure (*Course in General Linguistics*, 1966). The first is concerned with the function of myth as a means of objectifying basic antinomies, or oppositions, in the experience of life, and of coming to terms with them. The second is concerned with the functioning of language, in which it is possible to distinguish between what is said according to speech conventions and what is really meant. Putting these two insights together, we may say that a story will be told in connection with a problem of human existence, and structural analysis may be expected to reveal how this has been achieved. But precisely because myth objectifies problems in the life of every human being, the result of the analysis will have a direct application to the investigator. In this way ancient and seemingly irrelevant religious texts may yield fresh understanding of the human condition. The application of these ideas to biblical texts has been aided by the earlier work of V. Propp (*Morphology of the Folk-Tale*, 1928), who analysed the constantly recurring actions of the character-stereotypes in a huge range of Russian fairy-tales, and by the systematisation of such actions achieved by A. J. Greimas (*Sémantique structurale*, 1966). The results of these works of the structuralists have been applied to New Testament study particularly in the various writings of Paul Ricoeur and Daniel Patte.

The system of Greimas is very illuminating, but too complex to explain in detail here. Instead it must suffice to give an extremely simplified example of the analysis of a biblical passage along these lines, before making some more general reflections on the method.

A Case Study

My chosen example is Matthew's version of the temptation of Jesus (Matthew 4:1–11). Here we are not concerned with it as history, though it is historically significant that Jesus endured this inner struggle. Nor are we concerned with it as theology, though it is theologically important that Jesus was 'in every respect tempted as we are' (Hebrews 4:15). We shall make no attempt to answer the questions about the underlying tradition and setting-in-life which form criticism might bring to the text, or the question of the evangelist's understanding of it which would be the province of redaction criticism. The investigation is confined to the meaning of the text as it actually stands.

The first operation is to look at the materials of the story – the persons and situation and operative factors. These are the building-blocks of the narrative, but they also impose constraints on the story itself, which has to take a certain form simply because of its materials. One thing which the structuralists insist on is the cultural conditioning which lies behind the choice of materials and the restraints these exercise. In the temptations story the materials are: Jesus, the devil, the forty days, the wilderness, and the biblical model of Israel in Deuteronomy (which provides the answers of Jesus, and indeed much of the scenario). Thus the story is by a person whose understanding (and therefore achievement of the object of the story) is dominated by the Old Testament, which is the medium of the story in a web of ideas which constitute the New Testament world. Jesus and the devil obviously represent the opposed forces of good and evil, but the notion of good is defined and also constrained by the ideas associated with Jesus, and the notion of evil by the concept of Satan in New Testament times. Moreover, what constitutes temptation is defined by the symbolism in the story, which puts the conflict in terms of the testing of Israel in the forty years of the wilderness wanderings, as described in Deuteronomy.

The plot is concerned with the reconciliation of opposites, good and evil. The opposition surfaces at once in the suggestion of the devil: 'If you are the Son of God, command these stones to become loaves of bread' (verse 3). For the 'if' clause is a phrase which functions to express the good, but the command is only apparently an action that expresses the good. This becomes clear in Jesus' reply: 'Man shall not live by bread alone' – thus showing that the command is not a legitimate expression of the good – 'but by every word (i.e. command) that proceeds from the mouth of God' (verse 4 = Deuteronomy 8.3). Thus the devil sets up an opposition between God and God's will, and Jesus rebuts it by restoring the integrity of God and his will. Another way of putting this is to say that the reply of Jesus acts as mediator between the oppositions set up by the devil.

The same effect is produced by the second of the devil's suggestions, but this time it is backed up by a quotation from Psalm 91, which represents the speech of God himself. This reduces the opposition between God and the command (that Jesus should cast himself down from a pinnacle of the temple), because the claim that this is a divine command is reinforced by the word of God in Scripture. Hence Jesus' reply is reduced to one sentence which combines the command and God, and the issue is thereby revealed to be the devil's attempt to enlist God himself on his side: 'You shall not tempt the Lord your God' (verse 7 = Deuteronomy 6:16).

The third temptation makes this explicit by suggesting that God is not to be distinguished from the devil himself, who claims to have all the world in his power. The reply of Jesus ('You shall worship the Lord your God and him only shall you serve,' verse 10 = Deuteronomy 6:13) makes God primary, and excludes the devil altogether. Thus a specious distinction which was apparent in the first temptation, that God could somehow be identified with that which is known to be contrary to him, is refuted step by step, leading to the most basic assertion of the primacy of God. Thus the story is concerned with something that is a recurring experience in the psychic life of humanity, for the confusion of the good as we understand it with apparent goods that arise from our selfish desires is surely a universal experience. But the story has a specifically Christian understanding of this, because the concept of the good is defined by the meaning of Jesus and God in New Testament times.

Comment

The above example has been presented without the technical terms of linguistic and literary analysis, which give the method its precision, but also place a considerable barrier to the student, who is likely to be alarmed by the seemingly impenetrable jargon which is used. But perhaps enough has been said to show how the method of structural analysis is concerned with the dynamics of narrative. However, it is important to realise that this does not necessarily coincide with the intention of the writer, who may be unaware of the dynamics of his own composition. This point leads on to the further observation that one of the constraining factors in New Testament narrative is the complex pre-history of the material, which has passed through stages of oral transmission before being written down, and then been subjected to redactional changes before reaching its present form. This is one reason why the methods of historical criticism cannot be dispensed with, because the evangelist is bound by his sources and the finished product is not entirely a matter of free composition, and to treat it as if it were so would be a false basis of assessment.

2. NEW APPROACHES: NARRATIVE AND CANONICAL CRITICISM

Narrative Criticism

Allied to the interests of structural analysis is what may be called, for want of a better term, composition analysis, which is concerned with the mental stock of a writer, which supplies the materials out of which a narrative is built. In English literature, e.g. a poem like T. S. Eliot's *Little Gidding*, there is often a complex web of allusions to earlier literature and cultural traditions, and the poem derives its spiritual dynamic from its wealth of echoes and fleeting images, which have great evocative poser. Significantly the literary analysis of F. Kermode (*The Genesis of Secrecy: on the interpretation of narrative*, 1979) makes direct use of New Testament studies to illustrate this point. For the New Testament writers, like all Jews, were steeped in the Old Testament, and it is often possible to trace the influence of passages from it in the shaping of New Testament narratives. Thus the use of the Old Testament goes beyond explicit quotations and allusions, which may be used for purposes of argument or moral instruction. It is also a factor in narrative composition. It is universally recognised that Luke is indebted to the annunciation story of Samson (Judges 13) for much of the detail of his story of John the Baptist (Luke 1:5–25), and all sorts of Old Testament allusions abound throughout the infancy narratives of Matthew and Luke. The question then arises how far these stories owe their existence to the Old Testament models. Should they be regarded as evolved out of creative writing on the basis of these models with no foundation in actual historical memory at all? Are they products of creative imagination, supplying the gaps in an historical tradition which is felt to be defective? There are no simple answers to these questions, for it is not a matter of yes or no. Jesus' parable of the wicked husbandmen (Mark 12:1–9) has clear echoes of Isaiah's song of the vineyard (Isaiah 5:1–7), and its meaning is illuminated by the comparison, but it does not depend on the comparison to make its point. In his *Structure and Meaning in the Fourth Gospel* (1974), B. Olsson refers to an Old Testament 'screen' in certain passages of John, which carries the symbolism of the passages and helps to shape their meaning.

This use of the Old Testament as the groundwork for a New Testament narrative is often referred to as 'midrash', but the term needs to be used with caution. It is a technical term for a feature of Jewish homiletic writing, in which a scriptural text is glossed or rewritten, not only to clarify its meaning, but also to indicate its contemporary relevance. Thus midrash is aimed at reinforcing the point of the underlying passage. This is not usually the case in the New Testament. Here the object is to make the story of Christ more meaningful by suggesting a scriptural comparison. It is thus usually a matter of typology, in which Christ fulfils what has previously been foreshadowed. This is comparable to the use of Scripture in the Dead Sea Scrolls, in which the fulfilment is found in the rise of the Qumran Sect. It is significant that both earliest Christianity and Qumran have an overwhelming sense of living in the prelude to the final age, when all that God has revealed concerning his purposes will be fulfilled. Thus the focus of attention is the present and immediate future rather than the exact meaning of the ancient text. It may be for this reason that New Testament writers have no qualms about conflating texts (e.g. Matthew 24:30 = Zechariah 12:10 and Daniel 7:13, cf. Revelation 1:7; Romans 11:8 = Deuteronomy 29:3 and Isaiah 29:10), which scarcely ever happens in Jewish sources.

Genuine examples of midrash, however, are found in a few places in the New Testament. Thus in Romans 10:6–10 Paul creatively adapts and glosses a passage on the Law from Deuteronomy 30:12–14 in order to show that Christ is the reality to which this passage refers. He is thus exposing what he holds to be the true meaning of the passage, which has been brought to light by God's act in Christ.

Canonical Criticism

Concern for the actual, given text of the New Testament appears in the approach of canonical criticism. This was pioneered by J. A. Sanders in connection with the Old Testament (*Torah and Canon*, 1972), and has been applied to the New Testament by B. S. Childs (*The New Testament as Canon: an Introduction*, 1984). The method began as a protest against the tendency of historical criticism to be preoccupied solely with the recovery of what may be the original form of items in the Jesus tradition and with the question of the authenticity of the material. This had the effect of downgrading the existing form of the text, which tended to be regarded as a corruption of the original. The result was that preachers, trained in the discipline of historical criticism, found themselves reluctant to use the Bible as it stands. To redress the balance, canonical criticism shifts the focus back to the existing text. Following on from the insights of redaction criticism, the method seeks to expose the dynamic interaction between the text and the communities in which it has been preserved, whether in the oral stage or in the redactional handling of it by the New Testament writers. Thus attention is given to the meaning which the text has had at each stage in its history in relation to the developing life of the Church. The general acceptance of these particular books and the eventual delimitation of the canon have had further effects on their interpretation. So the formation of the canon is the result of dynamic interaction between text and community.

The method of canonical criticism, according to Sanders, is to determine first the text to be studied, using the appropriate tools of form and redaction criticism where necessary. Next an effort has to be made to understand the sociological context of the tradition or text in the life of the Church, again using the tools of historical criticism. The final step is to plot out the relationship between these two things, which enables the critic to perceive the text as a message in a particular situation. By repeating the process through the history of the fixation of the text and its acceptance into the canon, the critic can see the dynamic of the text as message in changing circumstances. Thus canonical criticism views the text in relation to a living process. This has a direct bearing on the hermeneutical problem of the New Testament, which requires larger treatment in our third main section.

Rhetorical Criticism

Finally brief mention may be made of *rhetorical criticism*, which shares some of the same interests. This also attends to the dynamic interrelation between writer and community, but the focus is on the literary devices which an author uses. It has often been observed that Luke, in writing for 'Theophilus' (Luke 1:3; Acts 1:1), adopted a style and adapted his material to suit the needs of an educated Gentile audience, which entailed certain literary conventions. Similarly the ways in which Paul follows, and significantly departs from, the norms of ancient letter-writing are well known. Recently, however, the New Testament letters have received more detailed analysis from the point of view of their rhetorical effects. H. D. Betz, especially in his major commentary on Galatians (1979), has argued that Paul adopted Greek rhetorical devices, as commonly used in the art of persuasion. These can be described as tricks of the trade, as when Paul uses the *captatio benevolentiae* (securing the goodwill of the readers) by gracefully modifying in Romans 1:12 the description which he has just given of his intentions in planning to come to Rome. The aim of rhetorical criticism is thus to study the ways by which the writer's objects are achieved from the point of view of effective communication with the readers.

3. INSPIRATION AND AUTHORITY

The more recent approaches to the New Testament have all drawn attention to the dynamics of the text in various ways. They are thus concerned with how the text speaks. Rhetorical criticism attends to the ways in which it spoke to the original readers. Canonical criticism studies the continuing interaction between text and community, which does not stop with the fixation of the text in its final form or with the closing of the canon. Structural analysis is concerned with the impact of the text at a deeper level of human understanding.

There is thus a preoccupation with the ways in which the meaning of the Bible can be appropriated today as a religious book, and this really has two aspects. There is on the one hand the hermeneutical problem, i.e. the problem of making its message accessible to contemporary understanding. Connected with this, there is on the other hand the problem of maintaining its spiritual authority in the light of the impact of modern criticism. To take the second point first, the whole critical approach treats the Bible as a work of human authors, just like any other book, so that it is difficult to see in what sense it can be said to be the Word of God. Moreover the presuppositions of criticism are neutral with regard to matters of faith, so that when, for instance, the appearance of an angel is mentioned, criticism looks at the functioning of the idea of angels in the world of the Bible, and refuses to be dogmatic about what 'really' happened in the given case. This takes us back to the other point, because it gives an example of the gulf that exists between the biblical world view and modern understanding. This problem has been stated forcefully by D. E. Nineham in *The Use and Abuse of the Bible* (1976).

The New Hermeneutic

We shall begin with this first point, and in order to do so we must recall what was said about Bultmann's method of demythologisation at the end of the last chapter. Responding to the challenge of Karl Barth to maintain the Lutheran tradition of the givenness of salvation through the Word of God revealed in Christ, Bultmann sought to make the notion of salvation meaningful in modern terms. He felt that the existentialist philosophy, which was coming into fashion at the time (the early twenties), especially in the work of Heidegger, offered a way through. According to this approach, reality is located in each person, and the universe in which we live has meaning only in so far as we, as individuals or communities, come to terms with it from the point of view of our own existence. On this view, faith statements are really statements about one's relation to, or understanding of, existence, of what it is to be a person, and God is the focus of existence rather than a mythical personality in the sky. Thus Bultmann saw the task of hermeneutics to be the translation of religious statements into existential statements, and because this is their 'real' meaning it follows that this is what Jesus was 'really' saying. The terms in which he spoke, with the paraphernalia of God, angels, spirits, heaven, miracles, etc., were appropriate for his own time and culture, but must be 'demythologised' in order to expose their meaning for our understanding today.

What has been termed the *new hermeneutic* arose partly as a result of criticism of Bultmann's programme of demythologising. Here the leading names are those of his pupils *E. Fuchs* and *G. Ebeling*. The main point of attack is that the programme is a conscious process of translation, which still treats the text as an object to be grasped. But, it is objected, for real understanding to take place the interpreter must be grasped by the text itself, and so he must allow it to speak to him and to act upon him. This point, of course, maintains the concept of Scripture as the Word of God. The reader is addressed by the Word.

For this process to take place the reader must first acknowledge the distance between himself and the text. There is the objective exegesis to be done, so as to expose the meaning of the text in its own terms of reference. At the same time the reader needs to examine his own presuppositions, which shape the questions which he brings to the text. Then, secondly, the interpreter needs to think his way into the text by an effort of imagination, so as to share the impact which it had on its original hearers. When this is done, there is the merging of two horizons, the world of the text and the world of the modern reader, who can then share in the experience of the original hearers and be addressed by the text, just as they were.

We can now see that the more recent work on structuralism can be helpful from this point of view. If we think again of the temptations narrative, the structural exegesis which was suggested above showed how it relates to universal experience of the confusion of the good in the mind of humanity. This enables a greater degree of empathy on the part of the reader, who is thus able to feel what the temptations narrative was saying when it was told and retold by Matthew. Reading the story with this awareness of the thought world of Jesus in his time, and also knowing oneself as one who takes part in the universal experience which it expresses, there can be a merging of the two horizons, so that the story speaks directly to one's own condition. If there is reason to believe that the story is at the service of God, then it can justly be claimed that in it and through it God speaks to the reader. An event of understanding has taken place. This effect is now usually referred to as a 'language event'.

The Parables of Jesus

Although what has been said applies to narratives and discourses of every kind, it is in respect of the parables of Jesus that it has been most fully worked out and most convincingly presented. Form criticism has shown that the parables have survived in the tradition because they were valued as illustrations of teaching, and easily acquired fresh applications in the changing life of the Church. The new hermeneutic, however, regards the parables, not as illustrations used by Jesus to clarify his teaching, but as extremely arresting items of the teaching itself. They are aimed at bringing the hearers round to a fresh realisation of what is involved in the kingdom, or rule, of God. Analysis of a parable shows that it produces its effect by involving the hearers in a familiar situation through the picture part of the story – like the sower sowing seed in the field – but the story builds up to a climax which forces the hearers to rethink their whole understanding of what is at stake. Thus the parable of the sower refers to the important part played by the different kinds of soil for the agreed object of producing a good harvest, and so each hearer has to face the question, what kind of soil am I? To split this up into different categories of persons, as in the given interpretation (Mark 4:14–20), is ruinous, for it fails to observe that all the kinds of soil may apply to every person. This interpretation also gives full value to the varied nature of the produce of the good soil (twentyfold, thirtyfold and sixtyfold), for it suggests the potential for increasing fruitfulness. Thus the story achieves its effect by involving the hearers, who find that it has had an effect on their understanding. A language event has taken place. Some parables, like the prodigal son, so completely reverse conventional ideas of what is good and what is bad that they are calculated to have a radical effect on those who grasp the meaning and are grasped by it in facing out the consequences for their own lives.

Unfortunately parables fail because they are too familiar! It has been observed that the modern reader automatically identifies with the tax-collector rather than the Pharisee in the well known parable of Luke 18:9–14, so that the intended effect, which depended on identification with the Pharisee, fails to come off. This is why the process of hermeneutic must begin with placing a distance between oneself and the text, so that it is understood within its own terms of reference first.

The new hermeneutic has been criticised for making the individual's response the sole content of biblical exposition, and neglecting the central message of the gospel of redemption through the sacrifice of Christ. But of course the method can equally be used in connection with the faith-statements of the New Testament, such as the argument of Paul's Letter to the Romans. The importance of the new hermeneutic has been expounded from the standpoint of conservative and evangelical faith in the major study of A. C. Thiselton (*The Two Horizons*, 1980).

Inspiration

Another objection to the new hermeneutic is that it can be attached to a form of Christianity which is ambiguous with regard to belief in God. This is not surprising in view of its origin in Bultmann's method of demythologising, since the concept of God was there replaced by the idea of authentic existence. But this is a matter of the philosophy of religion, not of biblical exegesis. The hermeneutic, as just shown, does not in any way presuppose dismissal of belief in God, even if the understanding of God in contemporary Christianity is part of the distance between the modern reader and the text.

The problem of biblical inspiration, however, necessarily starts from the reality of God. It is not a matter of the inspiration of the biblical authors as creative artists, like poets, though that is not a negligible aspect of the literary quality of the Bible. It is the question of the sense in which it can be claimed that the Bible is uniquely derived from God. In order to understand the debate on this issue it will be helpful to recall some points of the history which we have reviewed in previous chapters. It will be seen that the question of inspiration belongs to two different areas of conflict. The first is the relation of Scripture and tradition, which came to a head in the Reformation of the sixteenth century. The second is the relation of Scripture and science, which belongs to the nineteenth century and afterwards.

The rise of the concept of inspiration of Scripture was part of the canonisation process. Our opening chapter on the formation of the New Testament showed how the canon was established gradually, as a list of books approved for reading in church. It was naturally valued for its moral and spiritual teaching, but it was also constantly appealed to in matters of doctrinal controversy, precisely because it comprised the books which conveyed the authentic tradition. This is why apostolic authorship was considered to be such an important criterion for acceptance, though the deciding factor was really agreement with the Rule of Faith. All these factors contributed to the conviction that the New Testament was written by men who were inspired by the Holy Spirit to teach the truth (cf. John 16:13).

It is important to recognise that this was not a doctrine of verbal inerrancy, but of the unity of truth. Great efforts were made to see what the Bible means, because it is its meaning which conveys truth. The Fathers pay attention to the precise meaning of words. The various methods of interpretation, resulting in the traditional four senses of Scripture, were employed to expose its meaning in different contexts of Christian living and understanding. But there was never any doubt that the meaning of Scripture would always be in harmony with the doctrine of the Church. The great doctrinal controversies focus on the precise meaning of statements of Scripture, usually in the Gospel of John, and apparent contradictions must be resolved (as in the Arian controversy about the subordination of Christ to the Father) as part of the process of discovering the meaning.

Scripture and Tradition

This concept of the Bible as part of the unity of truth always continued in the east, but in the west, during the later Middle Ages, a rift began to appear between Scripture and tradition. We saw that Henri of Ghent (died 1293) is claimed to be the originator of the idea that Scripture and tradition (both of them equally inspired and apostolic) might differ, in as much as their contents are different. Thus the apostolic witness in the New Testament and the tradition handed down orally from the apostles, though ideally always in agreement, could be played off one against the other as two equally valid sources of truth. This enabled the canonists to promote the Papacy in spite of protests based on the New Testament by Wycliffe. The Reformation was then bound to be centred on the relative values of Scripture and tradition. Luther's *sola fide* (by faith alone) was directly opposed to the tradition represented by the papal bulls that the Church controlled reconciliation of the individual with God. It was bound to lead to the rallying cry of *sola scriptura* (Scripture alone) and the abandonment of tradition as a source of divine truth altogether. Though this could not be carried through absolutely, and Lutheranism developed its own new scholasticism and reformed Churches produced their own carefully guarded traditions out of sheer necessity, it is true to say that the Bible became central and normative for the Reformation Churches. It is to this period that the idea of verbal inerrancy of Scripture belongs, as the Bible was held to be the only guarantee of the truth. The faithful needed to be assured that it could not lie or lead them astray.

The Enlightenment and Reaction

Confidence in the unique inspiration of Scripture was, however, shaken by the effects of the Enlightenment. The discovery of scientific laws put the factual accuracy of the Bible in doubt, especially with regard to miracles. What is more important, the development of scientific method when applied to the study of history led to the rise of biblical criticism. This was widely perceived to be allied to rationalism, and indeed the speculations of the Tübingen school on the rise of Christianity owed much to rationalist attempts to explain the origins of religion in terms of human development. Thus those who sought to uphold belief in the supernatural in the debate on science and religion also had to make up their minds about the status of the Bible. This led to two extreme positions, the centralised dogmatism of the Roman Catholic Church, which prohibited biblical criticism altogether, on the one hand, and the biblical fundamentalism of the Bible-centred Protestant Churches on the other.

It is now widely agreed that we must distinguish between the quasi-fundamentalism of the pre-critical period and the fundamentalism which appeared in the nineteenth century (though the label fundamentalism is a twentieth century coinage), and which is still held by many evangelical Christians. The older period had its concept of the unity of truth, and always simply assumed that the Bible was true at face-value (at least mostly), but the meaning was what mattered. Now, however, supernatural religion was threatened altogether, and criticism appeared to be a traitor inside the Christian camp. The issue can be illustrated from the empty tomb story in the resurrection accounts. If it is said on critical grounds that all four accounts go back to Mark (source criticism), then that excludes the appearance to the women (added in Matthew and John). If it is then said further on traditio-historical grounds (using 1 Corinthians 15:3–8 as the primary source) that the resurrection of Jesus was established as a belief without the aid of the empty tomb story, and on form-critical grounds that this story should be classified as an example of 'confirmation of a miracle' without necessarily having an historical basis, then those who feel that supernatural religion is under threat will at once assume that the critic is destroying the basis of belief in the resurrection. There is thus a strong motive to save the historicity of this story, as it makes a bulwark to defend the threatened belief.

The result of this reaction to the impact of criticism is a new version of the two-source theory of divine truth, and there are many fundamentalist scientists who implicitly take this position, as they hold together the truth as revealed through science and the truth as enshrined in the inspired writings of the Bible. These need not come into conflict, because they serve different purposes: science serves practical knowledge, and the Bible serves the knowledge of God and the human response to him. But if this division of purpose is accepted, it is really no longer necessary to insist on the verbal inerrancy of Scripture, for a critical view of the Bible is equally capable of acknowledging the inspiration of Scripture from this point of view. Do we need to have miracles to receive the knowledge of God? Is the perception of New Testament times, when the pre-scientific understanding of life was very different from ours, indispensable, or can we not rather acknowledge that miracles were commonly reported about holy people, and what matters is the teaching which these traditions convey?

The Roman Catholic Situation

Although the Roman Catholic Church has now accepted the legitimacy of biblical criticism, verbal inerrancy remained part of the dogmatic tradition, and the long process of emancipation before 1965 included various attempts to define biblical inspiration. Something akin to Luther's distinction between the Word of God and the human words in which it is expressed was put forward at the end of the nineteenth century by J. B. Franzelin, who had taken a prominent part in the Vatican Council of 1869–70. On this view the Holy Spirit is considered to be the originator of the ideas in the minds of the sacred authors, rather than the director of every word they wrote. A more recent view, promoted by P. Benoit, takes up the theory of the *sensus plenior* (fuller sense), and attempts to preserve the patristic tradition of exegesis by suggesting that the work of the Holy Spirit is to bring truth to light through Scripture, and that this is not confined to the literal sense or the direct intention of the author, but is reached through the cumulative witness of the biblical revelation as a whole, and indeed through further clarification after the closing of the canon. The chief value of this view is in showing how the messianic prophecies of the Old Testament, which did not refer directly to Jesus in their original form, were nevertheless intended by God to apply to him, as can now be seen from the fuller revelation available in the New Testament. The theory is open to the objection that it requires the supposition that God has planned the process in advance as the method of revelation, in which the biblical writers are reduced to the status of unconscious instruments. Another recent alternative is that of N. Lohfink, building on the insights of the biblical theology movement. He sees the truth of the Bible in its wholeness as the revelation of the history of salvation, to which even small and apparently useless details make some kind of contribution. However both these views tend to devalue the Old Testament, which is seen to be provisional and to lack fulness of inspiration until it can be put into relation with the revelation in Christ.

Conclusion

The clue to a more satisfactory understanding of the inspiration and authority of the Bible is, however, provided by the Bible itself, and this comes close to the view of Lohfink, but overcomes the objection just raised. This is quite simply the fact that the Bible is a record of human response to God. *The inspiration of Scripture is best seen, not in terms of verbal inerrancy, but in the dynamic interaction between God and his people to which it bears witness.* Humanly speaking the Bible records what people thought about God and how they reacted to him. Seen from the divine point of view it is a continuous divine disclosure adapted to the capacity of mankind to receive the truth. Some facets of this interaction show the limitation of human perception so strongly that they make little or no permanent contribution. Others are of such fundamental importance that they remain valid for all time.

Moreover it is important that this disclosure should not be seen just in terms of propositions. The inspiration belongs not just to the past, but continues into the present. This is because, whenever people share through study of the Bible in the experience of the people of God, they are challenged to hear the Word of God which speaks through Scripture. Through Christ crucified and risen, and through the whole nexus of events leading up to Christ in Israel's history and stemming from him in the formation of the Church, God addresses the Church now. The story of redemption in both Testaments is a story of the initiative of God for the salvation of the people whom he has made. This carries with it ethical consequences, that God alone is to be given ultimate allegiance, and spiritual consequences, that God alone is to be trusted for ultimate salvation. These are reflected in the preaching of Jesus on the kingdom of God, in the sacrifice of Jesus as the supreme response to God, and in Paul's insight that justification is through the act of God alone, to be received by faith.

Christian doctrine is not only a matter of statements about God and Jesus. It is also a matter of response to God through Jesus. The New Testament, when critically studied, not only reveals the processes which lie behind Christian doctrine, but also makes its impact on the reader as the Word of God. Structuralism and the new hermeneutic represent ways in which this function of the New Testament has been analysed in recent research. But the crucial point is that the New Testament is concerned with the living God, who addresses every reader. Critical study may appear to deflect attention away from this vital, personal address to historical and literary problems. But the sensitive reader of the New Testament cannot study it without being challenged by it. There is no necessary conflict between academic study of the New Testament and the response of faith.

FOR FURTHER READING

Childs, B. S., *The New Testament as Canon: an Introduction*, SCM, London 1984.

Harvey, A. E., ed., *Alternative Approaches to New Testament Study*, SPCK, London 1985.

Henry, Patrick, *New Directions in New Testament Study*, Westminster, Philadelphia 1979, and SCM, London 1980.

Nineham, D. E., *The Use and Abuse of the Bible*, Macmillan, London 1976.

Patte, Daniel, *What is Structural Exegesis?*, Fortress, Philadelphia 1976.

Patte, D. and Aline Patte, *Structural Exegesis: From Theory to Practice* Fortress, Philadelphia 1978.

Perrin, Norman, *Jesus and the Language of the Kingdom*, Fortress, Philadelphia, and SCM, London 1976.

Thiselton, A. C., *The Two Horizons: New Testament Hermeneutics and Philosophical Description with Special Reference to Heidegger, Bultmann, Gadamer, and Wittgenstein*, Paternoster, Exeter, and Eerdmans, Grand Rapids 1980.

Vawter, Bruce, *Biblical Inspiration*, Westminster, Philadelphia 1972.

SUBJECT INDEX

NAME INDEX

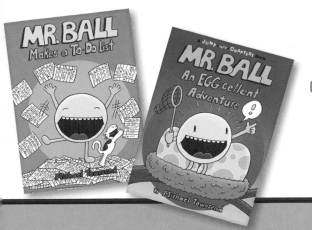

MR. BALL
Makes a To-Do List

Michael Townsend

A JUMP-into-CHAPTERS Book
MR. BALL
An EGG-cellent Adventure
by Michael Townsend

COMING
IN
SPRING
2015

A JUMP-into-CHAPTERS Book
It's Me,
CLOVER!

Lola Schaefer
Illustrated by
Susan Noes

Welcome to a new series created to cross the bridge between "read-to-me" books and "read-on-my-own" books!

Discover a series of books created to help new readers move from simple picture books to the challenges of chapter books. These engaging stories are between 72 and 96 pages in length, but with just a few words on each page—while the page count increases, the word count remains low.

Best of all, each of the books features fresh-and-funny characters. Kids will feel like they've made some great new friends who reflect their lives and feelings.

Downloadable activity and discussion materials for kids, parents, and educators are available on the Blue Apple Books website: **www.blueapplebooks.com**.

The End

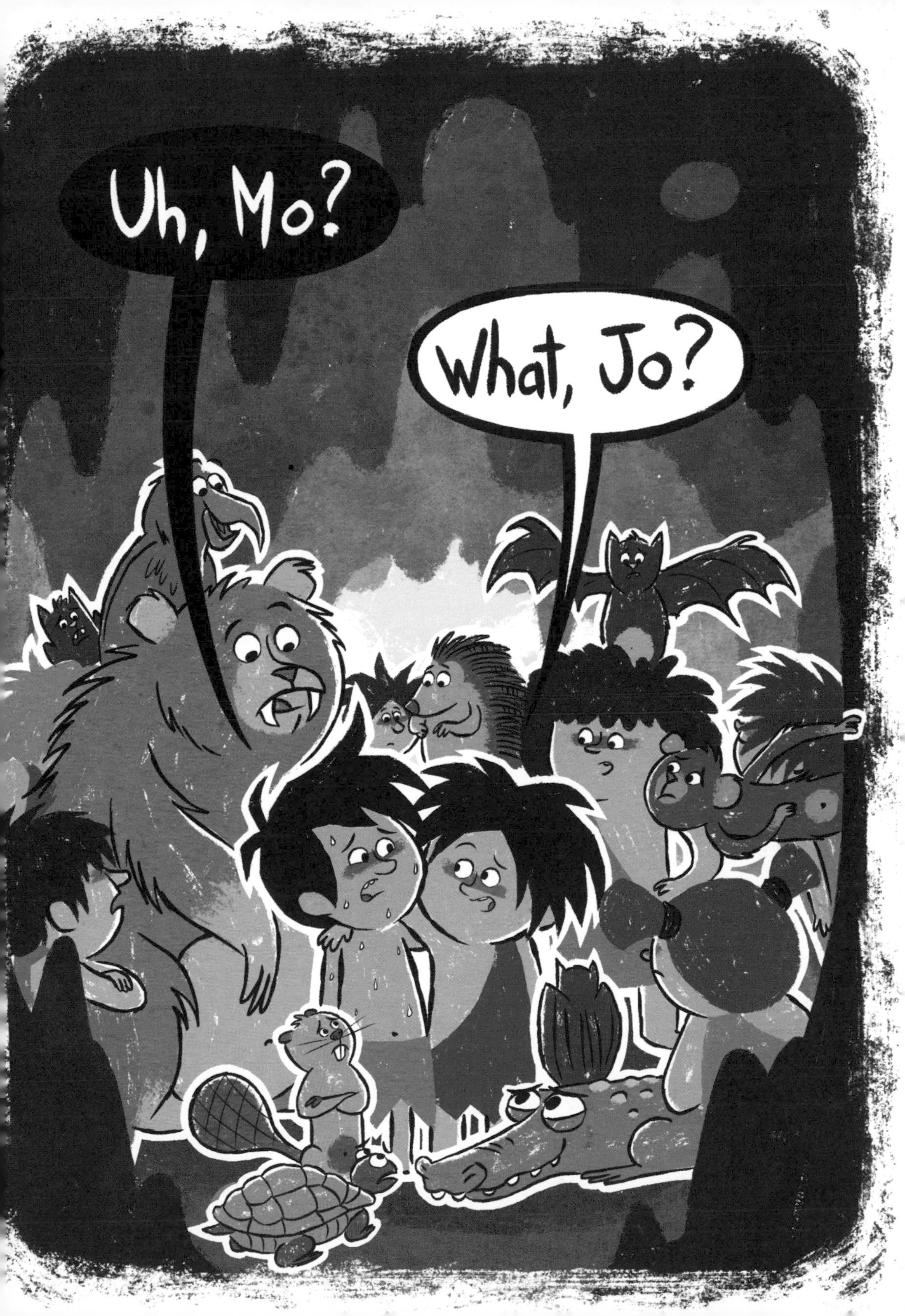
Uh, Mo?
What, Jo?

Mo and Jo sit down to rest.

But now they are cold again! So...

Mo and Jo run for a long time.

Me not cold!

Running make warm!

This is not a good idea.

How can Mo and Jo get some fur?
Mo and Jo try to pull the fur.

Jo and Mo see a bear.
The bear doesn't look cold.

Mo and Jo find leaves.

Mo and Jo find feathers.
Is this a good idea?

Jo sees some birds.
The birds do not look cold.

Feathers keep warm.

Mo and Jo think and think.
How can they get warm?

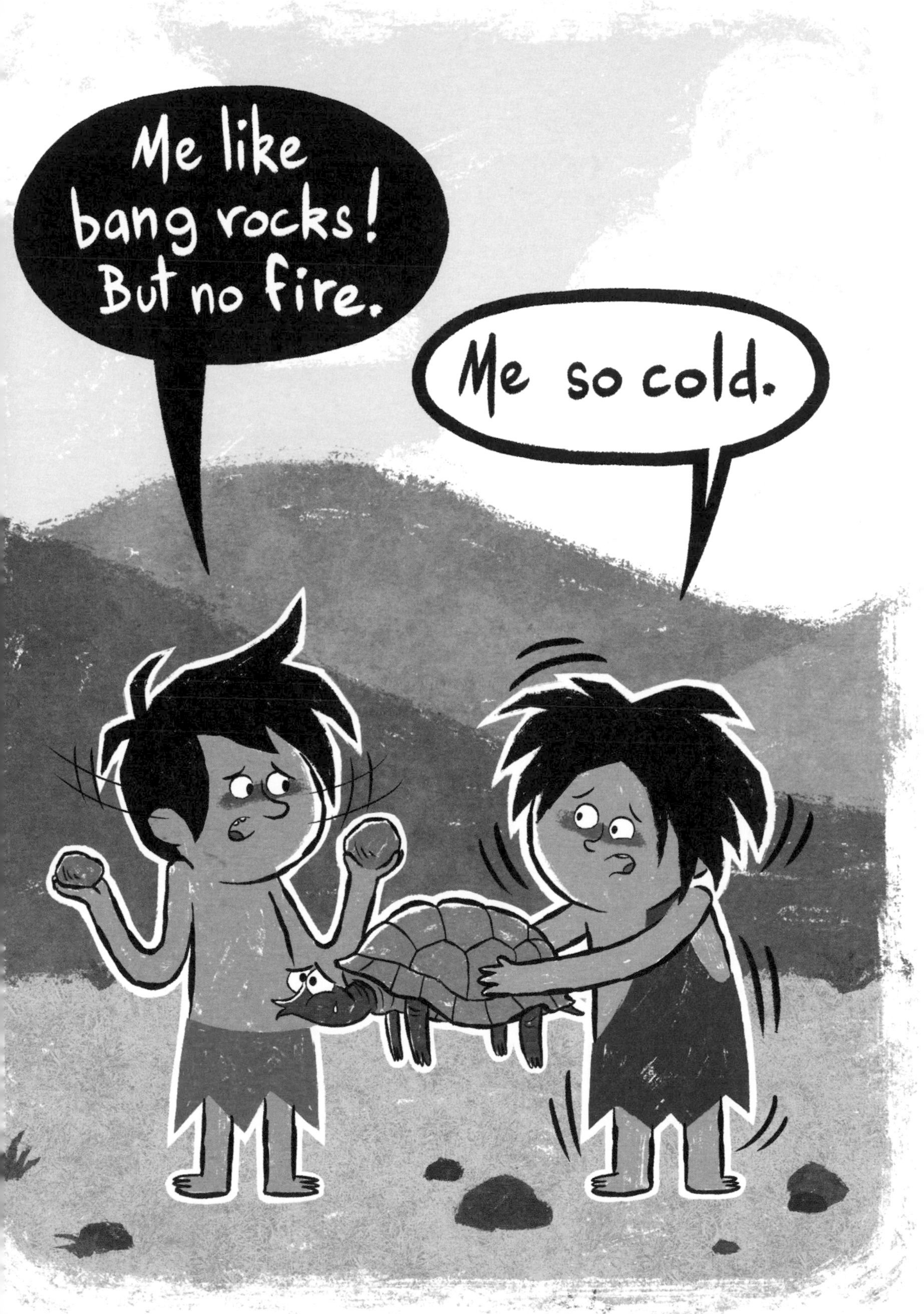
Me like bang rocks! But no fire.
Me so cold.

Mo has a new idea.

Bang rocks?

BANG BANG

BANG BANG

BANG BANG

Mo and Jo try to make fire.

Mo and Jo want to warm up.

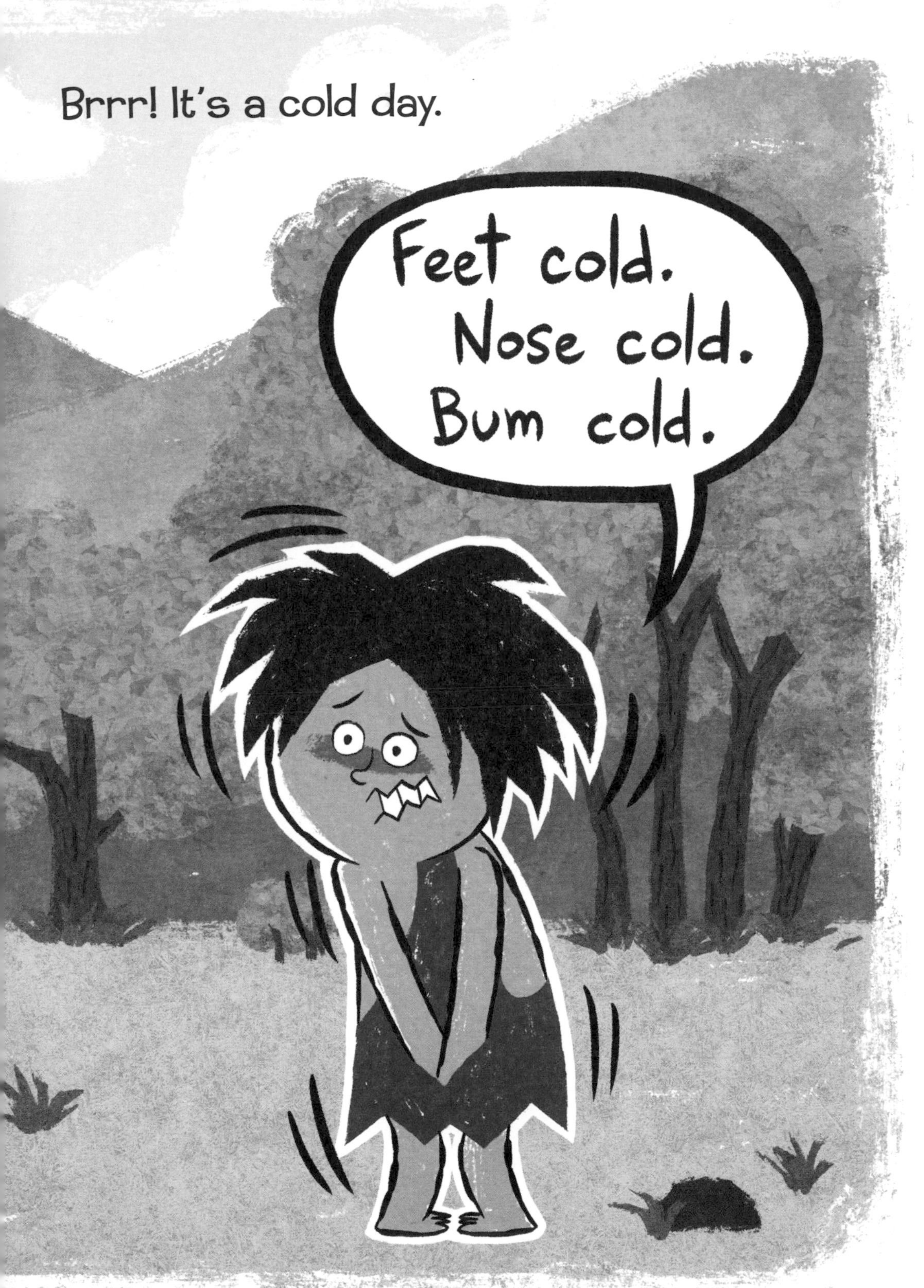
Brrr! It's a cold day.
Feet cold. Nose cold. Bum cold.

Who will win the game?

Mo has an idea.

Jo, you hide.
Me seek.

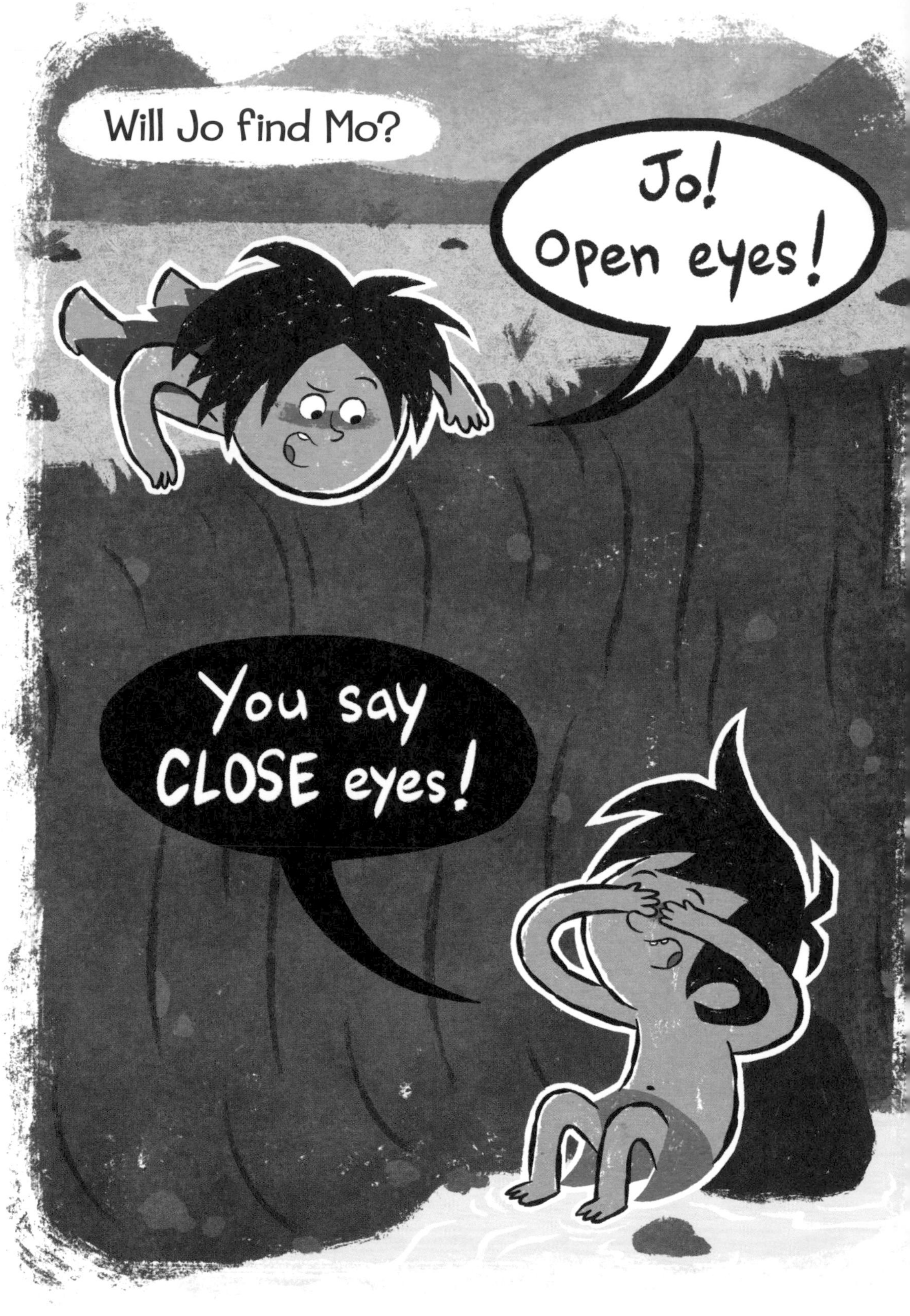
Will Jo find Mo?
Jo! Open eyes!
You say CLOSE eyes!

Now Mo can't find Jo!

Green Eggs and Ham

Ham

By Dr. Seuss

BEGINNER BOOKS

A Division of Random House, Inc.

This title was originally catalogued by the Library of Congress as follows: Geisel, Theodor Seuss, Green eggs and ham, by Dr. Seuss [pseud.] New York, Beginner Books; distributed by Random House, 1960. 62 p. illus. 24 cm. (Beginner Books, B-16) I. Title. PZ8.3.G276Gr 60-13493 ISBN: 0-394-80016-8 ISBN: 0-394-90016-2 (lib. bdg.)

3

4

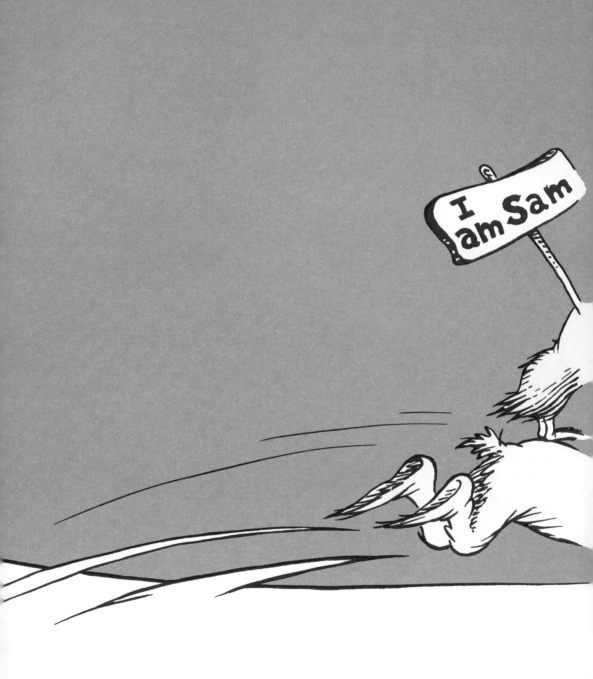

5

That Sam-I-am!
That Sam-I-am!
I do not like
that Sam-I-am!

Do you like

green eggs and ham?

11

I do not like them,
Sam-I-am.
I do not like
green eggs and ham.

13

Would you like them
here or there?

15

I would not like them
here or there.
I would not like them
anywhere.
I do not like
green eggs and ham.
I do not like them,
Sam-I-am.

Would you like them
in a house?
Would you like them
with a mouse?

I do not like them
in a house.
I do not like them
with a mouse.
I do not like them
here or there.
I do not like them
anywhere.
I do not like green eggs and ham.
I do not like them, Sam-I-am.

Would you eat them
in a box?
Would you eat them
with a fox?

Not in a box.
Not with a fox.
Not in a house.
Not with a mouse.
I would not eat them here or there.
I would not eat them anywhere.
I would not eat green eggs and ham.
I do not like them, Sam-I-am.

Would you? Could you?
In a car?
Eat them! Eat them!
Here they are.

I would not,
could not,
in a car.

You may like them.
You will see.
You may like them
in a tree!

I would not, could not in a tree.
Not in a car! You let me be.

I do not like them in a box.

I do not like them with a fox.

I do not like them in a house.

I do not like them with a mouse.

I do not like them here or there.

I do not like them anywhere.

I do not like green eggs and ham.

I do not like them, Sam-I-am.

A train! A train!
A train! A train!
Could you, would you,
on a train?

Not on a train! Not in a tree!
Not in a car! Sam! Let me be!

I would not, could not, in a box.
I could not, would not, with a fox.
I will not eat them with a mouse.
I will not eat them in a house.
I will not eat them here or there.
I will not eat them anywhere.
I do not eat green eggs and ham.
I do not like them, Sam-I-am.

Say!

In the dark?

Here in the dark!

Would you, could you, in the dark?

I would not, could not,

in the dark.

Would you, could you,
in the rain?

I would not, could not, in the rain.

Not in the dark. Not on a train.

Not in a car. Not in a tree.

I do not like them, Sam, you see.

Not in a house. Not in a box.

Not with a mouse. Not with a fox.

I will not eat them here or there.

I do not like them anywhere!

You do not like

green eggs and ham?

I do not
like them,
Sam-I-am.

Could you, would you,
with a goat?

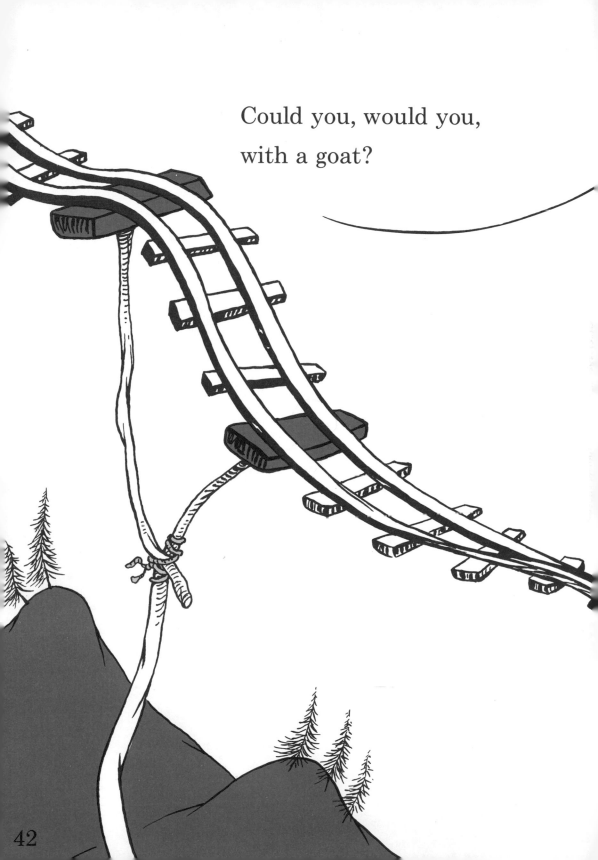

I would not,
could not,
with a goat!

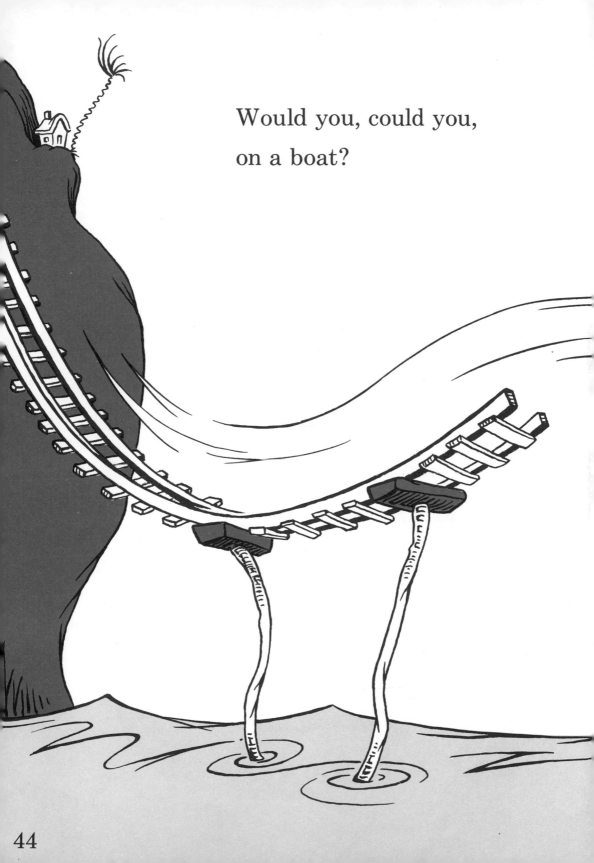

Would you, could you,

on a boat?

45

I could not, would not, on a boat.

I will not, will not, with a goat.

I will not eat them in the rain.

I will not eat them on a train.

Not in the dark! Not in a tree!

Not in a car! You let me be!

I do not like them in a box.

I do not like them with a fox.

I will not eat them in a house.

I do not like them with a mouse.

I do not like them here or there.

I do not like them ANYWHERE!

I do not like
green eggs
and ham!

I do not like them,
Sam-I-am.

You do not like them.

So you say.

Try them! Try them!

And you may.

Try them and you may, I say.

Sam!

If you will let me be,

I will try them.

You will see.

55

Say!

I like green eggs and ham!

I do! I like them, Sam-I-am!

And I would eat them in a boat.

And I would eat them with a goat . . .

59

And I will eat them in the rain.

And in the dark. And on a train.

And in a car. And in a tree.

They are so good, so good, you see!

So I will eat them in a box.

And I will eat them with a fox.

And I will eat them in a house.

And I will eat them with a mouse.

And I will eat them here and there.

Say! I will eat them ANYWHERE!

I do so like
green eggs and ham!
Thank you!
Thank you,
Sam-I-am!

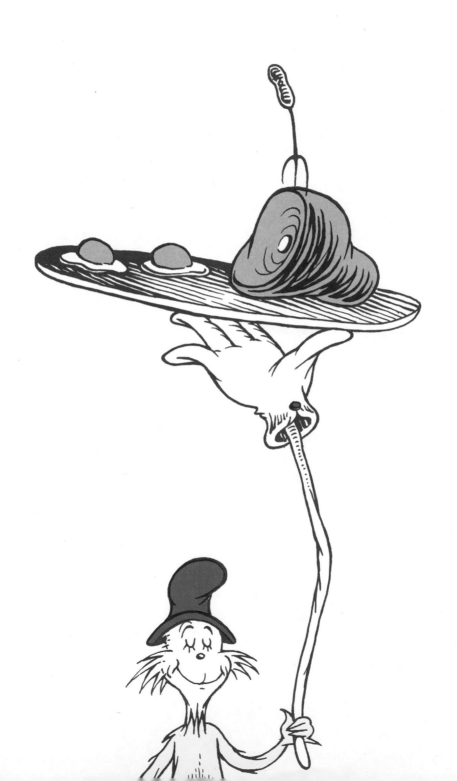